RECLAIMING PARADISE

RECLAIMING PARADISE

❖　❖　❖

The Global Environmental Movement

JOHN McCORMICK

Indiana University Press

BLOOMINGTON AND INDIANAPOLIS

© 1989 by John McCormick

Manufactured in the United States of America

Library of Congress Cataloging-in-Publication Data

McCormick, John
Reclaiming paradise.
Bibliography: p.
Includes index.
1. Environmental policy—Citizen participation.
I. Title.
HC79.E5M39 1989   363.7′058   87-46408
ISBN 0-253-34952-4

1 2 3 4 5 93 92 91 90 89

CONTENTS

Introduction

Of all the conceptual revolutions of the twentieth century, few have wrought so universal or so fundamental a change in human values as the environmental revolution.

Spawned by Victorian nature-lovers and philanthropists, nurtured by amateur naturalists and professional planners, and finally thrust onto the public policy agenda by a rebellious and idealistic new generation, environmentalism has cut across religious, national, and political divides and spread to almost every country on earth. It has won tens of millions of adherents, generated new bodies of legislation, hatched new political parties, encouraged a rethinking of economic priorities, and become an issue in domestic policy and international relations. Above all, it has changed our perceptions of the world in which we live. In just a few decades, the assumptions of centuries have been overturned. For the first time, humanity has been awakened to the basic truth that nature is finite and that misuse of the biosphere ultimately threatens human existence.

The change has been a long time coming. Although the environmental movement is a postwar phenomenon, environmental destruction has a long lineage. Nearly 3,700 years ago, Sumerian cities were being abandoned as the irrigated lands that had produced the world's first agricultural surpluses became increasingly saline and waterlogged.[1] Nearly 2,400 years ago, Plato bemoaned the deforestation and soil erosion brought to the hills of Attica by overgrazing and the cutting of trees for fuelwood.[2] In first-century Rome, Columella and Pliny the Elder warned that poor husbandry threatened crop failures and soil erosion.[3] By the seventh century, the complex Mesopotamian irrigation system built 400 years before was beginning to break down under the strain of mismanagement.[4] Population growth meanwhile was sowing the seeds of the tenth-century collapse of the Mayan civilization.[5] Shipbuilding for the fleets of the Byzantine Empire, of Venice and Genoa and other Italian maritime states, reduced the coastal forests of the Mediterranean.[6] Air pollution from coal-burning so afflicted medieval England that by 1661 the diarist and naturalist John Evelyn was deploring the "Hellish and dismall Cloud" which made the City of London resemble "the Court of Vulcan . . . or the Suburbs of Hell, [rather] than an Assembly of Rational Creatures."[7]

For all these early warnings, there was little sense of alarm or concern until well after the Industrial Revolution. The broader change in human attitudes began with the age of scientific discovery, when the signs of deterioration became evident to more than just a few of the more percipient observers of the condition of nature. The roots of a broader "movement" can first be discerned in the second half of the nineteenth century. The first protectionist groups were created in Britain in the 1860s. In the United States, a two-pronged movement of wilderness preservationists and resource conservationists began to emerge at the turn of the century. The public following of the early movements was small, but as science revealed more about the structure of nature, and as people became more mobile and looked beyond their immediate surroundings, the movement grew and spread. But the true environmental revolution came only after 1945, with the period of greatest change after 1962.

- In 1863, Britain passed the first broad-ranging air pollution law in the world and created the first pollution control agency. By 1971 there were still only 12 national environmental agencies in the world; today there are more than 140.

- The world's first private environmental group (the Commons, Footpaths, and Open Spaces Preservation Society) was founded in Britain in 1865; today the world has more than 15,000 such groups, a third of them founded after 1972.

- The first international agreement on the environment was signed in 1886; today there are more than 250, three-fourths of which were signed after 1960.

- In 1972 the United Nations created a new environmental program; by 1980, almost all the major international organizations—from the World Bank to the European Community and the Organization for Economic Cooperation and Development—had taken policy positions on the environment.

- Still dissatisfied with the political response, new Green parties have arisen to challenge the old order. The first was founded in New Zealand in 1972; by 1988, 14 countries had functioning Green parties, eight had returned members to their national assemblies, and 11 Green members sat in the European Parliament. For many, Green politics offered a potent new alternative to the inconsistencies and insufficiencies of the traditional left/right axis.

Not all the private groups have been effective, few of the national agencies have adequate powers or logical responsibilities, many of the laws are still inadequate or ignored, too few political pronouncements are more than bombast, and Green parties (but not their philosophies) may eventually prove a transient phenomenon. There is no denying the emergence of a substantial global movement, however. In the United States alone, 17 million people describe themselves as "environmentally active," and 55 percent of the population claims to support the aims of the movement.[8] Three million Britons are members of environmental groups,[9] making the movement the biggest in British history.

Environmentalism has indeed spawned a conceptual revolution of Copernican proportions. This makes it all the more surprising that little has been written about the history of the movement. American and West European scholarship has grown rapidly in the last ten years,[10] it is true, but little of it goes beyond narrow national movements, the notable exceptions being the work of Max Nicholson and Lynton Caldwell.[11] Yet it is difficult—even artificial—to assess environmentalism solely in terms of isolated national movements. To do so can lead to misconceptions.

There is the claim, for example, that conservation was one of America's great contributions to world reform movements and that its ideas were eventually exported to other nations.[12] In truth, American conservation was heavily influenced by German forestry, and conservation was practiced in parts of Europe—and even in South Africa and India—before it appeared in the United States.

There is the suggestion that national parks were an American "invention."[13] The world's first national park was Yellowstone, it is true, and the concept was indeed spelled out by George Catlin in about 1830; but Wordsworth had written ten years before of his hopes that the English Lake District be regarded as "a sort of national property, in which every man has a right and interest who has an eye to perceive and a heart to enjoy."[14]

There is the mistaken belief that many latter-day issues and problems are "new." Acid pollution, for example, is often portrayed as an issue of the 1980s. Yet it was suspected as early as the seventeenth century and confirmed in the 1850s. Much of the population debate of the 1960s merely echoed Thomas Malthus (1766–1834), who compared the exponential increase of human numbers to the arithmetical increase in food production—and even he was preempted by 150 years by Sir William Petty.[15] The idea that the industrial way of life was unsustainable, outlined in 1972 in *A Blueprint for Survival*, had already been explored at least as early as 1899 by the geographer Peter Kropotkin.[16]

Such myths and misconceptions may stem at least in part from the lack of clear, or consistent, definitions of the nature and parameters of environmentalism. Is it a way of life, a state of mind, an attitude to society, or even a political philosophy? Perhaps it is all of these, or only some of them. Why is it sometimes also (confusingly) called the "ecology" movement or the "conservation" movement? How does "protection" differ from "preservation"? How does "conservation" differ from "sustainable development"? What *is* "sustainable development"? Is ecology a science, a philosophy, a political doctrine, or all three?

Those searching for a working definition of environmentalism could do worse than refer to Roger Scruton, who defines it simply as "concern for the environment . . . when elevated into a political pursuit."[17] But the environmental movement goes beyond this. Few reform "movements" have ever been homogenous because few of society's problems have simple or universal answers. Environmentalism is no exception. Just as the civil rights movement is fundamentally concerned with racial equality, so environmentalism is fundamentally concerned with the protection and management of the natural and human environment. But just as the philosophies of civil rights have ranged from the nonviolence of Martin Luther King to the uncompromising black power of Malcolm X or the Black Panthers, so environmental groups have disparate ideologies, objectives, and methods.

In 1970, *New Republic* was moved to describe the American environmental movement as "the biggest assortment of ill-matched allies since the Crusades— young and old, radicals of left and right, liberals and conservatives, humanists and scientists, atheists and deists."[18] In his study of American environmentalism, Joseph Petulla identifies three main traditions: the biocentric (nature for and in itself), the ecologic (based on scientific understanding of interrelationships and interdependence among the parts of natural communities), and the economic (the optimal use of natural resources, otherwise described as the utilitarian approach to conservation). He lists different arguments (ranging from nature preservation to human ecology to the antigrowth philosophy), and a variety of ethical bases, ranging from the puritan tradition (waste is evil) to health and corporate ethics.[19] Allied to this is the rift between "deep ecology" and "shallow ecology"; the former sees man as a part of nature and subordinates economic considerations to ecological considerations; the latter is dismissed by "deep ecologists" as a belief that man is separate from nature, and measures environmental protection only by its usefulness to human interests. O'Riordan, for his part, notes the divergent evolution of two ideological themes: the ecocentric (believing in a natural order and natural laws) and the technocentric (believing that man is able to understand and control events to suit his purposes).[20]

Taken to the global level, the diversity of philosophies, tactics and aims is am-

plified. The issues range from the protection of orchids to the protection of
whales, from the actual destruction of wetlands to the theoretical dangers of nuclear winter, from the effects of affluence to the effects of poverty. Environmental
groups range from multimillion member organizations operating out of designer
offices in Washington, London, or Geneva to Himalayan village associations
fighting to save their very livelihood. Tactics range from careful and sustained
lobbying in national legislatures to occasionally violent confrontation on the high
seas. Philosophies range from accommodation between the needs of development and economic growth to uncompromising antigrowthism. Overarching everything is the fundamental question of whether the environment is a political,
economic, or a scientific issue, or all three.

This is the "environmental movement." Whatever the philosophies and methods of the parts, the ultimate aim of the whole is the maintenance of the quality of
the human environment. *Reclaiming Paradise* sets out to remedy some of the many
misconceptions about this complex movement and to provide the first history of
environmentalism as a global social, economic, and political phenomenon. It is a
study of how and why the state and condition of the environment was transformed from a private into a public issue. The principle vehicle for this transformation was a popular mass movement. As private concerns became public concerns,
so the efforts of this movement were increasingly reflected in legislation, public
policy, the creation and operation of public environmental agencies, and changes in
social, economic, and political values. This process has not yet ended. Although
Reclaiming Paradise draws heavily on the British and American experiences, its
central argument is that environmentalism must be seen not as a series of separate national movements, but as part of a wider and more long-term change in
human attitudes. Only in this way can it be properly assessed and understood.

Chapter 1 provides a necessary prelude to the rest of the book by looking at the
roots of environmentalism in nineteenth- and twentieth-century Britain and the
United States. In order to show how parallel developments occurred elsewhere,
there is a brief description of events in Australia, South Africa, and India. These
developments are then related to one of the first truly regional environmental
issues (the African wildlife question) and, finally, to the first signs of an international nature protection movement. The treatment here is not intended to be
comprehensive; readers seeking more detail on early national movements are referred to the cited sources.

Chapter 2 follows these threads through to the post-Second World War era: the
first major international conservation conferences, the creation of the first international conservation bodies, early neo-Malthusian alarums, and the beginnings of
an understanding of the conservation/development debate in postcolonial Africa.

Chapters 3 and 4 concentrate on the radical departure into New Environmentalism between 1962 and 1972. Chapter 3 assesses some of the reasons why the
new movement emerged when it did: the reaction to affluence, the fear of nuclear
fallout, the influence of Rachel Carson, the impact of environmental disasters,
and the influence of other social movements. Chapter 4 then looks at the debate
generated by the so-called prophets of doom.

Chapter 5 focuses on a single event: the 1972 Stockholm conference on the human environment. This was such a watershed that global environmentalism can
be divided into two phases—before and after Stockholm. The performance of the

most tangible institutional outcome of Stockholm—the United Nations Environment Programme, is reviewed in Chapter 6.

Chapter 7 assesses the politicization of the environment in more developed countries. Slightly before, but mainly after, Stockholm, New Environmentalism began to be translated into political action by governments: new legislation, the setting up of new government departments, and the agreement of international conventions. Non-governmental organizations played a key role in initiating and monitoring the development of public environmental policy. By the late 1970s, dissatisfaction with the response of Western governments had helped spawn new Green political parties.

Chapter 8 deals with a major outcome of the Stockholm conference and one of the most difficult problems faced by contemporary environmentalism: resolving the conflict between development goals and sustainable environmental management in the Third World. Without coherent policies, accurate data, broad-based economic development, a reduction in population growth, and a more equitable distribution of resources (natural and financial), the future for the human environment in less developed countries looks bleak.

Chapter 9 takes the broad view by assessing the prospects for greater international cooperation in addressing global and regional environmental problems.

Finally, the conclusion sums up the significance of environmentalism and looks at prospects into the twenty-first century.

Reclaiming Paradise began life as a master's dissertation for the University of London. It took six years and several redrafts to bring it to this final version. Making sense of one of the largest mass movements in history has been no easy task, and this book owes much to the input and influence of others. I owe a special debt of gratitude to Philip Lowe of University College London, who guided the development of the original dissertation; his well-chosen comments kept it on track and stopped it from becoming unmanageable. Max Nicholson took time to talk in some depth about the early years of IUCN and commented on the first two chapters. Martin Holdgate provided comprehensive comments on chapters 5 and 6. Lynton K. Caldwell of Indiana University, Richard N. L. Andrews of the University of North Carolina, and Tim O'Riordan of the University of East Anglia read through the whole manuscript and made many useful comments. David Brower, Czech Conroy, Duncan Poore, Robert Prescott-Allen and Richard Sandbrook discussed specific aspects of the movement with me and in some cases commented on sections of the manuscript. A World Wildlife Fund grant helped the dissertation through its early stages, and my colleagues in Earthscan and the International Institute for Environment and Development provided me with an inspiring weekday environment when the bulk of the work was under way.

To all these my sincere thanks.

Acronyms and Abbreviations

ACC	Administrative Committee on Coordination
ASP	African Special Project
CCOL	Coordinating Committee on the Ozone Layer
CDSN	European Committee for Conservation of Nature and Natural Resources
CEQ	Council on Environmental Quality (United States)
CFCs	chlorofluorocarbons
CIDA	Canadian International Development Agency
CITES	Convention on International Trade in Endangered Species of Wild Fauna and Flora
CND	Campaign for Nuclear Disarmament
CPRE	Council for the Protection of Rural England
CSE	Centre for Science and Environment (India)
DDT	dichlorodiphenyltrichloroethane
DESCON	Consultative Group for Desertification Control
DGSM	Dasohli Gram Swarajya Mandal (India)
DoE/DOE	Department of the Environment
ECB	Environment Coordination Board
ECOSOC	United Nations Economic and Social Council
ECY	European Conservation Year
EEB	European Environmental Bureau
EEC	European Economic Community
EIS	environmental impact statement
ELC	Environment Liaison Centre
EMEP	Co-operative Programme for Monitoring and Evaluation of Long-Range Transmission of Air Pollutants in Europe
EPA	Environmental Protection Agency (United States)
FAO	Food and Agriculture Organization of the UN
FoE	Friends of the Earth
GEMS	Global Environmental Monitoring System
GNP	gross national product
IAEA	International Atomic Energy Agency
IAWGD	Inter-Agency Working Group on Desertification
IBP	International Biological Programme
IBPGR	International Board for Plant Genetic Resources
IBRD	International Bank for Reconstruction and Development (World Bank)
ICBP	International Council for Bird Preservation
ICIDI	Independent Commission on International Development Issues (Brandt Commission)
ICSU	International Council of Scientific Unions
IGO	inter-governmental organization
IGY	International Geophysical Year
IIEA	International Institute for Environmental Affairs
IIED	International Institute for Environment and Development

ILO	International Labor Organization
IMCO	International Maritime Consultative Organization
INFOTERRA	International Referral System
IOPN	International Office for the Protection of Nature
IRPTC	International Register of Potentially Toxic Chemicals
ITC	International Technical Conference on the Protection of Nature
IUBS	International Union of Biological Sciences
IUCN	International Union for Conservation of Nature and Natural Resources
IUPN	International Union for the Protection of Nature
IWC	Inland Waterways Commission (United States)
IWRB	International Waterfowl Research Bureau
LDC	less developed country
LRTAP	long-range transboundary air pollution
MAB	Man and the Biosphere
MAP	Mediterranean Action Plan
MDC	more developed country
MEP	Mouvement d'Ecologie Politique
MIT	Massachusetts Institute of Technology
MOI	Memorandum of Intent Concerning Transboundary Air Pollution (United States/Canada)
MS	Movement for Survival
NAS	National Academy of Sciences (United States)
NATO	North Atlantic Treaty Organization
NCS	National Conservation Strategy
NES	National Environment Secretariat (Kenya)
NGO	non-governmental organization
OAS	Organization of American States
OAU	Organization of African Unity
OECD	Organization for Economic Cooperation and Development
OIPN	L'Office International pour la Protection de la Nature
OPEC	Organization of Petroleum Exporting Countries
PACD	Plan of Action to Combat Desertification
PSAC	President's Scientific Advisory Committee
RFF	Resources for the Future
RSP	Regional Seas Programme
RSPCA	Royal Society for the Prevention of Cruelty to Animals
SCEP	Study of Critical Environmental Problems
SCOPE	Scientific Committee on Problems of the Environment
SPB	Society for the Protection of Birds (Britain)
SPWFE	Society for the Preservation of the Wild Fauna of the Empire
SST	supersonic transport
SWMTEP	System-Wide Medium-Term Environmental Programme
UNCHE	United Nations Conference on the Human Environment
UNCOD	United Nations Conference on Desertification
UNCTAD	United Nations Conference on Trade and Development
UNDP	United Nations Development Programme
UNECE	United Nations Economic Commission for Europe
UNEP	United Nations Environment Programme

UNESCO	United Nations Educational, Scientific and Cultural Organization
UNFPA	United Nations Fund for Population Activities
UNICEF	United Nations Children's Fund
UNSCCUR	United Nations Scientific Conference on the Conservation and Utilization of Resources
UNSO	United Nations Sudano-Sahelian Office
USAID	United States Agency for International Development
WCS	World Conservation Strategy
WHO	World Health Organization
WLCSC	Wild Life Conservation Special Committee
WMO	World Meteorological Organization
WWF	World Wildlife Fund (from 1988– World Wide Fund for Nature)

RECLAIMING PARADISE

ONE

The Roots of Environmentalism

The environmental movement had no clear beginning. There was no single event that sparked a mass movement, no great orator or prophet who arose to fire the masses, few great battles lost or won, and few dramatic landmarks. The movement did not begin in one country and then spread to another; it emerged in different places at different times, and usually for different reasons. The earliest environmental issues were local issues. Once the most immediate and personal costs of pollution or hunting or the loss of forests were appreciated, individuals formed groups, which formed coalitions, which became national movements and finally a multinational movement. This evolution was episodic, with periods of dynamic expansion interspersed with times of somnolence.

The stimuli and the responses often differed, but there were certain objective criteria that had to be met before a broader movement could emerge: progress in scientific research, a growth in personal mobility, the intensification of industry, the spread of human settlement, and broader changes in social and economic relationships. These and other factors exerted varying levels of influence.

In Europe, the environment had been manipulated by man for centuries. Agriculture had reformed the landscape, restricting nature to forests, unusable land, and whatever small islands it could find in the sea of human habitation. When these remaining vestiges were threatened by industry and more efficient agriculture, protectionists rose in response. Elsewhere, in those regions experiencing new European settlement—North America, Australia, South Africa, and selected African colonies—conservation and protection emerged as a form of economic and political control. The unrestrained exploitation of natural resources in the absence of metropolitan control could not be allowed to continue. In North America, the eastern seaboard increasingly reflected human dominance of the European variety, but the lands west of the Appalachians were relatively unchanged. They also proved rich in natural resources. This led some to argue that the American West should be protected from the kind of man-made changes that had occurred in the East and led others to argue that the resources should be exploited, but in a rational and sustainable manner.

Eventually, intranational influences spread. The knowledge of Germany's foresters was exported to the United States, to India via Britain, to Australia via India, and beyond. Romanticism and Darwinism altered human perceptions far beyond their respective birthplaces. By the end of the nineteenth century it was difficult to disaggregate the aims of national movements. While differences in methods and goals may have remained, the stage was set for the rise of the global environmental movement.

VICTORIAN BRITAIN: IN SEARCH OF ARCADIA

The origins of British environmentalism lie in the age of scientific discovery. The growth of interest in natural history revealed much about the consequences of man's exploitative relationship with nature. This led first to a movement to protect wildlife, and then to demands that rural amenity be provided as an antidote to life in the burgeoning industrial conurbations. The first major influence on early British environmentalism was the study of natural history. The foundations of modern botany, zoology, and other life sciences were laid by the work of a succession of amateur field naturalists during the sixteenth, seventeenth, and eighteenth centuries.[1] The most notable was Gilbert White, whose seminal work *The Natural History of Selborne*, published in 1788, became the fourth most published book in the English language and influenced succeeding generations of naturalists, including Darwin. White epitomized the Arcadian view of nature, which advocated simplicity and humility in order to restore man to peaceful coexistence with nature.

"If there were few as yet willing or able to look at nature with the extraordinary maturity of Gilbert White," notes David Allen, "there were many gradually awakening to the attractions of natural scenery . . . and learning to respond with steadily increasing assurance."[2] This awakening encouraged, and found support among, the Romantics and the primitivists, who found emotional solace (but not necessarily scientific or intellectual challenge) in a natural world previously considered alien and forbidding. Their aesthetic sensibilities were offended by the human subjugation of nature. Poets and painters bemoaned the changes being wrought on the countryside by agriculture. Wordsworth wrote of the "violated rights" of nature. The writer and aesthete William Gilpin noted that "wherever man appears with his tools, deformity follows his steps. His spade and his plough, his hedge and his furrow, make shocking encroachments on the simplicity and elegance of landscape."[3]

Eighteenth-century England became a Mecca for naturalists and botanical illustrators.[4] The invention of lithography in 1796–98 brought the visual beauty of nature to a wider public, notably through the work of Thomas Bewick. The discoveries of the Swedish botanist Carl von Linne (Linnaeus), whose work on botanical taxonomy was ecology in its infancy, and of the English naturalist John Ray combined with the findings of the age of exploration to encourage research in the natural sciences, culminating in the theories of Darwin and Wallace. Natural history became a popular Victorian pastime, fueled by the feeling that it brought man closer to God. The study of nature was itself a devout act, as expressed in the recurring phrase "through Nature to Nature's God."[5]

The understanding of the natural environment that emerged from eighteenth- and nineteenth-century research profoundly affected man's view of his place in nature. The Victorian age was one of great confidence and self-assurance, although the Victorian ideal of civilization almost always depended on the conquest of nature by science and technology.[6] Mastery over the environment was seen as essential for progress and for the survival of the human race. But a "biocentric conscience"[7] gradually emerged, supporting a recovery of the sense of kinship between man and nature and acceptance of a moral responsibility to protect the earth from abuse. The work of Darwin provided a major stimulus to this view; evolution suggested that man was one with all other species and that he distanced himself from nature at his peril.

For Lowe, the term "balance of nature" in the eighteenth century had implied "a robust, pre-ordained system of checks and balances which ensured permanency and continuity in nature. By the end of the nineteenth century it conveyed the notion of a delicate and intimate equilibrium, easily disrupted and highly sensitive to human interference."[8] Changes that in the past had been considered advantageous now aroused passionate opposition, at least among an influential minority of intellectual and upper-class Victorians.[9] The imperative to "improve" the environment (by demolishing buildings, controlling pests, draining marshes, and so on) was often interpreted as vandalism and was increasingly rejected, a change of view founded in the intellectual reaction to many of the tenets of economic liberalism.[10]

The improvement of transport in the nineteenth century made the countryside accessible to the increasing number of Victorians who, in the prosperity of the age, sought education, leisure and self-improvement. By the 1880s, there were several hundred natural history societies and field clubs in the country, with a combined membership of about 100,000.[11] The emphasis at this time was on contemplation and study rather than the preservation of nature, but this was to change. The growth in popularity of natural history and ornithology led to widespread specimen collecting in mid-century and a corresponding growth in the damage inflicted upon wild plants and animals. While much collecting was undertaken for bona fide research purposes, the more thoughtless naturalists vied with one another to build collections of birds, eggs, and plants.

The desire to preserve nature now became implicit in the study of nature, and clubs and naturalists became concerned at the damage inflicted both by their own kind and by others. As naturalists learned more about nature, so they recognized its value and the scale of the threats posed by human activity. The vogue for collecting, coupled with the growing efficacy of firearms and the growing popularity (even among naturalists) of field sports, took its toll of wildlife. Hunting in itself did not cause concern, but wanton slaughter and cruelty did.[12] The indiscriminate killing of seabirds off Flamborough Head in Yorkshire attracted much condemnation.

Out of the same humanitarian zeal that had spawned the antislavery movement came the second major influence on British environmentalism: the crusade against cruelty to animals. Although the Society for the Protection of (later Prevention of Cruelty to) Animals, founded in 1824 and given a royal charter in 1840, first campaigned against cruelty to domesticated animals, it soon turned its attention to wild animals; by the 1870s it was investigating vivisection, pigeon-shooting, stag-hunting and rabbit-coursing. Cruelty to animals was seen as an expression of the most savage and primitive elements in human nature. Protectionists believed that in saving wildlife, they were helping preserve the very fabric of society.[13] Nothing so clearly illustrated the firm middle- and upper-class roots of British protectionism as the support the RSPCA derived from these sectors.

Popular social reform movements sometimes borrow techniques from one another and attract support from the same quarters. In the 1950s and 1960s, the environmental movement overlapped for a time with protests against nuclear testing, racial injustice and the Vietnam war (see chapter 3). Similarly, the methods of Victorian abolitionists and those opposed to cruelty to animals began to influence naturalists. David Allen identifies a turning point in the 1860s when the protectionist crusade mustered its forces around the issue of the killing of birds, particularly gulls, to provide plumage for women's fashions.[14] The plumage issue was almost certainly the first popular protectionist cause and was important in bringing protectionism closer to natural history.

The East Riding Association for the Protection of Sea Birds, founded in 1867 to campaign against the annual shoots off Flamborough Head, may have been the first wildlife preservation body in the world,[15] and others soon followed. Four acts of Parliament—in 1869 (Sea Birds), 1872 (Wild Birds), 1876 (Wild Fowl), and 1880 (Wild Birds)—gave some protection to wild birds and helped stem the flow of feathers from local sources, but new supplies were brought from the tropics in the 1880s. In the five months prior to April 1885, for example, the plumage of nearly 775,000 West Indian, Brazilian, East Indian and other birds were sold on the London market.[16] The opposition to the killing of birds for plumage was led by women themselves, who made up most of the membership of the earliest bodies—the Plumage League (1885), the Selborne League (1885), the (later Royal) Society for the Protection of Birds (1891), and the Fur, Fin and Feather Folk (1889). The SPB pledged its members not to wear plumage and set up a network of national and overseas branches; the Indian branch was behind one of the earliest pieces of legislation against international traffic in wildlife: the 1902 Indian government order banning the export of bird skins and feathers.[17]

The wildlife protection movement was only one consequence of the late Victorian reaction to development. Urban social conditions also came under increasing scrutiny, notably in the work of Charles Dickens and Friedrich Engels.[18] Optimistic belief in boundless prosperity was replaced by pessimism about the prospects for social and economic advance, with self-confidence sapped by the economic depression of the 1880s and the intellectual crisis of the post-Darwin era. The depression underlined the growing belief that industry was not necessarily the Great Provider: the source of the nation's economic and political power was now portrayed as destructive of the moral and social order, human health, traditional values, the physical environment, and natural beauty.[19]

The threat to human health had already been addressed in the campaign against the alkali industry. Production of sodium carbonate, used in the manufacture of soap, glass, and textiles, produced damaging emissions of hydrochloric acid. Preventing the pollution was a simple matter of washing the emissions with water, but without legal controls, producers were unwilling to take action unless their competitors did likewise. The *Times* reported on 12 May 1862 that "whole tracts of country, once as fertile as the fields of Devonshire, have been swept by deadly blights till they are as barren as the shores of the Dead Sea." Farmers and landowners complained, but little was done until Lord Derby, whose estate near St. Helens in Lancashire was affected, took up the matter in the House of Lords. Derby's parliamentary campaign was instrumental in the passage of the Alkali Act of 1863. Ashby and Anderson argue that the act "made explicit a social attitude that had been implicit for some years, namely that central government ought to do something about the protection of air against pollution by noxious vapours."[20]

Revulsion at the squalor of life in the industrial towns combined with the yearning for solace in open space and nature to produce the third major thrust of early British environmentalism: the amenity movement. The world's first private environmental group—the Commons, Open Spaces, and Footpaths Preservation Society (founded in 1865)—campaigned successfully for the preservation of land for amenity, particularly the urban commons that were often the nearest "countryside" available to urban workers. David Allen sees the concepts of recreation, preservation, sanctuary, and wilderness coalescing in the 1860s and being overlaid with economic and scientific arguments to give the amenity movement its strength.[21] The Commons Society's pressure tactics met with success, but it lacked corporate status and so could not buy land.

The need for a body to acquire and hold land and property for the nation was met in 1893 by the creation of the National Trust, which aimed to protect the nation's cultural and natural heritage from the standardization caused by industrial development.

The National Trust enjoyed some early success in acquiring land for preservation. By 1910 it counted 13 sites of natural interest among its acquisitions, but it was as much interested in sites of cultural and historic interest, and naturalists expressed concern at the almost random way in which potential nature reserves were acquired, with apparently little regard for the national significance of their plants and animals.[22] In 1912 the Society for the Promotion of Nature Reserves was created, not to own nature reserves itself but to stimulate the National Trust to give due regard to the creation of reserves. This it did by making a nationwide inventory of sites worth protecting and mobilizing public support for the acquisition of these sites. Even so, the need for protected areas was seen as less urgent than the need to curb the desires of collectors and to tackle cruelty to animals. Nature reserves were regarded by most people as a subsidiary and expensive means of supplementing legislation.[23] Although the first had been created on the Norfolk Broads in 1888, it was not until after the Second World War that the idea of habitat protection won wider support in Britain.

Ironically, the National Trust was condemned by its own success in acquiring properties to expend more and more of its resources on land agency and management. This opened the way for the creation in 1926 of the Council for the Preservation (later Protection) of Rural England (CPRE), founded to coordinate the voluntary movement, promote legislation, give advice to landowners, and "make a single, simple and direct appeal to everyone concerned with the preservation of the countryside."[24] In 1929 the CPRE made a direct request to Prime Minister Ramsay MacDonald for an enquiry into national parks. The Addison Committee was set up and presented a report in 1931 that advocated the creation of national parks to protect flora, fauna, and areas of exceptional natural interest and to improve public access. British national parks did not come until after the Second World War, though, and then took on a very different meaning from parks elsewhere. Instead of protecting wilderness, they preserved the countryside at large, in areas where the land remained in diverse ownership and people lived and made a living.[25]

TOWARD CONSERVATION IN THE EMPIRE:
INDIA, AUSTRALIA AND SOUTH AFRICA

No one knew more about forest science in the nineteenth century than the Germans. University instruction in forestry had been available for 150 years, and concepts of sustained yield forestry had been introduced in the late eighteenth century. Curiously, India was to prove an influential testing ground for German forestry science and helped not only to spread forestry more widely, but to lay the foundations of global conservation. Britain had appointed the first conservator of forests in Bombay in 1847, and the second in Madras in 1856;[26] both were charged with managing forests as a direct source of revenue to the state. Also in 1856, Britain acquired Lower Burma; the Governor-General of India, Lord Dalhousie, appointed the German forester Dietrich Brandis[27] (a relative by marriage) as forest superintendent for the region, charged with preventing deforestation. In 1864, Brandis was appointed inspector-general of forests for India, and the first Indian Forest Act was passed the following year. In 1866, the organized recruitment of forestry officers from Britain began, overseen by Brandis and his new German assistant, William Schlich. British forestry instruction at the time was patently lacking, so all British foresters spent time in Germany, France, and Switzerland as part of their education. After a time in the Indian Forest Service, many moved on to other parts of the Empire, notably Australia and East Africa.

The earliest settlers in Australia, like those in the United States, saw forests as obstacles in the path of progress. The first warnings of environmental deterioration were not long in coming. In 1803, the "improvident" cutting of timber on the banks of the Hawkesbury River in New South Wales and the cultivation of river banks was causing serious soil erosion and flooding, "which might have been prevented in some measure if the trees and other native plants had been suffered to remain."[28] Later in the nineteenth century, the clearing of forest for sheep grazing led to overgrazing and the laying waste of vast areas of inland Victoria, New South Wales, and Queensland. Bolton argues that Australia's slowness in practicing enlightened forest husbandry was largely an attitude inherited from Britain, which in some respects lagged behind the rest of Europe in the art of reforestation.[29]

Introduced plant species spread rapidly, often replacing native species; introduced animal pests (notably the domestic dog and cat, and the rabbit) contributed to the widespread extermination of wildlife, a process that had begun with whaling and sealing in the late eighteenth century and early nineteenth century. By the 1830s there were too few seals left to make sealing economically viable, and by the 1850s whaling, too, had dwindled, thanks largely to the practice of killing females at the time of calving. The idea of game laws was anathema to many Australians. In Britain, the right to hunt game had been a privilege of landowners and contravention of game laws the crime for which many convicts were shipped. The apparent abundance of Australian fauna suggested that it should be the right of all to kill animals without hindrance: "because Australia was a free and expanding young society, it would reject the notion of conservation of fauna as a hated relic of the feudal past from the Old Country."[30] As the killing spread, bustards, emus, wallabies, and smaller marsupials became increasingly rare. One British visitor to Western Australia noted in 1849 that although vast herds of kangaroo existed in the interior, the trade in kangaroo skins had taken such a toll that "no increase can bear up against this wholesale animal slaughter."[31]

The first signs of a response came in the late nineteenth century. From the 1860s, state governments began reserving coastal foreshore and lake and river banks for public pleasure.[32] In 1866 a reserve was established at Jenolan Caves in New South Wales. In 1879 the New South Wales government declared the Royal National Park south of Sydney, but more for public recreation than wilderness preservation. The Tasmanian parliament had begun legislating to protect selected bird species in 1860, and natural history societies were formed in Victoria and New South Wales in the 1880s. New South Wales introduced legislation protecting selected marsupials in 1903, and in 1909 a Wildlife Preservation Society was formed in Sydney. Commissions of enquiry in Tasmania and Victoria (1898) and Western Australia (1903) argued that forests could not be regarded as a limitless resource, but should be managed sustainably. A forests and national parks act in Queensland in 1906 empowered the government to create national parks in areas with little marketable timber, and in 1915 Tasmania passed a Scenery Preservation Act. But laws passed by other states were intended to set up parks for recreation rather than for wilderness preservation. Although forestry commissions—owing more to the Indian than the American model, with ex-officers of the Indian Forest Service playing an influential role—were set up in every state between 1907 and 1920, the result was not always improved forestry management.

In southern Africa, environmental destruction and legislation followed within years of the first permanent European settlement in 1652. By 1658, proclamations had to be issued to curb reckless clearance of forests for firewood and to protect penguins shot for food, seals for skins, and elephants for ivory (although the latter were imposed because the Dutch East India Company intended to monopolize the trade in ivory). However, it was difficult to enforce such laws in a colony whose settlers were becoming increasingly dispersed and isolated and for whom such resources as wood, skins, hides and ivory were a useful and accessible form of barter and a valuable source of income. Hunting spread during the eighteenth century, with some elephant hunters embarking on journeys of up to nine months duration. By the 1830s the elephant population of the Eastern Cape had all but disappeared.

The uncontrolled clearance of forests, and subsequent soil erosion and sand blow, prompted the passage of an 1846 ordinance aimed at the "better preservation" of the Cape Flats area near Cape Town; from this event, argues Grove, can be dated "the continuance of a concerted measure of aesthetically and urban-based environmental thinking."[33] Grove notes the parallels between the coincidental advent of environmental legislation of this kind close to cities in South Africa, Britain, Australia, and New Zealand. A forest commission was set up in the Cape in 1854, and forest conservancies were set up in the George region in 1856. In 1859 the Forest and Herbage Preservation Act was passed, surviving (although slightly modified in 1888) until 1910; Grove believes this was the most comprehensive form of conservation legislation passed in the British colonies in the nineteenth century. He pinpoints a serious drought in 1862 as a turning point in settler and farmer attitudes, emphasizing the need for new legislation on land management.

A Select Committee on soil erosion, drought, and associated problems set up in 1864 noted the links between soil erosion and veldt-burning and the clearance of vegetation. A one-man crusade was undertaken by J. C. Brown, Cape Botanist from 1862 to 1866, whose official reports on agriculture and aridification outlined the links between human activity and environmental degradation. The apparent abundance of land for settlement and the influence of the timber trade conspired to reduce the effect of the warnings of men such as Brown, who enjoyed little credibility within the settler community.[34] Of more immediate concern was the question of wildlife preservation. Despite the imposition of legislation to protect wildlife in Natal, the South African Republic, and Orange Free State in the second half of the eighteenth century, the number of animals killed grew. In 1858 ivory was Natal's most valuable export. In the peak year of 1877, more than 19 tons left the colony (roughly the produce of 950 elephant); by 1895 the annual export had fallen to just 66 pounds (30 kilograms). In 1866 one Orange Free State company alone exported 152,000 blesbok and wildebeest skins. In 1873, 62,000 zebra and wildebeest skins were exported.[35]

Professional hunting became a major occupation further north in the mid-nineteenth century, the objectives being ivory, ostrich feathers, rhino horns, hippo teeth, hides, and meat.[36] The major hunting grounds were in present-day Botswana and Zimbabwe. In 1872–74 alone, an estimated 50 tons of ivory—the spoils of about 2,500 elephant—were taken by Ndebele and European hunters. In 1876 a further 18 tons of ivory (approximately 900 elephant) was traded. As the herds diminished, hunters had to travel further north, and by 1880, elephant were so rare south of the Zambezi that it was impossible to make a living shooting for ivory in the area.[37] The first state game reserves in Africa were set up in 1857 in the Knysna and Tsitsikama forests, and private game reserves were created elsewhere by large landowners from 1875. In August 1883, the last quagga died in Amsterdam Zoo, emphasizing the degree of the threat faced by southern African wildlife; in the same month the first wildlife conservation body in South Africa, the Natal Game Protection Association, was founded. The concern for disappearing wildlife felt by

President Paul Kruger of the Transvaal Republic encouraged the establishment in 1894 of a game reserve at Pongola in the eastern Transvaal. This later became part of the Kruger National Park.

THE ROOTS OF AMERICAN ENVIRONMENTALISM

There are parallels between the growth of interest in the natural environment in Western Europe and North America. There was a similar flowering of interest in natural history, and the influence of Romanticism was comparable. But there was a major obvious difference in the fact that Europe had long been settled and exploited, whereas vast new areas of western North America were being opened to settlement in the same way as they had been in Australia and South Africa.

There had been instances of nature preservation on the eastern seaboard during the early years of European settlement. For example, William Penn had decreed at the foundation of Pennsylvania in the late seventeenth century that settlers leave an acre of trees for every five acres cleared.[38] But most settlers saw wilderness as a threat and as a barrier to the provision of safety, comfort, food, and shelter. The hope that the New World was a second Eden was shattered by the discovery that the land was often hostile and desolate. Nash argues that the settlement of the continent offered abundant opportunity for the expression of Judeo-Christian biases against wilderness.[39] Already by 1700, over 500,000 acres (200,000 hectares) of woodland had been cleared for farming in New England.[40] By 1880, 60 percent of the woodland in Massachusetts had been cleared. From about 1620 to 1870, wood was the major source of energy in the United States and the primary building material, but there was little understanding of woodland management techniques. For Huth, the axe was the symbol of early American attitudes toward nature.[41]

At the same time, the growing popularity of natural history alerted scientists (as it had in Britain) to the breadth of environmental change. The beauty of North American wilderness inspired the writings of Romantics, philosophers, and travelers throughout the eighteenth and early nineteenth centuries. The Scottish-born scientist, writer, and poet Alexander Wilson (who was better known in his time than John James Audubon) expounded on the beauties of nature and published a nine-volume study of American birds which raised interest in ornithology. The publication in London between 1827 and 1838 of Audubon's The Birds of America, which for the first time showed birds in their natural habitat, brought the beauty of nature to a wider audience. The writings of Ralph Waldo Emerson and Henry David Thoreau further influenced the early American philosophy of man and nature. Thoreau studied woodland management, and warned of the consequences of clearing forest and planting rye for short-term profits, "a greediness that defeats its own ends."[42]

While the westward advance of settlement during the nineteenth century pitted settlers and mining and lumber companies against the wilderness, it also consolidated the influence of nature lovers, who expounded upon the spectacular beauty of the Rocky Mountains and the Far West. A recurring theme in Romanticism was a fascination with biology and the study of the natural world: the Romantics saw nature as a system of necessary relationships that could not be disturbed without changing, perhaps destroying, the equilibrium of the whole.[43] Rather than accepting traditional Christian theology, they emphasized the primacy of nature as a source of inspiration.

Two seminal events in American environmentalism occurred in 1864. The first was the publication of *Man and Nature* by George Perkins Marsh,[44] a book remarkable for espousing ideas that would not be more widely discussed for another century. The book was a product of Marsh's upbringing in rural Vermont, his capacious memory and lifelong pursuit of knowledge, and his travels in Europe and North America (he had a reading knowledge of 20 languages). In it Marsh argued that wanton destruction and profligate waste were making the earth unfit for human habitation and ultimately threatened the extinction of man, who had "too long forgotten that the earth was given to him for usufruct alone, not for consumption, still less for profligate waste."[45] Society, he warned, was "breaking up the floor and wainscoting and doors and window frames of our dwelling, for fuel to warm our bodies and seethe our pottage, and the world cannot afford to wait till the slow and sure progress of exact science has taught it better economy . . . the teachings of simple experience . . . are not to be despised." Marsh's ideas had much influence in the later establishment of a national forestry commission,[46] and influenced French writers and Italian and Indian foresters. For Stewart Udall, the book represented the beginning of land wisdom in the United States.[47]

The second event was the 1864 act of Congress transferring the Yosemite Valley and the Mariposa Grove of Big Trees to the State of California on the conditions that "the premises shall be held for public use, resort and recreation and shall be held inalienable at all times."[48] The setting aside of an area for recreational enjoyment had never before been adopted as an element of land management in the United States. Roper traces the idea that democratic government should preserve regions of scenic beauty for the enjoyment of all its citizens to Jefferson in 1815.[49] During travels in the American West in 1829–32, the artist George Catlin concluded that buffalo and American Indians alike were threatened with extinction. He believed that the "primitive" was worthy of preservation and wrote that Indians, buffalo, and wilderness alike might be effectively protected if the government was to establish "a nation's Park containing man and beast, in all the wild[ness] and freshness of their nature's beauty!"[50] Similar ideas were expressed by Henry David Thoreau in 1853 when he wrote of the desirability of "national preserves"[51] and suggested that wilderness preservation was ultimately important for the preservation of civilization.[52] George Perkins Marsh took the argument further by suggesting that wilderness preservation had "economical" as well as "poetical" justifications, that is, it could be managed sustainably for the benefit of all.[53]

A second piece of legislation, signed into force in 1872, designated an area of two million acres (800,000 hectares) in Wyoming as Yellowstone National Park, the world's first national park. For Nash, the "American invention" of national parks was made possible by the existence of land in the public domain, the existence of wilderness at a time when demand for its preservation developed, and the pattern of American settlement (where developed and undeveloped land coexisted).[54] Runte suggests that American national parks originated in the search for a national identity and the glorification of the natural beauty revealed by westward expansion.[55] The establishment of Yellowstone and Yosemite gave substance to the philosophies of Catlin, Thoreau, Marsh, and others, and provided a model that was imitated in other countries from the late nineteenth century, although it adopted different meanings in different circumstances. National parks were created, for example, in Australia (Royal National Park, 1879), Canada (Banff National Park, 1885), and New Zealand (Tongariro National Park, 1894), but in the case of Australia at least, the parks were less for wilderness preservation than for public recreation.

MUIR VERSUS PINCHOT: THE AMERICAN MOVEMENT DIVIDES

At the turn of the century, American environmentalism divided into two camps: the preservationists and the conservationists. The former sought to preserve wilderness from all but recreational and educational use and the latter to exploit the continent's natural resources, but to do so rationally and sustainably. The former view was perhaps philosophically closer to the view of British protectionism; the latter was founded in the tradition of rational forest science of the German variety.

As a champion of wilderness preservation, no one could equal the naturalist John Muir.[56] His earliest campaigning was instrumental in the creation of Yosemite National Park in 1890, the first preserve consciously designed to protect wilderness.[57] Buoyed by this success, but wary of the need to watch closely over utilitarian claims to wilderness, Muir in 1892 helped found the Sierra Club, which worked to make the mountain regions of the Pacific Coast accessible to those who sought to enjoy wilderness. The Club became a rallying point for the preservationist cause. With motives based more on emotion than rationality (even though he often used practical justifications when arguing his case), Muir spoke and wrote of wilderness in religious terms, remarking that while God's glory was written all over his works, in the wilderness the letters were capitalized. When Ralph Waldo Emerson visited Yosemite in 1871, Muir hoped he could persuade Emerson to join him "in a month's worship with Nature in the high temples of the great Sierra Crown beyond our holy Yosemite."[58] He felt that civilization had distorted man's sense of his relationship to other living things.

While Muir and the preservationists spoke of "protecting" or "preserving" the environment, often implying that wilderness be totally excluded from anything but recreation, others spoke of "conservation," or sustainable exploitation of such resources as land, forests, and water. One of the earliest conservation issues was the protection of forests. Tree planting had begun in the prairie states in the 1860s,[59] and a Forestry Division had been created within the Agriculture Department in 1876, but it had neither money nor power. The real work was undertaken by amateurs, such as the financially independent botanist Charles Sprague Sargent. Inspired by Marsh's book, Sargent surveyed American forests for the federal government in 1880 and recommended that federally owned timber be protected until a comprehensive study could be made by experts. The first suggestion for a forest service of scientifically trained specialists came from Gifford Pinchot,[60] a wealthy Pennsylvanian who had studied forestry in Europe, where he had learned that forests could be both protected and managed for sustained yields. (The European influence continued when, in 1886, the German forester Bernhard Fernow became the first trained forester to be appointed to direct government forest work in the United States.)[61]

Pinchot, Sargent, and others pursued the idea of a government-sponsored commission and won the sponsorship of the National Academy of Sciences. The work of the commission confirmed that American forests were in a parlous condition but that they should not be withdrawn completely from future occupation or use: they should be made to contribute to the economy of the country, Pinchot argued.[62] How this could be achieved brought the breach between preservationists and conservationists into the open. Nash argues that Pinchot's ultimate loyalty was to civilization and forestry; Muir's to wilderness and preservation.[63] Pinchot found the preservationist ethic of the Muir school hard to understand and always sought to minimize their influence. He believed that conservation should be based on three main principles: development (the use of existing resources for the *present* generation), the prevention of waste, and the development of natural resources for the many, not the few.[64] He claimed that his conservation policy was "breaking new ground" (indeed, this was to be the title of his autobiography). Worster argues, however, that such a claim ignores a tradition of progressive, scientific agriculture that stretched back to the eighteenth century. Pinchot's contribution was, rather, to bring the tradition of progressive agriculture to the management of public lands, particularly forests.[65]

Early American conservation is often represented as a battle between morality (represented by the people) and immorality (represented by private interests set on exploiting the nation's natural resources for their own ends). For McConnell,[66] conservation had become closely identified with the Progressivism that swept the United States in the period 1900–1917, which was itself often depicted as a morality play.[67] Bates suggests that although the Progressive movement was in part a protest against monopoly and stressed free competition, it also marked the decline of laissez faire and the development of a social conscience.[68] Organized conservationists, he argues, were more concerned with economic justice and democracy in the handling of resources than with mere prevention of waste; conservation was a democratic crusade "to stop the stealing and exploitation . . . [and] to distribute more equitably the profits of the economy."

Hays concurs that American conservation did not arise from a broad popular outcry but also argues that it did not direct its fire primarily at the private corporation.[69] Unlike the amateur preservationists in contemporary Britain, American conservation leaders were professionals in fields such as forestry, hydrology and geology. They were influenced less by public opinion than by loyalty to their professional ideals in ensuring rational planning and efficient exploitation of natural resources. They bitterly opposed those who sought to withdraw resources from commercial development. Hays emphasizes the application of new technology, arguing that grassroots democracy, for the conservationists, would have defeated the "gospel of efficiency."[70] Jones suggests that Progressive leaders were not the product of popular discontent but the self-appointed guardians of the public interest.[71]

Pinchot's utilitarian philosophy was keenly supported by Vice-President Theodore Roosevelt, who became president following William McKinley's assassination in September 1901. Pursell argues that Roosevelt was attracted to conservation particularly because it was an issue he hoped would not raise fundamental social questions.[72] Pinchot in effect became Roosevelt's "Secretary of State for Conservation," and resource management became a matter of public policy. Roosevelt also sought Muir's opinions, and the demands of the preservationists were met during the Roosevelt era by the addition of Yosemite Valley to the surrounding national park and the creation of 53 wildlife reserves, 16 national monuments and five new national parks.[73] On the whole, though, Roosevelt's term saw the promotion of professional conservation based less on emotional principles of preservation than on rational management of natural resources.

If forestry was one inspiration of American conservation, water was another. Conservationists emphasized the importance of rivers in inland transport, domestic and commercial water supply, flood and erosion con-

TABLE 1:

Foundation of Selected Private Environmental Organizations, 1865–1914

Year	Organization	Country
1865	Commons, Open Spaces and Footpaths Preservation Society	- Britain
1867	East Riding Association for the Protection of Sea Birds	- Britain
1870	Association for the Protection of British Birds	- Britain
1880	Fog and Smoke Committee (National Smoke Abatement Institution from 1882)	- Britain
1883	American Ornithologists Union	- United States
	Natal Game Protection Association	- South Africa
1885	Selborne Society	- Britain
1886	Audubon Society (lapsed 1889, revived 1905)	- United States
1891	Society for the Protection of Birds	- Britain
1892	Sierra Club	- United States
1895	National Trust	- Britain
1896	Massachusetts Audubon Society	- United States
1898	Coal Smoke Abatement Society (now National Society for Clean Air)	- Britain
1903	Society for the Preservation of the Wild Fauna of the Empire	- Britain
1905	National Association of Audubon Societies	- United States
1909	Swiss League for the Protection of Nature	- Switzerland
	Swedish Society for the Protection of Nature	- Sweden
	Wildlife Preservation Society	- Australia
1912	Society for the Promotion of Nature Reserves	- Britain
1913	British Ecological Society	- Britain

trol, and hydroelectric power and noted that water power was the only major resource still in public possession. Multipurpose river development was seen as a prime example of the planned and efficient use of resources. American business was less interested in the management of water as a resource than in its exploitation, but even its leaders had to admit that inland navigation needed to be managed to prevent a monopoly on transport being won by the railways.

In March 1907, Roosevelt, at the suggestion of Pinchot,[74] created the Inland Waterways Commission (IWC), ostensibly to prepare and report a comprehensive plan for the improvement and control of American river systems. In fact, it went far beyond this. Roosevelt insisted that any plan for the utilization of inland waterways should consider flood control, the prevention of erosion and siltation, and the construction of dams. The commission concluded that any plans for the use of inland waterways should regard rivers as a national asset and take full account of the conservation of all resources connected with them. Its findings were published in February 1908 and immediately opposed by the influential Army Corps of Engineers (which had a narrow view of water use and development)[75] and by Congress (which was against the idea of a super planning agency).

In 1908–09, as his term drew to a close and his conservation program appeared to be ebbing, Roosevelt launched what Penick describes as a "crusade . . . born to some extent of frustration,"[76] aimed at taking conservation to the people. At an IWC meeting in May 1907, Frederick H. Newell (an engineer in the U.S. Geological Survey, a colleague of Pinchot's, and a member of the IWC) suggested that the Commission stage a national conference to help draw attention to conservation. The plan was agreed, and the White House Conference of Governors on Conservation was held on 13–15 May 1908. Some 44 state governors and representatives of 70 national organizations attended, but Muir, Sargent and other preservationists were not invited. Although initially limited to a discussion of national water resources, the agenda was widened to take in all natural resources. States rights was a key issue, with most governors declaring their opposition to more than the most marginal involvement of federal government in the control of resources. They recommended that each state create a conservation commission to work with other state commissions and the federal government. Thanks to the publicity surrounding the conference, conservation became a matter of public debate and was brought to the attention of the wider American public for the first time.

Within three weeks, Roosevelt had announced the creation of a National Conservation Commission, entrusted with making the first survey of natural resources in the United States. Pinchot headed the executive committee, which remarkably succeeded in having the inventory completed within six months. It was laid before Congress on 22 January 1909 as a basis for future legislation. Roosevelt described it as "one of the most fundamentally important documents ever laid before the American people."[77] The Commission was, however, short-lived. Congress refused to approve government funding because of a prevailing resentment at Roosevelt's expansion of executive power.[78]

Pinchot, meanwhile, aware that a new president was unlikely to be as sympathetic to conservation as Roosevelt had been, pursued two further conservation conferences, this time to be international in their scope. The first was the North American Conservation Congress, held in Washington, DC on 18 February 1909 under the chairmanship of Pinchot. Ten delegates from Canada, Newfoundland, Mexico, and the United States discussed the principles of conservation espoused by Roosevelt, Pinchot, and the governors' meeting. The most notable outcome of the congress was its agreement that conservation was a problem broader than the boundaries of one nation. The conference thus proposed that Roosevelt call a world conservation conference. The North American Congress was still in session when Roosevelt issued invitations to 58 countries to attend a world conservation congress in The Hague. Roosevelt left office in March, and nearly half the countries had accepted when the conference was called off by President Taft. Pinchot was bitterly disappointed. Further conservation congresses were held in September 1910, September 1911, October 1912, and November 1913, but Taft had not repeated his request to Congress, made as president-elect, to maintain the National Conservation Commission and appeared undecided over whether or not to embrace conservation policy. Pinchot was removed from office in 1910 and became president of the National Conservation Association (founded in 1909).

THE AFRICAN WILDLIFE QUESTION: 1895–1933

Although Roosevelt's North American Conservation Congress and his planned international conservation conference were the first attempts to discuss conservation at an intergovernmental level, the protection of nature, and particularly of birds, had already been the subject of international discussion. During the second half of the nineteenth century, bird protection organizations had become politically active in a number of European countries and had developed the argument for more universal protection of wild birds.[79] The idea for an international agreement to protect animals useful to forestry and agriculture (thus strongly utilitarian) was first suggested at a meeting of German foresters and agriculturalists held in Vienna in 1868. It was not until 1902, however, that a convention to protect birds useful to agriculture was finally signed by twelve European countries (excluding Britain).[80] Opposition to its utilitarian character, combined with its restriction to birds, formed a rallying point for groups seeking both a more ambitious document and a permanent international institution to work in the area of nature protection.[81]

An issue of perhaps greater long-term significance and greater pan-European import was the African wildlife question. The nineteenth century hunting and plumage debates in Britain drew the attention of some naturalists to the problems of the colonies. The wildlife of the East African colonies had begun to attract hunting parties, with game made suddenly accessible by the declaration of German and British protectorates, in 1885 and 1896 respectively. The abundance of game in southern British East Africa was thanks largely to the ascendancy of the Maasai (who did not kill or eat game themselves) over much of present-day southern Kenya and northern Tanzania. The building of the Uganda railway in 1895–1902 (and of the Tanga-Moshi railway in 1896–1912) made the interior accessible to white settlers and hunters. The latter returned to the coast and their home countries with reports of abundant game. From 1895 the number of visiting hunters grew rapidly, and the number of game animals diminished.

In 1897 the British Prime Minister, Lord Salisbury, responding to pressure from preservationists and hunters equally concerned (but for obviously different reasons) about the future availability of game, proposed to the German government the need to control ivory exports from East Africa. A note was circulated to other governments in 1899, and in 1900 the world's first international environmental agreement—the Convention for the Preservation of Animals, Birds, and Fish in Africa—was signed in London by Britain, France, Germany, Italy, Portugal, and the Belgian Congo. Game preservation was at the root of the convention, and there was little interest in nongame animals, which it was presumed were in no danger because they were not being hunted.[82] The convention was designed to control the trade in ivory, fish, skins, and trophies and suggested protective measures such as closed seasons. Although signed, it was never put into effect; its lasting importance lay in the precedent it created for later legislation.

The protection of animal life in the British colonies was taken a step further in 1903 with the foundation of the world's first international environmental organization, the Society for the Preservation of the Wild Fauna of the Empire (SPWFE, now the Fauna and Flora Preservation Society), sponsored by hunters (including Frederick Courtenay Selous) and naturalists (including Sir Ray Lankester). The Society aimed to encourage the protection of fauna (in effect, birds and the larger mammals) in the colonies. Within a year, its hunter sponsors were being nicknamed "the penitent butchers."[83]

Among those who warned of the decline of African game were Sir Harry Johnston, Special Commissioner in Uganda (1899–1901) and a founding member of SPWFE, and the sagacious German naturalist C. G. Schillings, who collected specimens for German museums and pioneered wildlife photography in the region. In 1906 Johnston wrote that funding was desperately needed to pay for the protection of future national parks in East Africa, that public opinion should be encouraged to strengthen government action, and that the lessons being learned in Africa should be learned also in Britain. He wrote disparagingly of European hunters: "It seems to be still the accepted panacea in Britain or Continental society that a young or middle-aged man, who has been crossed in love, or who has figured in the Divorce Court . . . must go out to Africa and kill big game."[84] Reserves created in East Africa at the end of the nineteenth century were planned as an amenity for the use of soldiers and administrators with a penchant for hunting.[85]

Schillings, who had attended the 1900 conference and was concerned that the destruction of South African wildlife should not be repeated in East Africa, wrote of the "tragedy of civilisation" in man bringing more and more of nature under his control and killing animals at an unprecedented rate. He found it regrettable that Germans knew so little of the animal life in their colonies, and, in his books *With Flashlight and Rifle* and *In Wildest Africa*, made impassioned pleas for greater protection and more research. He felt the most urgent task was to amass accurate data on wildlife and then devise practicable measures for protection. Like Marsh before him, Schillings argued that no epoch had seen such progress in industry and knowledge, yet was still blinded to the effects: water and air pollution, deforestation, the extinction of animal species, and the reckless exploitation of coal reserves.[86] He also pointed out that traders and black hunters were putting additional pressure on game, noting that in the German Cameroons, 452 tons of elephant tusks were exported in the period 1895–1905. By 1910, about 150–200 shooting parties were visiting British East Africa annually, taking about 10,000 animals.[87]

The vogue for hunting began to recede almost as suddenly as it had begun, due largely to the influx of permanent white settlers, which reduced the area of public hunting territory. By 1919 there were two game reserves in British East Africa: the Northern (between Lake Rudolf, now Turkana, and Mount Kenya), and the Southern (between Nairobi and the Tanganyika border, running down as far as Mt. Kilimanjaro). The Northern reserve covered semi-desert unsuitable for settlement, while the Southern had been created almost arbitrarily, and it was only during World War I military operations that it was found to contain land suitable for settlement. Lord Cranworth observed that there was little likelihood that the reserve would be kept inviolate unless settlers were convinced that it did not retard development of the colony: "Wherever you pick the area to be reserved for game, it is sure to be a Naboth's vineyard to someone, and . . . game is likely to get a worse name through this supposed usurpation than if such land were actually thrown open for settlement."[88] (This prescient observation was to apply equally well to the problems that were to arise much later when newly independent African governments tried to balance the need to exploit natural resources against demands that wildlife be protected.)

Although much reduced, hunting was to remain fashionable for several decades yet. But the spread of European settlement brought two more immediate problems in its wake. First, there was a growing suspicion that animals such as the eland and the buffalo carried tsetse fly and other parasites that posed a direct threat to domestic livestock. Second, speculators were beginning to see the commercial possibilities in exploiting East Africa's forest resources. The British colonial government, which was in favor of conserving forest resources, felt it would be premature to sell off concessions until it had a workable reforestation scheme. Nevertheless, an estimated 250,000 acres (100,000 hectares) of forest (or a quarter of the proclaimed forest area) were destroyed in the period 1894–1919.[89] The direct cause was clearance and conversion to crops by peasant farmers; the indirect cause was most likely government administrative policies that obliged peasant farmers to move off their traditional agricultural land. The Forest Ordinance of 1911 protected just over 2 million acres (800,000 hectares) of forest from cutting except under license.

The extermination by colonial authorities of wild animals regarded as agricultural pests or carriers of disease to domestic stocks began taking a heavy toll following the First World War; a total of 321,518 animals were killed, for example, in anti-tsetse fly operations between 1924 and 1945 in Southern Rhodesia alone.[90] Concern for the implications was one of the main motives behind the convening in London, on Britain's initiative, of the 1933 International Conference for the Protection of Fauna and Flora. This resulted in the signing of a convention on the Preservation of Fauna and Flora in Their Natural State, which was later ratified by most of the colonial powers. Superseding the long defunct 1900 Convention, it was designed to curb threats to African wildlife by creating protected areas, such as national parks and reserves. It brought preservationists, scientists and governments together in common cause, made its signatories aware of the problems of each other's African colonies, and established the precedent of nongovernmental organizations playing a technical advisory role in such initiatives.[91] It even included appendices of endangered and rare animal species. The signatories, however, were not bound by its rules, there was no provision for regular follow-up meetings, and no monitoring committee. It may also have begun making local populations antipathetic to the concept of wildlife protection, for animals were being protected for no practical reason and with no regard to traditional hunting rights. This would later become a critical factor in postindependence attempts to promote conservation (see chapters 5 and 8).

THE NEW DEAL AND THE DUST BOWL

Following the First World War and the wane of the influence of Roosevelt, Muir, and Pinchot, Fox sees American conservation losing its connection with political liberalism and becoming an adjunct to the business-minded Republican party of the 1920s. Thus, when Franklin D. Roosevelt took office in 1933 to preside over a nation in deep financial crisis, he inherited a Republican conservation movement in close alliance with business interests, a marriage that Fox believes fitted perfectly the New Deal's ideals of professional management and efficiency.[92] Roosevelt nevertheless harkened back to Pinchotism, and his New Deal administration applied it as a cornerstone of economic recovery, notably in the Tennessee Valley Authority, the apogee of the multipurpose development philosophy. Similarly, the Civilian Conservation Corps deployed unemployed men in forestry, soil erosion prevention, and flood control.

Elsewhere, attitudes to "rational management" were changing, as exemplified in the extermination (begun with federal funding by Theodore Roosevelt) of animal species regarded as pests. The wolf, the prairie dog, and the coyote were particular targets. Pinchot apparently had little interest in wildlife and paid little heed to the ecological implications of eradicating a species that interfered with the productivity of resources in which man had an interest.[93] Opposition to the extermination of predators was led in the postwar years by the American Society of Mammalogists, and by 1936, the killing of all predators in national parks had stopped. The changing view is encapsulated in the career of Aldo Leopold.[94] Leopold, a graduate of Yale Forestry School, in 1933 published his book *Game Management*, which became a key text for the wildlife profession. In it he declared that "effective conservation requires, in addition to public sentiment and laws, a deliberate and purposeful manipulation of the environment."[95] He had however, early become concerned at the Forest Service's obsession with forestry to the exclusion of wildlife management. He was instrumental, in 1924, in the creation of the Gila National Forest in New Mexico as a wilderness, and in 1935, he helped found the Wilderness Society.

Leopold's conversion from Progressive conservation was confirmed in his enormously influential *Sand County Almanac*, published posthumously in 1949. In it he called for a new land ethic based on the belief that man was not a conqueror of the "land-community" but a member and citizen of it; a weakness of conservation based on economic notions was that it ignored the elements in the land-community that lacked commercial value, but were essential to its healthy functioning.[96] He warned of the inadequacy of land conservation as a purely economic question: "We abuse land because we regard it as a commodity belonging to us. When we see land as a commodity to which we belong, we may begin to use it with love and respect."[97]

Meanwhile, the wilderness preservation movement underwent a revival during the New Deal. As the United States emerged from the Depression, visits to national parks soared from 6.3 million in 1934 to 16.2 million in 1938. Despite his deep concern about land, trees, and water for human use,[98] Roosevelt was personally unimpressed by many parks, but he saw them as essential in the process of national spiritual rejuvenation. He hoped they could be made more accessible, particularly for residents of the overpopulated eastern states. He was opposed in this by the wilderness preservationists, who argued that the roads being built into parks to make them more accessible threatened to destroy wilderness. The continuing rift between conservationists and preservationists came to a head in 1935–39 with the debate over Kings Canyon in the Sierra Nevada. Muir had long before campaigned without success to have it declared a national park; in 1935 the planned construction of an access road and the commercial development it would bring helped bring the Sierra Club out of the rut into which it had settled. Concentrated campaigning resulted in the declaration of Kings Canyon National Park in 1939.

The mid-1930s saw one of the greatest man-made environmental disasters in history: the Dust Bowl. Between 1934 and 1937, more than 200 regional dust storms hit the Great Plains.[99] Some were dense enough to blot out the sun and create drifts up to 20 feet (6 metres) high; others blew dust as far as Chicago, Washington, DC, and the Atlantic. By 1938, more than half the Great Plains—some 500,000 square miles (1.29 million sq km)—had been eroded; 16 states were affected, and the United States had been obliged to import wheat. Immediate blame was placed on the wind and on the drought of 1931–34. But the real blame lay with more than half a century of ill-advised agricultural practices: plowing long straight furrows, leaving fields bare of vegetation, reliance on a single cash crop, and the destruction of the native sod that was a vital buffer against wind and drought.[100] The Great Plains Committee, in its report of 1936, emphasized the effect of disturbances to the balance of nature, the pursuit of self-interest and unregulated competition, and the belief that nature could be shaped at will to suit man's convenience.[101] Before the Dust Bowl, resource management in the United States had been uncoordinated and founded in immediate economic needs; as a direct consequence of the Dust Bowl, Worster believes, conservation began to move toward a more inclusive, coordinated, ecological perspective.

The effects of the Dust Bowl were felt far beyond the borders of the United States. Anderson argues that the alarm created by images of the Dust Bowl was one of several factors that combined to encourage a reassessment of agrarian policies in Britain's African colonies;[102] the others included the effects of the Depression on export markets for colonial produce, recognition that rapid increases in the human and stock populations of African reserves were exerting serious pressure on the land, and concern for the consequences of an increasing incidence of drought in much of East Africa. By 1938, soil conservation had become a major public policy issue in East Africa, a development that Anderson sees as part of a wider transition in British colonial thinking.

NATURE PROTECTION: FIRST STEPS TOWARD AN INTERNATIONAL ORGANIZATION

In 1909, European nature protectionists met at the International Congress for the Protection of Nature, in Paris. Reviewing the progress (or lack thereof) of nature protection in Europe, they proposed the creation of an international nature protection body.[103] The idea was taken up by Paul Sarasin (the founder, in 1914, of the Swiss National Park). With the blessing of the Swiss Federal Council, he approached the governments of Austria, Argentina, Belgium, Britain, Denmark, France, Germany, Hungary, Italy, Japan, the Netherlands, Norway, Portugal, Romania, Russia, Spain, Sweden, and the United States. All but Japan and Romania agreed in principle. In 1913, an Act of Foundation of a Consultative Commission for the International Protection of Nature was signed in Berne by

17 European countries. It was to collect, classify, and publish information on the international protection of nature and propagandize on behalf of the cause. The first step was an international conference to talk about such issues as whaling, international trade in skins and feathers, and migratory bird protection. But the outbreak of war both prevented the conference and effectively laid the 1913 Commission to rest. The only progress made during the war years was the signing, in 1916, of a migratory bird agreement between the United States and Britain (on behalf of Canada).

Postwar attempts to revive the Commission met with little success. It was clear that the idea of an international body was little more than the pipe-dream of a few committed enthusiasts, among the most tireless of whom was the Dutch preservationist P. G. van Tienhoven. In 1925, van Tienhoven founded the Netherlands Committee for International Nature Protection as a base from which he could promote his dream of an international body to take over the mantle of the 1913 Commission. The foundation of national nature protection bodies in Belgium and France in 1925–26 seemed to augur well, but there was no support from Britain.[104] In 1928, van Tienhoven created—and won some support for—a Dutch-subsidized international coordinating office, which was reconstituted in 1934 as L'Office International pour la Protection de la Nature (OIPN) and charged with promoting international nature protection. Its work was inconclusive, though, and, like the 1913 Commission, it was destined to fail. It was premature; both the 1913 and the 1934 bodies lacked an international authority that they might lobby,[105] and mature national bodies that might form the basis of a firm international network.

Any progress that there might have been on international cooperation during the mid-war years belonged to the ornithologists. The International Committee (later Council) for Bird Protection (later Preservation) (ICBP) was founded at a meeting in London in June 1922. The moving light was Gilbert Pearson, president of the Audubon Association from 1910 to 1934, who hoped that the ICBP would strengthen links between American and European bird protection groups. The Committee had less ambitious aims than the 1913 Commission, seeking "transnational coordination rather than international integration."[106] The key to ICBP's success lay in the autonomy it gave to its national committees. It had an important formative influence on the international protection movement, drawing attention to the depletion of some species, the threats faced by migratory species, and the international trade in feathers.[107] The need for international action and legislation was on the agenda of other gatherings of ornithologists during the 1920s and 1930s, notably of the International Conference on the Protection of Migratory Waterfowl, held in London in 1927.

While Europe was diverted during the late 1930s by the escalating threat of Nazism, the Americans reached two notable international environmental agreements of their own. The first was the 1937 Migratory

Birds Treaty, signed with Mexico and Canada. The second, the Convention on Nature Protection and Wild Life Preservation in the Western Hemisphere (the Western Hemisphere Convention), was opened for signature in 1940 to all American countries. Wildlife, scenery, geological formations, wilderness, and regions and objects of aesthetic, historic, or scientific value were all included. Contracting governments undertook to set up new national parks, consolidate existing parks, maintain wilderness preserves, draw up legislation, encourage research exchange with one another, protect migratory birds, control trade in wildlife, and afford particular protection to species listed in an annex. This was all very impressive, but by the end of the war only eight states had signed, and the convention, lacking adequate administration, was to lie almost forgotten until 1976 when the Organization of American States launched a campaign to revive it. By then, though, it had little practical value.[108]

The SPWFE, IOPN, ICBP, the two African conventions and the Western Hemisphere convention represented the seeds of an interest in international cooperation, an acceptance (if only as yet by a minority) that national conservation and protection movements ultimately had interests that transcended national frontiers. But it was to take another world war before the climate was right for the hopes of a few to be converted into the actions of many.

TWO

Protection, Conservation, and the United Nations (1945–1961)

The Second World War transformed values and attitudes toward internationalism, which in turn radically altered the agenda of environmentalism. Even before the war had ended, plans were being drawn up to promote reconstruction and economic assistance, particularly through the new United Nations and its specialized agencies. In this receptive climate, the period 1943–46 saw the resurrection of two environmental initiatives that predated the First World War: the convening of an international conference on the conservation of natural resources and the establishment of an international organization for the protection of nature. Once more, however, the conservationists and the protectionists followed separate paths, and it was to be another decade before they began to agree.

Since the cancellation by Taft of Theodore Roosevelt's proposed international conference in 1909, Gifford Pinchot had periodically attempted to revive the idea. He had approached Wilson, Harding, Coolidge, and Hoover in turn with no success. Then his friendship with Franklin D. Roosevelt once again gave him influence in the White House. In a speech to the Eighth American Scientific Congress in May 1940, Pinchot argued that every nation's "fair access" to natural resources was "an indispensable condition of permanent peace."[1] He felt that peace could only be achieved by removing the incentives to war, one of the commonest of which was the demand for land and natural resources. In June 1944, he finally raised the matter with Roosevelt, who responded favorably. "I am surprised that the world knows so little about itself," Roosevelt later wrote to his secretary of state, Cordell Hull. "Conservation is a basis of permanent peace."[2]

The State Department was less than enthused. It argued that the new UN Economic and Social Council (ECOSOC) and the planned Food and Agriculture Organization (FAO) intended to make conservation part of postwar economic policy planning, and it doubted whether significant international agreement could be reached on conservation without considering the orderly development and marketing of natural resources. Conservation, it argued, was only one part, albeit an important part, of the total problem of international collaboration in the wisest use of the world's productive resources. Conservation as it related to agriculture, fisheries, and forestry would be assessed by FAO; the Anglo-American Petroleum Agreement then before Congress included the basic objective of an "orderly" development of world petroleum resources; and conservation had already been raised in international commodity discussions.[3] Roosevelt dismissed these arguments, saying that they had failed to grasp the real need for finding out more about the world's resources. In January 1945 he told Pinchot that he would take up the idea of the conference as a basis of permanent peace with Stalin and Churchill at Yalta later that month.[4]

There is no evidence that he did raise the matter at Yalta, however, and although Pinchot's plans for the conference were awaiting Roosevelt upon his return, the president appears to have been swayed by the State Department view. He drafted a memo to Pinchot in March suggesting that, given the elements of conservation being worked into the programs of FAO, ECOSOC, and the World Bank, the conference be postponed. "We would not want to have a separate international organization to recommend plans and projects with respect to conservation except subordinate to, and related to, [ECOSOC]," he wrote.[5] The memo was never sent, however, and Pinchot now presented Roosevelt with a detailed draft plan for the conference. It might consider the setting up of an international organization to promote the conservation of natural resources, fair access to necessary raw materials by all countries, information exchange, and the drawing up of an inventory of natural resources and a set of principles on their conservation. Pinchot pointed out that Lewis Lorwin, a senior member of the U.S. Foreign Economic Administration, had suggested that the Dumbarton Oaks proposals outlining the purposes of the UN might include the encouragement of international cooperation in the conservation of natural and human resources.[6] Pinchot also established with the chairman of the UN Interim Commission on Food and Agriculture that there would be no conflict between the world conference and the plans of FAO. Those in government to whom Pinchot had spoken were all supportive, he claimed; only the State Department was opposed.

With Roosevelt's death in April 1945 came an end to direct White House interest in the matter. In a subsequent letter to the State Department, William Clayton, the assistant secretary of state for economic affairs, pointed out that Pinchot's draft plan of March "confirms our early misgivings. The suggested agenda [and recommendations and conclusions] . . . all indicate a coverage of discussion that would overlap at almost every turn" with the functions of FAO, ECOSOC, and a proposed World Trade Conference. Clayton felt it unnecessary to call a conference to collect information, which could be better done by technicians communicating with each other through "normal channels," and that it was unlikely that countries could agree on collaborative conservation action until the larger problems of trade and commodity arrangements had been resolved.[7] Pinchot was advised to approach Truman, Averell Harriman, and Clayton. In May he spoke to Truman, and in December he gave him another set of plans for the conference.[8] But the initiative was now out of Pinchot's hands, and he was left to devote his last months to his autobiography. He died in October 1946, at the age of 81.

Ironically, the United Nations had already begun thinking about an international conference on the conservation and use of resources, to be based on the "need for continuous development and widespread application of the techniques of resource conservation and utilization."[9] In September 1946, the American representative at the United Nations wrote to the acting president of ECOSOC on behalf of the United States proposing that a scientific conference be held in the United States to "consider the conservation and effective utilization of natural resources."[10] The primary motive was the need to look at conservation in the light of the wartime strain on natural resources and their importance to postwar reconstruction. Despite the U.S. State Department's earlier reservation that the conference would duplicate ECOSOC's own activities in the area, ECOSOC for its part was agreeable and adopted a resolution recognizing the need for the development and application of techniques of resource conservation and development. It called a conference to be "devoted solely to the *exchange of ideas and experience* on these matters among engineers, resource technicians, economists and other experts in related fields" (my emphasis).[11] The conference—the United Nations Scientific Conference on the Conservation and Utilization of Resources (UNSCCUR)—was scheduled for the summer of 1949. In form and content, it was all but identical to Pinchot's stillborn conference.

FOOD SECURITY, THE UNITED NATIONS, AND THE NEO-MALTHUSIANS

The provision of food and the elimination of starvation was one of the immediate priorities of the UN's agenda of social and economic rehabilitation. In October 1942, Frank McDougall, adviser to the Australian representative to the League of Nations and someone long involved in League activities on nutrition, had outlined in a memorandum circulated to governments a proposal for a UN campaign for freedom from want of food. He submitted this suggestion to Roosevelt, who, with little notice, announced in February 1943 that a conference would be held that spring to explore long-term food problems. Discussion at the conference (held at Hot Springs, Virginia, in May 1943) centered on food supply and demand, increased production to meet consumer needs, and better distribution. There was passing mention of the value of soil management; the proposed new Food and Agriculture Organization, noted the report of the conference, would be "dedicated to furthering good use and good management, in all ways and by all peoples, of this most basic of man's resources."[12]

FAO was founded at a conference in Quebec in October 1945, and Sir John Boyd Orr was elected first director-general.[13] The new organization was "born out of the idea of freedom from want";[14] Orr's first priority was to cope with a world food crisis, at the time predicted to last well into 1947, and then to deal with long-term food supply. He proposed a World Food Council that would buy, hold, and sell important agricultural commodities entering world trade, thereby controlling prices and supplies. The Council would be closely related to ECOSOC and the International Bank for Reconstruction and Development (the World Bank, created in 1944). It would build up food reserves large enough to cope with famine emergencies. This proposal was, however, rejected in late 1947, a defeat that was to be instrumental in Orr's decision to resign his post in the following year.

FAO emphasized the development and exploitation of natural resources in support of its short- and longer-term aims of tackling world nutrition problems and bettering the condition of rural populations by improving efficiency in the production and distribution of food and agricultural products, but it also recognized the importance of conservation. One means of achieving its goals, as outlined in Article I of its constitution, was "the conservation of natural resources and the adoption of improved methods of agricultural production."[15] Allied to the food problem was the issue of the restoration of the timber industry, to which end FAO promoted the protection and extension of forest cover to check soil erosion, protect watersheds, control floods, act as windbreaks, and shelter wildlife. For example, it ran training courses and workshops in forestry, studied timber trends, and convened conferences in 1947, 1948, 1949, and 1952 to discuss, respectively, the provision of timber in Europe, Latin America, Asia and the Pacific, and the Near East, as well as long-term plans for forest rehabilitation and the use of forest products. Technical assistance to less developed countries was prominent in the FAO agenda.

In 1951, FAO held a conference in Ceylon on land use in Asia and the Far East. Population was at the core of the debate, and shifting cultivation was blamed for the reduction of soil fertility, the clearance of vegetation, flooding, soil erosion, river siltation, and the reduction of water supply. Two critical points were made at the conference:

1) Research into tropical soils was urgently needed; there had been too great a tendency to apply in the tropics the results of research and experience in temperate zones, resulting in the failure of agricultural development programs. An example of such a failure was the attempt made in 1947–48 to develop a groundnut scheme in Tanganyika. A lack of preliminary planning, and a failure to plan the scheme according to local climatic conditions, led to its abandonment in 1950.[16]

2) More attention needed to be given to the needs of peasant farmers; land reform might be needed to create efficient small farms. A research project was launched in 1949 to look into Latin American forestry resources and the best ways of managing and exploiting them.

In his presidential address to the annual meeting of the British Association for the Advancement of Science in September 1949, Sir John Russell spoke of the essential role of science in feeding growing populations. Warning of the social and political roots of soil erosion, and alluding to the anti-soil erosion programs then being carried out in the United States, the USSR, South Africa, and African colonies, he concluded that ecology was being used increasingly to help crop production: "The old idea that science would enable the farmer to go anywhere and produce anything has given place to the more realistic principle that every acre of land should, as far as possible, be used in the way to which it is best adapted. Extensions of the cultivated area, treatment of eroded land and improvement of wild pasture are already seen as ecological problems but the range is much wider and the possibilities great."[17] It became clear to several economists and conservationists that resource mismanagement and population growth were obstacles to the solution of the food crisis. Orr wrote in 1953 of the "wasting asset" of fertile land, caused by soil erosion, which was in turn caused by the clearance of trees (especially on sloping land) and by overgrazing and overcultivation. "The present world food shortage," he noted, "has raised again the spectre of Malthus."[18]

Many others had ventured their opinions since Malthus, some only a few years before Orr. In 1936, the liberal economist Stuart Chase had written alarmedly of the depletion of natural resources.[19] In 1937, at the height of the Dust Bowl, Paul Sears had written of the dangers of spreading deserts in his book *Deserts on the March.*[20] In 1939, Hugh Bennett[21] of the U.S. Soil Conservation Service, and R. O. Whyte and G. V. Jacks[22] had warned of the dangers of soil erosion and the need for conservation. In 1945 Frank Pearson and Floyd Harper had written about the relationship between hunger, population and land in their book *The World's Hunger.*[23] Concerns about the relationship between population growth and resource depletion were now revived in two influential books published in the United States in 1948: *Our Plundered Planet* by Fairfield Osborn and *Road to Survival* by William Vogt.

Osborn (1887–1969) had been president of the New York Zoological Society since 1940 (and from 1948 to 1962 was president of the Conservation Foundation). Prompted partly by the memory of the Dust Bowl and partly by wartime shortages of food and wood, and quoting numerous examples from history of human misuse of the land, he argued that the story of forests, grasslands, wildlife, and water resources in the United States in the previous century had been "the most violent and most destructive of any written in the long history of civilization." He bemoaned the fact that few people were aware of the processes of mounting destruction being inflicted on natural resources: "Action of government, in the last analysis rests mainly . . . on the point of view of the people. The fact that more than 55 per cent of the population of the USA lives in cities and towns results inevitably in detachment from the land and apathy as to how living resources are treated." He argued that international discord could be traced to diminishing productive lands and increasing population pressures and warned: "The tide of the earth's population is rising, the reservoir of the earth's living resources is falling. . . . There is only one solution: Man must recognize the necessity of co-operating with nature."[24]

In *The Limits of the Earth* (published in 1953), Osborn argued: "When resources have proved adequate not only to meet the basic needs of peoples but also to support their economies, nations and cultures have flourished. The so-called 'great periods' of history are intimately identified with this favorable relationship. Lacking it, apparently indestructible empires have dissolved."[25] Like Marsh before him, Osborn traced the links between environmental destruction and social decay in Greece and Rome. He now asked how the earth could continue meeting the needs of a rapidly growing population.

Vogt (1902–1968) was even more alarmist. His wartime experiences in Peru and Chile, with their poverty and large families, and the Catholic Church's resistance to birth control, turned him into a neo-Malthusian.[26] From 1943 to 1948 Vogt was head of the Conservation Section of the Pan-American Union. *Road to Survival*, which anticipated the prophets of doom of the 1960s, became a best-seller. In it, Vogt argued that the United States was over-populated, self-indulgent, wasteful (of topsoil, timber, water, coal, and gasoline particularly) and doomed to extinction. "The methods of free competition and the application of the profit motive have been disastrous to the land. . . . Land is managed on the basis of so-called economic laws and in very general disregard of the physical and biological laws to which it is subject. Man assumes that what has been good for industry must necessarily be good for the land. This may prove to be one of the most expensive mistakes in history."[27] Surveying the effects of an imbalance between human demands and the carrying capacity of land in five continents, Vogt concluded that man had "moved into an untenable position by protracted and wholesale violation of certain natural laws; to re-establish himself he needs only to bring his behavior into conformity with natural limitations." Vogt argued that everyone was responsible and that governments were unlikely to act without people leading the way. People had to appreciate the complex relationships between man and resources that made it impossible to isolate the lot of one nation from another and to understand their dependence on resources. It was also essential that people be made aware of the dilemma.[28] Among those influenced by Vogt's assessment was Paul

Ehrlich, then a student and later a professor of biology at Stanford University (see chapter 4).

The warnings of Osborn and Vogt were widely read, but their impact was dampened by the fact that they came just as the United States reached the end of two decades of enforced austerity and embarked on a decade of unparalleled prosperity and consumption. Good weather produced repeated bumper harvests, incomes rose, and consumer spending and energy consumption grew. Half a century before, American conservation had been allied to Progressivism, which in turn was a product of an era of prosperity. But prosperity now produced a very different reaction; in such a climate, predictions of doom seemed premature, and talk of resource shortages irrelevant. Nevertheless, in 1952, a government commission chaired by William Paley of CBS agreed with Vogt's contention that the United States was running out of resources. Meetings between Osborn, Horace Albright, and others resulted in the foundation in the same year of Resources for the Future (RFF), set up with a large grant from the Ford Foundation, which charged RFF with the task of devising a rational plan for resource consumption. But the presence on the RFF Council of Sponsors of representatives from chambers of commerce and trade associations influenced RFF's outlook on conservation; in 1963 it published a report that in effect refuted Paley's findings.[29]

NATURE PROTECTION: UNESCO AND THE CREATION OF AN INTERNATIONAL ORGANIZATION

Postwar attempts to set up an international nature protection organization were initially sidetracked by a curious little struggle between British and American protectionists on the one side and Swiss, Belgians, and Dutch on the other. The latter were particularly keen to set up an organization independent of the new UN system; the former thought it ill-advised. The continental Europeans prevailed, thus denying environmentalists an effective input into UN affairs for nearly thirty years.

As part of a study of the feasibility of establishing national parks in Britain, a National Parks Committee was set up, and a Wild Life Conservation Special Committee (WLCSC) was established under the chairmanship of Julian Huxley.[30] Huxley concluded that the WLCSC could usefully study the Swiss National Park, founded 32 years before. Its administration had many years of the kind of experience that could prove useful to the WLCSC in its deliberations. A team of six scientists and administrators, including Max Nicholson,[31] was thus dispatched to Switzerland in June 1946 to meet with the scientific committee overseeing the park and discuss the scientific management of national parks.

The team was surprised, and more than a little dismayed, to find upon its arrival that the Swiss had convened a meeting of their counterparts from Belgium, France, Norway, the Netherlands, and Czechoslovakia, countries where a revival of the prewar conservation network had already been informally discussed. The International Office for the Protection of Nature (IOPN), which had moved from Brussels to Amsterdam in 1940, had maintained only routine work until 1947 when, in an attempt to revive interest, it produced a report on international wildlife protection activity during the war. Dr. Charles Bernard, president of the Swiss League for the Protection of Nature, now decided to submit the matter to wider scrutiny. The purpose of the Swiss meeting was to discuss "informally and without commitments" the future of international nature protection.[32] Bernard had, however, pursued his goal of reviving IOPN with such energy that he was accused of planning to bring IOPN, or its successor, to Switzerland. Nicholson believes that the Swiss saw this 1946 gathering as an opportunity to out-manoeuvre the Dutch and the Belgians, who had maintained IOPN before the war.[33]

Bernard assured the meeting that decisions could not be taken: "Our aim is to enable each of us to state his ideas on the subject. Our conversations will be informal, as none of us have come in our official capacity. Also there are not enough nations represented here."[34] The British delegation insisted that no minutes be taken and no commitments be made. Thus agreed, discussions centered on the usefulness of an official intergovernmental body, and it was proposed that the Swiss League ask the Swiss government to restore the 1913 Commission. Van Tienhoven suggested that UNESCO be approached for assistance, but was overruled. At a final meeting on 6 July, two provisional conclusions were reached: that it was "desirable" that there be an active international organization ("adequately financed, and with adequate terms of reference") to facilitate cooperation between national bodies and that national bodies might well consider this.[35] The British delegation returned home resolved that it was too early to be talking about international initiatives in the field of nature protection.[36] While Switzerland had remained neutral, they argued, the rest of the world had been fighting a devastating war, and not only was extensive reconstruction an overriding priority, but few countries had either the resources or the national agencies needed to make up a viable international network.

While his colleagues in Britain now turned to the question of a national body (the Nature Conservancy was set up in 1949), Julian Huxley brought his influence as the new director-general of UNESCO to bear. Always a keen naturalist, he was convinced of the relevance and urgency of nature protection. In his memoirs,[37] he was to describe IUPN as "the organisation foi Nature Conservation I had founded and built up while at UNESCO," a claim that was exaggerated but should not detract from his role. UNESCO had been founded in November 1946 to promote international cooperation in education, science, and culture. Its agenda for 1947 centered on measures to assist in postwar reconstruction, especially in the field of education; its only official involvement with the natural sciences was in the promotion of scientific exchange and education. Its Department of Natural Sciences (one of seven UNESCO departments), had 12 percent of UNESCO's budget for 1948 but employed less than 6 percent of its staff.[38] Within the department, natural resource conservation was a minor element, although a project was launched in April 1947 to look into the "needs and possibilities" of the Amazon forest, essentially intended to research and relay scientific data and information on the area.[39] The word "conservation" appeared in UNESCO's constitution only in relation to books, works of art, and "monuments" of history and science.

As a new body, UNESCO was obliged to seek advice on technical matters from existing international non-governmental bodies, one of which was the International Council of Scientific Unions (ICSU). At the suggestion of the Cambridge biochemist Joseph Needham, ICSU became attached to UNESCO in Paris. UNESCO had also given itself powers to help create new international non-governmental organizations if necessary. Huxley began by submitting a proposal to the General Conference in Mexico City in 1947 that UNESCO include the protection of nature in its brief. He succeeded eventually in persuading the conference that "the enjoyment of nature was part of culture, and that preservation of rare and interesting animals and plants was a scientific duty."[40] It had been thanks to Huxley and Needham that science had been included in UNESCO's brief at all; but for Huxley, notes Nicholson, "science would have been either formally eliminated or would never have appeared as a serious factor in UNESCO."[41] It was only Huxley's personal interest that now gave rise to any discussion at all on the subject of nature protection within UNESCO. Another contribution came from the New York Zoological Society, which was promoting the idea of an international foundation with a brief to pursue the *conservation* of animal life, forests, and other plant life, water resources, and soils.

The new international nature protection body proposed by the Europeans was meanwhile discussed in greater depth at a second meeting sponsored by the Swiss and held between 28 June and 3 July 1947 at Brunnen. Better organized than the informal Basle meeting the year before, it was attended by 70 delegates from 24 countries (all European except Argentina, Australia, Guatemala, the Dutch East Indies, New Zealand, and the United States); 14 governments had given their representatives powers to speak on their behalf, leaving Britain, Belgium, and Switzerland as the only Western European countries without government representation. Again, it was made clear that no final decisions could be taken; the task was "first and foremost to establish the basis of an organisation that would be definitively created in the near future."[42] Despite the better organization, the conference was confused in its intentions. Some delegates saw it merely as the opportunity for further preparatory discussions, while others pressed for the immediate foundation of an international body. Some delegates favored swift action, arguing that it would "not be practical to leave to UNESCO the initiative [because] UNESCO . . . had not, any more than UNO, the special knowledge required to put such an organisation on its feet."[43]

There was clearly some concern that the initiative not be lost to the United Nations, and that IOPN preserve its independence. The British delegation, however, differed and proposed that UNESCO be asked to convene a congress, preferably in Paris in 1948, to consider the form of an international nature protection body, using the terms of the 1913 Commission as the basis for a new agreement. There was some confusion over UNESCO'S possible role. The more hopeful of the delegates at Brunnen found it difficult to ignore Huxley's now well-known personal support for nature protection. Huxley and Needham had, however, told the Swiss League that UNESCO had no wish to undertake immediate specific action in the field of nature protection, and no evidence of tangible UNESCO support was forthcoming. A French delegate, Professor Bresson, who had been closely involved in the foundation of IOPN in 1926, summed up: "Without governmental help, I think we can do nothing in the matter of an international organisation."[44] The Americans supported the British view that the help of a UN agency was mandatory if governments were to take the proposed new body seriously; certainly the United States government would give no support unless UN sponsorship was achieved. And how, the Americans asked, could the new body be truly international when countries such as the USSR, China, India, Canada, and South Africa were not represented at Brunnen?

Despite the doubts, a draft constitution was adopted by the conference establishing a Provisional International Union for the Protection of Nature (IUPN). Based in Basle, IUPN would "facilitate co-operation between Governments and national and international organisations concerned with . . . the protection of nature."[45] Scientific research, public awareness, education, regional planning, the creation of protected areas, the preservation of wildlife and habitats, and the preparation of a global convention were all to fall to IUPN. A copy of the draft constitution was to be sent immediately to UNESCO with the request that they pass it on to governments for comment. UNESCO was to be asked to convene a congress at Paris in July 1948 to adopt the constitution.

By deciding that UNESCO should be asked to represent the draft IUPN constitution to governments, IUPN had manoeuvred UNESCO into identifying itself with IUPN, thereby attracting government support. At the same Mexico City conference in 1947 at which he had convinced UNESCO of the importance of nature protection, Huxley succeeded in having UNESCO agree to convene a technical conference on nature protection to be held at the same time as UNSCCUR, the planned UN scientific conference in 1949. There was some opposition to this, especially from the U.S. National Commission for UNESCO, which believed that

UNESCO should transfer its support directly to the UN conference and ensure that emphasis be given to the preservation of natural areas.[46] Huxley's wishes nevertheless prevailed, and UNESCO even promised financial assistance to IUPN for the convening of the technical conference. Natural resource conservation and nature protection were thus to be treated as separate issues.

Of more pressing concern to the Swiss League and UNESCO was the Paris conference suggested by delegates at Brunnen. UNESCO saw it as a conference to set up a non-governmental organization (NGO), while IUPN hoped for government involvement. After heated discussion, a compromise was reached whereby UNESCO and the French government agreed to invite government representatives, while the Swiss League invited NGOs. The conference was held from 30 September to 7 October 1948 at Fontainebleu and was attended by representatives from 18 governments, seven international organizations, and 107 national organizations. Most of the discussion revolved around the issue of a constitution for IUPN. The draft discussed at Brunnen had, in Nicholson's view, been lacking, and he had had a new draft drawn up by the British Foreign Office that provided the basis for most of the discussion,[47] with amendments proferred by UNESCO and the United States delegation. The most controversial issue was the relative power of government and private representatives, with the governments not wishing to be in the position where they could be outvoted by private groups. The solution accepted was to give governments two votes at General Assemblies and the private groups one vote between them.

In its final form, IUPN was a hybrid of governmental and non-governmental bodies that, even today, is almost unique. The Constitutive Act of the Union was signed on 5 October 1948. IUPN was to promote the *preservation* of wildlife and the natural environment, public knowledge of the issues, education, scientific research, and legislation, and would collect, analyze, and disseminate data and information. Work would also be begun on the preparation of a global convention for the protection of nature (an undertaking that would prove overly optimistic and unrealistically broad). For IUPN's purposes, nature was defined as an important facet of spiritual life, its development and exploitation formed the foundation of human civilization, and the depletion of natural resources had led to a depression in human standards of living. This was an overlap of protection and conservation. The constitution emphasized that the destruction of nature could be reversed if people were "awakened in time to a full realisation of their dependence upon exhaustible natural resources and [recognized] the need for their protection and restoration as well as for their wise and informed administration in order that the future peace, progress, and prosperity of mankind may be assured."[48] So despite the fact that much of the discussion surrounding the formation of IUPN had centered on nature protection, IUPN's principles touched on resource conservation. Aesthetic considerations were minimized, and the ethics of conservation mentioned not at all. IUPN's philosophy saw man standing firmly at the heart of the natural system with conservation directly serving his interests and needs.

The headquarters of the new body were moved from Basle to Brussels, where ad hoc commissions were established to deal with education, nomenclature, and publications. One of the Union's most pressing tasks was to draw up a contract with UNESCO for the technical conference planned for the following summer. This was agreed and signed in November, with UNESCO pledging financial support for the preparations for the conference. Although IUPN now existed on paper, it faced the two enormous problems of turning its principles into tangible results, and of establishing its authority and credibility. In this it was hindered by financial restrictions that were to grow increasingly serious over the next decade. Much now depended upon the results of UNSCCUR, where experts in resource conservation and management would be able to exchange views "on past experience in order to compare the economic advantages of different methods,"[49] but there were to be no recommendations laid down for future action.

THE UN SCIENTIFIC CONFERENCE ON THE CONSERVATION AND UTILIZATION OF RESOURCES(UNSCCUR)

In anticipation of UNSCCUR, it was agreed that delegates should have at their disposal the findings of regional conferences on conservation. This need was met in part by the Inter-American Conference on the Conservation of Renewable Natural Resources in September 1948 in Denver, and the Seventh Pacific Science Congress in New Zealand in February 1949. The Denver conference was convened by the U.S. government at the request of the Pan-American Union and resolved to ask the Union to take the lead in helping the UN promote cooperation between Western governments in dealing with the conservation of natural resources. The 21 American governments represented were urged to set up national conservation bodies and to ratify the Western Hemisphere Convention.[50]

UNSCCUR was held at Lake Success in New York State between 17 August and 6 September 1949. Organized jointly by FAO, WHO, UNESCO, and the International Labor Organization, it was attended by more than 530 delegates from 49 countries (excluding the USSR). At 54 meetings held under sections on minerals, fuels and energy, water, forests, land, and wildlife and fish, the conference discussed global resource questions: increasing pressure on resources; the interdependence of resources; a review of critical shortages of food, forests, animals and fuels; the development of new resources by applied technology; educational resource techniques for underdeveloped countries; and the integrated development of river basins. It discussed science, not policy (although questions of policy were inevitably touched upon); it had no power to bind governments and did not make recommendations to them, nor attempt to reach international agreements. The conference was intended solely as a forum for the exchange of ideas and experience on the techniques of resource conservation and utilization.[51] Much of what was discussed could not anyway hope to be put into practice until the financial resources were available, but the principles discussed were to provide a useful framework for future action. A central issue on the agenda was the adequacy of natural resources to meet growing demands; it was argued that scientific knowledge could discover and create new resources and help better understand those already in use. Another recurring theme was the wasteful depletion of resources due to war.

Many of UNSCCUR's themes and conclusions were undoubtedly precocious, so much so that although they generated much discussion at the time, it was to be another two decades before they were more widely reflected in international conservation policy. Most environmental historians unfairly ignore UNSCCUR; in Nicholson's view it was successful only inasmuch as "it marked a breakthrough for conservation onto the agenda of intergovernmental business."[52] But this underrates the remarkable breadth and foresight of its agenda, which would not be repeated again until the 1968 Biosphere Conference and the 1972 Stockholm Conference (see chapter 5). Without question, it was the first major landmark in the rise of the international environmental movement.

Although the concurrent IUPN conference was titled the International Technical Conference on the Protection of Nature (ITC), it also discussed the conservation of renewable natural resources. Noting, for example, that the UN agencies were looking at technical assistance to less developed countries, and that such projects "to be effective require the application of human ecological principles,"[53] IUPN resolved to recommend to these agencies the promotion of the study of human ecology. ITC was attended by representatives from 32 countries and 11 international organizations, including FAO, WHO, ICBP, ICSU, and the Organization of American States, and focused on education and human ecology. A total of 23 resolutions were passed, many going beyond nature protection and being remarkably conservationist—for example, calling for a careful study of human ecology; the promotion of conservation education; consideration of the ecological impact of large-scale development projects; the controlled use of pesticides ("more attention should be drawn to the control of [pesticides] and biological methods from the point of view of protecting the equilibrium of nature");[54] detailed research into the plight of threatened fauna and flora; and cooperation between UNESCO and FAO on the conservation of food resources. Perhaps the most far-sighted resolution was No. 7, which suggested that IUPN should investigate the possibility of promoting, with development aid agencies, the execution of surveys detailing the ecological impact of development projects. Such a policy would not be actively pursued by environmental groups or aid agencies for another twenty years or more.

The resolutions that came out of the ITC could have formed the basis of an organization that early based its activities on the relationship between development and the environment. In fact, the promise of the ITC was to pose a stark contrast to the reality of the far more limited interest in nature protection that characterized IUPN policy in the following 15 years.

IUPN—EARLY YEARS

IUPN was not the product of a popular movement, but the creation of a few enthusiasts. Nicholson recalls that, until the 5th General Assembly in Copenhagen in 1954, when the administration was taken over by "scientists," the Union was run by "emotionally inspired missionary individuals and groups."[55] It began life with a healthy supply of enthusiasm and dedication, but little else. It was a small and exclusive body concerned with a narrow range of interests. It had little organizational ability and financial support, few national bodies or committees with which it could work, and very little hard scientific evidence upon which to base an agenda and design policies. By holding the ITC separately, it may have distanced itself from the UN system and perhaps missed an opportunity not only to encourage preservation activity within the UN but to benefit from the political influence and financial resources that closer involvement with the UN might have brought. At its 2nd General Assembly in Brussels in 1950, a note of frustration was evident in the words of Secretary-General Jean-Paul Harroy: "It is not unreasonable to claim that the UN should place the Union on a level with its principal specialized agencies and endow it with numerous collaborators disposing of very substantial credits."[56] Without money it could not sponsor research or fund conservation, and it could barely afford the kind of professional staff needed to establish it as an international scientific organization.

Nicholson believes the Union was an imaginative organization that foresaw problems such as the effect of toxic chemicals and the problems likely to arise from accelerated attempts to find and develop new stocks of energy.[57] Yet it fell short of the promise contained in the preamble to its constitution, which defined nature protection as "the preservation of the entire world biotic community, or man's natural environment, which includes the earth's renewable natural resources of which it is composed";[58] it chose instead to devote itself almost exclusively to nature protection. During his term as secretary-general (1948–1955), Jean-Paul Harroy "continually heard the Union criticised as being behind the times" because of its limited view.[59] Few governments had more than a passing interest in nature protection; in Britain, Nicholson recalls, it was regarded as "the amiable eccentricity of a number of people who had to be humoured."[60] At the 1952 General Assembly in Caracas, a group including Vogt, Osborn, Coolidge, and Harroy tabled a resolution suggesting that IUPN request the UN secretary-general to assign one of the specialized agencies to consider population. This led to a debate so bitter that Charles Bernard (the president of IUPN) feared for the stability of the Union and requested the withdrawal of the resolution.[61] (The resolution was eventually adopted at the 1954 General Assembly.)

Of all IUPN's handicaps, few were greater than the sheer lack of hard data. Scattered records and the independent work of individual scientists had long before established that some species were threatened with extinction, but often the only clue lay in depleted numbers; the source of the threat and the appropriate corrective action were often conjecture. The ITC had, however, shed some light on the state of existing knowledge, and a tentative list of threatened species was immediately compiled. State members of IUPN were encouraged to draw up national lists of threatened species, but none did so until the late 1960s. The Survival Service was created as an advisory network linking specialists in different countries, and the *IUPN Bulletin*, launched in 1952, provided a forum for the exchange of news and information. But the Survival Service faced the problem of finding individuals and organizations qualified, capable, or even willing to provide current and satisfactory information. Lack of progress in mammal conservation led the American Society of Mammalogists to resign from IUPN in 1954.

An injection of private funding from the United States in 1955 finally allowed IUPN to undertake field research. An American ecologist, Lee Talbot,[62] was commissioned to undertake a survey to determine the status of threatened mammals, notably those on the IUPN list. He traveled widely through Africa, south Asia, and the Near and Middle East during 1956–57. His survey not only added weight to IUPN's information resources but was immediately used for education and publicity. Talbot's work, together with other surveys carried out during the late 1950s in cooperation with the Fauna Preservation Society, resulted in a much clearer picture of the situation and the first hesitant corrective action. The information collected and classified during the 1950s—coordinated by the Survival Service—resulted in the publication in 1958 of a list of 34 endangered species. This led in turn to the publication in 1960 of the Red Data Book, a loose-leaf file of 135 endangered mammal species. ICBP and IUCN together drew up an additional list of threatened birds. Both lists grew during the 1960s and ultimately formed the basis of the current series of Red Data Books, the major reference source on the status of threatened and endangered species.

The Lake Success conference had concluded that the number of threatened species of fauna *and flora*[63] was growing, but plants were all but ignored in the early work of IUPN, as were smaller mammals, reptiles, amphibians, insects, and mollusks. "Fauna" in effect meant only the larger (and more visible and popular) mammals. The Survival Service Commission Threatened Plants Committee was established only in 1974, and a plants Red Data Book was finally published in 1978. Boardman believes that this reflected less a lack of appreciation of the ecological importance of plants than the difficulties involved in listing and assessing threats to the thousands of species involved.[64] Mammals and birds were more visible, the threats they faced more easily identified, and corrective action more readily suggested. Nicholson believes that much can also be ascribed to historical accident;[65] ornithology had entered a dynamic growth phase in the 1920s, and so tended to eclipse the other sciences for some time. Botany was simply in a recession of interest following the war.

The second of IUPN's major networks, in addition to the Survival Service, was the Commission on Ecology. This was set up in 1954 under the chairmanship of the American ecologist Edward Graham to coordinate ecological research and promote coordination between ecologists. By 1956 the Commission had concluded that its priority was research into the biotic conditions governing certain types of "landscapes," the study of human influences, and the best long-term use of these landscapes. There were early suggestions that plants could only be protected if habitats were protected; by 1980 the Red Data Books confirmed that 67 percent of all threatened species were threatened by the loss or contamination of their habitats.[66] Inaction by IUPN over the problem of habitat destruction had early caused some discontent, notably in the United States. At the International Zoological Congress in London in 1958, Coolidge noted the "greater realization of the importance of preserving habitats instead of individual species."[67] The importance of conserving representative ecosystems now attracted greater attention.

Between 1948 and 1956, influenced by the Commission on Ecology's warnings that people should be aware of the ecological consequences of their activities, IUPN's interests gradually broadened to encompass conservation. This was confirmed in 1956 by the Union's decision to change its name (largely on American insistence)[68] to the International Union for *Conservation* of Nature and Natural Resources (IUCN). The new emphasis on conserving representative ecosystems began with a focus on wetlands at the turn of the decade. In 1961, IUCN launched Project MAR (a name derived from the common three letters of the word for "marsh" in different languages) to underline the threats to wetlands, and a conference (jointly organized by IUCN, ICBP, and the International Waterfowl Research Bureau [IWRB]) was held in the French Camargue in November 1962. The second focus was on national parks. For nearly 90 years now, parks had developed in national isolation, with individual states responding to domestic needs and making little reference to international developments. The belief that more coordination was needed, and a concern that some countries had not yet even established national parks, was behind the IUCN-sponsored First World Conference on National Parks, held in Seattle, Washington, in July 1962.

THE WORLD WILDLIFE FUND

Of all the problems that plagued IUCN during the 1950s, lack of money was the most serious; the Union could barely support itself, let alone finance outside projects. Some funding had come initially from UNESCO, but this had proved irregular, and it became increasingly clear that an organized fund-raising structure was needed. The idea for a separate fund-raising body cannot be credited entirely to any one individual; against the background of IUCN's financial problems, it must have weighed heavily on more than one mind during the 1950s. But it was Julian Huxley and Max Nicholson who started the ball rolling. Nicholson—by now director-general of Britain's Nature Conservancy—recalls that while the Nature Conservancy had, within the United Kingdom, adequate statutory powers and a small but growing income, there was concern at the "lack of a strong support movement to share the burdens and provide political muscle. [The] . . . threat (to nature) was worldwide. . . . It would be morally obligatory and also a source of added strength to use our British base to build up an effective world network."[69] In May 1961 IUCN issued the Morges Manifesto, a piece of rhetoric that served partly to state IUCN's belief that the ability and skill needed to tackle threats to wildlife existed, but not the "support and resources," and that money was the most essential of all needs.[70]

Following a visit to East Africa in 1960, Julian Huxley wrote three articles for the London weekly *The Observer* on the growing threats to African wildlife, particularly from the extension of cultivation, increasing numbers of cattle, poaching, deforestation, overgrazing, and the transformation of land into semidesert. Huxley broached the fund-raising idea with Max Nicholson, whose involvement with IUCN during the 1950s had convinced him that the Union was incapable of running its own affairs (especially financial affairs) efficiently and had given him the idea of a twin body to IUCN that would be responsible for fund-raising. The priority of this body was to "salvage" IUCN.[71] Nicholson proposed a new body consisting of a trust registered in Switzerland, an operations group responsible for establishing priorities and allocating funds, a supporters club of wealthy members, and several national appeals. The concept was discussed at the Arusha conference (see below) in September, and the World Wildlife Fund (WWF) was launched in London later that month. In December, national appeals were launched in the United States and Switzerland, to be followed by appeals in the Netherlands in 1962 and West Germany and Austria in 1963. Altogether, twenty national appeals were launched during the first ten years of operation.

According to Harold Coolidge, WWF "was founded without question for the purpose of raising funds to finance the budget of IUCN,"[72] but this is questionable. WWF rapidly set off on a parallel rather than an auxiliary course to IUCN. "Instead of taking care of us first," Coolidge recalled, "[WWF] stated we were the highest priority, but they had to take care of their own administrative expenses and then they also had certain projects they wanted to fund."[73] This caused problems, with IUCN constantly in deficit and WWF consistently performing well financially and eventually outgrowing IUCN.[74] (By the mid-1980s, the artificiality of many of the divisions between the two organizations led to an attempt to mold their shared Swiss headquarters into a "World Conservation Center.")

WWF funded projects in five categories: individual species, wilderness areas, support for existing organizations, conservation education, and "miscellaneous" conservation matters. WWF also made direct representations to governments. In 1965, it made representations to the Ugandan government not to build a hydroelectric power station in the Murchison Falls National Park. In 1968 the Tanzanian government was persuaded not to build a new hotel in the Ngorongoro crater. Representations were made to several countries to set up specific national parks or to launch national conservation plans. By 1967, WWF was spending more than $370,000 per year on conservation and had funded 183 projects, but there were marked imbalances in the way the money was spent. While the majority of projects (56 percent) were in Africa and Asia, they attracted only 26 percent of the funds. Inversely, Europe and North America, with 27 percent of the projects, attracted 52 percent of the funds. This could be explained (WWF claimed) by the fact that most of the European and North American projects involved the purchase or rent of land for the establishment of new protected areas at relatively high costs. That Africa had more projects and attracted more money than the rest of the Third World combined was explained by that fact that it had simply submitted the most applications.[75]

By 1969 the proportion of money paid to North American and European projects had risen even further, to nearly two-thirds of total expenditure, with Africa, Asia, and Latin America combined receiving just 15 percent. These were perhaps not, WWF admitted, the percentages "the founders of WWF had in mind at the time of its inception, [but] it is clear that if WWF wishes to raise considerable funds in future it has to show tangible results in the countries in which money is available *now*."[76] The proportions were to change significantly over the next eight years: the proportion of funds spent in Europe fell from 50 percent in 1971 to 10 percent in 1977; in 1969, North America received 40 percent of the funds, and in 1975 just 0.5 percent; funds for Africa fluctuated wildly, while the proportion spent in Asia rose from 6.5 percent in 1968 to nearly 20 percent in 1975. As for IUCN, only 12.8 percent of WWF expenditure between 1962 and 1967 went directly to the Union, and by 1969 the proportion had dropped to 9 percent.[77] This figure did not, however, include funds given to IUCN-approved projects.

CONSERVATION, DEVELOPMENT AND THE AFRICAN SPECIAL PROJECT

As IUPN/IUCN struggled through its first decade, it realized just how inadequate its preservationist policies were as a response to the postwar demand for resources and development; conservation clearly had to be pursued as an integral part of development. This notion had been reflected in key resolutions agreed at the Lake Success ITC. Resolution No. 1 related the importance of understanding the implications of UN technical assistance to less developed countries (LDCs) in terms of human ecology; No. 3 resolved that "organizations concerned with nature protection and conservation, and those concerned with the utilization of resources, should collaborate to the greatest possible extent;" No. 7 noted that large development projects could have serious unforeseen effects on natural conditions and that IUPN should promote detailed ecological surveys of their impact.

European interest in the African environment had already produced the 1900 and 1933 conventions, both of which set nature aside in protected areas. While colonial administrations had been free to design and impose—for better or for worse—their own concepts of wildlife protection without much reference to the wishes or needs of local people, this would clearly no longer be possible in the postcolonial era. As Africa emerged from colonialism, European conservationists felt it was essential to encourage African governments to publicly associate themselves with conservation and to agree in principle to reconcile conservation with national development plans.

On Belgian initiative, the Third International Conference for the Protection of the Fauna and Flora of Africa was held in Bukavu in the Belgian Congo in 1953. It was to discuss African resource issues and a possible revision of the 1933 convention to bring it "up to date and in line with modern conservation concepts."[78] In what amounted to a tangential departure from previous thinking, delegates agreed that nature protection in Africa involved far more than the fauna and flora protection provisions of the 1933 convention. The vital problem of protecting the human environment of Africa, they noted, could not be solved "solely by the creation of nature reserves and the protection of certain species;" governments should consider a new, broader-based convention designed to conserve natural vegetation, soil, water, and natural resources, "primarily in the interest of the populations of Africa."[79]

At its 1956 General Assembly, IUCN noted that "landscape-planning based on ecological research" should be the starting point for development in LDCs.[80] At its 1960 General Assembly, IUCN concluded that conservation was a particularly urgent priority in Africa and that foreign aid was "prone to overlook conservation and the value of wildlife and habitat as a continuing economic, scientific, and cultural asset."[81] IUCN's response was to launch the African Special Project (ASP) in an attempt to encourage new African leaders to publicly identify themselves with conservation and to convince them of "the virtue of living off the income of their natural resources, not the capital."[82]

The ASP had three stages. In the first, the FAO forestry officer for Africa, Gerald Watterson, on secondment to IUCN as its secretary-general, toured 16 African countries and reported on the conservation of natural resources in each. Stage II was the Pan-African Symposium on the Conservation of Nature and Natural Resources in Modern African States (or Arusha Conference), held in Arusha, Tanganyika in September 1961, three months before Tanganyikan independence. Attended by representatives from 27 countries (21 in Africa), and cosponsored by FAO and UNESCO, it was notable for being the first occasion on which Africans themselves had been fully represented at a forum for the discussion of their own natural resources. (The 1900 and 1933 conferences had involved only representatives of the European colonial powers, and so had reflected their particular perspective.) The Arusha Conference, by attempting to draw newly independent and near-independent states into the debate, opened discussion on the needs of local people and their attitudes to nature.[83] Opening the conference, Sir Richard Turnbull, the governor of Tanganyika, outlined three issues for consideration: that wildlife and nature were valuable sources of revenue and so should be rationally exploited where this was the best form of land use, that the support of public opinion was essential, and that international aid was needed if African wildlife was to be preserved.[84]

The journalist John Hillaby, noting IUCN's "chequered history," reflected the week before the conference that the Union now appeared to have been "entirely revitalised."[85] There was marked emphasis during discussions at the conference on the utilization of wildlife, whether for food or recreation. The point was made that "only by the planned utilization of wildlife as a renewable natural resource . . . can its conservation and development be economically justified in competition with agriculture, stock ranching and other forms of land use."[86] The value of wildlife as a resource was in no way incompatible with the demands of agriculture and forestry, nor with the overall economic and social development of a country. A Sudanese forester, Sayed Kamil Shawki, argued that natural resources were "comparatively more fundamental to the economic development of underdeveloped countries than they are to more highly developed states."[87] Wildlife management outside and adjacent to national parks depended on the needs, way of life, and cooperation of local communities and their maximum involvement in management projects. Traditional African bonds with nature, which had been undermined by European economic development models of the sort that had caused the destruction of nature in Europe, needed to be revitalized. The point was raised in discussion that preservation alone was not the answer and that rational management based on clear objectives was needed. Among the major recommendations of the conference: land-use policies should be developed aimed at avoiding intensive occupation of unsuitable land by farmers and pastoralists, greater attention should be paid to the economics of resource development programs, and African governments should draw up wildlife policies. IUCN offered to help governments integrate wildlife management with overall land-use development plans.

Stage III of the ASP was originally to have involved the creation of a specialized unit within IUCN to provide consultancy services to African governments; in actuality, it took the form of a tour of African states during 1962–63 by two land-use specialists (Thane Riney and Peter Hill) to advise governments on integrating resource use and economic development. Their tour of Sahelian and West African countries in early 1962 revealed an "urgent necessity for an international service to emphasize the need for close integration in the development of . . . renewable natural resources, for overall land-use planning, and for introducing ecological thinking into such planning."[88] There was also clearly a need for a convention binding African states to the conservation of nature, as had been suggested at Bukavu. FAO had, in fact, set up a working party in 1960 to draft just such a convention. Two resolutions drawn up at the Seattle national parks conference referred to the importance of conservation in development programs and the need for development agencies to incorporate environmental considerations into their planning.[89]

In December 1962 the UN adopted a resolution supporting the argument that natural resources were vital to economic development and that economic development in less developed countries could jeopardize natural resources if it took place "without due attention to their conservation and restoration."[90] At its 1963 session, the Commission for Technical Cooperation in Africa approved a draft charter, endorsed by the 1963 IUCN General Assembly held in Nairobi (the first time it had been held in Africa and only the second time outside Europe or North America), which concentrated on the problems of tropical environments. The technical papers before the conference, and much of the discussion, concentrated on the balance between population and environment and the effects of population pressure on land. IUCN concluded that "if the purely political considerations which have dominated the African scene during the last few years can now be subordinated to the more precise consideration of primary human and animal needs—which are usually complementary—plans can be prepared which, if realistically implemented, will lead to a reasonable and improving standard of living for the African peoples."[91] Speaking at the assembly, U.S. Secretary of State for the Interior Stewart Udall said the world was in need of a conservation ethic: "The burgeoning of populations jeopardizes the conservation idea, and furthers the obsession of over-exploitation. This is simply a 'plunder now, pay later' policy. The expansion of populations everywhere makes all the more necessary a wise policy of conservation. Conservation is not a luxury; it is a necessity."[92]

Speaking at the 1967 WWF Congress in Amsterdam, Russell Train, then president of the Conservation Foundation in Washington, DC, warned against the tendency among conservationists to think of man and nature as separate and mutually exclusive concepts; this approach was self-defeating. He was encouraged to note, though, that conservationists were increasingly understanding that long-term conservation objectives "cannot be pursued successfully in isolation from other national objectives but can best be achieved as integral elements of overall national development programs."[93]

Between 1963 and 1967, FAO and IUCN worked on rival drafts of the proposed African convention, FAO having proceeded independently in the belief that the IUCN draft paid too little heed to wildlife as a resource to be exploited and that FAO was more experienced than IUCN in the drafting of conventions.[94] But it was the IUCN draft that was eventually accepted by the Organization of African Unity (OAU) in 1967 and formed the basis of the African Convention for Conservation of Nature and Natural Resources. Adopted by 33 OAU member-states in Algiers in September 1968, it entered into force in 1969. The philosophy of the convention was founded on the "conservation, utilization and development of soil, water, flora, and faunal resources in accordance with scientific principles and with due regard to the best interests of the people."[95]

The changed emphasis in IUCN's thinking was confirmed at its 10th General Assembly in New Delhi in 1969 when it was agreed that, after 21 years of a "fire brigade" approach to curing individual conservation problems as they arose, the time had come for an approach based on prevention *and* cure.[96] The assembly defined conservation as the "management (which includes survey, research, administration, preservation, utilization . . .) of air, water, soil, minerals, and living species including man, so as to achieve the highest sustainable quality of life."[97]

Even as IUCN and WWF developed a broader and more universally useful definition of the concept of conservation, however, the conservation movement was already being rapidly overtaken by a new, independent and much more activist movement concerned with much broader environmental issues. At some time in the late 1950s and early 1960s, circumstances conspired to give rise to a new protest movement based on concerns about the state of the human environment and about human attitudes to the earth. Nature and natural resources were now no longer the sole concern; the new movement addressed everything from overpopulation and pollution to the costs of technology and economic growth. New Environmentalism went beyond the natural world; it challenged the very essence of capitalism.

THREE

The Environmental Revolution
(1962–1970)

In the late summer of 1962, a new book by Rachel Carson went on sale in American bookstores. Despite its seemingly impenetrable topic, synthetic pesticides and insecticides, *Silent Spring* struck a chord with its readers, sold half a million copies in hard cover, stayed on the best-seller list of the *New York Times* for 31 weeks,[1] and prompted the creation of a presidential advisory panel on pesticides.

In April 1970, 300,000 Americans—perhaps more—took part in Earth Day, the largest environmental demonstration in history. Cover stories and newspaper headlines proclaimed the arrival of the environment as a primary public issue. For *Time* magazine, the environment was *the* issue of 1970;[2] for *Life*, it was a movement that promised to dominate the new decade.[3] Work had meanwhile already begun on one of the biggest United Nations conferences ever held, which would take the representatives of 113 nations to Stockholm to discuss the problems of the global environment.

The intervening eight years had seen environmentalism transformed; there had been an environmental revolution, most notably in the United States. If in 1962 there was unease about the state of the environment, by 1970 there was vocal—occasionally strident—insistence on change in a global society seemingly bent on self-destruction. The concerns of a few scientists, administrators, and conservation groups blossomed into a fervent mass movement that swept the industrialized world. Many of the old, established conservation and protection organizations, temporarily stalled in the apathy of the 1950s, were bypassed and left to catch up as best they could. The transformed movement—New Environmentalism— was more dynamic, more broad-based, more responsive, and won much wider public support. Some of the older organizations flowed with the tide, but a wave of new organizations emerged,[4] differing from their precursors in at least two major respects.

In the first place, if nature protection had been a moral crusade centered on the nonhuman environment and conservation a utilitarian movement centered on the rational management of natural resources,

environmentalism centered on humanity and its surroundings. For protectionists, the issue was wildlife and habitat; for the New Environmentalists, human survival itself was at stake. There was a broader
conception of the place of man in the biosphere, a more sophisticated
understanding of that relationship, and a note of crisis that was greater
and broader than it had been in the earlier conservation movement.[5]
Nash argues that fear underlay the growth of popular American concern
for the environment—fear not of running out of resources and losing its
position in world politics, nor of ugliness in the world, but fear for the
future of life and the vulnerability of man; man "was rediscovered as being part of nature."[6] Americans were not just limiting their perception to
"the great outdoors," but were applying their moral and aesthetic appreciation of nature to the total environment.[7]

Secondly, New Environmentalism was activist and political. Many of
the older preservation groups pursued essentially charitable aims, while
the conservationists based their arguments on economics; the new environmentalists, by contrast, sought a more direct political impact. Their
message was that environmental catastrophe could be avoided only by
fundamental changes in the values and institutions of industrial
societies.[8] New Environmentalism can be seen as part of a wider social
transformation then taking place in Western society. The new movement
took positions that were both reactive and antiestablishment. Its leaders
responded more to events and challenges than to scientific evidence
alone. Certainty of the consequences of environmental mismanagement
was regarded as less important than evidence beyond reasonable doubt.
New Environmentalism was a social and political movement, and the issues it addressed were ultimately universal.

Like its precursors, New Environmentalism was not an organized and
homogeneous phenomenon, but an accumulation of organizations and
individuals with varied motives and tendencies, with roughly similar
goals but often different methods. Sandbach makes the distinction between the older ecological/scientific form of environmentalism, and the
newer antiestablishment form.[9] The first, embodied in the writings of
George Perkins Marsh and in the Progressive conservation movement of
Roosevelt and Pinchot, saw the sustenance of a viable physical and biological environment as the priority, attempting to influence policy by pre-
senting a valid, scientifically argued case. The second, embodied in New
Environmentalism, was more anarchistic, less concerned with systems
analysis and more with humanism. But there were many other ways of
categorizing the movement; it contained elements of anarchism, evange-
lism, social reform, political reform, and—through its relationship to
ecology—science. Indeed, in its early years it was often called the ecology movement; a professional ecologist told a U.S. congressional committee in 1970 that "ecology is no longer a scientific discipline—it's an
attitude of mind."[10] For Michael McCloskey, executive director of the Si-

erra Club, the components of the new movement in the United States reached beyond the old alliances to include "the consumer movement, including the corporate reformers; the movement for scientific responsibility; a revitalized public health movement; birth control and population stabilization groups; pacifists and those who stress participatory democracy in which decisions are made consensually; young people who emphasize direct action; and a diffuse movement in search of a new focus for politics."[11]

Why did the New Environmental movement emerge when it did, and why did the transformation occur so suddenly and so completely? Neat and straightforward explanations are always tempting, but revolutions are rarely that simple. The environmental movement was a product of forces both internal and external to its immediate objectives. The elements of change were emerging long before the 1960s; when they finally intersected with one another, and with wider socio-political factors, the result was a new force for social and political change. Six factors in particular seem to have played a role in the change: the effects of affluence, the age of atomic testing, the book *Silent Spring*, a series of well-publicized environmental disasters, advances in scientific knowledge, and the influence of other social movements.

NEW ENVIRONMENTALISM AND THE AFFLUENT SOCIETY

The sudden growth of new environmental groups in Britain in the early 1970s has been characterized as part of a pattern of similar occurrences (in the 1890s, late 1920s, and late 1950s) discernible at similar phases in the world economic cycle; such growth had in each case occurred toward the end of periods of sustained economic expansion.[12] Hence the simultaneous heightening of environmental concern in all industrialized capitalist countries as more and more people turned to count the mounting external costs of unbridled economic growth and sought to reassert nonmaterial values.[13] O'Riordan suggests that conservation movements peak at times of economic anxiety, not in an attempt to slow down economic growth but "to ensure continued progress in economic well-being and reasonable spread of the benefits of growth across the population at large . . . maybe the threat of scarcity is necessary to remind a greedy population enjoying the hedonism of affluence of the need for efficiency and frugality."[14]

The emergence of New Environmentalism was part of a broad, cumulative process of social and political change. The Suez Crisis, the Cold War, the threat of nuclear war, and the injustices of racial inequality generated public concern and even mass protest in the late 1950s. Concurrently, prolonged and steady economic growth came to all the industrialized economies. The juxtaposition of these two trends ultimately gave rise to frustration with government and the belief that only direct action could bring issues outside conventional political paradigms to the attention of the political establishment.[15] This was to be extended in the 1960s to the view that environmental degradation posed as great a threat to material security as did war; hence the many parallels between environmentalism and the antiwar movement. Both were social reform movements, and both derived much of their support from young and well-educated activists.

In the United States, the 1950s was a time of apparent calm, equanimity, consensus, and affluence. Big business reestablished the reputation it had lost in the Depression. To Americans with adequate incomes, it was a time of material comfort and increased leisure time. Commenting on the weakened state of American conservation in 1952, Steven Raushenbush noted that "the ultimate function of all the raw materials in the world is that of supporting the high American standard of living," and that conservation was in danger of becoming a lost cause.[16] By the middle of the decade, the United States, with 6 percent of the world's population, was producing and consuming over one-third of the world's goods and services.[17] Large families were considered desirable, and the death rate was declining, so population grew rapidly. Intellectuals retreated from social criticism; the middle class had faith in the ability of government—in the context of a booming economy—to attend to such problems as pollution, inner city conditions, and unemployment. Britain, too, enjoyed some of the hedonism of affluence. Even if the boom of the Macmillan years was only brief and superficial, it did appear for a time that the British really had never had it so good. Keynsian economics appeared to have brought permanent full employment and steady economic growth, and the young had more disposable income than ever before, giving them increasing independence.

Yet the contentment and conformity of the late 1950s was apparently superficial, for there was in truth a deep and latent discontent, particularly among the young. Although the United States in the 1950s appeared calm and equanimous, and the 1960s by contrast were marked by activism and change in politics and society, the struggles that brought reform in the 1960s were already emerging in the 1950s.[18] Postwar prosperity obscured the more significant reality of economic inequality; although the share of national income received by the wealthiest 5 percent of the American population had fallen in the Depression and war years, it remained constant at about 21 percent thereafter.[19] Similarly, the poorest 20 percent of the population received a constant 5 percent of the national income. For industrial workers, life became dull and mechanical, there was little room for personal pride in mass-produced goods, and the prospect of growing automation brought a feeling of insecurity.

In the affluence of the 1950s, the middle-class young of America enjoyed home comforts and extended education, and were generally conservative and conformist. But they became increasingly critical of the complacency and apparent indifference of their society. Increased leisure time and greater prosperity helped shift attention from the accumulation and enjoyment of material security, and the very comfort of middle-class existence served to draw attention to social inequality. The young were alarmed by the prospect of nuclear conflict that seemed to be concomitant upon the creation of what Eisenhower described as the "military-industrial complex"—the accumulation of power by military and business elites.

The drawbacks of the affluent society became increasingly evident in the early 1960s, partly through their environmental consequences. In 1958, John Kenneth Galbraith, then professor of economics at Harvard, published *The Affluent Society*. Motivated partly by the postwar market revival and the belief that all social ills could be cured by more production and also by concern at the remarkable degree of poverty and deprivation that remained in a country that enjoyed apparent prosperity and wealth, he criticized materialistic consumption. Increased production was not the final test of social achievement, he warned.[20] Downs suggests that affluence brought with it a marked increase in the aspirations and standards of Americans concerning what their environment ought to be like. Rising dissatisfaction with the "system" in the United States did not result primarily from poorer performance by that system, he argues. Rather, it stemmed from a rapid escalation of people's aspirations as to what the performance of the system ought to be.[21]

THE ADVENT OF THE ATOMIC AGE

The first truly global environmental issue of the postwar era—and perhaps the first ever—was the danger of fallout from atmospheric nuclear testing. Following the first explosion of an atomic bomb by the Soviet Union in 1949, the development of nuclear devices entered a new and competitive phase. The United States launched its test program in 1951, followed by Britain and the USSR in 1953, and France in 1960. The earliest British tests were carried out in Australia and the Pacific, the first device being detonated on a British frigate off the Australian coast in October 1952.[22] Eleven more major tests were carried out there and in the interior of South Australia until 1957, and more between 1956 and 1958 around Christmas Island. The official secrecy that surrounded the tests encouraged the circulation of fearful rumors, generating strong local opposition.[23] France began testing in Algeria, but miscalculated meteorological conditions, with the result that a radioactive cloud crossed into the Iberian peninsula.[24] The French test site was subsequently moved to French Polynesia.

Between 1945 and 1962, a total of 423 nuclear detonations were announced by the United States (271), the USSR (124), Britain (23), and France (5).[25] Attempts to reach agreement on nuclear disarmament began within weeks of the Hiroshima bomb, but the first tangible result did not come until the signing in 1963 of the Partial Nuclear Test Ban Treaty, which brought atmospheric testing by the United States, the USSR, and Britain to an end. Ward, Dubos, and Commoner claim the treaty as the first victory in the campaign to save the environment.[26] Maddox takes a different view, suggesting that although the issue of radioactivity in the environment was an element in the equation, the powers signing the treaty were moved more by the fact that they had completed the development of long-range missile warheads, calculated that the treaty would help postpone the time when other nations could become nuclear powers, and so felt they could afford to accept the environmental argument.[27] Was the treaty indeed a victory for environmentalism?

An early indication of the environmental costs of nuclear testing came in October 1952, when abnormally radioactive hailstones fell 1,750 miles (2,820 km) from the first British test site off Australia.[28] In April 1953, radioactive rain fell in New York State, apparently contaminated by nuclear tests in Nevada. The debate about this new phenomenon soon spread within the scientific community.[29] In *The Closing Circle*, Barry Commoner recalled that he "learned about the environment from the United States Atomic Energy Commission in 1953. Until then, like most people, I had taken the air, water, soil, and our natural surroundings more or less for granted."[30] He now became deeply concerned by the new and destructive force of nuclear energy. The tests became a matter of wider public concern in March 1954 when an American hydrogen bomb test, code-named BRAVO, was held on Bikini Atoll in the western Pacific. The explosive yield was twice that anticipated, and an unexpected shift in the wind caused radioactive ash to drift over the inhabited Marshall Islands, instead of falling into the ocean as planned. Some 7,000 square miles (18,130 sq km) of ocean was seriously contaminated by a radioactive cloud that extended 220 nautical miles (410 km) and was as wide as 40 miles (75 km).

Two weeks after the test, a Japanese tuna trawler, the *Fukuryu Maru No. 5 (Lucky Dragon)*, returned to port with all 23 of its crew members suffering radiation sickness. The boat had been downwind of the BRAVO test; whether it was inside or outside the "off-limits" sector set by the United States was unclear. Fish subsequently arriving at Japanese ports from other vessels in the region were found to be contaminated. All of Asia, notes Voss, was "galvanized" into action to stop further testing.[31] Albert Schweitzer, Albert Einstein and Pope Pius XII joined the outcry. The death of one of the *Lucky Dragon* crew members six months later touched off a wave of anti-Americanism in Japan and strained U.S.-Japanese relations.[32] Matters were perhaps made worse—then and later—by the secrecy with which the U.S. Atomic Energy Commission approached the question of fallout, raising public suspicions that something frightening was being withheld.

Media and public opinion in the United States on the cessation of testing was nonetheless divided. Opinion polls indicated a steady (albeit inconsistent) majority in support of testing, with the figures fluctuating according to the level of Cold War tensions (e.g., a 71 percent majority in support in 1954 changed to a 77 percent majority against in 1959, but was back to 55 percent in support in 1961, following the U-2 incident and the Cuban missile crisis).[33] Although the 1955 Geneva disarmament conference (and continuing UN discussions) failed to reach agreement, in 1958 the United States, USSR, and Britain all announced a moratorium on nuclear testing pending further discussions. Testing became an issue during the 1956 presidential campaign; moved by the BRAVO incident, Adlai Stevenson called for a ban on hydrogen bomb tests. During his 1960 election campaign, John F. Kennedy committed himself to seeking an accord on nuclear testing.

In the wake of all the tests, fears had grown about the presence in the atmosphere of strontium 90 and other toxic ingredients of fallout. In hearings before a Senate sub-committee on disarmament in the late 1950s, scientists, church leaders, and congressmen voiced concern about the dangers of fallout, particularly to human health.[34] But opinion was divided, and there were those—notably Edward Teller, then a senior scientific advisor to the Eisenhower administration—who argued that radiation was a minor worry. In the view of Barry Commoner, the tests revealed how little was known about the environment, because it was mistakenly assumed that much of the fallout would remain in the stratosphere for years, out of harm's way; in fact it returned to earth within months.[35] In 1958, Commoner and others at Washington University in St. Louis formed the St. Louis Committee for Nuclear Information with the object of drawing attention to the implications of fallout.

Despite such fears, fallout was at first only a minor public concern. In 1961, only 21 percent of Americans felt there was enough fallout in the atmosphere to constitute a danger.[36] *Familiarity* with fallout, however, grew. In 1955 only 17 percent of Americans could correctly define fallout; by 1961 the figure had risen to 57 percent.[37] As segments of the mass media (and President Kennedy himself) expressed themselves increasingly in support of a test ban treaty during 1963, not only did public support for the treaty grow, but so did the importance of fallout as an issue. In July 1963, 52 percent gave unqualified support to the treaty, and 12 percent quoted fallout as the major consideration. By September, the figures were respectively 81 percent and 21 percent, with fallout replacing a general need to end tests as the most oft-quoted justification for the treaty.[38]

The view in U.S. government circles was similarly divided. Kennedy was deeply concerned about the fallout issue,[39] as were his scientific advisors and the Arms Control and Disarmament Agency created in 1961. In his radio and television address to the nation in July 1963, Kennedy listed the abolition of fallout as a key advantage of the treaty, second only to the reduction of world tension. In other government agencies and the Senate, however, the issue was much less important than military considerations; some senators even saw contamination as an acceptable cost for continued testing.[40] Congressional opinions varied from that of Senator Wayne Morse, who felt that fallout control was the central purpose of the treaty, to conservative Republican Senator Strom Thurmond, who dismissed the fallout issue as "propaganda," to Senator Bourke Hickenlooper who argued that radiation, in moderation, could actually be beneficial to health.[41]

In 1961, with negotiations on a test ban apparently stalled,[42] the USSR and the United States resumed their tests, followed in 1962 by Britain. The Geneva disarmament conference was adjourned, to be resumed in July 1963 after bilateral contacts between the United States and the USSR. By then, it was clear that there was growing international opposition to atmospheric tests, motivated partly by significant increases in fallout levels following the 1962 test series. Furthermore, U.S. stockpiles of nuclear weapons had by 1962 reached such a high level that there were fears about command problems leading to an accidental war.[43] In August, the Partial Test Ban Treaty was finally signed in Moscow by the United States, the Soviet Union and Britain, banning tests in the air, above the atmosphere or at sea (but not underground). Because the United States and the USSR were unable to agree on methods of verifying compliance with underground tests, the final treaty—much to Kennedy's dismay—could only be partial. Commoner argues that one of the benefits of the treaty was that it established that nuclear weapons were a *scientific* failure inasmuch as regardless of the outcome of nuclear war, neither major power would survive the holocaust—the failure of nuclear "defense" thus lay in the ecological disasters it would set off.[44]

To claim that the Partial Test Ban Treaty was the first global environmental agreement is not the overstatement it may at first seem. The question of global security would have been enough reason in itself, but the environmental element was a key supporting factor, even though it apparently played only a minor role until just before the actual signing of the treaty. The preamble to the treaty itself lists the principal aim as "the speediest possible achievement of an agreement on general and complete disarmament . . . which would put an end to the armaments race"; the desire to "put an end to the contamination of man's environment by radioactive substances" was a secondary aim.[45] In the text of the treaty tabled at the 17-nation Geneva disarmament conference in August 1962, the preamble made no mention at all of fallout; that particular clause was included only in the final few months of negotiations.[46] Irrespective of the *primary* motives of the treaty, however, the fallout question undoubtedly alerted many people to the idea that technology could cause unlimited environmental contamination and that everyone could be affected; there was the first inkling of the concept of a global environment and of

universal environmental problems. This concept was now further reinforced with the publication of *Silent Spring*.

RACHEL CARSON AND *SILENT SPRING*

The single event most frequently credited as signifying the beginning of
the environmental revolution was the publication in 1962 of *Silent Spring*
by Rachel Carson.[47] The book detailed the adverse effects of the misuse
of synthetic chemical pesticides and insecticides, generated much controversy, and heightened public awareness of the implications of human activity on the environment and of the cost in turn to human society. Shea
argues that the book showed for the first time "that a meticulously re-
searched and lucidly written account of a faulty technology could arouse
the public to demand a more rational approach to problems of the
environment."[48] For Schnaiberg, the book provided a sinister worldview
in which the forces undermining the ecosystem operated much less dramatically but with greater impact than any lay observer could
appreciate.[49] It exposed some of the social, economic, and scientific infrastructure that had *knowingly* permitted ecological degradation to occur.

Rachel Carson had already established a reputation as a writer during
the 1950s with the publication of books such as *The Sea Around Us*
(1951)—a best-seller in the United States for 96 weeks and translated into
33 languages—and *On the Edge of the Sea* (1955). Both were unpolemical
studies in natural history and reflected her primary interest: the sea. *Silent Spring*, for which she is now best remembered, differed from these
inasmuch as it grew out of her observations of the *threats* posed to nature. As she familiarized herself with the issue of chemical pesticides,
Graham notes, so "she clearly saw that man was, more than ever before,
approaching the earth not with humility, but with arrogance."[50] Besides
the threat of nuclear war, Carson wrote, "the central problem of our age
has . . . become the contamination of man's total environment with . . .
substances of incredible potential for harm."[51] The use of chemicals to
control insect pests was, she warned, interfering with the natural de-
fenses of the environment itself; "we have allowed these chemicals to be
used with little or no advance investigation of their effect on soil, water,
wildlife, and man himself."[52]

Carson had first become concerned about the effects of DDT in 1945,
while working for the U.S. Fish and Wildlife Service.[53] *Silent Spring* was
by no means the first public warning of the environmental impact of persistent pesticides; such forecasts had been made as early as 1945.[54] (The
insecticidal properties of DDT were discovered in 1939. Cheap and easy
to make, it was hailed as the universal pesticide and became the most
widely used of new chemical pesticides, before its environmental effects
had been intensively studied.) The message of *Silent Spring* was clear and
direct, and—boosted by prepublication serialization in the *New Yorker*—it

became an immediate best-seller, selling half a million copies in hard cover. During 1963 it was published in 15 countries. It came under immediate attack from the U.S. Department of Agriculture and several chemical companies, one of which had apparently attempted to suppress its publication.[55] The book also fell foul of the scepticism with which scientists often greet works that attempt to popularize scientific information. Carson was variously criticized for misusing the word "mutagen," misciting or misrepresenting the writings of medical authorities, giving credence to cancer theories that were speculative or had already been discarded, and so on.[56] Despite the detractors, President Kennedy was sufficiently impressed to refer to Carson's work in an August 1962 press conference and to request his scientific advisor to study the pesticide issue. A special panel of the President's Scientific Advisory Committee (PSAC) was set up and released a report in May 1963 that was critical of the pesticide industry and the federal government. The report, noted *Science*, was "a fairly thoroughgoing vindication" of *Silent Spring*. By corroborating Carson's thesis, Brooks notes, the report of the PSAC had changed the nature of the debate; no one could any longer deny that the problem existed.[57]

Why was *Silent Spring* so influential? Its impact stemmed from a combination of its moralism, the controversy it caused, and from the effect it had of taking the pesticide issue out of academic circles and technical journals and into the public arena. While almost all previous writing on the subject had been phrased in economic terms, notes Graham, *Silent Spring* was essentially an ecological book; it was, furthermore, designed to shock people into action against the misuse of chemical pesticides.[58] Fox notes the relative failure of a book published only six months earlier (*Our Synthetic Environment* by Murray Bookchin, written under the pen name of Lewis Herber), which examined a broad range of the incidental effects of modern technology, from air pollution to contaminated milk, and suggests that it failed because it was too comprehensive.[59] Carson, by contrast, concentrated on a single issue. Inaccurate and alarmist she may occasionally have been, but her essential message stood. Pesticides became a public issue not only in the United States, but elsewhere. *Silent Spring* can be implicated in instigating changes in local and national government policy in the United States (e.g., some states banned the aerial spraying of DDT, and procedures for registering chemical pesticides were improved) and several European countries (e.g., Britain, Sweden, Denmark, and Hungary). The public debate over pesticides continued throughout the 1960s, and all twelve of the most toxic substances listed in *Silent Spring* were ultimately banned or restricted.[60]

ENVIRONMENTAL DISASTERS AND PUBLIC ALARM

The disquiet spawned by the effects of nuclear fallout and the warnings of *Silent Spring* was compounded in the period 1966–1972 by a series of "environmental disasters"—headline events that had the effect of cata-lyzing environmental fears.[61] There had been comparable environmental disasters before, some of them in the very recent past. In 1948, for exam-ple, 20 people had died and 43 percent of the population of Donora, Pennsylvania, had fallen ill following a sulfurous fog. A winter smog that descended on London between 5 and 10 December 1952 was impli-cated by the London County Council in the immediate deaths of 445 peo-ple; altogether, more than 4,000 people died, most from long-term circulatory or respiratory disorders brought on by the smog.[62] The event was directly related to the passage in Britain of the 1956 Clean Air Act. In October 1957, a fire broke out at the Windscale nuclear plant in northern England when one of the reactors overheated. The fire burned for more than 85 hours, but although radioactivity was released, contamination was limited.[63] While the event caused deep concern within the nuclear power industry, the public and the media —still unfamiliar with the nu-clear power process and therefore with the implications of such acci-dents—barely responded. Besides, nuclear power was still in its infancy and was being hailed as the fuel of the future.

The accidents that occurred from the mid-1960s had much greater im-pact because of the heightened public sensitivity to environmental prob-lems. One of the first in the new round of disasters was the collapse in October 1966 of a pit-heap above the village of Aberfan in South Wales, resulting in the deaths of 144 people, 116 of them children in the local school. Stanley Johnson suggests that Aberfan was important not be-cause it had a clear place in the genealogy of pollution but because it prepared the way for a greater understanding of the implications of pollution.[64] Even more influential than the hazards of derelict land, how-ever, was the problem of oil pollution, which had immediate, visible, and often catastrophic side-effects, and hence much attraction to news editors.

The size and number of operating oil tankers had grown dramatically since the Second World War. In 1950 there was only one tanker bigger than 50,000 dead weight tons; by the late 1960s there were 602 tankers above that weight.[65] The first major disaster was the wreck of the tanker *Torrey Canyon* in March 1967. Some 875,000 barrels (117,000 tons) of crude oil was spilled after the tanker struck a reef off the southwest tip of En-gland, between Land's End and the Isles of Scilly. Hundreds of miles of Cornish coastline were polluted. "It was a national event of international dimensions" notes Stanley Johnson.[66] The use of untested detergents to break down the oil only added to the biological damage. The incident dramatically illustrated the threat posed to marine ecosystems by tanker traffic through coastal waters. With the cost of Royal Air Force bombing sorties intended to set fire to the spilled oil and the £6 million bill for cleaning up the polluted coastline, it also impressed upon British tax-payers—by being on their own doorstep—the financial costs of pollu-tion. The disaster revealed a lack of government preparedness for such eventualities and gaps in the organization of scientific research and of scientific advice to the British government.[67] The government response led ultimately to the creation of the Royal Commission on Environmental Pollution in 1969. The incident was also foremost in the minds of signatories to the 1969 Convention Relating to Intervention on the High Seas in Cases of Oil Pollution Casualties and the Convention on Civil Liability for Oil Pollution Damage.

Two years after *Torrey Canyon*, a blowout at a Union Oil Company platform off the coast of Santa Barbara, California, brought serious pollution to miles of Californian coastline. Because the spill came from a drill hole in an unstable area of the continental shelf, it took several weeks to bring the flow fully under control. It was also impossible to be sure of the precise quantity of oil spilled; estimates varied widely.[68] The blowout occurred on 28 January 1969, and took two days to bring under control, but there was a second eruption on 12 February. Seepage continued for weeks, and beaches were still being polluted in July. Although there have since been far greater disasters (for example, 2 million barrels of oil were spilled after a 1979 tanker collision in the Caribbean, and 3.1 million barrels in the 1979–1980 blowout of the Mexican Ixtoc I well in the Gulf of Mexico), the *Torrey Canyon* and Santa Barbara spills were the first such incidents and so had far greater public impact.

"Santa Barbara was neither the worst nor the most frightening environmental disaster the nation has experienced," reflected the Council on Environmental Quality in 1979; "no one was killed . . . no one suffered permanent health damage . . . no large numbers of people were threatened. . . . Yet the event dramatized what many people saw as thoughtless insensitivity and lack of concern on the part of government and business to an issue that had become deeply important to them. It brought home to a great many Americans a feeling that protection of their environment would not simply happen, but required their active support and involvement."[69] The effect of the spill was reinforced by the indignation of the disproportionately upper- and upper-middle-class nature of Santa Barbara's population.[70] Johnson[71] and Molotch[72] note the significance in what the spill revealed of the change in political priorities and the nature of power in the United States. Interior Secretary Walter Hickel took immediate action by closing down wells in the Santa Barbara Channel area, but within 24 hours he had ordered a resumption of drilling and production, confirming the worst fears of local residents about government priorities.[73]

Torrey Canyon and the Santa Barbara spill were the most publicized oil spills of the time, but they were by no means the only spills; in 1968, 714 oil spills greater than 100 barrels were reported in United States waters alone, and in 1969 more than 1,000 were reported.[74] Altogether, an estimated 10,000 spills of oil and other hazardous materials annually polluted the navigable waters of the United States during the late 1960s.[75]

Pollution of other kinds now began to capture wider public imagination. The parlous condition of Lake Erie was often singled out as an example of the extreme effects of pollution; Barry Commoner, for example, devoted a chapter of *The Closing Circle* to the subject.[76] The lake had long been used as a sink for organic effluent from major industrial centers such as Detroit and Toledo. Yields from the Lake Erie fishery had begun to diminish at the turn of the century and became progressively smaller. Annual yields of cisco, for example, which once constituted 50 percent of the fish crop of the lake, fell from 6,187 tons before the 1930s to 3.6 tons in 1960–64. Pollution was suspected, but it took biological surveys conducted over several years before it could be confirmed in the early 1950s that the lake was suffering from eutrophication.[77]

The human costs of environmental pollution were illustrated in the late 1960s and early 1970s by events at Minamata in Japan. Chemical production had begun on the shores of Minamata Bay (opposite Nagasaki) in 1939, and spent catalysts containing mercury were discharged into the bay. In 1953 it was noticed that cats and birds in the area were acting strangely, and by 1956 neurological disorders were noticed among fishing families. Concentrations of mercury were discovered in fish from the bay and in local people who had died from what became known as "Minamata disease." The chemical company involved denied any relationship between mercury and the disease but, between 1961 and 1964, paid out small compensations to disease victims. A second outbreak of the disease occurred at the city of Niigata, where another factory was discharging mercury into a river. Niigata victims won a civil action against the factory in 1971, and in 1973 the Minamata factory was found similarly culpable and ordered to pay reasonable compensation.[78]

There were lesser-known but equally significant incidents elsewhere in Japan. In 1972 the Mitsui Mining and Smelting Company was ordered to pay compensation to victims of *itai itai*, a disease that had appeared as early as 1920 and afflicted people drinking water from the Jinzu River (on the north coast of central Japan), into which the factory had poured untreated cadmium, zinc, and lead wastes over a period of several decades. At Yokkaichi in central Japan, site of the country's first oil-refining and petrochemical complex, air pollution—already a problem by 1959—led to a growing incidence of respiratory diseases. An action brought by nine victims in 1967 resulted in a 1972 decision in their favor. Stimulated by the outcome of the incidents at Minamata, Niigata, Mitsui, and Yokkaichi, more than 450 antipollution campaigns had been launched in Japan by 1971.[79] Most took issue with the kind of single-minded economic growth pursued by Japan since the war. Pollution control and waste treatment were of low priority in Japanese industrial planning, which added to the problems created by the new energy-intensive industrial development that had replaced prewar light industry.[80] By the late 1960s, pollution had become a critical problem in Japan. Photochemical smog afflicted urban connurbations and had spread to the countryside, Tokyo Bay was seriously polluted, and mass production and consumption had created a wasteful society—about 10 percent of Tokyo's garbage was plastic.

The effect of these and other environmental disasters was to draw wider public attention to the threats facing the environment. People were sensitized to the potential costs of careless economic development and now lent growing support to a series of local and national environmental campaigns, which were often given wide media attention. In the United States, for example, there was debate over a planned jetport near the Everglades National Park, the proposed Alaskan pipeline, polluted beaches off New York, lead in gasoline, and phosphates in detergents. In Britain in 1969, there was debate over the siting of the third London airport, with the inhabitants of short-listed localities organizing vocal, and ultimately successful, opposition. New Environmentalism replaced traditional concerns with new concerns. For example, a National Wildlife Federation survey in the United States in 1969 showed that an established issue (water pollution) and an issue of more recent interest (air pollution and its links with vehicle emissions) had joined concern over pesticides to leave open spaces and wildlife well behind in the issues regarded as most important by the American public.[81]

ADVANCES IN SCIENTIFIC KNOWLEDGE

Rachel Carson and others were prone to criticism on scientific grounds; lack of scientific certainty was a stick that the opponents and critics of environmentalism continued to wield twenty years later (see acid pollution debate, chapter 9). There was no question that greater scientific certainty was needed and that environmentalism could not feed indefinitely on instinct or supposition. Scientists realized this just as much as environmentalists, and the rise of New Environmentalism paralleled substantial new initiatives in international scientific research. A major impetus came in 1957–58 with International Geophysical Year (IGY), which showed how research could benefit from international cooperation. Inspired by IGY, senior members of the International Council of Scientific Unions (ICSU)—notably the president, Sir Rudolph Peters—and of the International Union of Biological Sciences (IUBS) talked of applying the IGY model to biological research. Professor C. H. Waddington, president of IUBS, noted that ecology was at that time (the early 1960s) "emerging from a descriptive to an experimental stage. . . . Prominent ecologists were communicating with each other and this made the time ripe for a coordinated international effort."[82] There was concern that the study of environmental biology was lagging behind other fields, such as cell biology and molecular biology.

After discussions between ICSU, IUBS, IUCN, and biologists in a number of countries, the International Biological Programme (IBP) was launched in July 1964. Its theme was "the biological basis of productivity and human welfare"; its aims were to promote international study of organic production, the potential and uses of new and existing natural resources, and human adaptability to changing conditions. It was a direct response to the threats to natural ecosystems that were now the subject of so much attention. A year was regarded as too short a time in which to collect a significant body of biological information, so three phases were planned, taking the IBP through to 1974.

The enthusiasm for IBP was by no means universal. On the one hand, few questioned the need for better understanding of environmental biology, and biologists saw that the sum of national efforts was nowhere near enough to meet the world's future needs for national parks, nature reserves, and "field laboratories." Britain was probably the most enthusiastic proponent of IBP, supported by most of the countries of east and west Europe. On the other hand, there were biologists who felt that national scientific programs were adequate and feared the diversion of funds from those programs to IBP. The United States, where the structure and priorities of biological research were very different, early opposed the IBP (although it subsequently provided active support).[83]

Lack of funding proved a major handicap, particularly as relatively few countries had the funds to provide sustained support. Total income for IBP from 1962 through 1974 was $1.88 million, of which 43 percent came from national dues and special contributions, 15 percent each from ICSU grants and loans and UNESCO contracts, and 12 percent from publications.[84] Even so, IBP was generally regarded as a success. IBP's *modus operandi* was to define a problem, bring together a small team of competent specialists, set up an action plan, put the plan into operation, and finally assess the results. This had the effect of putting specialists in different countries in touch with one another. It encouraged ecological research in many countries, produced reliable research methods, had a catalytic effect on new environmental research programs,[85] and produced 40 volumes of findings. Holdgate and colleagues believe it had a notable impact on sensitizing the world to threats to the global biosphere, and as such was an important input to the Stockholm conference[86] (see chapter 5). UNESCO took particular interest in the program, and IBP for a time overlapped with, and transferred interests to, UNESCO's subsequent Man and the Biosphere program (see chapter 9). If IBP had a defect, it was that it was too broad and ambitious. Bourlière noted that the name itself was misleading, and it might more realistically have been called the International Environmental Program.[87]

THE INFLUENCE OF OTHER SOCIAL MOVEMENTS

During the late 1950s and 1960s, a number of social and political issues galvanized mass publics—particularly the young—into protest, creating a new climate of heightened public activism from which environmentalism benefited. The first such issues in the postwar United States were poverty and racism. In December 1955, the black workers of Montgomery, Alabama, began a boycott of the city bus system to protest segregation on the buses. This gave a much needed fillip to the civil rights movement, which went from strength to strength over the following dozen years. Schnaiberg suggests that it was the first social movement to (a) capture the energies of substantial numbers of the college population (shifting their concerns from private to public goals) and (b) extend and develop new techniques of participation in resistance to existing social forces.[88] Inspired by the examples of black students demonstrating against racial prejudice and segregated schools in the late 1950s, some white students hoped to encourage social democracy, idealistically believing that this could be achieved quickly and painlessly, without revolution.

There were no formal links between the civil rights and environmental movements; indeed they had very different values and very different constituencies. Many studies (in the late 1960s and since) have argued that environmentalism was elitist and that it drew most of its support from the (mainly white) middle class.[89] For the black citizens of the United States, the most immediate and urgent issues were social and economic justice and civil rights. While the poor were fighting for jobs, education, and political and social equality, the environmental lobby included among its aims such apparently nonessential demands as the protection of wilderness. For many black activists, the environmental movement even threatened to divert dollars and the conscience of the middle class. During the 1960s, the more radical segments of the civil rights movement began to exclude white liberals. The radical journalist James Ridgeway went so far as to suggest that the ecology movement was remote, separate and "cut off from the revolutionary surge sweeping through American society . . . it had no bearing on the war, political repression, blacks, the poor, or any other factor which created the currents of stress in the society."[90] Yet the civil rights movement showed what could be achieved through mass protest, and the techniques used by Martin Luther King and other civil rights leaders to bring about peaceful confrontation with authority undoubtedly educated a new generation in the methods of effective protest.

In terms of the influence it had on alerting a generation to social problems and methods of protest, the nearest British equivalent to the civil rights movement was the Campaign for Nuclear Disarmament (CND). The Suez crisis and the Hungarian uprising of 1956 created a new mood of idealistic purpose on the British Left, giving rise to a crusading spirit, new humanistic socialism, and mistrust of old ideologies and institutions.[91] The nuclear arms race was seen as symptomatic of the problems of the old order; demonstrations during the early 1950s revealed a groundswell of public concern over nuclear weapons, and in

1957 the Emergency Committee for Direct Action Against Nuclear War (DAC) was set up to protest a British nuclear test at Christmas Island. CND was created in 1958. Between 1958 and 1965, a number of mass demonstrations were held, notably the marches between London and the nuclear weapons establishment at Aldermaston in Berkshire. Although the majority of disarmament campaigners became involved for moral, political, or religious reasons, there were significant links between the disarmament movement and the later environmental movement, if only because both groups sought human, rational control over the high technology created by advanced industrial society.[92] Certainly by the early 1970s it was difficult to disassociate the campaigns against nuclear weapons and nuclear energy.

The second American protest movement of note—with which New Environmentalism had much closer links—was the anti-war movement. In 1965, the first acknowledged American combat troops were landed in South Vietnam, and "nonretaliatory" air strikes began at the same time; the first student protests against the war followed in short order. Growing knowledge about the nature of the war, the course of the war itself (and the fact that official predictions were not borne out by events), bitterness at the hollowness of President Johnson's 1964 campaign posture as a man of peace, and opposition to the draft all combined to produce escalating protest in the second half of the decade. The main bases of support were found among white professionals, students, and clergy.[93] Students were exempt from the draft, so college campuses became the headquarters of the movement, whose moral underpinnings overlapped for a while with wider and deeper student discontent with society. Demonstrations became almost an everyday event; in the 1967–68 academic year alone, there were 221 demonstrations on 101 campuses.[94] The anti-war movement revealed a campus population that, according to the Cox Commission report on disturbances at Columbia, was "the best informed, the most intelligent, and the most idealistic this country has ever known. . . . It is also the most sensitive to public issues and the most sophisticated in political tactics."[95] At the root of the phenomenon was a society apparently unable to live up to the ideals taught in schools and churches. For many student activists, noted the 1968 National Commission on the Causes and Prevention of Violence, the university represented a qualitatively different kind of social institution, one in which radical social criticism could be generated and constructive social change promoted.[96]

Student disaffection came to many industrialized nations in the late 1960s, the watershed of protest being 1968 (cf., France, West Germany, and Spain). Lipset notes that "one would learn to expect a sharp increase in student activism in a society where, for a variety of reasons, accepted political and social values are being questioned, in times particularly where events are testing the viability of a regime and where policy failures seem to question the legitimacy of social and economic arrangements and institutions."[97] Searle notes three features of the student unrest of the time: the search for sacred goals and values, the creation of an adversary relationship with authority, and the rejection of authority.[98] Heightened student concern and sensitivity created a constituency receptive to all issues where the prevailing social and economic system was seen to be working against an ideal. In the same way as racial discrimination and the immorality of the Vietnam war seemed to be symptomatic of the sickness of the system, so environmental degradation seemed an equally acceptable agenda item for protest. Nash suggests that sections of the American college population were at this time attributing social problems—from imperialism to racism—to "unecological attitudes."[99] Student disaffection spread to the obsession with success and security of the older generations. Materialism, technology, power, profit, and growth were characterized as symbols of all that was worst about Western society and as posing a threat to the environment.

Environmentalism also provided expression for the counterculture, which, notes Cotgrove, was "profoundly anti-industrial, with its decisive rejection of the work ethic, its condemnation of consumerism and material values, and its questioning of the rationality of a society which harnessed science to what were seen as the inhuman atrocities of the Vietnam war, and the ecological damage wrought by insecticides and industrial waste."[100] The hippie movement of the late 1960s embodied the moral and antiestablishment school of environmentalism in the United States, when a return to wilderness and nature was seen as the only way of retaining earthly values in a materialist world. Nash believes it no accident that Charles Reich chose *The Greening of America* as the title for his influential 1971 book,[101] because "the green world, the wild world, held essential truths."[102]

Environmentalism in the United States finally matured when it intersected with the heterogeneous social movements of the day. Reaching its crest at the end of a decade of social activism, the environmental revolution, argues Fox,[103] borrowed from all the major movements, the primary link being chronological, in that activists turned to the environment at the end of the 1960s as the civil rights and antiwar movements lost momentum. In both Britain and the United States, many of the young supporters of the environmental movement had been introduced to activism through the experiences of other protest campaigns.

THE DOWNS MODEL

The "issue-attention cycle" outlined by Anthony Downs[104] reveals much about the advent of New Environmentalism in the United States. He argues that the interest of the American public in social problems is short-lived, intense, and capricious. Public perception of most "crises" in

American domestic life does not reflect changes in real conditions so much as it reflects the operation of a systematic cycle of heightening public interest and then increasing boredom with major issues. He suggests that the rise and fall of many social issues in the United States follows five stages: (1) a preproblem stage when an undesirable social problem exists but has not yet captured public attention; (2) a stage of alarmed discovery—often triggered by a series of events that reveal the existence of a problem—and euphoric enthusiasm about society's ability to respond (Downs notes the "great American tradition" of optimistically viewing most obstacles to social progress as external to the structure of society, and as being capable of being eliminated without any fundamental reordering of society itself); (3) a realistic stage when the true cost of "solving" the problem is appreciated; (4) a gradual decline in intense public interest, brought on by discouragement, alarm, boredom, or the emergence of a new issue; and (5) a postproblem stage when the issue moves into prolonged limbo, a time of lesser attention or spasmodic recurrences in interest.

The first three of Downs's stages undoubtedly applied to New Environmentalism, in western Europe as much as in North America. But while a veritable flood of writing in the early 1970s (and later)[105] suggested that environmentalism had entered the fourth stage by about 1972, this was true only insofar as interest fell from the perhaps artificial peak attained in 1968–72. Rather than enter a decline, environmentalism gradually became tempered by a less emotional and more carefully considered response to the problems of the environment. It shifted from euphoria to reason and temporarily became lodged in stage three, where, instead of discouragement in the face of the costs of action (which were often high, but perhaps no higher than the potential costs of inaction), the environment became a central public policy issue. Certainly it has not yet entered stage five, nor may it ever. Downs himself suggested that while the environmental issue must inevitably decline, it would maintain more attention than problems that affected smaller numbers of people. It was more visible and more clearly threatening than most other social problems; it was a universal threat (which made it less politically divisive than, for example, attacking racism or poverty); it could be blamed on a small number of wealthy and powerful "public enemies"; there was the possibility of firm technological answers to environmental problems; most of the costs of pollution control could be passed on to the public through higher product prices rather than higher taxes; the issue could generate a large private industry with strong vested interests in continued spending against pollution; and the issues themselves were ambiguous— improving the environment was a broad and all-encompassing objective.

Downs's model fails to take account of the integration of popular social issues with the political fabric of societies. Time and again, such social movements achieve some or all of their intended goals by transforming society; this happened with the civil rights and women's movements, it has happened with antiwar movements, and it happened with environmentalism. By no means have all the goals of all these movements yet been achieved, but in most cases the social reformers successfully scaled the walls and entered the citadel of public policy.

NO LONGER A QUIET CRISIS

Social revolutions have complex roots. The roots of New Environmentalism were many and varied, and it is difficult to dissociate one from the other. It was not a single issue or sudden crisis that led to the formation of the movement, argues Bowman.[106] It seems more than coincidental that the rise of environmental awareness coincided with the maturation of the first generation to grow up in postwar affluence; the outcry over environmental quality was probably more a function of changes in attitude than changes in the actual state of the environment,[107] but the former might not have happened without the latter. New Environmentalism was mainly concerned with the quality of life and how it was compromised by the pollutive by-products of economic growth. Affluence, youthful discontent, headline disasters, and broader social and economic trends all played their part in eliciting the change.

Other explanations have been offered. Means suggests that the goals of the traditional conservation movements may have been too narrow and were being questioned—paradoxically—because they had been surprisingly successful.[108] Schnaiberg points to the growing interest in wilderness recreation and camping, in part a reflection of metropolitan decay and the expansion of urban areas.[109] Downs suggests that so many Americans were able to participate in certain activities that were formerly only available to a small, wealthy minority (such as car ownership and access to national parks, suburban housing, and resort areas), that the environment of the elite was deteriorating.[110] Enzensberger suggests that the environmental impact of new technological developments had become more universal, which meant that—for the middle and upper-middle class—geographical mobility was no longer an answer to avoiding problems like nuclear fallout and oil pollution.[111] Solesbury suggests that problems such as poverty, housing, and racial tension had become less important in the affluent 1960s, and environmentalism had taken their place in the public imagination.[112] Hardin suggests that environmental concern may have been a displacement from other, more intractable problems.[113] Golub and Townsend argue that the myth of an ecological crisis was developed by business interests as a means of encouraging greater international cooperation, thus enabling planned industrial growth by an increasing number of multinational corporations.[114]

Whatever the cause, by 1970, there had been a revolution in environmental attitudes. In 1969–70, annual membership in the five major U.S.

conservation groups was growing at 16–18 percent; membership of the Sierra Club alone had tripled since 1966.[115] Environmental spokesmen such as Paul Ehrlich and Barry Commoner (see chapter 4) were traveling the country, occasionally speaking before audiences of up to 10,000. In a cover story in February 1970, *Time* noted that the environment "may well be the gut issue that can unify a polarized nation."[116] New Environmentalism peaked on 22 April 1970, when Earth Day, the largest environmental demonstration in history, was held in the United States. The idea came from Senator Gaylord Nelson of Wisconsin; with federal funding, an organizing committee chaired by Denis Hayes orchestrated a nationwide show of concern for the environment. Rallies and teach-ins were held at an estimated 1,500 colleges and 10,000 schools; both houses of Congress recessed; Nelson himself spoke at nine college campuses, from Harvard to Berkeley; cars were banned from New York's Fifth Avenue for two hours, allowing 100,000 pedestrians to fill the thoroughfare; and in Washington, DC, 10,000 people surrounded the Washington Monument for 12 hours of revelry. Shortly before Earth Day, *New Republic* dismissed "the ecology craze" as "a cop-out for a President and a populace too cheap or too gutless or too tired or too frustrated or too all of them to tangle with some old problems that have proved resistant and emotionally ungratifying to boot." Six months later, it devoted an issue to the environment and admitted that Earth Day had been "not just a channel for frustrated antiwar energies, as we thought. It signaled an awakening to the dangers in a dictatorship of technology."[117]

In 1963 Stewart Udall, Secretary of the Interior in the Kennedy and Johnson administrations, had written *The Quiet Crisis*, a personal review of the history of American environmental philosophy, from the land wisdom of the American Indians to the urban planning of Frederick Law Olmsted. The "quiet crisis," he argued, lay in the fact that "America today stands poised on a pinnacle of wealth and power, yet we live in a land of vanishing beauty, of increasing ugliness, of shrinking open space, and of an overall environment that is diminished daily by pollution and noise and blight."[118] Udall argued that the postwar obsession with "hot and cold wars" had diverted attention from the conservation concept and that progress in science had encouraged a false sense of well-being that had resulted in urgent conservation and management needs being ignored.

In July 1965, five days before his death, Adlai Stevenson (then United States ambassador to the United Nations) gave a speech before the UN Economic and Social Council in Geneva on the problems of urbanization throughout the world. In the speech (originally drafted by Barbara Ward),[119] he used the metaphor of the earth as a spaceship on which humanity traveled, dependent on its vulnerable supplies of air and soil. The theme was developed further by Kenneth Boulding, an economist at the University of Michigan, in his 1966 essay "The Economics of Coming

Spaceship Earth," in which he compared the open "cowboy economy" (reckless, exploitative, romantic, where consumption and production were good things) with a future "spaceman" economy concerned primarily with stock maintenance, where "throughput is by no means a desideratum, and is indeed to be regarded as something to be minimized rather than maximized. The essential measure of the success of the economy is not production and consumption at all, but the nature, quality, and complexity of the total capital stock."[120] The notion of Spaceship Earth was graphically underlined by the publication in 1966 of the first photographs of earth taken by Lunar Orbiter satellites, which showed the planet as a lone, finite, and seemingly vulnerable oasis in space. For millions on earth, suggests Arthur C. Clarke, these photographs "must have been the moment when the Earth really became a planet."[121]

By 1970, the environmental crisis was no longer a quiet crisis. A new mass movement had arisen, and a new issue was beginning to find its way onto the public policy agenda. Mounting scientific evidence confirmed many of the fears of activists and amateur ecologists; the human race was rapidly using up its stock of natural resources and fouling its nest in the process. Concern mounted, and a controversial debate on the limits to growth was born, centered on the Malthusian postulation that crisis and collapse were inevitable unless growth in population and resource exploitation were brought under control. The prophets of doom had arrived.

FOUR

The Prophets of Doom (1968–1972)

Multiple disasters, argues Barkun, serve to destroy the commonly held theories that have served sufficiently well in the past, and also, typically, the response to such stress is the rise of charismatic leaders who offer ideas and a philosophy that can be interpreted in a salvationist manner.[1] While the civil rights movement had such leaders, the same was less true of environmentalism. In the growing atmosphere of alarm about the welfare of the environment in the 1960s, there emerged instead—in the United States at least—environmental theorists and philosophers (charismatic occasionally, controversial often). Most were academics, for example, Paul Ehrlich of Stanford, Barry Commoner of Washington (St. Louis), LaMont Cole of Cornell, Eugene Odum of Georgia, Kenneth Watt of the University of California at Davis, and Garrett Hardin of UC Santa Barbara. They offered no unifying creed for the movement, nor did they give it a particular sense of direction, nor could they be called "leaders." The more pessimistic among them quickly earned such unflattering sobriquets as "the prophets of doom" or "the New Jeremiahs."

Yet they provided a degree of intellectual focus. The debates they raised drew attention to three key issues: pollution, population growth, and technology. The contention that none of these theories *alone* fully explained the environmental dilemma in turn led to the view that the crisis stemmed from exponential growth and that there were clear limits to economic growth.

THE EHRLICH-COMMONER DEBATE

The earliest controversy was aroused by the differences of opinion between two biologists, Paul Ehrlich and Barry Commoner. Ehrlich took a well-worn theme—population growth—and made it his own; Commoner, for his part, focused on the quality of economic growth. The population question had a long history, dating back to the British physician Sir William Petty (1623–1687), who had written in 1650 of the multiplication of human population,[2] speculating that it would take 2,000 years for the earth's carrying capacity to be reached. Not surprisingly, his views drew little notice. Nearly 150 years later, much greater public impact was achieved by the British classical economist Thomas Malthus.[3] In his *Essay on Population*, written in 1798–1803, Malthus argued that the natural rate of population growth was exponential and that of food production was arithmetical. Unless population growth was checked, the population would outstrip the available food supply and there would be widespread famine.[4] Vogt, Osborn, the Wilderness Society, the Sierra Club, and others raised the question of overpopulation again in the late 1940s and 1950s. In 1966, David Brower, then executive director of the Sierra Club, argued that there could be no conservation policy without a population policy.[5] In 1967 Brower heard Ehrlich,[6] a professor of biology at Stanford University, talk at the Commonwealth Club in San Francisco and commissioned him to write a short book on population for the Sierra Club. The book, *The Population Bomb*, was published in 1968. It subsequently became one of the best-selling environmental books of all time, with three million copies in paperback by the mid-1970s.[7]

Ehrlich was an unashamed neo-Malthusian. Criticisms that he was an alarmist did not upset him: "I *am* an alarmist," he told *Playboy* in 1970, "because I'm very goddamned alarmed. I believe we're facing the *brink* because of population pressures."[8] It was the battle to provide for an ever-increasing human population that caused most of the problems, he argued, and the most effective environmental safeguard was birth control; "no changes in behavior or technology can save us unless we can achieve control over the size of the human population."[9] Ehrlich warned that (1) hundreds of millions of people faced starvation in the 1970s and 1980s, (2) the limits of human capability to produce food by conventional means had nearly been reached, (3) attempts to increase food production would cause environmental deterioration and reduce the earth's capacity to produce food, (4) population growth could lead to plague and nuclear war, and (5) the only solution lay in a change in human attitudes.

Barry Commoner,[10] then professor of biology at Washington University, St. Louis, offered a different view. Commoner's environmental activism had begun in 1953 with his concern for the effects of nuclear fallout. The publicity generated by his Committee for Nuclear Information is often credited as a telling factor in public support for the 1963 Partial Test Ban Treaty. The fallout issue for him was symptomatic of the destructive impact of technology on the environment. He took his message to American campuses in the late 1960s, and by early 1970 had earned a *Time* cover story hailing him as the Paul Revere of ecology. He outlined his fears in *The Closing Circle*, published in 1971. While population growth and affluence had intensified since the Second World War, he noted, the increases were too small to account for rises in pollution levels since 1946 of 200 to 2,000 percent. An additional factor must, therefore, be "flawed technology" resulting in a massive growth in the use of synthetics, disposable products, pesticides, and detergents. The issue was not so much the growth in economic activity, but *how* that growth had been achieved. It was not so much that *more* goods were being consumed, but that their production and disposal were more costly in environmental terms. The increased output of pollutants per unit production resulting from the introduction of new productive technologies since 1946 had, he argued, come to account for 95 percent of the total output of pollutants.[11] He emphasized that some of the most dangerous environmental perils were those that could not be seen, notably air, food, and water contaminated by polluting substances.

Their positions stated, Ehrlich and Commoner entered into an often vitriolic debate of questionable merit, perhaps based as much on academic competitiveness as on any genuine philosophical differences. Popular opinion among physical and social scientists at the time was that both men were carrying their views to the extreme, Ehrlich being an "alarmist" and Commoner strangely obstinate in exonerating population growth.[12] There was also concern that ideological commitments on both sides were obscuring the scientific questions; Ehrlich spoke from a scientific perspective, whereas Commoner considered politics to be very much part of the equation.[13] Commoner opposed coercion in limiting population growth, arguing that action to eliminate poverty would result in a demographic transition; that is, as societies became wealthier and more industrialized, population growth would slow. He suggested that most of the serious pollution problems of the United States either dated from the postwar years or had worsened since the war[14] (although *The Closing Circle* relates many examples of pollution that predated the war, often by decades). Commoner argued that pollution and the exhaustion of mineral resources would continue without population growth. Indeed, in *Science and Survival*, he had fleetingly described population growth as a major source of pollution; following the opening of the debate with Ehrlich, he tended to dismiss the population issue.

Ehrlich felt *The Closing Circle* to be "inexplicably inconsistent and dangerously misleading." He saw three principal defects in the book: it assumed that environmental deterioration consisted only of pollution (leading Commoner to discuss the environmental crisis "as if it had begun in the 1940s"); the argument that the cause of pollution lay in faulty technology was based on faulty research and interpretation of data; and Commoner's misconceptions about certain aspects of demography led him to draw erroneous conclusions about human "self-regulation" and viable strategies for population limitations.[15]

Ehrlich occasionally appeared more open-minded than Commoner, admitting, for example, that his views changed with time and with his understanding of the issues. Commoner recalled how, in early conversation with Ehrlich and his followers, the latter "conceded [in contrast with the position expressed in *The Population Bomb*] . . . that population growth is not *alone* responsible for environmental impact, and that technological factors are also significant. I was gratified by this indication that they were prepared to modify their position on the basis of the new data."[16] In 1973[17] and again in 1974,[18] Ehrlich appeared to soften his disagreement with Commoner by suggesting that the components of the environmental crisis caused by population growth, affluence, or technological errors were difficult to differentiate; it was preposterous, he argued, "to try to sort out which of three multiplicative factors is responsible for the whole thing, when quite obviously we have to attack all three."[19] Some curious contradictions crept into Ehrlich's argument. In 1970 he pointed out that he had written *The Population Bomb* because he thought too many people were emphasizing only pollution; "I'm not in any way trying to minimize the problem of pollution," he argued. "At the moment, it is at least as serious as, or possibly more serious in the United States than population growth."[20] Yet in 1973, he observed that "from the point of view of an ecologist . . . [air pollution is] one of the relatively trivial problems. . . . It's amenable to rather rapid technological cure and is just a symptom of some of the things we're doing, rather than something ecologically serious."[21] Similarly, while arguing that overpopulation would lead to famine and ecocatastrophe, he also argued that "in the long view the progressive deterioration of our environment may cause more death and misery than the food-population gap."[22] Ehrlich's contention that the earth was producing as much food as it could has since been shown to be erroneous, and by the early 1980s it was increasingly widely accepted that the root cause of hunger was not a shortage of food so much as an imbalance between supply and demand. Ehrlich's argument made no allowances for the inefficiency of food production techniques, falling production rates, or poor land management practice, and his suggested solutions made no mention of the need to use existing resources more efficiently or to reduce waste. He never alluded, for instance, to the potential for land reform and agricultural intensification.

Ehrlich also criticized Commoner for being preoccupied with pollution almost to the exclusion of other forms of environmental deterioration, yet was himself preoccupied with the single issue of population and looked at *that* from a limited perspective. As a cause of resource depletion, population growth has since been joined—if not eclipsed—by the inefficient and unsustainable use of resources. In other words, it is less a question of sheer numbers of people than of how resources such as food are used and distributed. Both Commoner and Ehrlich were guided more by what they saw happening in Western industrialized countries, and less by what was happening—or has since been shown to have been happening—in centrally planned economies and LDCs.

If anything, subsequent events and scientific and demographic evidence have proved both men to have been largely correct in their central theses (as far as they went) but suffering in similar proportion from parallel obsessions and misconceptions. Ehrlich himself pinpointed one of the dangers to which he had fallen prey when he noted that scientists were often criticized either for being too narrow or for stepping out of their field of speciality; but he often felt moved to go beyond the boundaries of his formal training to seek solutions to human problems, and saw "no other course than for scientists in all fields to do the same— even at the risk of being wrong."[23] Similarly, in 1973 he observed that "most of the criticism of environmentalists implies that they should never make errors. But there are going to be continuing errors in the statements of environmentalists because they are dealing with systems that we don't understand completely and where there is a great deal of uncertainty."[24]

THE TRAGEDY OF THE COMMONS

A similarly controversial doomsday thesis was the essay written by the biologist Garret Hardin[25] on the "tragedy of the commons."[26] It was first presented as a presidential address to the Pacific Division of the American Association for the Advancement of Science in December 1967. As Hardin himself pointed out, the commons theme was not new and was well known in social science circles.[27] What were new—and what generated the controversy—were his conclusions. He argued that there were no "scientific" solutions to problems such as overpopulation. The "tragedy" lay in the inevitability of the destruction of communally owned resources; Hardin suggested that the inevitability of global destruction predetermined the choices that mankind should make to ensure its survival. He used the parable of a commons on which a number of cattle herders grazed their cattle. A particular number of cattle at a particular time ate grass at the same rate as it grew—supply and demand were in perfect balance. Then one herder concluded that he could add one more cow and reap the benefits while the costs were spread among the other herders, whose cows had to settle for less. He also concluded that if he did not add an extra cow, the other herders might, and they would then reap the benefits at his expense. The only rational solution was to add a cow. But every other herder reached the same conclusions and decided that they must introduce additional cows.

Thus "each man is locked into a system that compels him to increase his herd without limit—in a world that is limited. Ruin is the destination towards which all men rush, each pursuing his own best interest in a society that believes in the freedom of the commons. Freedom in a commons brings ruin to all." Hardin suggested that pollution was the reverse of the tragedy of the commons in that man was not taking from but was giving to the commons in the form of noxious waste. "The rational man finds that his share of the cost of the wastes he discharges into the commons is less than the cost of purifying his wastes before releasing them. Since this is true for everyone, we are locked into a system of 'fouling our own nest', so long as we behave only as independent, rational, free-enterprisers." How, Hardin asked, could we "legislate temperance" in, for example, human procreation? Prohibition was easy to legislate, but temperance not so, and he took issue with the view of the Universal Declaration of Human Rights that "any choice and decision with regard to the size of the family must irrevocably rest with the family itself, and cannot be made by anyone else." Temperance could not be achieved by appeal to conscience, but only through "mutual coercion, mutually agreed upon by the majority of the people affected," especially where applied to the control of population growth. In other words, man must be coerced into a sense of communal responsibility because he would never adopt it voluntarily.[28]

GLOBAL MODELS AND THE LIMITS TO GROWTH

Overpopulation was not the only old theory revived by New Environmentalism. An idea with an even more impressive intellectual pedigree— the limits to exponential growth—was dusted off and revisited with even greater controversy. Thomas Malthus, David Ricardo, John Stuart Mill, W. Stanley Jevons, Karl Marx, and Friedrich Engels had all at one time or another looked at this or related issues.[29] As recently as 1953, the lawyer Samuel Ordway had outlined his own "Theory of the Limit to Growth" in a slim and largely ignored volume that anticipated many of the sophisticated and expensive computer simulations of the 1970s.[30]

The principal product of the 1970s revival was *The Limits to Growth*, published in 1972. The roots of the report went back to the late 1940s, when Jay Forrester[31] pioneered the application of the digital computer, tactical military decision-making, and information-feedback systems to studies of the interacting forces of social systems.[32] During the late 1950s, he refined his theories of industrial dynamics as a management technique. The system dynamics method argues that models are needed to describe the organization of systems, their internal relations, and assumptions about external contacts across the system boundaries. Components of relationships can then be changed in order to simulate alternative outcomes. The method holds that mental models are inferior to computer models because only computer models enable relationships and their consequences to be made explicit.[33]

During the mid-1960s, Dr. Aurelio Peccei, an Italian management consultant,[34] had begun to reflect on the problems of the world. He saw them as embodied in a set of interconnected relationships and felt they could only be understood through an overview that outlined the links between seemingly unrelated occurrences and conditions. He outlined his thoughts in *The Chasm Ahead*.[35] In 1968, he brought together an informal group of 30 economists, scientists, educationalists, and industrialists at a meeting in Rome. Out of this meeting emerged the Club of Rome, a loose association of scientists, technocrats, and politicians. By 1970 the Club had 75 members from 25 countries. Its professed goal was to foster understanding of the interdependent economic, political, natural, and social components of "the global system" and to encourage the adoption of new attitudes, policies, and institutions capable of redressing the problems. Environmental degradation was just one of these problems. Others included urban sprawl, loss of faith in institutions, rejection of traditional values, and economic disruption, all of which the Club saw as of such complexity as to be beyond the competency of traditional institutions and policies.

Forrester's system dynamics method had already come under severe criticism,[36] but the Club saw in it considerable potential for their own interests. In 1970 it launched a Project on the Predicament of Mankind and invited Forrester to Switzerland to outline his method. The "predicament" was that human society, despite its knowledge and skills, did not understand the "origins, significance, and inter-relationships of its many components and thus is unable to devise effective responses."[37] The failure had occurred because society continued to examine single issues without understanding that the whole was more than the sum of its parts.

Meanwhile, during their study of the preparations being made for the UN Conference on the Human Environment, to be held in Stockholm in 1972 (see chapter 5), a group at the Massachusetts Institute of Technology (MIT) concluded that a Study of Critical Environmental Problems (SCEP) would help the conference planners. Under the aegis of a steering committee, 70 scientists and professionals and 45 observers met during July 1970 in Williamstown, Massachusetts, to study and discuss the effect on global climatic and terrestrial conditions of specific atmospheric, terrestrial, and marine pollutants and to examine research and monitoring procedures.

"The existence of a global problem," SCEP emphasized, "does not imply the necessity for a global solution."[38] Most corrective action, it concluded, would have to be taken at national, regional, or local levels, but the potential for international cooperation in research and monitoring was high. SCEP's general recommendation was for new methods of standardized global data gathering. The report made two particularly important points: that the available data, especially at the international level, were fragmentary, contradictory, sometimes unreliable, and often unavailable (because of inconsistent reporting and lack of standardization); and that environmental problems had to be considered from the different perspectives of more developed and less developed countries. "There is little reason to believe that the developing countries can be diverted from their preoccupation with the first-order effects of technology to a concern about the side effects upon the environment. Currently, and in the foreseeable future, the advanced industrial societies will have to carry the load of remedial action against pollution."[39] The MIT report called for a more complete and satisfactory study of such issues as marine oil pollution, atmospheric carbon dioxide build-up, and the potential effects of supersonic transport airliners (SSTs) on the atmosphere; the formulation of new priorities; and the abandonment of the assumption that the environment must bear the costs of industrial and technological development.

The Club of Rome project was launched at a meeting in Cambridge, Massachusetts, in late July 1970. Forrester had outlined a global model, called World I, identifying specific components of the problem and suggesting techniques for analyzing the most important of these components. He argued that the human mind was incapable of understanding, predicting, or controlling the activities of very complex patterns, and that human intuition often misled people into pursuing remedies that either had no effect or the opposite effect to that desired;[40] computer simulation was, thus, vital to helping man cope with macropolicy questions. Forrester developed his model into World 2, outlined in his book *World Dynamics*; looking only at the broad aspects of the world system, he neither addressed the difficulties of implementing changes in human attitudes, nor allowed for changes in human aspirations and values brought on from recognition of the predicament facing mankind.[41] He set up a team under the direction of 28-year-old Dennis Meadows[42] to make a yet more detailed and polished version—World 3. Five basic factors were identified as determining and ultimately limiting growth: population, agricultural production, natural resources, industrial production, and pollution.

Using the Forrester model, the team reached three main conclusions:

(1) If existing trends in world population, pollution, industrialization, food production, and resource depletion continued unchanged, the limits to growth on the planet would be reached within one hundred years. The most likely result would be a sudden and uncontrollable decline in both population and industrial capacity.

(2) It was possible to alter these growth trends and to establish a condition of ecological and economic stability that was sustainable far into the future. The state of global equilibrium could be designed so that the basic material needs of each person on earth were satisfied and each person had an equal opportunity to realize their individual human potential.

(3) If the world's people decided to strive for this second outcome rather than the first, the sooner they began working to attain it, the greater would be their chances of success.[43]

The essential thesis of the MIT model, released on 2 March 1972 as *The Limits to Growth,* was that the roots of the environmental crisis lay in exponential growth. Catastrophe was inevitable by the end of the century, brought on by the exhaustion of resources and rising death rates from pollution and food shortages. Increased food supply, the discovery of new sources of energy, and technological advances to control pollution could reverse the trend. Ultimately though, there was an urgent need to achieve global equilibrium through recognizing the limits to economic and population growth. "Technological optimism," the team argued, "is the most common and the most dangerous reaction to our findings from the world model. Technology can relieve the symptoms of a problem without affecting the underlying causes . . . [and] can thus divert our attention from the most fundamental problem—the problem of growth in a finite system."[44] The authors recommended, among other things, a 40 percent reduction in industrial investment, a 20 percent reduction in agricultural investment, a 40 percent reduction in the birth rate, and a massive transfer of wealth from rich to poor countries.

Drawing on the findings of Worlds 2 and 3, the Club of Rome reached a number of its own conclusions,[45] many of them remarkably perceptive:

(1) It was essential that the quantitative restraints of the world environment be realized; population pressure alone was enough to compel society to seek a state of global equilibrium; such equilibrium could only be achieved if the lot of the Third World was substantially improved.

(2) Global development was so closely interlinked with other issues that an overall strategy needed to be evolved to tackle all major problems, particularly man's relationship with the environment.[46]

(3) If society was to embark on a new course, concerted international measures and joint long-term planning on an unprecedented scale was needed; imposing a break on population and economic growth should not lead to a freeze on economic development; rather, the MDCs should take a lead by decelerating their growth and helping LDCs advance their economies more rapidly. (These views were to gain wider currency in the late 1970s and early 1980s [see chapter 8].)

The authors of World 3 did not claim infallibility. They admitted that their model was "imperfect, over-simplified, and unfinished," and that much further study was needed. Yet in spite of its preliminary state, they felt it important to publish the findings when they did because decisions with far-reaching global physical, economic, and social implications were constantly being made and could not await perfect models and total understanding. The purpose of publishing *The Limits to Growth,* a nontechnical summary of their findings, was to open the debate on accelerating global trends to a wider community than that of scientists alone; in this they succeeded. Meadows and his team positively welcomed constructive criticism and discussion, as indicated by their association with the Sussex team (see below).

One of the motives behind the Club's work was the belief that scientists and politicians had become too complacent and willing to believe that man could always pull a solution out of the air when things seemed to be on the point of going too far. The Club hoped to shock people out of their complacency, "to provide warnings of potential world crisis if . . . [current] trends are allowed to continue, and thus offer an opportunity to make changes in our political, economic, and social systems to ensure that these crises do not take place,"[47] and to shock society into initiating a transition from growth to global equilibrium. The Club of Rome saw Worlds 2 and 3 as means to their ends and hoped that by quantifying the human predicament, the models would encourage people to look for solutions. Unlike Hardin, the Club believed that the improvement of the lot of the Third World was essential to the achievement of equilibrium. But like Hardin, who believed that "no technical solution can rescue us from the misery of over-population,"[48] the Club believed "technological solutions alone"[49] could not extricate man from the vicious cycle of growing population and the overexploitation of the natural environment. The Club concluded that redress of global imbalance was a challenge for the present generation, not the next, and that this demanded concerted international measures and long-term planning on a scale without precedent.

Across the Atlantic, meanwhile, a second "doomsday hypothesis"—*A Blueprint for Survival*[50]—had been published as a radical response to what were regarded as the rather staid attitudes of the British conservation establishment. The immediate fillip came from an August 1971 article in the *Observer* by its environment correspondent, Gerald Leach. In it he observed that while the main lines of the changes needed to move toward the spaceship economy were becoming clear, no one had sketched out the details. Edward Goldsmith, editor of the *Ecologist*, organized a conference at which it was decided to construct a model for Britain. The *Blueprint*, which drew heavily on the SCEP model and was influenced by *The Limits to Growth*, was published in the *Ecologist* in early 1972. It started from a similar premise to that of the MIT model, that "if current trends are allowed to persist, the breakdown of society and the irreversible disruption of the life-support systems on this planet . . . are inevitable."[51] Population growth and resource consumption necessitated radical changes in attitudes and practices; indefinite growth could not be sustained by finite resources. Among the recommendations: the use of fewer pesticides and fertilizers, efficient disposal of sewage and reduction of industrial waste, protection of genetic resources, social accounting (e.g., making polluters pay), the stabilizing of population growth, and the creation of a new decentralized social system. Like MIT, the *Blueprint* team acknowledged their debt to the ideas of John Stuart Mill. To implement its ideas, the team proposed a Movement for Survival (MS), a coalition of environmental organizations working to persuade governments to take measures leading to a stable society; although Friends of the

Earth and the Conservation Society, among others, expressed early interest, MS came to naught.

The theme of nongrowth was taken further in 1973 by the British economist E. F. Schumacher. In his book *Small is Beautiful*,[52] he criticized the waste and squandering of resources and the over-reliance of Western industry on capital- and energy-intensive technology. Criticizing the value system that allowed such a state of affairs to continue, he challenged people to reexamine their values and lifestyles and to make a transition from the belief that "more is better" to "small is beautiful." Schumacher's thesis was given special significance by the decision of the OPEC nations in October 1973 to impose an oil embargo, leading to a quadrupling in the price of oil.

APOCALYPSE TOMORROW

By the beginning of the 1970s, many Western Europeans and North Americans were thoroughly alarmed by the apparently dismal prospects for the future. Despite the lack of complete scientific data, speculation became a popular pastime. In the wake of the prophets came a flood of often fantastic apocalyptic predictions, many of which have since come back to haunt their authors. Paul and Anne Ehrlich, for example, warned that "mankind itself may stand on the brink of extinction."[53] Elsewhere, Ehrlich often warned of the prospect of "eco-catastrophe," worldwide plague, and nuclear war if population growth continued. Barbara Ward and René Dubos predicted that by 1985 all land surfaces other than the coldest and highest would be occupied and utilized by man.[54] Fears for the effect on the atmosphere of supersonic transport planes (SSTs), combined with predictions that up to 500 SSTs would be flying within a few years, led to the suggestion that by 1985, a fleet of 300 Concordes, together with an expanded Boeing SST fleet, would consume 2.2 billion barrels of oil per year, or one-ninth of world demand in 1971.[55] In 1970, *Life* listed a number of predictions for which scientists claimed "solid experimental and theoretical evidence": air pollution combined with a temperature inversion would kill thousands in a U.S. city in the early 1980s; urban dwellers would be wearing gas masks to survive air pollution; by 1985 air pollution would have halved the amount of sunlight reaching the earth; and a major ecological system would have broken down somewhere in the United States.[56]

In 1969, Paul Ehrlich made a whole series of predictions of collapse, an exercise that might, in retrospect, seem both unwise and uncharacteristic of a rational scientist. Based on trends then apparent, he predicted the failure of the Green Revolution, the incompetence of aid programs to LDCs, and the collapse of the Peruvian anchovy industry (it collapsed in 1972, three years earlier than Ehrlich predicted). However, he also incorrectly predicted:

(1) the collapse of the whaling industry in 1973 (it did not collapse);

(2) the reduction of the annual ocean fish catch to 30 million tons by 1977 (in fact, it was more than twice that figure, although the possibility of a collapse in world fisheries persisted as catches continued to be unsustainable);

(3) an annual rate of deaths from malnutrition of 50 million (It is impossible to reach more than an approximate figure of deaths from malnutrition in any given region or period, but mortality figures from countries experiencing famine between 1960 and 1983 indicate that just over 12 million people died.[57] Even the most pessimistic projections of annual deaths from all forms of malnutrition would fall well short of Ehrlich's prediction. Of course, whatever the estimates, 12 million deaths was a tragedy of gigantic proportions.);

(4) diatom blooms in the oceans and the extinction by 1979 of all important marine animal life (marine life was to prove considerably more resilient than many scientists expected).

What these and other predictions emphasize is that the environmental crisis seemed much worse in 1968 than it was to seem 10 or 15 years later. By then, some action at least had been taken that may have allowed the world to avoid an apocalypse; even so, it is questionable whether some of the predictions would have ever come true. Much of the alarmism was created and fed by the prophets of doom. When Ehrlich wrote *The Population Bomb*, the population of the United States was growing at nearly 1.5 percent annually, enough to double the American population in about 60 years. Given the high average per capita consumption of natural resources by American consumers, the implications of this growth seemed serious. By the late 1970s, however, the American population growth rate had fallen below 1 percent annually. In 1978, Ehrlich admitted that no one had anticipated the rapid change of reproductive behavior which occurred in the early 1970s.[58] But he was still only marginally more optimistic. Those who claimed that there was no population problem, only a problem of distribution, were wrong, he argued; the only sensible strategy remained that of ending population growth as rapidly and humanely as possible.

RESPONSES TO *THE LIMITS TO GROWTH*

As the number of New Jeremiahs proliferated, so too did the ranks of their critics. In his review of these critics, Sills suggests that there were two analytically distinct positions concerning the nature of the environmental problem: pessimism and optimism.[59] Environmentalists by this definition were pessimists, and critics of the movement were optimists.

The two sides differed over projections on natural resources, food, pollution, and population; the most common criticism of the environmentalists was that they were alarmist, a view encapsulated in one oft-quoted review of *The Limits to Growth*: "The Computer That Printed Out W*O*L*F*."[60] *The Limits to Growth* itself became a notable subject of debate and criticism. Particular invective was directed at the recommendation for massive nongrowth; not only would this produce a major industrial slump in more developed countries, but it would put a brake on development in LDCs. The World models began with a recipe of doom, argues O'Riordan, "and one can only assume that this enormously complicated computer programme was produced to estimate the timing of the cataclysmic result that was so predetermined"; Peccei's "evangelical passion for an earth-awakening 'commando operation'" furthermore threw a certain amount of scientific caution to the winds. The report interested hard-line conservative politicians, who "sought a politically respectable rationale for blocking what they regarded as exceptionally progressive social reform."[61] In his review of the 3rd Conference in the Countryside in 1970 series, the British environmentalist Robert Boote said, "If we underestimated the task in 1963, this is no cause to accept the clamour of the neo-Malthusians that we face impending doom."[62] The Marxist view was that *The Limits to Growth* ideology was aimed at breaking working-class resistance to authority.[63] *The Limits to Growth* (and the "doomsday syndrome" generally) was also criticized for suggesting the hopelessness of taking reasoned action and for ignoring the ability of humans to make social and political adaptations[64] (see also Kahn and Simon debate in chapter 7).

Forrester probably had an interest in promoting the system dynamics methodology, comment the authors of *Global 2000*, while the members of the Meadows team "probably had less well-defined aspirations. They were relatively young (average age below 30) and for the most part at the start of their careers. Meadows and his wife had just returned from a year in Asia, during which they had become concerned about problems of development and the environment, and were eager to explore the causes and possible cures of such problems. Most of the team members were formally trained in science, engineering or system dynamics, rather than the social sciences."[65] Significantly, the 17-member team consisted of ten Americans, three Germans, a Norwegian, a Turk, an Iranian, and an Indian; in other words, it was heavily weighted toward the United States, had little Third World representation, and no members were from the Eastern bloc.

The most comprehensive critique of *The Limits to Growth* was that undertaken in 1972 by 13 essayists associated with the Science Policy Research Unit of the University of Sussex in Britain.[66] Their report focused on the weaknesses in the methodology of the MIT analysis, the technical value of the model, and the ideological values of the modelers. The

Sussex authors stressed that they did not underestimate the positive importance of the MIT work and acknowledged that as a result of reading *The Limits to Growth*, many people were thinking about and discussing the problems; "in particular, they are discussing once again whether or not the world is likely to run up against physical limits."[67] The open public debate surrounding the MIT work was its most important achievement, argued the Sussex team. (By the late 1970s, about 4 million copies of *The Limits to Growth* had been sold in 30 languages.)[68]

The team argued that the social sciences could benefit from the use of computer modeling, but models had their limitations. The MIT team had set itself the task of drawing up a model in which relationships were an accurate representation of the real world as it was in 1970, but their model fell short of requirements. The basic problem lay in a lack of data (for which the MIT team could not be blamed, and which it indeed admitted), the assumptions made about relationships, the choice of assumptions, and the relative neglect of economics and sociology. Hence the dangerous self-deception of the assertion by Meadows in the introduction to *The Limits to Growth* that "the basic behavior modes we have already observed in this model appear to be so fundamental and general that we do not expect our broad conclusions to be substantially altered by further revisions."[69] It was, the Sussex team argued, "essential to look at the political bias and the values implicitly or explicitly present in any study of social systems. The apparent detached neutrality of a computer model is as illusory as it is persuasive." Stressing that subjective values and attitudes influence forecasts (and indeed admitting that its own views on *The Limits to Growth* reflected its own political biases and subjective limitations), the Sussex team identified a second major weakness—"computer fetishism, [which] . . . endows the computer model with a validity and an independent power which altogether transcends the mental models which are its essential basis."[70]

The views of the Sussex team differed in three fundamental respects from those of the MIT team:

(1) It put much greater emphasis on the political and social limits to growth than on the purely physical limits (poverty, they argued, was a major problem, in the light of which the MIT goal of zero growth was not ideal); "the Growth versus No Growth debate has become a rather sterile one . . . because it tends to ignore the really important issues of the *composition* of growth in output, and the *distribution* of the fruits of growth." The problem was one of stimulating more equitable distribution.

(2) The MIT group was underestimating the possibilities of continued technical progress. The Sussex team argued that "the inclusion of technical progress in the MIT model in sectors from which it is omit-

ted has the effect of indefinitely postponing the catastrophes which the model otherwise predicts." Studies made 100 years before the MIT study (which made forecasts 130 years ahead) could not have foreseen the dependence on oil and the growth of nuclear power, the Sussex team argued.

(3) The Sussex team was not fully convinced that world models based on system dynamics could develop into satisfactory tools of forecasting and policymaking. Robert Golub, a physicist at Sussex, argued that the MIT approach was inherently dangerous because it gave the spurious appearance of precise knowledge of quantities and relationships which were unknown (and often unknowable), stimulated gross oversimplification, and encouraged the neglect of factors difficult to quantify, such as policy changes or social values.[71]

There was no question that exponential growth could not continue indefinitely, but the Sussex team took particular exception to the MIT contention that existing growth should end within the lifetime of many people then alive and that unless drastic steps were taken, global disaster would occur. *The Limits to Growth* has been additionally criticized by Sandbach[72] and O'Riordan[73] for basing all its predictions on known reserves of resources (although the MIT team was careful to point out that new discoveries "would only postpone shortage rather than eliminate it").[74] Sandbach cites the example of a 1944 American study where, if the predicted reserves of 41 commodities had remained static, 21 would by 1980 have been exhausted.[75] Technological progress has repeatedly shown that resources have become easier to extract and substitute, that the efficiency of industrial processes has grown,[76] and that the volume of known exploitable resources has often grown with demand.

It is now clear that the MIT models were constructed at a time when understanding of environmental processes and resource issues was incomplete (it remains incomplete today), when computer modeling was in its infancy, and when perceptions were likely to have been influenced by the prevailing Malthusian gloom of the times. The weaknesses of *The Limits to Growth* lay not so much in its broad conclusions (although many of these were disputed) as in its methodology. Some critics felt the method to be too simple and, thus, insufficient to provide policy guidelines. Still others felt that since *The Limits to Growth* was basically a "sensationalized" version of *World Dynamics*, publication of *Limits* could have been delayed until some of its structural problems had been resolved.[77]

The Sussex team was not itself immune to misconception. In criticizing the MIT model pollution subsystem, it argued that "most disasters caused by material pollutants are likely to be local . . . or to be caused by one pollutant or class of pollutants." By aggregating all pollutants, the Sussex team argued, "and assuming that they behave in some composite way, attention is drawn away from what are urgent, and still soluble problems, and diverted into speculation upon an imaginary race against time between 'Life' and 'Global asphyxiation'." Even as the team wrote, there was growing evidence of the emerging problem of acid pollution (the MIT team had touched on sulfur dioxide pollution), which has gone on to disprove the Sussex contention; it may be caused by one class of pollutants, but the paths to acid damage are enormously complex, and the problem is neither entirely local nor always capable of local solution.[78]

A decade later, the authors of *Global 2000* criticized the Worlds 2 and 3 models on a number of counts. "They are general, strategy-oriented models and make no attempt to develop specific, detailed analyses. They familiarize one with the basic tendencies in population-resource-environment systems but do not speak to the problems of specific regions."[79] Further problems identified by *Global 2000* include the following: the models were based on a series of controversial assumptions (including the inability of technology to alleviate natural limits to growth); they focused on metal resources without giving attention to fossil fuels; they omitted social factors, such as income distribution and the international order, which "may pose limiting problems well before actual physical limits are encountered"; they suffered from a weak data base and an aggregation of items with dissimilar behavior in the pollution subsystem; and they failed to allow for qualitative changes in the nature of economic growth that could make it less demanding on limited resources. *Global 2000* concluded that while the World models helped clarify the nature of long-term global problems, "their limitations render them unsuitable as primary tools of analysis or as tools for detailed analysis of global problems and their solutions."[80] For Hecox, the lasting contribution of *The Limits to Growth* lay more in the questions it raised than in the answers it provided and more in focusing public attention on crucial issues of global futures than in specific descriptions of those futures.[81]

THE DOOMSDAY SYNDROME

If the prophets of doom elicited reasoned scientific rebuttal and scholarly analysis, they also drew passionate and occasionally reactionary attacks on their alarmism. If the doom-critics had a standard-bearer, it was probably John Maddox, the editor of the British science journal *Nature*. The opening line of his 1972 book *The Doomsday Syndrome* reads: "This is not a scholarly work but a complaint."[82] He objected to the models and essays ignoring the ways in which "social institutions and human aspirations can conspire to solve the most daunting problems." He felt that the doomsday debate was too dogmatic—you were either far-sighted and for the preservation of the environment, or you were heartless and against it. By spreading gloom and alarm, he argued, the doomsday syndrome could undermine the capacity of the human race to look out for its survival and "be as much a hazard as any of the conundrums which society has created for itself." Maddox viewed with scepticism the values and the history of the entire environmental movement: the environmental argument in support of the Test Ban Treaty of 1963 was acceptable to the signatories only because they had by then achieved the strategic objectives of the test program; Rachel Carson had to an extent seriously misled her readers, and the influence of *Silent Spring* depended much on Carson's "technique of calculated overdramatization"; and the claim that the decision of the U.S. Congress in 1971 to abandon its SST project was an environmental victory was misplaced—far more important was the unwillingness of Congress to be coerced into agreeing to a development project of questionable economic benefit.

Other doom-critics were less guarded in their attacks. Few were more indignant than Thomas R. Shepard, Jr., the publisher of *Look* magazine. In his remarkable 1973 book *The Doomsday Lobby*, coauthored with Melvin Grayson, he clearly allowed outrage to divert him from the path of reason. Particular invective was reserved for *Silent Spring*. The book was, the two men argued, an attack on the business establishment, an attack on scientific and technological progress, an attack on the United States, and an attack on man himself. Rachel Carson had become a standard-bearer for the "left-wing academic brigade." (They stopped just short of calling her a communist.) Millions of Americans had bought the book "as avidly as the buxom hausfraus of Bavaria had bought the garbage of Adolf Hitler, and for much the same reason." In 1961, they related, there were 110 reported cases of malaria in Sri Lanka (then Ceylon) and no deaths; in 1968 there were 2.5 million cases and 10,000 deaths. There were many who believed, wrote Grayson and Shepard, that these new cases and deaths could be attributed in large measure to the impact of *Silent Spring* on producing a ban on DDT. It was, they wrote, "The Book That Killed."[83]

Shepard may have been upset, but his views paled against those of Petr Beckmann, an electrical engineer at the University of Colorado. In his book *Eco-hysterics and the Technophobes*,[84] he expressed himself unobliged to observe the niceties of scientific etiquette because he was not arguing with scientists but with "benighted fanatics" preaching "vicious nonsense." For him, *The Limits to Growth* was "one of the major cripples begotten by the philosophy of apocalypse," the word ecology had lost all meaning, and the prophets of doom were ignorant about demography, economics, and science. He had no quarrel with the idea that the environment should be protected and preserved but felt that "econuts" and the "ecocult" had come to dominate the environmental movement to the point where the movement was beginning to degenerate into blind technophobia. Science itself was under attack, he wrote; environmentalists were curtailing scientific activity and reducing new enrollments in schools of physics and engineering. The fray was finally joined by the Nobel laureate Norman Borlaug (the father of the Green Revolution), who denounced "hysterical environmentalists" for attempting to block the use of agricultural chemicals. "If agriculture," he continued, "is denied the use of agricultural chemicals because of unwise legislation that is now being promoted by a powerful group of hysterical lobbyists who are provoking fear by predicting doom for the world through chemical poisoning, then the world will be doomed not by chemical poisoning but from starvation."[85]

Beyond these views, there was growing evidence of the emergence of what Killian calls a "counter-social movement."[86] At one level, environmentalism raised the ire of those who believed in the sanctity of "traditional values," such as the right to determine the size of one's own family. At another level, attempts were made to relate the environmental movement to a larger conspiracy. The Daughters of the American Revolution felt Earth Day was subversive; a state administrator from Georgia mounted a small campaign to draw attention to the fact that Earth Day fell on Lenin's birthday;[87] the president of the American Coal Association warned that the environmental movement could be radicalized to the point that it could weaken the United States by denying it necessary minerals and other resources.[88] Finally, there was the issue of "pollution versus payroll," in which many threatened industries argued that they would no longer be able to operate if forced to meet stringent environmental controls, and thus many of their employees would lose their jobs.[89]

There is no longer any doubt that some of the prophets did to some extent overstate the problem. More traditional environmentalists may have feared that the doomsday syndrome would do more harm than good to the environmental cause. Robert Allen, one of the authors of *A Blueprint for Survival*, observed that most ecologists cast themselves as moderates.[90] Maddox warned that the environmental movement could find itself "falling flat on its face when it is most needed, simply because it has pitched its tale too strongly."[91] Daniel Luten, president of Friends of the Earth, reflected in 1985 that the prophets predicted immediate crisis "because they were afraid that the public's attention span wasn't long enough to look at the deeper issues they felt needed attention. When there was no immediate crisis they were discredited."[92] In fairness, most of the prophets were outlining scenarios that illustrated what *could* happen, not what necessarily *would* happen. The authors of *The Limits to Growth* emphasized (clearly to little effect) that "our posture is one of very grave concern, but not of despair."[93] The models and essays drew bleak pictures it is true, and some of the prophecies proved false, thus engendering doubt; yet the prophets made people think. It may have been crude—or even a dangerous gamble—to use such shock tactics, but the intense interest generated in the welfare of the environment, if often lacking the support of credible scientific data and relying too heavily on postulation, nevertheless cleared a path for change in social, and subsequently political, attitudes.

Like Smith, Malthus, Mill, Marx, and Keynes before them, the new prophets of doom touched off heated debate, so that their arguments became less important than the effects of the arguments. In *The Poverty of Philosophy*, Marx observed of Malthus's book on population that "in its first edition it was nothing but a 'sensational pamphlet' and *plagiarism* from beginning to end into the bargain. And yet what a *stimulus* was produced by this *libel* on *the human race!*"[94] Whatever inaccuracies or delusions marked the writings of Ehrlich, Commoner, Hardin, Meadows, and others, their contribution to New Environmentalism was that they challenged people to think about the issues. To that extent, the prophets of doom succeeded in their stated aims.

FIVE

The Stockholm Conference
(1970–1972)

In 1968 and 1972, two international conferences were held to assess the problems of the global environment and, more importantly, to suggest corrective action. The first was the Biosphere Conference, held in Paris in September 1968. Concentrating on scientific aspects of the conservation of the biosphere, it was partly a product of the growth in the coordination of ecological research encouraged by the International Biological Programme (see chapter 3). The second was the United Nations Conference on the Human Environment, held in Stockholm in June 1972. Stockholm was without doubt the landmark event in the growth of international environmentalism. It was the first occasion on which the political, social, and economic problems of the global environment were discussed at an intergovernmental forum with a view to actually taking corrective action. It aimed to "create a basis for comprehensive consideration within the United Nations of the problems of the human environment" and to "focus the attention of Governments and public opinion in various countries on the importance of the problem."[1] It resulted directly in the creation of the United Nations Environment Programme (UNEP). It also marked a transition: from the emotional and occasionally naive New Environmentalism of the 1960s to the more rational, political, and global perspective of the 1970s. Above all, it brought the debate between LDCs and MDCs—with their differing perceptions of environmental priorities—into open forum and caused a fundamental shift in the direction of global environmentalism.

THE BIOSPHERE CONFERENCE

The Biosphere Conference continued the theme of international cooperation in ecological research that had first been explored at UNSCCUR in 1949. At the 1962 national parks conference in Seattle, a comparable meeting on endangered species was mooted.[2] This was discussed at the IUCN 1963 General Assembly, and plans were drawn up in 1965–66 by a multi-NGO steering committee. UNESCO then suggested that a more general conference on the rational use and conservation of the biosphere was needed if emerging nations were to be persuaded of the virtues of conservation. The Biosphere Conference (the Intergovernmental Conference of Experts on the Scientific Basis for Rational Use and Conservation of the Resources of the Biosphere) was held under the auspices of UNESCO in Paris from 1 September to 13 September 1968. The biosphere was defined as "that part of the world in which life can exist, including therefore certain parts of the lithosphere, hydrosphere and atmosphere."[3] The conference discussed human impact on the biosphere, including the effects of air and water pollution, overgrazing, deforestation, and the drainage of wetlands.

A number of themes emerged from the debate on the national reports distributed at the conference:

(1) Although some changes in the environment had been taking place for decades or longer, they seemed to have reached a critical threshold.

(2) In industrialized countries this was "producing concern and a popular demand for correction."

(3) Parallel with this concern was a realization that traditional ways of developing and using natural resources had to be changed, with careless development being replaced by development that recognized that the biosphere was a system, the whole of which could be affected by activities in any one part of it.

(4) A new interdisciplinary approach to the planned use of natural resources was needed; the natural sciences and technology alone could not solve resource management problems—the social sciences, too, needed to be considered.

(5) A vast amount of new research was needed, in MDCs and LDCs; since there was no universal solution to the problems of the biosphere, understanding and techniques would have to be adapted to areas within countries and to regions of two or more countries.

The conference agreed on a list of 20 recommendations. The first eight were based on the need for more and better research on ecosystems, human ecology, pollution, and genetic and natural resources, and on the need for an inventory and monitoring of resources. Recommendations 9 to 13 argued the need for new approaches to environmental education. A proposal had by then been adopted by the UN Economic and Social Council (ECOSOC) for a conference on the human environment; delegates at Paris welcomed this, noting that the rational use and conservation of the human environment depended on understanding not only the scientific problems but the economic, social, and political dimensions as well, which were outside the purview of the Paris conference. Recommendation 19 noted the need for taking ecological impacts into account in large-scale development projects. Delegates feared that industrialization and the intensive exploitation of natural resources in less developed countries could cause irreparable damage to little-disturbed and ecologically fragile environments and so inhibit socio-economic development.

An important outcome of the Biosphere Conference was the emphasis on the interrelatedness of the environment. Delegates concluded that the deterioration of the environment was the fault of rapid population growth, urbanization, and industrialization. A massive rural exodus had led to the disappearance of traditions, customary rights, and changes in lifestyles, leading to particularly serious problems in less developed countries. The world "lacked considered, comprehensive policies for managing the environment. It is now abundantly clear that national policies are mandatory if environmental quality is to be restored and preserved."[4]

Recommendations 1 and 20 argued the case for a new international research program on man and the biosphere. "Many of the changes produced by man affect the biosphere as a whole," the conference noted, "and are not confined within regional or national boundaries . . . These problems cannot be solved on a regional, national or local basis, but require attention on a global scale."[5] The International Biological Programme was due to close in 1974; it had made a valuable start, but it was a nongovernmental endeavor and so had only limited capabilities. UNESCO believed that the IBP put too little emphasis on studying the areas where neighboring ecosystems met, that because it was run solely by specialists in the natural sciences, it took little account of social and economic data in the study of ecosystems, and that it lacked a training component.[6] A successor to the IBP was discussed, and the Man and the Biosphere program (MAB) was eventually launched in November 1971 (see chapter 9).

PREPARATIONS FOR STOCKHOLM

The significance of the Biosphere Conference is regularly overlooked, mainly because of the much greater public and political impact of the 1972 Stockholm conference. Yet initiatives credited to Stockholm were in some cases only expansions of themes raised at Paris. Some of the intellectual foundations of Stockholm reflected those of Paris, and some of the recommendations were common to both conferences. The real difference lies in the fact that while Paris specifically addressed the scientific aspects of environmental problems, Stockholm looked at the wider political, social and economic questions. This not only gave NGOs (i.e. the citizens' movement) greater involvement in the discussions, but it made for more dramatic newspaper copy.

If there was any single issue that spawned Stockholm, it was acid pollution. Swedish research during the late 1960s had revealed a disturbing increase in the acidity of rain falling in the region (see chapter 9), prompting Swedish scientists to demand preventive action. Sverker Astrom, the Swedish ambassador to the United Nations, submitted a proposal for an international conference in a resolution put before ECOSOC in July 1968. Doud suggests that the speed with which the resolution was adopted by the General Assembly the following December reflected to some extent the impact of New Environmentalism.[7] The resolution emphasized the environmental work already being undertaken by intergovernmental organizations (IGOs), NGOs, and UN specialized agencies (it actually listed ILO, FAO, UNESCO, WHO, WMO, IMCO, and IAEA, which suggests a very loose definition of what constituted "environmental activity"). The conference, it went on, was needed to provide a framework within which the United Nations could comprehensively assess the problems of the human environment and focus the attention of governments and public opinion.[8] It should also identify those aspects which could only or best be solved through international cooperation and agreement.[9] This was the critical point. It was no coincidence that acid pollution—a transnational issue—had helped spark the conference; American and European environmentalists were preoccupied at the time with pollution, and to a lesser extent with the destruction of wilderness.

But the most significant outcome of the preconference discussions was the tenacious new role of LDCs in the environmental debate. Pollution, an MDC problem, may have been the spark for the conference, but LDCs used their General Assembly voting power to make sure that the Third World perspective was appreciated from the outset. The General Assembly resolution expressed the hope that less developed countries would "derive particular benefit from the mobilization of knowledge and experience about the problems of the human environment, enabling them . . . to forestall the occurrence of many such problems."[10] Subsequent UN General Assembly and ECOSOC resolutions reflected Third World wariness of the nongrowth philosophy that spawned *The Limits to Growth*. A progress report on conference preparations in July 1970 warned that the popularization of environmental problems "raised the danger of a concentration on the more spectacular aspects of environmental deterioration (such as pollution) in a few advanced countries, to the neglect of less obvious aspects of a cultural and economic nature." An information program aimed at legislators, government policymakers, and leaders of industry and agriculture was needed to put issues such as pollution in perspective and to draw attention to the environmental problems of LDCs.[11]

LDCs clearly feared that environmental safeguards and restrictions imposed by industrialized nations would retard development, that trade restrictions might follow as MDCs prohibited the importation of food contaminated by pesticides, and that they might not benefit from the management of shared natural resources. "Debates on doomsday theories, limits to growth, the population explosion, and the conservation of nature and natural resources," noted UNEP, "were thought of as largely academic, of no great interest to those faced with the daily realities of poverty, hunger, disease and survival."[12] Of much greater urgency was short life expectation, the shortage of basic necessities such as shelter, clean drinking water, and adequate sanitation, and, above all, the need to feed and employ rapidly growing numbers of people. There was a strong temptation for LDCs to concentrate all their energy and resources on the short-term resolution of these problems and to take care of any resulting environmental problems at a later stage. On the other hand, a number of Third World governments felt that they might learn from the environmental mistakes of the industrialized world. In December 1971, the General Assembly passed a resolution devoted largely to outlining the reservations of LDCs. It stressed that the Stockholm action plan must recognize that "no environmental policy should adversely affect the present or future development possibilities of the developing countries . . . [and that] the burden of the environmental policies of developed countries cannot be transferred . . . to the developing countries."[13] The United Kingdom and the United States were the only two countries to vote against this resolution.[14]

Many of the LDC concerns were raised at two preparatory meetings held during 1971: the Panel of Experts on Development and Environment (Founex, Switzerland, 4–12 June) and the SCOPE/UNCHE (Scientific Committee on Problems of the Environment/UN Conference on the Human Environment) working party on environmental problems in less developed countries (Canberra, Australia, 24 August–3 September). The Founex panel tried to assure LDCs that environmental protection would not go against their interests; it would not affect their position in international trade, and they could maintain their industrial development plans while avoiding the pitfalls experienced by the more developed world. Rather than a confrontation between developers and conservationists, observes Rodgers, "what emerged was a consensus forged under the leadership of Third World development economists which identified environment as a critical dimension of successful development."[15] Founex, argue Holdgate and colleagues, began to clarify the links between environment and development, destroyed the idea that these concepts were necessarily incompatible, and began to convince LDC representatives that environmental concerns were both more widespread and more relevant to their situation than they had appreciated and that they should not be a barrier to development, but should be part of the process.[16]

Maurice Strong,[17] who had convened the Founex meeting and was secretary-general-designate of the Stockholm conference, now took part in a 27-nation Preparatory Committee set up to prepare for Stockholm and draw up an agenda. The reservations of the LDCs, he later recorded, "made it clear that they thought under-development and poverty constituted the most acute and immediate threat to the environment of their peoples." As a result, the agenda of the conference and the very concept of environment were broadened to include issues such as soil loss, desertification, tropical ecosystem management, water supply, and human settlements. LDCs had "forced a clear recognition of the relationship between environment and development."[18] A conference agenda was agreed at the February 1971 meeting of the Preparatory Committee. It included the management of human settlements, natural resource management, control of pollutants, education and information, and environment and development.

Attention now turned to the question of the institutional arrangements to follow the conference. It was agreed that some new structure was needed, but there was no agreement on the form it should take. At its third session in July 1971 the Preparatory Committee had before it a report from outgoing UN Secretary-General U Thant outlining criteria for these arrangements. This included the proviso that "all functions that can best be performed by existing organizations should be assigned to those organizations, both international and national, most capable of carrying them out effectively. *No unnecessary new machinery should be created*" (my emphasis).[19] The report further suggested that it would be more logical to think in terms of separate sectoral organizations linked by "switchboards" rather than in terms of a global "super agency." This was in marked contrast to an earlier proposal made by U Thant for just such a "super agency," which had clearly met with the active opposition of existing UN agencies.[20] Any policy center, warned the report, "that is expected to influence and co-ordinate the activities of other agencies should not itself have operational functions which in any way compete with the organizations over which it expects to exercise such influence."[21]

In a barely disguised exercise in salesmanship, the existing UN agencies put their case in a subject paper prepared for governments before the conference. Drawn up by a committee of the UN agencies, the paper amounted to a defense of existing UN environmental protection activities. They were systematic, noted the report, and they had dealt with a variety of problems related to the environment. Considering the complexity and variety of issues, the cooperative arrangements between UN organizations had provided "an effective and dynamic mechanism."[22] The UN's sectoral pattern was still the best approach to dealing with a large number of environmental problems, both nationally and internationally, because it could "provide the flexibility required to combine . . . these sectoral activities" on an ad hoc basis.[23] Admittedly, there were gaps (notably in research, data exchange, and the provision of technical assistance), there was new ground to be broken, and many issues had received inadequate attention; the multidisciplinary approach had been applied only in a limited number of instances. But recognition that many of the problems of the human environment were intersectoral had led to greater coordination in such areas as water resource development, population, and environmental research.

The report went on to outline existing UN activities in the field of the human environment, including human settlements, natural resource management, and pollution. This would help Stockholm delegates fully appreciate the potential offered by the UN system for "broadened worldwide efforts toward a better human environment." The UN system had not been designed for many of the tasks it now regularly and effectively undertook; however, "new responsibilities do not automatically require new institutions and mechanisms, but do mean an adaptation of existing mechanisms and arrangements. . . . The institutions, the experience and a large measure of expertise needed, exist."[24] The specialized agencies were clearly concerned that any changes agreed at Stockholm might threaten their future independence.[25] This disquiet was not raised in open forum at Stockholm, but there were apparently enough private discussions during the conference to move Maurice Strong to make a public declaration to the conference that the ultimate authority for programs rested with each of the specialized agencies.[26]

A parallel paper prepared by the conference secretariat offered the opposite view to the UN report, arguing that decentralization was not the most effective form of management. It recommended the establishment of a new intergovernmental body within the UN, backed by a small secretariat and a limited budget. Population would not be one of its concerns since the UN had recently set up the UN Fund for Population Activities (UNFPA). Both Britain and the United States had actively promoted the idea of limited institutional arrangements, but while Britain had suggested that no new funds at all be provided for UN environmental work, an Advisory Committee of the U.S. State Department had recommended a Voluntary Fund for the Environment, with a minimum annual budget of $100 million (of which half would be designated for human settlements). This should be administered by a "strong, high-level executive (i.e. a single officer supported by a small staff) for environmental affairs" established in the office of the UN secretary-general.[27] The committee also recommended the creation of a UN Intergovernmental Body for the Environment as a subsidiary of the General Assembly, to advise and support the executive. The Advisory Committee, which reported in April 1972, suggested that funding might be worked out through national assessments based on each country's rate of energy consumption. In February 1972, President Nixon had proposed a fund to be contributed voluntarily by UN members, with a five year target of $100 million.[28]

A panel had meanwhile been set up by the National Academy of Sciences (at the request of the State Department) to examine the mandate of the United States at the conference. It recommended that, given the diffuse aims of the conference and the breadth of environmental problems, "we envisage not a choice between the principal existing structure for international cooperation, the United Nations, or a new international structure, but the emergence of flexible federations of networks of institutions—public and private, global and regional, ongoing and ad hoc—to deal with international environmental problems."[29] The panel recommended that the United States advocate a single focal point in the UN system for environmental problems, an independent research and advisory board, a global monitoring system, an environmental fund, and support for the work of transnational or regional organizations to address common problems where national capabilities were inadequate. The conference secretariat ultimately agreed that the form of the new institution could not be decided until the functions to be performed by the UN had been determined.

National reports were submitted to the Preparatory Committee by 80 countries, regional seminars were held to air the reservations of LDCs, and meetings were held to negotiate the publication of three new environmental conventions: making illegal the dumping of wastes at sea, conserving sites of cultural or natural heritage value, and preserving wetlands and islands as sites of special ecological significance (see chapter 8). Preparations like these made the going at Stockholm itself much smoother. What happened at the conference was just the tip of the iceberg, notes Sohn; "a whole mountain of arduous preparatory labor was the necessary prerequisite of the final success."[30] The reports ultimately gave Stockholm a sense of direction, focused the minds of delegates, and avoided much time-wasting preliminary discussion. What Landsberg calls the "patient missionary work"[31] of Maurice Strong had also helped avoid major disagreement between MDCs and LDCs. Strong had constantly emphasized the compatibility of development and environmental quality in his preparatory talks with Third World governments. Landsberg believes that the discussions about development and environment at Founex, Canberra, and other meetings had helped reduce what otherwise could have been "a great deal of rhetoric and sharp controversy at Stockholm. In a way, the impression had taken hold that all these problems had been talked about, and with exceptions, there was almost a reluctance to go over the familiar ground once again."[32] Differences of opinion remained, but they did not polarize the conference irretrievably. Fears that the LDCs would discount environmental concerns were not borne out.[33]

In May 1971, Maurice Strong commissioned Barbara Ward and René Dubos[34] to prepare an unofficial report that would provide Stockholm delegates with the intellectual and philosophical foundation for their deliberations; Strong described it as providing "a conceptual framework."[35] The report, later published as *Only One Earth*,[36] was reviewed by a corresponding committee of 152 consultants with backgrounds in industry,

scientific research, planning, international relations, economics, and development. All this reviewing and editing produced a document that was
often bland and rhetorical and occasionally alarmist, and that provided
general guidance rather than specific proposals (which, it was assumed,
would come out of the conference itself). The book summed up by outlining three very broad requirements for future progress: a "collective
international responsibility" for learning more about natural systems and
how they were affected by human activity and vice versa; the adoption of
global (rather than national) and coordinated policy on questions of global proportions, such as climate and oceans; and unity of purpose based
on "loyalty to the earth," a belief in the need to protect and enhance the
environment, and recognition of the concept of the planetary interdependence of life on earth. Ward and Dubos criticized existing international
institutions for lacking "any sense of planetary community and commitment." They assessed the characteristics of environmental problems in
LDCs and MDCs separately. Pollution, the waste and misuse of land,
urban growth, the consumer society, and pressure on resources were
listed as "problems of high technology," that is, MDC problems. Population pressures, the potential problems of the Green Revolution, industry
and pollution, and urban growth were assessed in the context of less
developed countries.

Despite its sweeping nature, *Only One Earth* was well received and
provided a useful philosophical peg for the conference. Its publication
was undertaken by a new research institute, the International Institute
for Environmental Affairs (IIEA), set up in 1972 under the sponsorship of
the Aspen Institute for Humanistic Studies in Colorado. IIEA was to help
prepare for Stockholm and thence to follow up its findings and to some
extent act as a bridge between LDCs and MDCs.[37] It would concentrate
on the sociopolitical impact of environmental management and on the
international implications of environment/society relationships, acting as
a source of reliable information and as a communications focal point for
institutions, people, and ideas.[38] A memorandum on a proposed structure for IIEA noted that Stockholm was a pressing political opportunity
to begin encouraging increased international cooperation in the environmental field, yet a "real danger exists that the outcome could be more
divisive than anything else. Almost inescapably, the Stockholm Conference will bring to a head an incipient but necessary political collision
between environmental goals and development goals. . . . It will at least
impinge upon questions of international standards and enforcement procedures and thus upon international law."[39]

The philosophical foundations of IIEA lay in the results of a four-
month feasibility study conducted in February–May 1970 by the Anderson Foundation. The study found that national and international
government institutions were concerned almost exclusively with the
physical symptoms of the environmental issue, rather than the implications for social or institutional change; that public interest (at least in the

United States) was focused almost entirely on domestic environmental problems; and that while there were strong pressures to halt environmental degradation, there were few pressures to address values or to "help guide the 'environmental movement' along constructive, dynamic paths of reform in traditional attitudes, values and institutions."[40]

IIEA began by hosting a series of workshops at Aspen on the international management of environmental problems and passed on its recommendations to the Stockholm organizers. IIEA's cochairman, Robert O. Anderson (chairman of Atlantic Richfield and the seed funder of the institute) believed that the institute should "steer a steady mid-course between doom and gloom alarmists and those who resist acknowledging the clear danger to which the human environment is being subjected."[41] In January 1973, Barbara Ward became full-time president of the institute, moved the headquarters to London, and renamed it the International Institute for Environment and Development (IIED), reflecting the outcome of the discussions on LDC/MDC priorities at Stockholm. IIED subsequently functioned as a policy research group, investigating the theme that development without proper regard to environmental constraints was both unsustainable and wasteful (see chapter 8).

THE STOCKHOLM CONFERENCE

The United Nations Conference on the Human Environment was held in Stockholm, Sweden from 5 June to 16 June 1972. It was attended by the representatives of 113 countries, 19 intergovernmental agencies, and 400 other intergovernmental and nongovernmental organizations. Although China was represented, notable for their absence were all the East European countries but Romania, which boycotted the conference because of an argument over the the voting status of East Germany. They had all, however, taken part in the preparatory discussions. The conference, said Maurice Strong at the opening, would launch "a new liberation movement" to free humans from environmental perils of their own making; while the "no-growth" concept was not a viable policy for any society, the traditional concepts of the basic purposes of growth needed to be rethought.[42] It was concerned mainly with "the characteristics of the environment which affect the quality of human life—a very subjective and ill-defined concept."[43] Though the concept of the "human environment" had emerged before the conference, it was the emphasis on this theme that distinguished Stockholm from previous international gatherings at this level. Recalling Stockholm some years later, Barbara Ward observed, "Before Stockholm, people usually saw the environment . . . as something totally divorced from humanity . . . Stockholm recorded a fundamental shift in the emphasis of our environmental thinking."[44]

Many reports of the conference convey a prevailing feeling of excitement and anticipation. Lee Talbot, who attended as a member of the U.S. Council on Environmental Quality, believes this was partly because many of the participants were new to the UN system, partly because of the hope that lofty declarations would be converted into firm action, and partly because Stockholm was the first UN theme conference.[45] (Later theme conferences focused on population [1974], habitat [1976], desertification [1977], and new and renewable sources of energy [1981].) There was also an air of youthfulness about the conference; it followed closely on the heels of New Environmentalism and was seen by many as official UN sanction that the problems identified during the 1960s deserved government attention (although some national governments had already begun to address them—see chapter 7). Holdgate recalls that "the dominant feeling, certainly among delegates with a professional background in the environmental sciences, was that environmental issues had 'broken through'. For the first time the environment was being discussed by the world's governments as a subject in its own right."[46] Barbara Ward noted in her speech to the conference that it was impossible to be taking part "without wondering whether we may not be present at one of those turning points in man's affairs when the human race begins to see itself and its concerns from a new angle of vision."[47] She later recalled, "Those of us who were there experienced . . . a feeling that at last we were getting going."[48]

The enthusiasm was by no means universal. Although IUCN, along with other major conservation organizations, had taken part in Preparatory Committee meetings, it was lukewarm toward the conference. It recorded rather pompously in its annual report for 1971 that "few who had worked closely with the [organizing] programme held out hope that Stockholm would produce any basically new approach to the problems of the environment." It did concede that there had been a recent awakening in governmental concern and that existing organizations would most likely "find their environmental programmes strengthened as a result of the conference."[49] At the conference itself, Gerardo Budowski, who attended as director-general of IUCN, conceded only that "the time and place were favourable."[50] In its annual review for 1972, the Union listed its own 11th General Assembly, the Second World Conference on National Parks, the World Heritage Convention, and closer links with WWF and UN organizations before noting its collaboration in the preparations for Stockholm. It noted that while there had been general recognition at the conference itself that the conservation of nature and natural resources should be an integral part of sound development and environment programs, "the theme of wilderness and the need to maintain and enhance diversity was given little attention."[51] While it enthused in its 1972 Annual Report about the achievements of the national parks conference and the adoption of the World Heritage Convention, it appeared reserved in its judgments on Stockholm.

The major breakthrough at the conference was the new perception of the position of less developed countries. Despite the earlier attempts to allay the concerns of LDCs, many had remained sceptical. The publicity attached to pollution-related incidents in the years before Stockholm had encouraged LDCs to equate environment with pollution. Because many in turn saw pollution as external evidence of industrial development, efforts to control it were seen as efforts to constrain development. Ambassador Keith Johnson, the Jamaican rapporteur-general of the conference, observed that many LDCs had "a lingering fear that Stockholm was merely another ploy by the developed countries to avoid supporting the development revolution."[52] A theme running through many Third World speeches was that environmental factors should not be allowed to curb economic growth. The point was well taken; Aaronson noted that, following Stockholm, it would "be difficult for Western environmentalists ever again to view 'the environment' in a parochial way."[53] The view of LDCs dominated the discussions in almost every respect and forced Western environmentalists to abandon their parochialism and begin to see environmental problems in a global perspective. MDCs had gone to the conference determined to discuss their own definitions of critical environmental problems and found the discussions leading them to a compromise position on the relative priorities of LDCs and MDCs.

The role of the Chinese delegation deserves special mention. The Chinese had arranged to come to Stockholm only at the last minute, and there was some concern over its plans for the conference sessions, particularly that it would assume the leadership of the less developed countries.[54] Indeed the positions taken by many Third World countries were strengthened by China's presence.[55] In a major address to the conference, Tang Ke, the chairman of the Chinese delegation, argued that China supported the LDCs in exploiting their natural resources in accordance with their own needs; "each country has the right to determine its own environment standards and policies in the light of its own conditions, and no country whatsoever should undermine the interests of the developing countries under the pretext of protecting the environment."[56]

Otherwise, the delegation played a passive role. Its main interest appeared to be in the Declaration on the Human Environment, a draft of which had been drawn up in the 18 months prior to the conference by the Preparatory Committee. A motion by China led to renewed discussion, tempered by concern that a text be agreed on by the end of the conference; Maurice Strong argued that it would be one of the key measures of the success of Stockholm. The Chinese initially took an extreme view, arguing, for example, that the Preamble should be enlarged to state that the environment was, in some places, endangered by "plunder, aggression and war by the colonialists, imperialists and neocolonialists." It suggested an amendment to Principle 13 to the effect that overpopulation was caused by "plunder, aggression and war" and that "the notorious Malthusian theory is absurd in theory and groundless in fact."[57] Toward the end of the discussions it suggested that all principles on which consensus had not been reached should be omitted. But when the Declaration came to a vote on the final day of the conference, the Chinese were the only delegation not to receive it with acclamation.

The United States delegation found itself in a curious position. One of the strongest advocates of the Stockholm conference from the outset, it opposed many of the principles or amendments proposed or supported by less developed countries, attempted to weaken the proposed International Register of Potentially Toxic Chemicals, abstained from voting on a resolution condemning nuclear weapons tests (especially those in the atmosphere), and opposed the expansion of the proposed governing council of the new UN environmental program. It was also consistently criticized (by, for example, Sweden, India, China, Iceland, and Tanzania, and by radical American activist groups outside the conference hall) for the human and environmental costs of the war in Indochina. By contrast, the United States won wide popular acclaim for sponsoring a ten-year moratorium on commercial whaling, an issue that attracted wide attention among delegates, NGOs and the media.

A significant factor in the quality of Stockholm was the role of NGOs. More than 400 were officially represented, mainly international and MDC NGOs. The presence of many unaccredited groups had raised fears for security at the conference, but these were dispelled by the arrangements made for NGO involvement. Provision had been made during the preparations for an Environment Forum (the Miljöforum), ostensibly as the official arena for accredited NGOs at Stockholm, sanctioned by the UN. The sceptics felt that rather than offering NGOs the opportunity to express their view, the Forum was designed to divert their attention away from the official conference, thereby minimizing the attention drawn to controversial issues.[58] The Forum was handicapped by funding limitations and fears that it would be either too radical or too conservative, but it was nevertheless able to arrange a series of useful briefings and meetings, albeit away from the conference hall itself. The *Ecologist* and Friends of the Earth collaborated on the publication of *Stockholm Conference Eco*, a newsletter designed to provide a constructive appraisal of conference sessions. An alternative People's Forum (the Folkets Forum) was set up on the initiative of PowWow, an alternative group formed in Stockholm in 1971, which argued that the problems of the environment could not be solved by governments. The more radical groups were concerned that the conference had no plans to deal with issues such as chemical and biological warfare, population, and the "ecocidal" activities of the United States in Indochina. Some felt that the conference was inadequate because government representatives would be bound to promote the vested interests of their governments, whether or not these interests coincided with those of improving the human environment.[59] Strict security over admission to the conference sessions initially caused some ill-feeling among NGOs, but Barbara Ward arranged briefing sessions, tickets, and documents, and set up routes of access to the conference for the groups.[60]

Talbot recalls the excitement among NGOs and citizen groups, who believed that they were finally attracting the attention of governments. But, he notes, "it was clear to most in the governmental delegations that the NGO activities were quite separate from and had little discernible effect on 'the real action' . . . There has [since] been real disillusionment on the part of many NGOs as they have come to realize how little a role they actually played."[61] NGOs initially played an active role in UNEP affairs, but financial constraints, a falling interest in the global solution ("or at least," argues Sandbrook, "a falling interest in UNEP providing one"),[62] and the rise of activist groups had by 1980 resulted in falling NGO attendance at the annual UNEP Governing Councils. In 1974, more than 150 NGOs had registered to attend the Governing Council; by 1980 the number had fallen to less than 20. At the 1980 Governing Council, Sandbrook found very little evidence of governments from any region having consulted with NGOs about their position before attending the Council; many complained that the interest was not there even when sought. The most consistent link between UNEP and NGOs has remained the Environment Liaison Centre (ELC), a coalition NGO based in Nairobi (the site of UNEP) that regularly provides information and material on UNEP activities to more than 3,000 NGOs.

In spite of the limited NGO role in UN affairs, the post-Stockholm era saw renewed growth in the formation of new NGOs. By 1982, the ELC estimated that there were 2,230 environmental NGOs in less developed countries, of which 60 percent had been formed since Stockholm, and 13,000 in more developed countries, of which 30 percent had been formed since Stockholm.[63] New forms of NGOs had also emerged. Noting that pressure groups in Western democracies play a complementary role to government institutions, helping keep governments informed, responsive, and in check, Lowe and Goyder argue that it is logical to assume that as governments agree to form levels of decision-making higher than those within the nation-state, nongovernmental groups would similarly regroup to meet the new level.[64] This would appear to be the case, for example, with the European Environmental Bureau (EEB), the origins of which can be traced directly to Stockholm. The conference not only put national NGOs in touch with one another, but emphasized that they faced common problems demanding a concerted response. The first suggestion for a European NGO agency came from Julian Lessey of the Conservation Society in Britain. At a meeting in Brighton in 1974 between 20 representatives of groups from western Europe and North America, including IIED and the Sierra Club, it was agreed that the European Community was "progressively becoming more important for environmental matters,"[65] and that closer cooperation was needed between Community NGOs. The EEB was created in December 1974 to offer NGOs a direct channel of access to the European Community, whose first Environmental Action Plan had been published in 1973. The creation of the EEB suggested that after many previous false starts, when international NGOs had lacked international authorities that they might lobby, the emergence of political internationalism and the creation of international governmental organizations had given international NGOs contextual relevance and permanence.[66]

Despite the sceptics, there was optimistic expectation among many of the participants at Stockholm that the conference offered a real opportunity to begin to avert the dangers of environmental degradation. Under these circumstances, Holdgate argues, it was inevitable that "some of the euphoria . . . would not survive the harsh reality of making the action plan work."[67] Within a year of the conference, the energy crisis of 1973–74 had altered the international economic climate. Declining economic growth rates and instability in international relations further diverted interest away from the environment, which was widely regarded as a long-term concern. Barbara Ward later recalled that in retrospect the conference should have been more of a turning point than it became.[68] This suggests to some extent that much of the optimism and euphoria of Stockholm was based on political naiveté. But Ward noted that this high expectation was a characteristic of many conferences, where the build-up of interest and excitement tended to overwhelm participants with their own importance. Yet, she felt, the creation of a new UN body and of a focal-point where interests could be expressed, and the dissipation of Third World unease were major achievements.[69]

Stockholm was largely agreed on both the problems and the solutions, but, Ward noted, the "action [of governments] rarely matched their promises. For an increasing number of environmental issues the difficulty is not to identify the remedy, because the remedy is now well understood. The problems are rooted in the society and the economy—and in the end in the political structure."[70] Talbot observes that this oft-quoted feeling of disillusionment misses the true significance of Stockholm, which is that it was not an isolated event but was part of a process that brought the environment to the attention of governments, facilitated subsequent international agreements and conventions on key environmental issues, and resulted in the creation of the United Nations Environment Programme.[71] As Holdgate and colleagues observe, the Stockholm conference was "a focus for, rather than the start of, action on environmental problems."[72] Barbara Ward argued that people found it very much easier to identify needed changes than to actually begin implementing them. The difficulties were heightened if, in addition to identifying a new approach, it had to be linked with new institutions, methodologies, and perceptions.[73]

DECLARATION, PRINCIPLES AND ACTION PLAN

The Stockholm conference produced a Declaration, a list of Principles, and an Action Plan. The idea for the Declaration appears to have been first suggested at the Biosphere Conference and was immediately supported by the UN secretary-general.[74] It was not intended to make legally binding provisions, but was to be "inspirational," to put on record the essential arguments of human environmentalism and to act as a preface to the Principles, outlining broad goals and objectives. It was remarkable that so many countries—with differing political, economic, and social systems—should have been able to agree to such a broad-ranging and philosophical exercise. Wisely, the Declaration did not attempt to define the term "human environment," partly because it was felt that it would be difficult at that stage to achieve a definition that was not unduly restrictive.

The 26 Principles can be broken down into five main groups. These stated respectively that:

(1) Natural resources should be safeguarded and conserved, the earth's capacity to produce renewable resources should be maintained, and non-renewable resources should be shared.

(2) Development and environmental concern should go together, and less developed countries should be given every assistance and incentive to promote rational environmental management. (This group was designed to reassure LDCs.)

(3) Each country should establish its own standards of environmental management and exploit resources as they wished but should not endanger other states. There should be international cooperation aimed at improving the environment.

(4) Pollution should not exceed the capacity of the environment to clean itself, and oceanic pollution should be prevented.

(5) Science, technology, education, and research should all be used to promote environmental protection.

There were only minor disagreements on most Principles; the one exception was the Principle concerning the provision of information on national activities that might have adverse consequences beyond their borders. The UN General Assembly discussed the issue and concluded that information exchanges subsequent to Stockholm should not be seen as enabling one state to interfere with the development of natural resources in another. Principles 21 and 22 ultimately recommended that states had the right to exploit their own resources and the responsibility to ensure that they did not cause damage to other states, and that states should cooperate to develop international law on liability and compensation.[75] Principle 11 separately stated that the environmental policies of all states "should enhance and not adversely affect the present or future development potential of developing countries." Landsberg notes that the breadth of the agenda and the cumbersome nature of the processes that were involved in discussing and agreeing on recommendations posed potential threats to the success of the conference.[76] But a frenetic pace of discussion and amendment was maintained throughout, and the final business was compressed into the last three days. This gave the proceedings a sense of urgency which may have discouraged delays.

Sandbrook has summarized the general intent of the Action Plan as launching "a set of internationally coordinated activities aimed first at increasing knowledge of environmental trends and their effects on man and resources, and secondly, at protecting and improving the quality of the environment and the productivity of resources by integrated planning and management."[77] The Action Plan consisted of 109 separate recommendations, ranging from the specific to the general, and falling into one of three broad groups: environmental assessment, environmental management, and supporting measures. Almost half dealt with the conservation of natural resources, while the rest covered issues relating to human settlements, pollution and marine pollution, development and the environment, and education and information.

THE LEGACY OF STOCKHOLM

The Stockholm conference was the single most influential event in the evolution of the international environmental movement. It had four major results.

First, the conference confirmed the trend toward a new emphasis on the *human* environment. Thinking had progressed from the limited aims of nature protection and natural resource conservation to the more comprehensive view of human mismanagement of the biosphere. The nature of environmentalism itself changed: from the popular, intuitive, and parochial form which had emerged in MDCs in the late 1960s, to a form that was more rational and global in outlook and emphasized working toward a full understanding of the problems and agreeing on effective legislative action. New Environmentalism was transformed into terms that were politically more acceptable, encouraging more national governments to make the environment a policy issue.

Second, Stockholm forced a compromise between the different perceptions of the environment held by MDCs and LDCs. This is ironic because the conference was initially a product of concern in industrialized countries in the 1960s. But the conference organizers were never allowed to let the conference concentrate solely on MDC interests. During the early UN debates on the conference, LDCs used their UN General Assembly voting power to compel more developed countries to recognize the need to balance environmental management priorities with the aims of economic development. More developed countries were at least encouraged to begin to reinterpret the priorities of environmentalism, to take a broader view of the global interrelatedness of many problems, and to begin to understand how many of these problems were rooted in social and polit-ical problems, particularly in LDCs. Under any circumstances, it was per-haps inevitable that many of Stockholm's recommendations would be compromises; the concerns of the LDCs injected a much-needed note of realism into the proceedings of the conference itself and led ultimately to a much wider view being taken of the roots and causes of the environ-mental crisis. Before Stockholm, environmental priorities had been deter-mined largely by more developed countries; following Stockholm the needs of less developed countries became a key factor in determining international policy.

Third, the presence of so many NGOs at the conference—and the part they played—marked the beginning of a new and more insistent role for NGOs in the work of governments and intergovernmental organizations. The NGOs had little influence at the conference itself and have not al-ways achieved as much influence at UN fora as they might have, but there was a rapid growth in the number and quality of NGOs in the post-Stockholm decade. The conference not only put national NGOs in con-tact with one another, but emphasized that they faced common problems demanding a concerted response.

Finally, the most tangible outcome of Stockholm was the creation of the United Nations Environment Programme. It had limitations and de-ficiencies, but it was probably the best form of institution possible under the circumstances.

SIX

The United Nations Environment Programme (1972–1982)

For all their merits and for all the significance attached to the process of simply reaching agreement on their content, the Stockholm Declaration, Principles, and Action Plan would remain paper exercises until they had some practical result. Their true effectiveness would depend on the institutional arrangements made for turning principles into policies and active programs. UN specialized agencies had been concerned about the form that these arrangements would take. These and other concerns had been considered by the conference preparatory committee, particularly during its final session in New York in March 1972, but the committee ruled that the institutional arrangements should be left to the conference itself.

The arrangement eventually confirmed by UN General Assembly resolution 2997 of 15 December 1972[1] was not for the creation of a new specialized agency, but of a cross-cutting program of policy coordination; this took form in the United Nations Environment Programme (UNEP), created as recognition that "environmental problems of broad international significance" fell within the province of the UN network. The headquarters of every existing UN specialized agency was in North America or Europe, so when it came to the question of a secretariat for the new body, there was a campaign to have it set up in a less developed country.[2] This was opposed by several MDCs, which argued that in view of UNEP's coordinating role it should be sited closer to the existing UN agencies.[3] The LDC option prevailed, however, and UNEP was located in Nairobi, Kenya. This, it was hoped, would further appease those in the LDCs who doubted the benefits of environmental planning. Liaison offices were also set up in New York and Geneva, and regional offices in Bangkok, Beirut, Mexico City and Nairobi. Maurice Strong was appointed first executive director of UNEP.

IMPLEMENTING THE ACTION PLAN

The new organization had four parts: a governing council for environmental programs; a small secretariat that would be the "focal point for environmental action and coordination within the UN system"; a voluntary environment fund to which governments could contribute; and an environmental coordination board made up of members of all relevant UN bodies. The Governing Council would meet annually, promote international environmental cooperation, provide "general policy guidance for the direction and coordination of environmental programmes within the United Nations system,"[4] and ensure that governments gave emerging international environmental problems appropriate attention. The blueprint for UNEP was the Stockholm Action Plan. This would be implemented through three functional components: environmental assessment, environmental management, and supporting measures.

Global environmental assessment. This materialized in the form of Earthwatch, a UN-sponsored network designed to research, monitor, and evaluate environmental processes and trends, providing early warning of environmental hazards and determining the status of selected natural resources. Earthwatch in turn had three other rather disparate components. The first was the International Referral System (INFOTERRA), a decentralized "switchboard" for the exchange of information. The second component, the Global Environmental Monitoring System (GEMS), would put environmental surveys into effect, collecting information from governments and building a picture of regional and global environmental trends. The third component of Earthwatch was the International Register of Potentially Toxic Chemicals (IRPTC), which became operational in 1976. Based in Geneva, it was to build up a data bank on potentially toxic chemicals for the use of governments; they would be notified of any changes and advised on appropriate action. IRPTC was an ambitious exercise; to maximize its utility, a great deal of time had to be devoted to keeping up the quality of its data.[5] The siting of the IRPTC in Geneva, however, along with the Regional Seas Programme (see below), gave it better access to other UN agencies and greater freedom from the bureaucracy of the UNEP headquarters.[6]

Earthwatch was broad and often sweeping in its aims. The main obstacle to its development was the lack of an adequate organizational structure and the necessary financial resources.[7] The head of Earthwatch had a coordinating rather than an executive role; the program had only two to three professional staff; much of the money allocated to Earthwatch was spent on individual projects rather than on Earthwatch per se; the program structure of UNEP did not relate sufficiently to Earthwatch; and few governments even appeared to be aware of the existence of Earthwatch or its services. Earthwatch was supposed to be an activity of all relevant UN agencies, coordinated by UNEP, but its lack of manpower and money meant that there was virtually no environmental assessment activity within the UN, and the relevant activities undertaken by the individual agencies were not properly coordinated or evaluated.[8] An independent assessment of INFOTERRA in 1980, conducted under the auspices of UNESCO, concluded that it had fulfilled the mandate outlined at Stockholm. But while INFOTERRA was by then established, it was still considerably underused.[9] Ironically, monitoring and assessing the earth's "outer limits" was one area in which UNEP felt it could play a useful role, given the limitations imposed upon many of its other functions.[10]

GEMS early faced three major problems: the lack of evaluation and assessment within Earthwatch as a whole, reliance on the cooperation and work of others, and a prevailing climate of pessimism about the usefulness of global monitoring.[11] Many of the monitoring systems set up after Stockholm fell short of expectations, largely because of a lack of clearly defined objectives. Such monitoring as had existed before Stockholm tended to concentrate on pollution. The World Meteorological Organization was supposed to provide a working foundation for GEMS by setting up a network of ten baseline atmospheric stations in remote areas and 100 regional stations removed from centers of major environmental contamination. But in the first five years of GEMS only 12 air monitoring stations were established, giving some indication of the size of the undertaking. Within two years of its creation, plans for GEMS had broadened to include a system that would warn of threats to human health and impending natural disasters, a concept so broad that as late as 1977 most of GEMS was still in the design phase. At the 7th UNEP Governing Council in 1979, concern expressed by several governments at the apparent lack of progress in Earthwatch led to a hasty meeting of experts to review developments. Their report was descriptive rather than critical, but did suggest that one of the major limitations on environmental assessments was the variability in the quality, comparability, timeliness, and representativeness of data;[12] the development of methodologies had not been universal, nor were existing methodologies always compatible. This, UNEP argued, together with the relative paucity of resources allocated to Earthwatch, explained why there had been so few comprehensive assessments.[13]

Environmental management. The information gathered by Earthwatch was to help with the implementation of the second component of the Action Plan, environmental management. The aim here was to develop a comprehensive planning structure that would support environmental protection. International conventions would be drawn up, action taken to ensure the preservation of biological diversity and genetic resources, and a number of specific goals—including a moratorium on commercial whaling—promoted. This was generally a workable program with identifiable goals, but progress was uneven. UNEP felt that many governments lacked the political will to adopt the recommendations of their own experts and that some of the Stockholm recommendations touched on delicate issues relating to the sovereignty of states and their economic development.[14] UNEP nevertheless collaborated with other organizations—UN agencies, IGOs, and NGOs—in the drafting and agreement of international conventions, notably the Convention on International Trade in Endangered Species of Wild Fauna and Flora (CITES), the Bonn Convention on migratory species (in both cases UNEP funded the setting up of convention secretariats), and the Convention for the Protection of the Mediterranean Sea against Pollution (Barcelona, 1976). On whaling, a moratorium was agreed in 1982 (although Iceland, Norway, South Korea, the USSR, and Japan continued killing whales five years later). On development aid, UNEP helped encourage bilateral and multilateral aid agencies to include environmental assessment procedures in development grants (see chapter 8).

Supporting measures. These included education, manpower training, public information, and financial assistance. In 1975 a joint UNEP/ UNESCO Environmental Education Programme was created, and in 1977 the UNEP/UNESCO Inter-governmental Conference on Environmental Education was held in Tbilisi, USSR; both events resulted in a series of training workshops and seminars, the creation of an information network, and the training of environmental specialists. But education was ultimately a national issue, and the work of UN specialized agencies was to be less productive in this area than the work of national NGOs. In Britain, the United States, and other Western countries, education had long been an important element in the work of NGOs, and this continued during the 1970s. On public information, UNEP was less than successful. The institution in 1972 of an annual World Environment Day (5 June) had little effect; outside environmental NGOs, almost no one even knew it existed. To complicate matters, UNEP was unable to decide between running its own modest information program and devolving responsibility to outside agencies. In 1975 it provided the funding to set up Earthscan, a news and information service within IIED, which went on to produce a substantial body of information for media and NGOs. By 1986, when most of Earthscan's staff left to form The Panos Institute, its networks included newspapers, specialist journalists, and NGOs in 130 countries. It worked closely with UNEP, but the proportion of funding it received from UNEP steadily diminished.

UNEP: THE FIRST TEN YEARS

UNEP experienced mixed fortunes in its first decade. Its prospects were made no easier by the fact that it had what Sandbrook describes as "perhaps one of the most difficult jobs in the entire UN system."[15] The critical point is that it was *not* designed as an executive body with the same kinds of powers as FAO, UNESCO, or the other specialized agencies. It had to coordinate the work of some UN agencies, promote policy initiatives with others, and provide information to others. It had a huge constituency—effectively the entire natural environment—and paltry finances. It was compelled to involve itself in multifarious activities and concerns and often had to take action based on the chance emergence of opportunity rather than on any carefully considered long-term plans. It had no power to interfere in the affairs of nations in the management of local and regional environmental affairs. Broadly speaking, its problems fell into four main categories: financial, managerial, political, and constitutional.

The strength of UNEP had ultimately to be measured in terms of the finances it had available. It made a promising start, with $60 million pledged to the Environment Fund in just six months (the target was $100 million in five years). Governments (a total of 96 by 1983) made a voluntary contribution to the UNEP Environment Fund, varying in scale from that of the United States—which, during the first eight years of UNEP's existence, contributed $40 million (36 percent of the fund)—to those of 64 countries such as Zambia, Jordan, and Paraguay, which made no contributions at all between 1978 and 1981. In the first five years of operation, UNEP planned to raise $20 million per year, a target that it very nearly achieved. In the period 1978–81 it raised about $31 million per year (as against a planned $37.5 million per year). The target for the period 1982–83 was $60 million per year, but funding targets proved increasingly unrealistic and elusive, and UNEP had to settle for an average annual income of $30 million in the period 1979–83. Set against inflation, this was worth less and less. The complications of shortfalls in income were aggravated by contributions arriving late or at the end of the financial year or in nonconvertible currency (currency that can only be spent in the donor country, commonly in the Eastern bloc). Such problems made forward planning difficult. Just over one third of UNEP's spending (1980 figures) was in the form of assistance to other UN agencies, while 28.4 percent went to other institutions, 22.4 percent to projects directly implemented by UNEP, and 14.7 percent to UNEP's own Programme Activity Centres, set up to manage those UNEP projects that involved a number of different agencies.

UNEP's second major handicap lay in its own internal management. It was accused by its critics of having a limited perspective on global problems, of being inefficient, of failing to delineate its priorities, of being too centralized in the person of the executive director, and of trying to do too much with too little to show in the end. The responsibility for these problems was seen to lie partly in UNEP's own management policy and partly in the limitations inherent in UNEP's constituency. Maurice Strong, despite his role in Stockholm and in the foundation of UNEP, was new to environmental matters, so on his appointment as first executive director, he drew on the areas he knew best—business, politics, and international public service—when appointing senior staff to launch UNEP.[16] The long-term result was that UNEP suffered management systems based more on bureaucratic procedures than on professional approaches to the problems of the environment.

There was little improvement in the first four-year term (1976–1980) of Strong's successor, Dr. Mostafa Tolba.[17] By 1980, personnel issues had reached such a low ebb that the permanent representatives to UNEP of the European Community countries compiled a short report outlining what they saw as the key problems: autocratic management with no delegation of authority, and all decisions, no matter how small, centralized in the person of the executive director; low staff morale and high turnover (of 180 professional staff positions, 60 were vacant); and the unhealthy state of the Environment Fund which could be blamed partly on dissatisfaction with the performance of UNEP and its executive director.[18] An unsuccessful attempt was made in 1980 to replace Dr. Tolba at the end of his first term in office; the European Community representatives, and others, supported the Ghanaian scientist Dr. Ernest Boateng. Staff numbers were by no means large; in 1975, UNEP employed 99 staff (85 in the headquarters and 14 in regional offices) on an annual budget of $30 million. By 1980 it had 180 professional staff positions and the same budget. The impermanence of its headquarters arrangements and the postponement in 1980 of new building plans made the management problems no easier. Only in 1983, after being based temporarily in several different offices, did UNEP finally move into permanent office buildings on the outskirts of Nairobi.

The third source of problems was UNEP's location in Nairobi. It helped redress the imbalance in the location of UN agency headquarters, and it probably helped broaden the minds of European and North American environmentalists by drawing attention to the situation in LDCs. But it also isolated UNEP from the industrialized countries which held the balance of world economic and political power and, hence, made many of the key decisions affecting the global environment; Sills's observation that Nairobi was "far from the environmental battleground"[19] ignores the fact that many of the most dire environmental battles are being fought in LDCs (but many of the decisions that affect these battles are, it is true, made further north). UNEP itself felt that the location made it difficult to recruit highly qualified staff and demanded that UNEP create a new infrastructure from very little, whereas if it had been located within an existing UN agency it would have been able to draw from a common pool of personnel while directing its resources at substantive action.[20] The location in Kenya also tended to leave UNEP divided between the more developed world, which supported emphasis on global problems such as pollution, and the less developed world, which adopted UNEP as its own UN "agency," emphasized issues of environmentally sound development, and hoped that UNEP would have been particularly sympathetic to the needs of LDCs in any conflict of interest with industrialized countries. This reached the point where the Governing Council was accused of rejecting project suggestions from the Secretariat because they were not sufficiently Third World-oriented.[21] The division in turn helped sour relations between the Governing Council and the Secretariat.

The fourth source of problems was constitutional. From the outset, UNEP headquarters was divided between the Programme proper and the Fund. The former was responsible for devising programs, which may or may not have been put into effect in the form of projects. The latter was responsible for managing finances for these projects. This division demanded that all UNEP activities be approved by both Fund and Programme and involve staff from both sides in formulation and execution. A second division within UNEP was that between the Secretariat itself and the Governing Council. The Council was drawn from 58 member-governments, representatives of whom were voted onto the Council for three-year terms by the UN General Assembly. The Council met annually for two weeks to discuss and decide policy. At the outset, it was charged with a number of basic responsibilities: to promote international environmental cooperation, to guide policy and review progress in UN agencies, to draw the attention of governments to emerging global environmental problems, to ensure that development in LDCs was not handicapped by environmental management policies, and to manage the Environment Fund. Critics charged that the Council was successful in the last of these responsibilities, but not in the others. It was often accused of being too cumbersome and too obsessed with procedure, in common with the rest of the UN system. Martin Holdgate, president of the 11th session of the Governing Council in 1984, was concerned that during 1983 procedural matters had become so dominant that they tended to obscure the real justification of UNEP: "that people all over the world have environmental needs that the United Nations should meet." Too much time was spent by the plenary session "on discussions that were unlikely to help resolve these appalling problems."[22]

The most critical constitutional problem lay in the nature of UNEP's relationship with other UN agencies. Having no executive powers, it had little scope for carrying out its own programs and had rather to function through the other UN specialized agencies. Its task of persuading other agencies to execute programs was hampered by the fact that it had few incentives to offer and no means of enforcing its wishes;[23] furthermore, some of UNEP's slow progress reflected the fact that the environment had proved more complex, and more costly to monitor, than Stockholm delegates realized.[24] The Action Plan was widely regarded as too broad, too vague about priorities, and—above all—too lacking in means of implementation. The difficulty of assessing UNEP's effectiveness was amplified by the difficulty of assessing its precise role in a given project. Unlike WHO or FAO, observed Dr. Tolba, UNEP could not "say at the end of the day [that it had] eradicated a disease here or planted so many thousand hectares of rice fields there."[25]

In 1976, the UN General Assembly reviewed its institutional arrangements for the environment and concluded that they were adequate. But UNEP itself admitted their shortcomings.[26] The incompatibility between the desire for a small secretariat and the need to maintain the wider ranging aims of the program was a difficulty that had still not been resolved as late as 1982. Perhaps the most fundamental problem of all was that UNEP's role was consistently and widely misunderstood.[27] UNEP was never intended to be a full UN specialized agency, but simply the environmental program of the United Nations system. It was designed to be able to take a comprehensive view of the global environment and to develop an environmental program that could be carried out by all relevant agencies—its role was catalytic. As Holdgate observes, existing UN agencies—notably FAO, WHO, WMO, and the World Bank—were already concerned with environmental questions (as they had been at pains to emphasize before Stockholm) and the environment "was not a separate entity requiring its own operational body but a cross-cutting theme."[28] Holdgate points out that well-established and powerful organizations were bound to be cautious of any new superimposed coordination of their work, a dilemma of which Maurice Strong and the UNEP council were aware. Their answer was to develop a series of activities that met a real need and did not conflict with those of other established bodies.[29] The first three areas were those agreed on before Stockholm— the Global Environmental Monitoring System, marine pollution, and IN-FOTERRA. As its own activities evolved, so UNEP's credibility and capacity to do the job of coordination and compilation of a truly system-wide program increased.[30]

UNEP's relations with other UN agencies was a key determinant of UNEP's level of influence. In its first few years, these relations were poor, for three main reasons. First, the novelty of the situation made existing UN agencies particularly distrustful of UNEP; it would take time for them to become used to UNEP's existence and to accept its program. Second, UNEP—disregarding its limited powers—tended to comment upon or try to influence the activities of other agencies more than it had been allowed by its terms of reference. Tolba was not discouraged by the complaints this attracted and said in 1975, "We will never stop interfering in everyone else's business as long as it involves the environment. That is our mandate."[31] Third, the mechanisms through which UNEP was supposed to work with the other agencies were insufficient. The fourth element of the institutional arrangements recommended at Stockholm, the Environment Co-ordination Board (ECB), had been set up as a means by which UNEP could coordinate and influence the activities of other UN agencies and as a channel through which UN agencies could influence UNEP; initially, it was to provide more of the latter.[32] Requested by the Governing Council in 1976 to review its own functions, the ECB concluded that the cycle of its meetings needed to be planned to allow prompt responses to Governing Council decisions, that the concept of joint programming needed further development (involving all agencies concerned), and that there needed to be more multiagency programming rather than bilateral discussions between UNEP and the other agencies.[33] The joint programming that had taken place by February 1976 amounted to a series of meetings between UNEP and other UN agencies (e.g. FAO, UNESCO, WHO, and UNECE), which really did no more than identify areas of common interest and agree on mechanisms for keeping each other informed of developments.

At the fifth Governing Council in 1977, the ECB was charged with drawing up memoranda of understanding with other specialized agencies,[34] which it did subsequently with a number of them. But the memoranda, the ECB, joint-programming exercises, and thematic programming (planning whole program areas, such as water or food) were all unsuccessful. In 1978, as part of wider UN changes in interagency coordination, the ECB was merged with the Administrative Committee on Co-ordination (ACC). Robinson notes a perceptible improvement in relationships among the UN agencies, probably as a result of the work of the ACC.[35] In 1982 a new exercise—the System-Wide Medium-Term Environmental Programme (SWMTEP)—was introduced, designed to define precisely what each UN agency would do in the period 1984–89. Most of the descriptions of action to be taken by each agency have since been dismissed as bland and highly generalized; SWMTEP furthermore outlined areas of interest but spoke only in broad terms of appropriate action.[36] It was so broad that nearly every initiative on the environment could be fitted into one or another of its proposals. Rather than allowing UNEP to do a few things well, it ran the danger of further diluting the UNEP agenda. Yet ten years after Stockholm, UNEP confidently believed that its relations with other agencies had improved as the incidence of joint programming had grown.[37]

THE REGIONAL SEAS PROGRAMME

Oft-quoted as one of UNEP's major successes—if not its only real success in its first decade—was its Regional Seas Programme (RSP), in which UNEP successfully brought 120 countries and 14 UN agencies together to confront shared problems of pollution and coastal degradation in shared seas. Stockholm recommended action to end all significant marine pollution within three to four years, particularly in enclosed and semi-enclosed seas.[38] The idea for the RSP was born at a meeting of experts held in London in June 1971 in preparation for Stockholm. Reviewing the position of marine pollution, the meeting concluded that a sea-by-sea approach to the problem was more realistic and attainable than a broad-ranging global program.[39] This approach says much about why more broad-ranging global plans were not always able to achieve a degree of success comparable to that of the Regional Seas Programme.

The RSP was initiated in 1974 with a strategy carefully designed to respect national sensitivities, particularly over data on pollution, and to leave the actual implementation of each regional plan firmly in the hands of the coastal states concerned. The RSP involved most of the major UN bodies and illustrated exactly the kind of catalytic and part-executive role that UNEP could play.[40] Under the RSP, surveys of each region were carried out and a plan of action drafted. UNEP then arranged a meeting between relevant governments to have them agree among themselves that the regional sea was a common resource faced by common threats and then to agree to the action plan. This was followed by monitoring and information exchange, with national institutions meeting to discuss action. UNEP acted as the initial catalyst, and as each program grew, the states themselves took over funding and management, and national scientific bodies undertook monitoring and research work, drawing on UN agencies for specialist advice. In this way an international body was bringing a number of nations together on a problem of mutual interest.

The model for the RSP was the Mediterranean Action Plan (MAP), adopted by 16 Mediterranean states in Barcelona in January 1975. In February 1976 a second meeting was held in Barcelona to implement the legislative component of the action plan. This was historically the first real attempt to initiate effective management of the Mediterranean.[41] The first component of MAP was new legislation; the meeting adopted the Barcelona Convention for the Protection of the Mediterranean Sea against Pollution and two protocols: one to prevent dumping from ships and aircraft, the other to encourage cooperation in the event of emergency pollution by oil or other substances. The convention came into force in 1978. In 1980 a third protocol was adopted, concerned with pollution from land-based sources. The convention and the protocols were gentlemen's agreements—there were no means of enforcing them. The second component of MAP was monitoring and research, carried out by the national laboratories of coastal states; 84 such laboratories were involved by 1984. The third component was environmental management, consisting of a long-term program of study and research into development and environment (the Blue Plan) and a Priority Actions Programme concentrating on selected priority areas. The final component was the small secretariat set up to oversee the action plan. Using a similar blueprint, but allowing regional variations for specific regional needs, regional action plans were subsequently drawn up for ten regional seas, including the Red Sea (1976), the Kuwait region (1978), the West and Central African coastal seas, the Caribbean, the East Asian seas, the southeast Pacific seas (all 1981), and the southwest Pacific seas (1982).

By 1983, more than 120 countries, 14 UN agencies and 12 other international organizations were involved—to varying degrees—in the RSP.[42]

Unfortunately, the Programme's success was limited by a number of fundamental problems, several of which were outlined in the UNEP-commissioned Portmann report of 1982:[43]

(1) Other UN agencies were reluctant to fully support the Programme, and used different sources of information within countries when undertaking their own environmental activities.

(2) Financial support, because it was voluntary, was unpredictable, which made UN agencies even less willing to become involved. UNEP, for example, spent $8 million on the Mediterranean Action Plan in its first five years. When the governments involved took over responsibility, they reduced the budget by a quarter. Three countries (France, Italy and Spain) between them subsequently supplied 80 percent of governmental contributions.[44] Late payments meant that funds for the Mediterranean almost dried up in 1981–82.

(3) In many regions, the level of expertise and the facilities available for the implementation of the action plan were inadequate. (Stjepan Keckes, director of the RSP, demurred on this point and argued that the necessary infrastructure could grow with the RSP.)[45]

(4) A clear deficiency affecting all regional plans was the scarcity of information on pollutants and the limited reliable data on marine pollution levels. As of 1985, there was only one completed report on the state of a regional marine environment: that for the Mediterranean. Although the Mediterranean Action Plan was well progressed, combined problems with financing and disagreements over standards limited the improvement that actually occurred.

Despite these problems, the Regional Seas Programme was widely regarded as UNEP's most effective undertaking in its first decade of operation. UNEP attributed the Programme's success to the fact that it was regional rather than global, involving nations in urgent common problems that could only be solved by mutual action.[46] As a regional endeavor it also had more easily manageable proportions and more easily achieved aims. Other problems (such as acid pollution or pollution of shared rivers) have been proven to be best tackled by countries bilaterally or regionally where there are identifiable shared interests, economic costs, or political implications.

UNEP FOILED: THE PROBLEM OF DESERTIFICATION

An indication of how more broad-ranging schemes can fail, even where national or regional provisions are included, lies in one of UNEP's major failures, an area to which it devoted considerable time and resources, namely, the campaign against desertification. "Desertification" is a cumbersome word of relatively recent origin, commonly defined as the man-made degradation of land so that it loses its fertility and its capacity to provide economic returns under cultivation or grazing.[47] Desertification does not imply the spread of natural deserts so much as the increased incidence of desert conditions in semidesert areas. One-third of the earth's land area is semidesert and supports more than 600 million people; about half this area—supporting 80 million people—is thought to be threatened by desertification.[48] According to the UN Desertification Map of the World, more than 40 percent of nondesert Africa is at risk of desertification; half the world's people most menaced by desertification live in the West African Sahel.[49] The causes are complex, but they include deforestation, overcultivation (brought on by a combination of increased food demand from growing populations and an increase in cash crop cultivation and leading to declining soil fertility, wind and water erosion, sand dune encroachment and falling crop yields), overgrazing, and poorly designed and managed irrigation. The incidence of these phenomena in turn strikes at the heart of the resource management dilemma of many of the poorer LDCs.

Drought and famines are commonly perceived as acts of God; until perhaps 15 to 20 years ago, much of the literature on famine concentrated upon the link between absolute food supply and starvation. Sen rejects this notion, observing that while famines involve often widespread acute starvation, not all groups in famine-affected nations go without. His "entitlement" approach concentrates on ownership and exchange.[50] Timberlake argues that while drought may be a natural precursor of famine (i.e., an act of God), the Sahelian famine of 1984–86 was a direct result of unsound economic, agricultural, and environmental strategies (i.e., an act of man). African peasants, in their efforts to survive, were compelled to draw increasingly upon their "capital stock" of forests, soils, and rivers; this process "bankrupted" Africa's environment by undermining the ability of African nations to feed themselves.[51]

The 1968–73 drought in the Sahel illustrated some of the dangers associated with the spread of human settlement into marginal arid lands. Drought in the area is not unusual (there were major droughts in 1910–14, 1927–30, and 1940–44,[52] and again in 1984–85), but the circumstances of the 1968–73 drought gave cause for particular concern. "The ultimate cause of the Sahelian disaster [of 1968–73]," argues Murdoch, "was the destruction of a complex pattern of living arrangements that had previously allowed quite large numbers of people to live in a difficult environment."[53] Over a period of centuries, Sahelian nomads had created an agricultural, economic, and trading system designed to account precisely for the limitations of their environment. They raised mixed herds of camels, cattle, sheep, and goats; they staggered breeding patterns in order to have milk throughout the year; they moved their herds according to the incidence of rain, moving them during dry seasons to areas of permanent vegetation; they kept larger herds than they immediately needed, thereby assuring food security in times of drought; they took to hunting and gathering in times of extreme drought; and they maintained complex trading patterns with the savanna regions to the south, ensuring a regular supply of grain.

Colonialism brought taxes and export demands, forcing peasants into cash crop production, undermining indigenous agricultural systems, reducing soil fertility, increasing soil erosion, and impoverishing peasants. Land was worked more intensively to make up for lost fertility, and peasants moved into marginal lands to produce food and cash crops (meanwhile reducing fallow periods). The changes thus wrought in the economic and agricultural systems of the Sahel have persisted, accounting in large part for the significantly decreased resistance to drought that made the famines of 1968–73 and 1984–86 so disastrous. Murdoch concludes that the poverty of the peasants was "a causal mechanism in the vicious circle of underdevelopment that has prevented the sustained growth of an integrated economy, which would in turn provide more income, greater employment, and more capital for investment." He further notes the effect of the collapse of traditional nomadic trading in destroying the long-term strategy of the nomads.[54]

Years of good rain during the 1960s had encouraged the spread of rainfed cropping and livestock pasturing into marginal lands on the edges of the Sahara. When the rains failed in 1968, the herds of livestock were deprived of pasture (but not water) and began dying in large numbers. The rains failed again in 1970 and the harvest was quickly exhausted, leaving an estimated 3 million people in six countries in need of emergency food aid. By 1973, when the full extent of the drought became clear, it was estimated that 100–250,000 people and 3.5 million head of cattle had died. One of the lessons to be learned was the disastrous consequence of a combination of drought and the movement of large numbers of people and livestock into ecologically marginal land.

Under normal circumstances, nomadic pastoralism makes optimal use of drylands; moderate sustainable grazing can actually increase the productivity of pastures. But increases in the sizes of herds and decreases in the areas of pasture available to them led to overgrazing. In Niger, for example, between 1938 and 1961, the number of donkeys increased by 100 percent, of sheep and goats by 200 percent, of cattle by 480 percent, and of camels by 700 percent.[55] The growing numbers of livestock were partly a function of human population growth. Herds are regarded as an insurance against dry years. During years of good rainfall, the numbers are allowed to increase. When drought first appears, however, herdsmen are reluctant to reduce stock numbers, thereby placing greater pressure on drought-stressed pastures. Improved veterinary care has further increased stock numbers, and the widespread government policy of encouraging nomads to settle offers the land little relief from grazing. Furthermore, the building of wells has tended to concentrate nomads, often attracting many more animals than the wells were designed to support and intensifying the use of surrounding land.

The 1968–73 drought was one motive behind the convening in 1977 of the UN Conference on Desertification (UNCOD), held in Nairobi from 29 August to 9 September 1977. The object was to provide a forum for the discussion of the problem, which was seen to be reaching crisis proportions, and to plan action. The convening of the conference implied clear recognition that desertification was a primary element in the reduction of Africa's ability to feed itself; it also succeeded in firmly establishing the role of human activity in desertification. The conference resulted in a Plan of Action to Combat Desertification (PACD) consisting of 28 recommendations. These included national plans of action, improved livestock raising, rain-fed farming, and irrigated cropping; the monitoring of desertification trends; transnational projects aimed at linking countries in integrated antidesertification measures; the management of regional aquifers; and the creation of green belts to physically halt the spread of deserts. Emphasis, too, was placed on the importance of curbing population growth and learning to understand the social, economic, and political factors associated with desertification. The UN Sudano-Sahelian Office (UNSO) was made responsible for coordinating follow-up action in the Sudano-Sahelian region, and UNEP for the rest of the world.

Tolba argued that there was general agreement that UNCOD was "one of the best scientifically prepared UN conferences of the 1970s" and that the recommendations, if effectively applied, "would have put the international community in a position to have halted desertification by the year 2000."[56] As executive-director of UNEP, his assessment was obviously not disinterested, but there is much evidence to back up his conclusion. Unlike many other environmental problems, there was certainty about the causes and the necessary corrective action. But in May 1981, Tolba reported that progress on the implementation of the plan of action had been slow. In May 1984, a two-day meeting of the UNEP Governing Council (convened to discuss the UNEP General Assessment on Progress in the Implementation of PACD) confirmed that the objectives of PACD were still fundamentally sound and viable; but Tolba now admitted (in a remarkably candid and forthright speech) that the goal set by UNCOD of stopping desertification by the end of the century had been unrealistic.[57]

The assessment concluded that desertification had continued to extend and intensify, rates were unlikely to change in grasslands and irrigated lands and would grow to critical proportions in rain-fed croplands, and the cost of losses in production due to desertification amounted to five times the estimated cost of halting desertification ($4.5 billion per year for 20 years). The countries most affected were LDCs in tropical drylands, particularly those beset by low incomes, drought, and political unrest. Continuing drought in the Sudano-Sahelian belt, and an economic recession that had limited the availability of funds, had not helped the campaign against desertification. Four-fifths of the investment in desertification-related projects had been in the form of "preparatory or supportive" action such as building roads, supplying drinking water, providing housing, and extending irrigation. Only 20 percent of spending had been in the form of corrective action of the kind recommended by UNCOD. The transnational projects were stillborn, and little was done to monitor the situation or increase understanding of the process. Only 22 percent of all aid to the Sahel went into agriculture and about 1.4 percent into forestry. Few countries had produced national plans of action or tried to assess the extent and severity of desertification. Few corrective measures had involved the local community.

While the technical solutions to desertification were well known and understood, the economic, social and political means to apply them had not yet been found.[58] There were three levels of approach to the problem: national, regional, and international. At the national level, PACD had recommended that coordinating national machinery be established to combat desertification and draw up national plans of action. In all but three cases, responsibility had in fact been given to existing agencies. Of the three new national agencies created, only one was actually effective as of May 1984. In many cases, failure to establish national machinery reflected the low national priority accorded to combating desertification.[59] Tolba pointed out in his May 1984 speech that this had been encouraged by the lack of political power among the rural poor most immediately affected. LDCs had also felt that there were more immediate short-term problems in need of rectification and were reluctant to plan for the long-term. As for MDCs, aid agencies consistently preferred to finance visible "showcase" projects such as dams, roads, and factories, which utilized expertise and equipment from donor nations, creating jobs and profits in that nation. Rural projects were harder to identify, plan and implement, and were less visible.[60] There was also a prevailing lack of awareness in more developed countries—many of them far removed from the immediate causes and effects—about the extent of the problem.

At the regional level, four UN regional commissions organized meetings and began collecting data, but none drew up regional plans of action. UNEP blamed the failure on financial stringencies, civil strife and warfare, and strained political relations between the countries involved, rather than on the inadequacy of regional machinery.[61] One of the most effective regional agencies was UNSO, which helped produce a regional agreement on desertification strategy in the Sudano-Sahelian region, raised $40 million in 1978-83 for antidesertification programs in the 19 countries it served, and helped establish two regional study centers. But it also had its problems. One criticism was that the office, based in New

York, had more experience of technical assistance than of desertification problems and might have classified a project as "antidesertification" only because it was politically expedient so to do.[62]

At the international level, all UN agencies were encouraged to support antidesertification activities, and two ad hoc agencies were set up to encourage this: the Desertification Branch of UNEP, and the Inter-Agency Working Group on Desertification (IAWGD). UNEP believed that this system had "generally operated effectively,"[63] but financial constraints meant that the Desertification Branch had not had its full complement of professional staff, leaving it little opportunity to function effectively. "It is the key UN desertification unit," concluded UNEP, "and yet to date it has never had the resources to fulfil its functions."[64] IAWGD, by contrast, was moderately successful in bringing UN agency representatives together to coordinate research, training and information exchange within the UN.

Of all the obstacles to progress, none was more serious than the sheer lack of money. At UNCOD, Tolba had said that $2.4 billion would need to be spent annually for 20 years to halt desertification in the Third World. A special account was set up within the United Nations to finance antidesertification projects, but between 1977 and 1984 it attracted a paltry $48,524. The Consultative Group for Desertification Control (DESCON)—a hybrid of representatives from UN agencies and aid agencies—was set up to identify sources of finance and priority projects and bring the two together. In 1978–83, it reviewed 48 projects, arranging full finance for 12 and partial finance for seven. The amount actually secured by DESCON was $26 million, or about a quarter of the total needed. UNEP believed that both MDCs and LDCs alike had been confused about DESCON's aims and had not fully used its services. UNEP offered two explanations for the parlous financial situation: LDCs suffering from desertification had seemed unable (or perhaps unwilling) to give priority to antidesertification measures, and activities to combat desertification were generally not competitive in terms of short-term economic cost-benefit ratios. Mohammed Kassas, president of IUCN and an authority on drylands, pointed out that Egypt, for example, spent $13,800 per hectare reclaiming desert land. Invested in a bank, this sum could have earned $1,700 a year in interest, far more than the land could return.[65]

In 1982, Grainger warned that ten years after the climax of the 1968–73 Sahelian drought, the Sahel was moving steadily toward another disaster; experts disagreed whether the next crisis was just around the corner or some years away, but past experience dictated that it must come.[66] Despite the urgent need to increase food production, less than a quarter of aid to the region had been invested in agricultural development. Population in the Sahel was growing at 2.5 percent per annum, crop yields were declining (rain-fed cereal production was down to 75 percent of its 1968 level), and many countries had come to rely on food aid (much of which reached only the towns). The Club du Sahel estimated that self-sufficiency in food actually decreased between the mid-1970s and 1982. Drought did indeed return to sub-Saharan Africa, and famine followed. In May 1984, a group of 25 journalists visited Ethiopia under the aegis of the environmental information service Earthscan, to be shown the effects of desertification. It was immediately apparent that Ethiopia was already in the early stages of a famine of considerable proportions. All 25 journalists filed stories to their newspapers and journals, reporting that five million people faced starvation, but there was little interest and few of the stories were printed. In October 1984, a BBC television crew filmed a report on refugee camps in rural Ethiopia. Emphasizing yet again the power of television, the screening of the film resulted, over the next 18 months, in a worldwide public awareness and fund-raising campaign of unprecedented proportions. British rock artists led by Bob Geldof and Midge Ure formed Band Aid and in November recorded a best-selling single, "Do They Know It's Christmas," to raise funds for famine relief. They were followed by an American counterpart, U.S.A. for Africa with "We Are the World," and simultaneous Live Aid concerts in Britain and the United States. By 1986, a total of $100 million had been raised by Band Aid and Live Aid, and $51 million by U.S.A. for Africa.[67] By 1984–85, famine afflicted 20 countries (the Sudan, Ethiopia, Niger, Mozambique, Somalia, Chad, and Mali were affected the worst). An estimated 1 million people died from malnutrition and related diseases, 10 million were forced to abandon their homes and lands in search of food, water, and pasture, and 30 million in 20 countries had insufficient food on which to live.

Very little of the media publicity given to the famine in the West talked about environmental degradation as a root cause. Yet the famine/drought led to the realization among government officials, aid agencies, and development planners that African development programs over the preceding 20 years had failed. In 1984, the World Bank, a normally cautious institution, concluded that "the economic and social transformation of Africa, begun so eagerly and effectively in the early years of independence, could be halted or reversed" unless development policies changed.[68] Timberlake observes that the famine had the positive effect of starting "a painful reappraisal among those responsible for Africa's 'development', and brought a new willingness to admit mistakes."[69] The causes of the famine vindicated many of the warnings made before, during, and since Stockholm about the nature of the relationship between development planning and environmental management.

UNEP: A MIXED RECORD OF ACHIEVEMENT

UNEP was the most tangible result of the Stockholm conference. Although imperfect and, a decade later, still insufficient in many ways, it

TABLE 2:

The Performance of UNEP, 1982: An Assessment by the Sierra Club and the Ågesta Group

	Sierra Club	Ågesta Group
Good progress	Regional Seas conservation conventions/protocols INFOTERRA global monitoring	Regional Seas conservation conventions/protocols periodic reports
Fair progress	IRPTC microbiology rural technology industries interstate relations education periodic reports	IRPTC microbiology rural technology industries interstate relations global monitoring INFOTERRA
Limited progress	advice to governments development planning communications desertification	advice to governments development planning communications education
Slow progress	health disaster warning system technical assistance management	health disaster warning system technical assistance management desertification

SOURCES: Nicholas A. Robinson, Prepared statement before the Subcommittee on Human Rights and International Organizations, Committee on Foreign Affairs, U.S. House of Representatives, 20 April 1982; The Ågesta Group, *Twenty Years after Stockholm: A Summary of Comments Received* (Farsta, Sweden: Ågesta Gammelgard, April 1982), 4.

was probably the best form of institution possible given the limitations imposed by other UN specialized agencies and by the low level of funding from governments. But it had severe obstacles placed in its path from the outset. It has had too little money, too few staff, and too much to do. It has had the thankless task of coordinating the work of other UN agencies against a background of interagency jealousy and suspicion, and national governments have proved unwilling to grant UNEP significant powers. Hence, argues Eckholm, UNEP has simply not become the powerful global force that some once dreamed of.[70] Ten years after Stockholm, UNEP itself could claim only "a mixed record of achievement . . . [with] fair-to-good progress . . . in implementing some of the elements of the Action Plan . . . [while] for other elements, progress has been very slow."[71]

Apart from the Regional Seas Programme, UNEP's most notable success was its involvement in promoting agreement on the 1985 Vienna Convention for Protection of the Ozone Layer (see chapter 9). The UNEP-sponsored Coordinating Committee on the Ozone Layer helped build consensus on the dimensions of the threat to the ozone layer. This set a hopeful precedent for progress on other global threats. Through GEMS, UNEP also promoted the development of monitoring programs, through IRPTC it made a start on coordinating data on toxic chemicals, and it must take credit for helping get conventions like CITES off the ground. But the failures have outnumbered the successes. At its 1977 session, the UNEP Governing Council set out 21 specific goals to be met by 1982. In 1982, the Sierra Club and the Ågesta Group of Sweden made separate assessments of progress; the results, compared in Table 2, were not encouraging.

UNEP itself believed that it would never have been possible to set out immediately to implement the recommendations of the Stockholm Action Plan for three reasons: the small secretariat and limited funding, the immensity of its task, and the nature of the recommendations themselves, which varied from the specific (in terms of goals and necessary actions) to the general (in terms of necessary action rather than goals).[72] Under the circumstances, it can be credited with having achieved more than it was in reality empowered to do; a distinction must be made between what UNEP actually *could* do and what outsiders felt it *should* do. On balance, Tolba believed that UNEP's most important overall achievement was to raise the general level of environmental awareness in policymaking circles.[73] UNEP could claim to have helped draw the attention of governments both to their own national environmental problems and to shared global problems. But its principal handicap remains: it is rarely in a position to back up its warnings and advice with either money or technical assistance.

SEVEN

The North: Politics and Activism (1969–1980)

As the following for New Environmentalism intensified, so public concerns were increasingly reflected in public policy. While four major pieces of national environmental legislation had been passed in OECD member states between 1956 and 1960, ten were passed in the period 1961 to 1965, 18 between 1966 and 1970, and 31 in the years 1971 to 1975.[1] As of August 1971, 12 countries had either planned or implemented reorganization of their environmental programs;[2] by June 1972, the number had reached 25 (11 of them in the Third World); by 1985, more than 140 countries had environmental agencies.[3] Sandbach argues that the creation of new administrative agencies and legislation helped allay the fears of environmentalists and contain the environmental issue.[4] But the changes in policy and administration were often more quantitative than qualitative. Although many western European political parties had begun to grasp the expediency of adopting policies on the environment in the early 1970s, their responses were poor enough to help stimulate the growth of entirely new environmental parties, notably in West Germany, Switzerland, Belgium, France, and the Netherlands.

To make matters worse, few governments created environmental agencies with adequate powers. Whether they restructured the divided responsibilities of existing departments, created entirely new departments, or created new regulatory agencies with cross-cutting powers, the solutions rarely proved sufficient to deal with the problems. There were three main reasons for this.

First, the environment proved almost impossible to compartmentalize. A problem common to almost all attempts to create new government machinery has been that of deciding the delineation of responsibilities and of providing the necessary legislative authority. The environment really impinges on almost every other major policy area. In theory, a true "department of the environment" would have to be armed with an awesome array of legislative authority, cutting into agriculture, industry, trade, transport, energy, water supply, and other areas of resource planning. In practice, the new environmental agencies rarely enjoyed the backing of legislation adequate to the breadth of their responsibilities.

Second, the creation of new departments has often caused conflict with existing departments unwilling to give up their powers or responsibilities, resulting all too often in new agencies with mismatched, inadequate, or incomplete duties, or with much responsibility but little power. In the United States, 27 different agencies have responsibilities for different components of environmental policy. In Britain, the misnamed Department of the Environment probably has less real influence over environmental policy than the Department of Agriculture (and no British government department does as much in practical terms as the private environmental movement).

Third, many of the new agencies were plagued by a lack of human, technical, and financial resources; they tended to be junior members of government, the heads of such agencies often had to operate at middle levels without access to senior decisionmakers, and the monitoring and enforcement of legislation varied from close control to none at all.[5] The OECD concluded in 1985 that even among its member states, several countries were unable to devote the resources to environmental programs that were needed.[6]

Six elements in particular determined the nature of the response of most political systems to the environmental issue in the 1970s and 1980s: (1) the level of public political activism, particularly through interest groups; (2) the degree of faith in administrative ability (much greater in Britain, for example, than in the United States); (3) the role of law and the division of powers between central and local government (greater centralization in Britain than in the United States); (4) the degree of public consultation and of public access to the decisionmaking process (overt lobbying in the United States, private consultation in Britain); (5) the degree of public access to information (greater in the United States than in Britain); and (6) the nature of existing institutional arrangements.

The purview of the new environmental agencies often revealed much about the political and economic priorities of different political systems. The stimulus for most LDCs was the desire to plan natural resources in the interests of economic development. Thus LDCs often combined responsibility for natural resources, tourism, wildlife, population, and land-use under one or two agencies. In industrialized countries, pollution control was usually the major element in the responsibilities of new departments; this also provided a stimulus in some of the more industrialized LDCs, such as India, Brazil, and China. While MDCs began to address a new agenda of "anticipate and prevent," LDCs were still in the "react and cure" phase.[7] In MDCs there was also a marked shift toward addressing transboundary problems such as acid pollution, toxic chemicals, hazardous wastes, shared fisheries, and river basin management. There was the beginning of a true weighing of national with international interests, for example, in the issue of acid pollution (see chapter 9). In most cases, the initiatives in environmental policy were national responses to national problems, but the fact that many different countries almost simultaneously began addressing environmental problems suggests that national initiatives were influenced too by more general advances in scientific knowledge, by the well-publicized findings of global models, by events (such as environmental disasters) in other countries, and by membership of international treaties or intergovernmental organizations.

Nationally and internationally, an important element in environmental politics has been the role of interest groups, both in drawing attention to issues and in monitoring the implementation and effectiveness of legislation. As the number of state environmental agencies and pieces of legislation blossomed, so did the number of—and support for—NGOs. The trend amongst these groups was away from the more limited issues of nature protection and toward wider environmental questions, and, at the same time, increasingly away from purely charitable concerns and toward political activism and lobbying. While domestic issues remained the most immediately identifiable and accessible to most NGOs, the larger NGOs (or NGO coalitions) were not able to ignore the increase in the number of issues that had to be addressed at regional or global levels.[8]

The contrasting responses of Britain and the United States to environmental policymaking give some idea of the different issues at stake, the different national styles of regulation, and the inherent complexity of the environment as a political issue.

BRITAIN: NANNY KNOWS BEST

On the face of it, Britain has an impressive record in recognizing and responding to environmental degradation. In 1273 it passed what may have been the world's first piece of antipollution legislation (a decree prohibiting the burning of sea coal). In 1863 it set up the first pollution control agency (the Alkali Inspectorate). In 1947 it passed one of the most comprehensive planning acts in the world, the Town and Country Planning Act. In 1956 it was the first major industrialized nation to pass a Clean Air Act. In 1970 it created the world's first cabinet-level "environment" department. Yet, paradoxically, successive postwar governments have mainly proved slow to respond to trends in public opinion on the environment. Britain's position on acid pollution provides an example. The problem was first identified in Britain, Battersea power station in London (opened 1929) was the first power station in the world to fit antipollution scrubbers, and London was one of the first cities in the world to respond successfully to smog problems. Yet Britain consistently lagged behind other West European nations during the 1980s in agreeing to international action to curb acid pollution (see chapter 9). The answers to such paradoxes must be sought in the nature of the British political system.

British policymakers have traditionally viewed themselves as custodians of the public interest and have felt confident of understanding this interest with minimal reference to the public itself. One of the characteristics of British politics is the limitation imposed on public access to information and the belief that a passive public will accept what is thought to be in its interest (an attitude that is frequently challenged). This in turn has meant that much regulatory policymaking in Britain has been executed by selective consultation with interest groups, with no requirement to inform the public.[9] Voluntary compliance with "decent" standards of behavior has been a key element of pollution control, an attitude described by Jon Tinker in 1972 as the "Nanny knows best" syndrome, in which the government appeals to the sense of fair play of polluting industries. Some of Britain's pollution rules, he argued, were better suited to an Edwardian girl's school than to an advanced industrial society. Offenders, he noted, "are taken quietly on one side by the prefects and ticked off for letting the side down. There is no need for prosecutions: the shame of being found out is reckoned to be punishment enough."[10] The noncoercive approach to pollution control is reflected in the fact that the Alkali Inspectorate prosecuted just three cases between 1920 and 1967.[11] Stanley Johnson argues that Britain's approach to pollution control tended toward conservatism in believing in innocence until guilt had been proven.[12] In 1972, the Royal Commission on Environmental Pollution concluded in its second annual report that there was a need for more public openness in the environmental policy process.[13]

A second source of problems lies in the fact that although Britain is often held up as a model of democracy, the process of government is frustrated to some extent by the domination of an elitist civil service and a ponderous bureaucracy. British civil servants are commonly criticized for failing to adopt modern methods of management, for not being sufficiently systematic, for not planning ahead, and for being obsessed with procedure.

A third problem lies in the inadequacies of local government, where considerable control over the environment is vested. There is relatively little public interest in local politics, yet local government has much of the authority for ensuring public health. In the industrial heartlands of the Midlands, South Wales, and Scotland, the weaknesses of local government have been reinforced by a prevailing public unwillingness to acknowledge pollution as a problem, or—in coal mining areas—to accept less pollutive alternative energy sources such as natural gas. As has happened so often elsewhere, fears that environmental controls would undermine existing industry and drive away new industry at a time of economic hardship discouraged the implementation of pollution controls.[14]

Until 1970, authority for environmentally related policy in Britain was divided between a disparate group of agencies; air pollution control, for example, was divided between the ministries of housing and local government (Alkali Inspectorate), technology, transport, and agriculture, the Department of Social Services, the Board of Trade, and the secretaries of state for Scotland and Wales. Harold Wilson first proposed an amalgamation in 1969 and created both the Ministry for Local Government and Regional Planning[15] and the Royal Commission on Environmental Pollution. There was much discussion about environmental issues both within the Labour government and the Conservative opposition in 1969–1970, encouraged partly by the series of BBC Reith Lectures given by Sir Frank Fraser Darling in November 1969,[16] by the opening of European Conservation Year 1970, and by President Nixon's 1970 Message to Congress. The environment was not to be an election issue in 1970, the closeness of the election encouraging both major parties to concentrate on familiar issues. Following the Conservative victory, however, the word "environment" appeared for the first time in the Queen's Speech in July 1970. In October, the reorganization of government machinery originally planned by the Wilson government was outlined in a Heath Government White Paper, which noted that it was "increasingly accepted that maintaining a decent environment, improving people's living conditions and providing for adequate transport facilities all come together in the planning of development. . . . Because these functions interact, and because they give rise to acute and conflicting requirements, a new form of organisation is needed at the centre of the administrative system."[17]

The ministries of housing and local government, public building and works, and transport were thence amalgamated by the Heath government into a new Department of the Environment (DoE) responsible for "the whole range of functions which affect people's living environment." Peter Walker was appointed Secretary of State and immediately set the department four objectives. Only two—those relating to developing a "practical and positive approach" to pollution in all its forms and developing a positive approach to planning—were strictly policies on the environment (the others related to reforming local government and housing). One of the DoE's earliest activities in pollution control was a comprehensive reorganization of water services. Responsibility for water supply, sewerage, and water conservation in England and Wales lay with more than 1,400 local and regional agencies. Under the 1973 Water Act (in which environmental pressure groups played only a minor role), these were replaced with ten Regional Water Authorities based on natural watersheds rather than local governmental units. The 1974 Control of Pollution Act addressed several environmental problems, including waste disposal, and water, air, and noise pollution. Bennett sees it as "the first formal recognition of the environment as a single entity."[18]

The creation of the Department of the Environment—the first so-named department in the world—is often given greater significance than it deserves. The suggestion by Aldous that the new department was armed with "as wide a range of powers over the environment as it is politically acceptable for a single ministry to have within a demo- cratic . . . parliamentary system"[19] is questionable. The creation of the DoE was more a reorganization of government machinery than the cre- ation of a new department with additional powers. The very title Depart- ment of the "Environment" was a misnomer, because environmental policy proved to be a small (and not very important) part of its responsi- bilities; it gave considerably greater weight to its responsibilities in local government and housing. By 1985, it had become obvious that the struc- ture of the department was unsatisfactory, and the Labour party followed the lead of the Liberal-SDP Alliance in suggesting the need to reorganize the government structure relating to environmental management. Exactly how this would be implemented was not spelled out.

The most controversial and widely debated environmental issue of the 1970s and 1980s, and perhaps of the twentieth century, was the country- side. The rural ethic holds a place in the British psyche that is equivalent to the position of forests in West Germany or wilderness in the United States. Social and economic change over a period of 6,000 years has pro- duced the characteristic British landscape which has long enthralled writ- ers, artists, and poets: small fields and meadows divided by hedgerows and sprinkled with copses and small areas of woodland. It has also re- moved all but 7 percent of the natural forest cover of the British Isles. Very little, if any, true wilderness remains, and only the vestiges of once great natural forests remain in locales such as Sherwood, the New Forest, and the Forest of Dean. For the rest, wildlife must coexist alongside ag- riculture. In England alone, 70 percent of the land area is farmed.

During the Second World War, the need to become self-sufficient in food encouraged agricultural intensification, a process that continued through the postwar years, encouraged by tariffs on imports and subsi- dies to farmers—particularly those later made available under the Euro- pean Community's much-maligned Common Agricultural Policy. One result has been the removal of hedgerows and forests and the reclama- tion of wetlands at an unprecedented rate in order to create bigger fields and increase agricultural yields. For many, farming no longer enriches and conserves the landscape, but destroys it. Between 1946 and 1974, a quarter of the hedgerows in England and Wales—about 120,000 miles (193,000 km) in all—were removed.[20] Deciduous forests have been steadily replaced by commercial conifer plantations or converted to arable land—between 1947 and 1980, half the ancient woodlands in Britain were lost.[21] Grasslands, bogs, marshes, heaths, downs and moorlands have been similarly converted.

In 1980, the nature of the changes was documented by Marion Shoard in *The Theft of the Countryside*. Noting that Britain's planning system was widely considered the most sophisticated and effective mechanism in the world for curbing the inherent tendency of powerful private interests to override public interest in land, she asked what it was doing to safeguard landscape from the systematic onslaught of modern agriculture. "The answer," she wrote, "is almost nothing. The planning system does not attempt to reconcile the different priorities of food production and landscape or wildlife conservation in cases where the two interests conflict. . . . [Farming and commercial forestry] are effectively above the law as it applies to other activities which affect the environment."[22] Much of the conflict between conservationists and farmers came to a head during the formulation of the 1981 Wildlife and Countryside Act, which attracted a record 2,300 amendments before it was passed. Among the many anomalies in the Act was the fact that landowners whose land contained Sites of Special Scientific Interest (a curious form of designation created by the Nature Conservancy Council) were given no incentive to maintain such sites and plenty of incentive to develop them. Within months of the passage of the Act, it became clear that it was insufficient, and there was strong support among conservationists for its replacement.

Private environmental bodies are a key element in British policymaking. Where other industrialized countries may formulate and execute environmental policy through government agencies, many functions in Britain are carried out by private groups. The National Trust, for example, does considerably more than the government in acquiring and maintaining historic buildings and scenic landscape. Most nature reserves are run by local naturalist groups, which are coordinated in turn by the Royal Society for Nature Conservation. Many environmental groups receive direct government funding, and nearly half have representatives on one or more official advisory committees. Until the 1970s, these groups relied on private negotiations with government officials; thereafter, many became more involved in direct lobbying, political activism, and the mobilization of public opinion—this despite the fact that for many groups, overt political activity would threaten their charitable status. The change is exemplified by the comment of one senior official of the Council for the Protection of Rural England (CPRE), who noted that under the leadership of Sir Herbert Griffin, the CPRE did not seek attention and fastidiously avoided embarassing those who it influenced or sought to influence. Griffin, secretary-general of the CPRE since its foundation in 1926, finally retired in 1965. "Nowadays," the official noted, "we are not reluctant to go public. Indeed, we are very media-conscious. This is better suited to the general style of environmental politics which has become more conflict-oriented."[23] Members of both houses of parliament held official or honorary positions in many environmental organizations, and increased interest in environmental issues was reflected in parliamentary debates and questions.

Silent Spring, Aberfan, *Torrey Canyon,* and the rise of the global environmental movement all influenced British environmentalism, and the membership of environmental groups surged during the 1970s. Between

1967 and 1980, the membership of the CPRE and of the Ramblers Association more than doubled, that of the Society for the Promotion of Nature Conservation (now Royal Society for Nature Conservation) more than quadrupled. Membership of the Royal Society for the Protection of Birds rose from 38,000 to 300,000 and of the National Trust (whose interests go beyond nature protection) from 159,000 to 1 million. The number of local amenity societies increased sixfold between 1958 and 1975; by 1977 they had a total membership of 300,000.[24] By 1983, it was estimated that the British environmental movement had some 3 million members, or 5.3 percent of the total population.[25] This made it the largest mass movement in British history.

As in the United States, members of British environmental groups are generally more affluent and better educated than the average. Because class is still a major social division in Britain, and because it is in turn tied to labor and employment, amenity organizations are more active in the predominantly white collar and professional south of England than they are in the predominantly manual and industrial Midlands and in the north. The class identification of environmentalists is nowhere more marked than in the support given to many environmental groups by peers, and by the active role of the House of Lords in initiating, debating, and amending much environmental legislation. Lord Ashby, for example, was first chairman of the Royal Commission on Environmental Pollution, Lord Creighton plays an active role in the management of several environmental organizations, and Lord Melchett is both an active parliamentarian and an active member of several environmental groups.

THE UNITED STATES: CHECKS AND BALANCES

As in Britain, the United States had, until 1970, no single federal agency responsible for pollution control; responsibility lay with a confused coalition of separate agencies in the Department of Health, Education, and Welfare. Air and water pollution were generally considered local matters, and the role of the federal government in environmental policymaking was thus limited. Environmental organizations had, however, begun pressing for more vigorous and comprehensive action on the environment. In his 1970 Message to Congress, Richard Nixon had spoken of the "inadequacy of our institutions for dealing with problems that cut across traditional political boundaries,"[26] and ushered in a new decade of environmental policy formulation.

Despite attempts to rationalize environmental policymaking and implementation, the stratified nature of the American political system has placed enormous obstacles in the path of addressing an already complex policy area. Like all public policy areas, environmental programs in the United States have been shaped by the dispersal of government power through checks and balances and by the role of interest groups. Shared,

TABLE 3:

Membership of Selected British and U.S. Environmental Groups 1968–1984 (in thousands)

	1968	1972	1976	1980	1984
BRITAIN					
Royal Society for the Protection of Birds	41	108	204	300	340
Ramblers Association	15	26	30	32	37
National Trust	170	346	548	1000	1460*
Council for the Protection of Rural England	16	25	28	29	30
Royal Society for Nature Conservation	35	75	109	140	180
TOTAL	277	580	919	1501	2047
UNITED STATES					
National Wildlife Federation	364	524	620	818	820
Sierra Club	68	136	165	182	348
Wilderness Society	39	67	91	50	65
National Audubon Society	66	164	269	400	450
Izaak Walton League	56	56	50	52	50
TOTAL	593	947	1195	1502	1733

* 1982

SOURCE: This figure is based on information from Francis Sandbach, *Environment: Ideology and Policy* (Oxford: Basil Blackwell, 1980), 12; Stephen Fox, *John Muir and His Legacy: The American Conservation Movement* (Boston: Little, Brown & Co., 1981), 315; *The Conservation Directory* (Washington, DC: National Wildlife Federation, various years); and some of the listed organizations.

independent, and countervailing authority in the federal system makes it impossible to differentiate federal, state, and local functions; jurisdictional rivalries add the first layer of complexity to the management of environmental problems. Further complexity is presented by the fragmentation of environmental responsibilities among many institutions and attempts to apply federal environmental policies through state and local governments. The final layer of complexity is added by the division of powers for making, implementing, and assessing policy among the White House, Congress, the bureaucracy, and the courts. The problem of the bureaucracy (particularly the lack of coordination within and between departments) is illustrated by the example of the Department of the Interior: two of its agencies, the Fish and Wildlife Service and the Bureau of Land Management, are in direct competition. The one preserves wildlife on public lands, while the other has been traditionally inclined to protect the rights of those who wish to graze livestock or extract minerals.[27] Apart from the interior, agriculture, and energy departments, no less than 27 different organizations—from the Army Corps of Engineers to the Federal Aviation Administration, the Food and Drug Administration, the National Park Service, and the U.S. Coast Guard—are involved in implementing environmental policy.[28]

Despite all these jurisdictional claims, the Environmental Protection Agency (EPA) is the most important of the major regulatory agencies. The history of the EPA dates from 1969, when a President's Advisory Council on Executive Organization (the Ash Council) was set up to examine federal natural resource policy and pollution control programs. Among its recommendations was one for a huge new department of natural resources and the environment, replacing the Department of the Interior (long regarded as the unofficial department of natural resources) and drawing off relevant responsibilities from other departments. (Similar proposals had been made previously by the 1949 Hoover Commission, and again in a 1965 Senate bill.)[29] The Ash Council's guiding principle was to minimize the number of federal agencies reporting to the president.[30] It initially favored the consolidation of existing pollution programs under the proposed new Department of Natural Resources but recanted when Council members argued that this would submerge pollution control programs and result in decisions favoring resource development at the expense of improved environmental quality.[31]

On 1 January 1970, the National Environmental Policy Act was signed into law after rapid passage through Congress, despite White House opposition. It drew the attention of all government agencies to the environmental consequences of their activities and required an environmental impact statement (EIS) of all major federal programs "significantly affecting the quality of the human environment." More than 12,000 such EISs were prepared in the first decade of operation.[32] The act also created the Council on Environmental Quality (CEQ), based in the Executive Office of the President, to draw up an annual environmental quality report and to advise the president on national policies for improving environmental quality.[33] The CEQ was given no real powers, and Davies and Davies suggest that it derived what influence it had solely through its location in the Executive Office; it was doubtful, they noted, that the CEQ could "withstand the blows of a hostile president."[34] This was confirmed in 1981, when President Reagan first considered abolishing the CEQ and then settled on dismissing almost all the staff and halving its budget.

The compromise reached on pollution programs was the establishment in December 1970 of the EPA, an independent pollution control agency with consolidated responsibility for regulating and enforcing federal programs on air and water pollution, environmental radiation, pesticides, and solid waste, and, to a lesser extent, for research. The agency reported directly to the president. Quarles suggests that in political terms the decision to create the EPA was "a compromise that reduced opposition to the reorganization. The original proposal [for a new department of natural resources] might well have been too bold, since vested interest would have tried to lobby for its overturn in the Congress."[35]

The EPA became, in personnel and budgetary terms, the biggest regulatory agency in Washington. It began with a staff of 8,000 and a budget of $455 million; by 1981 it had a staff of nearly 13,000 and a budget of $1.35 billion.[36] It was responsible for major pieces of legislation, such as the Clean Air Act, the Clean Water Act, the Resource Conservation and Recovery Act, and the Toxic Substances Control Act. In addition to regulation, it also had powers of disbursement, notably through the administration of Superfund, a $1.6 billion program for cleaning up the nation's waste dumps. NEPA's first decade saw an impressive outpouring of federal environmental legislation. Despite pressures imposed on the Nixon administration by business interests, congressional support for environmental reform ensured the passage of key legislation on air and water pollution control, solid waste recovery, and pesticide regulation.

The new toxic waste legislation was put to the test by a major public controversy between 1976 and 1979. The manufacture, consumption, and disposal of chemicals, especially as used in fertilizers and pesticides, had often given cause for concern. In 1976, following several years of unusually heavy rain and snow, chemicals began seeping into the basements of homes near Love Canal, an uncompleted and abandoned nineteenth-century waterway in New York State. The canal had earlier been used as an industrial dump and then was sold to the Niagara Falls Board of Education, which built a school and playing field on the site. Some of the land was sold off to a developer, who built several hundred homes alongside the site of the canal. Studies now identified 82 different chemical compounds, including trichlorophenol, which contained dioxin. In August 1978, pregnant women and children under two years of age were advised to leave the area. By July 1979, 263 families had been evacuated and their homes purchased by the state, 1,000 additional families had been advised to leave the area, and nearly $27 million had been spent by municipal, state, and federal authorities to provide temporary housing, close off the contaminated area, and contain the seepage of chemicals.[37] Love Canal was only the most publicized of many such potential incidents; a 1979 report to the EPA estimated the number of disposal sites containing hazardous wastes in the United States at between 32,000 and 50,000, of which 1,200–2,000 could pose significant risks to human health or the environment.[38]

THE REAGAN ENVIRONMENTAL AGENDA

White House attitudes to the environment underwent a dramatic transformation under the early Reagan administration. Vig and Kraft suggest that the Reagan environmental agenda was based on (1) regulatory reform, (2) reliance as much as possible on the free market to allocate resources, and (3) the shifting of responsibilities for environmental protection to state and local government.[39] Two Reagan appointments exemplified the attitude of the new president: that of James Watt as Secretary of the Interior, and that of Anne Burford (nee Gorsuch)—a Watt protégé—as administrator of the EPA. Watt had served at the Interior Department for six years during the Nixon administration. Prior to his appointment as secretary, he had run the Mountain States Legal Foundation, an organization devoted to legal action to curb or repeal federal actions in Colorado and other western states. Watt believed that most resource problems could be solved by opening them to the free market. His outspokenness soon became as big an issue as his policies. In a January 1982 speech, he said he never used the words Democrat or Republican—"it's liberals and Americans." A year later he compared his environmentalist critics to Nazis and Bolsheviks.[40] A quintessential Sagebrush Rebel, his policies included the opening up of wilderness areas to oil and gas leasing, the privatization of lands owned by the Forest Service and the Bureau of Land Management, and an increase in the availability of federally owned coal, oil, and gas.

Anne Gorsuch was an attorney and one-term state legislator from Colorado with no management experience; her previous clients had included many industries opposed to federal environmental regulation. Environmentalists interpreted her appointment as a signal that the White House intended to move the EPA's sympathies away from environmentalists and toward business and other regulated interests.[41] Of the 15 subordinates named by Gorsuch, 11 had been connected with industries regulated by EPA. President Reagan early made it clear that he proposed to reduce the power of the EPA, instituting budget and personnel cuts (of 29 percent and 23 percent respectively)[42] between 1981 and 1983. Under Gorsuch's tenure, most of the agency's major programs were near-paralyzed, and staff morale at the EPA collapsed. Suggestions that the EPA administration was involved in political chicanery became a political embarassment. In December 1982, Gorsuch was cited for contempt of Congress for refusing—on presidential orders—to deliver subpoenaed documents on alleged mismanagement of the Superfund. In March 1983, she resigned (the month before, she had married Robert Burford, head of the Bureau of Land Management). The appointment of William Ruckelshaus (who had been first administrator of the EPA) seemed to augur well for the agency, but continued personnel and budgetary cuts continued to interfere with EPA's effective operation. Within six months of Burford's resignation, James Watt had also resigned. His comment that the members of a commission set up to examine his controversial coal-leasing policies comprised "a black . . . a woman, two Jews and a cripple" had so incensed public opinion that the Republican-led Senate appeared ready to pass a resolution calling for his removal; Watt resigned on October 9 rather than face "deconfirmation" by his own party.[43]

The principle implicit in American politics that the interests affected by public policies should have an active input into the formulation and assessment of policies has meant that the environmental lobby, like all other lobbies on Capitol Hill, has had a major role in environmental policymaking. Organizations such as the Sierra Club and Friends of the Earth formed their own political action committees (through which money could be directly contributed to political candidates); the League of Conservation Voters became increasingly active in presidential and congressional elections; and a number of organizations—notably the Environmental Defense Fund and the Natural Resources Defense Council—increased the size of their scientific and technical staffs in order to provide their own expert testimony and reduce their dependence upon studies provided by government agencies or regulated interests.[44]

Those who, in the post-prophets era, had talked of the faddishness of environmentalism had cause to revise their opinions a decade later. Not only did environmental issues retain a steady prominence in the public policy priorities of the American public, but alarm at the anti-environmentalist stand of the Reagan administration led to a surge in membership in 1981–82. The larger national environmental groups alone—including the Sierra Club, the National Wildlife Federation, and the National Audubon Society—had a combined membership of about five million. A 1980 RFF poll suggested that about 7 percent of the American population (17 million people) might be involved in the environmental movement, and a further 55 percent were sympathetic to its goals.[45] Sympathy for the movement was greatest among whites, the young, those with at least some college education, and those with higher incomes.[46]

THE RISE OF THE GREENS

In March 1983, environmental politics in Western Europe took on a new dimension with the arrival in the West German Bundestag of 27 parliamentarians representing *die Grünen* (the Greens), a party formed exactly four years before. The party had crossed the 5 percent barrier allowing them to be represented in the Bundestag. As the first new party to enter the Bundestag in 30 years, *die Grünen* seemed poised to displace the faltering Free Democrats as the third party in West German politics.[47] *Die Grünen* took their seats in the Bundestag between the conservative Christian Democrats and the liberal-left Social Democrats, but in truth they were not easy to categorize in conventional political terms.[48] An early slogan of the new movement was "We are neither left nor right; we are in front." Although espousing essentially an environmental platform, they also considered themselves the political voice of citizens' movements opposed to nuclear power and supporting peace, feminism, and Third World issues. Spretnak and Capra note four pillars in the

Green platform: ecology, social responsibility, grassroots democracy, and nonviolence.[49]

Die Grünen grew out of a complex network of environmentally-oriented "citizen's initiative associations," notably Grüne Aktion Zukunft (Green Action Future; GAZ), founded in 1978 by Herbert Gruhl, who had been elected to the Bundestag as a member of the Christian Democratic Union but defected on forming GAZ. Green parties contested Land (state) elections in Hesse and Bavaria without success in 1978. In October 1979 the Bremer Grüne Liste won enough votes in the Bremen state elections to take four seats. Prompted in large part by Gruhl and by Petra Kelly and Roland Vogt (then with the Union of German Ecological Citizens' Groups), the Sonstige Politische Vereinigung (SPV) Die Grünen (Alternative Political Alliance—The Greens) was founded in March 1979, and die Grünen was formally established as a national political party at a meeting in Karlsruhe in January 1980. Die Grünen variously espoused the creation of a national economy not based on growth, the breakdown of large companies into smaller units, a 35-hour work week, higher taxes for higher income groups, state investment to create jobs, an end to nuclear power, the sustainable use of natural resources, materials and energy conservation, zero population growth, and nuclear disarmament. Gruhl thought die Grünen too left-wing and too concerned with nonecological policies, so he and others left and formed a Grüne Föderation, and then in 1981 the Ökologisch-Demokratische Partei (ÖDP) (Ecological Democratic Party).

Within two months, die Grünen had won their first six Landtag seats when they took 5.3 percent of the vote in Baden-Württenburg. In 1982 they won enough seats in Hesse and Hamburg to hold the balance of power;[50] in August 1983 the Greens precipitated a new election in Hesse by refusing to approve the 1983 budget, and although they lost two of their seats in the new election, they retained the balance of power. Petra Kelly early emerged as their most energetic and visible leader,[51] a position she continued to maintain until removed by the party's system of rotating leaders in 1984. Along with the national breakthrough in the 1983 Bundestag elections, die Grünen also took 49 state and city seats, and more than 320 community seats.

Die Grünen has had more visibility and electoral successes than any other Green party, but it was neither the first to win seats in a national legislature (that distinction belongs to the Swiss Greens in 1979)[52] nor the first to contest a national election. Eleven years before, the Values Party had contested about half the seats at the 1972 general election in New Zealand, winning 1.98 percent of the vote (although polling as high as 9 percent in individual electorates).[53] Founded in May 1972 by Tony Brunt (a 25-year old journalist) and Norman Smith (a 29-year old public relations executive), Values appealed mainly to young, well-educated professionals. Despite leadership changes and internal problems, Values was sufficiently organized to contest every seat at the 1975 election, increasing its share of the votes to an impressive 5.2 percent, and taking third place in 29 of the 41 major city constituencies.[54] But members disagreed about its place in the political spectrum and even about whether it should be a political party at all, rather than simply an interest group.[55] It managed only 2.5 percent of the vote in 1978; by 1984, its share had fallen to just 0.2 percent. James notes that many party members considered Values less a potential governing party than a channel for influencing attitudes laterally and influencing public policy from below; by 1978 the novelty of the party's message may have worn off, the larger parties had become more environmentally conscious, and Values may have suffered from a switch to the Labour party by voters anxious to remove Prime Minister Robert Muldoon.[56]

The British Ecology Party was Europe's first, founded in 1973. Although it contested 106 seats in the 1983 general election and 133 in the 1987 election, the party has never been strong. Rüdig and Lowe offer four main reasons: the absence of environmentally controversial development projects that would have stimulated radical ecology, the integration of such radicalism as there was into the realm of Labour Party politics, the accession by authorities to strong resistance against particular projects (thereby reducing the potential for local opposition), and the traditional preference among British conservation groups for changing the system from within.[57] Neither has the Ecology Party (now called the Green Party) been able to overcome the plurality system which militates against smaller parties in Britain.

French ecology parties contested presidential and National Assembly elections throughout the 1970s and 1980s. An ecology movement born out of the 1968 student uprisings had first taken form in 1970. In 1974, with the support of French ecology groups, René Dumont (a professor at the National Institute of Agronomy and a member of the Club of Rome) ran in the presidential election, winning a modest 1.32 percent of the vote. An electoral alliance of ecology groups, established in 1977, ran in the 1978 National Assembly elections under the banner *Ecologie-78,* winning 2.1 percent of the first-round vote. In 1980, a nonaligned *Mouvement d'Ecologie Politique* (MEP) was established and fielded Brice Lalonde (a 35-year-old journalist and veteran of the 1968 student uprisings) in the 1981 presidential election. Lalonde won a creditable 1.126 million votes (3.88 percent of the total), but MEP was unable to capitalize on this and performed badly at the National Assembly elections later that year.

Elsewhere in Western Europe, the ecologists were more successful. Between 1978 and 1984, ecology parties were created in ten more countries (see Figure 1); Swiss Greens won two national seats in 1979, followed by the two Belgian parties (*Ecolo* and *Agalev*) in 1981, the West German Greens in 1983, *Di Greng Alternativ* in Luxembourg in 1984, the Austrian Greens in 1986, the Finnish and Italian Greens in 1987, and the Swedish Greens in 1988. By 1988, 104 Green representatives sat in eight national assemblies, 11 sat in the European Parliament, and many hundreds more sat in regional, local, and, municipal assemblies.

FIGURE 1: Chronology of the Green Party Movement (by country): 1970–1987.

1972
NEW ZEALAND. *Values Party* founded. Contested about half the seats at the 1972 national elections (winning 1.98 percent), and all of them in 1975 (5.2 percent of the vote). Share fell to 2.5 percent at the 1978 election. Although Values contested 1981 and 1984 elections, share of vote had collapsed to 0.2 percent.

1973
BRITAIN. *Ecology Party* founded under the name People. Contested the two general elections of 1974, but first rose to national attention in 1979 election, when it fielded 53 candidates and won an average 1.5 percent of the votes. Won its first local council seat in Cornwall in 1981. Although it fielded 108 candidates in the 1983 general election, average vote share was just 1 percent. Renamed *Green Party* in 1985.

1974
FRANCE. Ecology movement (founded in wake of 1968 student movement) fielded René Dumont in 1974 presidential elections and won 337,000 votes (1.32 percent). Fielded 200 candidates in 1978 National Assembly election under banner of *Ecologie-78* and won 2.1 percent of vote.

Mouvement d'Ecologie Politique (MEP) founded 1980. Fielded Brice Lalonde of Les Amis de la Terre (Friends of the Earth) in 1981 Presidential elections and won 1.126 million votes (3.88 percent of total). MEP polled only 1.08 percent in 1981 National Assembly elections.

MEP formally constituted as political party in 1982, adopting name *Les Verts-Parti Ecologiste* (VPE). Won 6 percent of votes and several dozen seats at 1983 municipal elections. In 1984, VPE merged with other green groups to form *Confédération Ecologiste et Parti Ecologiste*. Ecologists contested nearly a third of metropolitan districts in 1986 National Assembly elections, winning 1.21 percent of the vote.

1978
BELGIUM. *Parti Ecologiste (Ecolo;* (Ecologist Party) and *Anders Gaan Leven (Agalev)* (Live Differently) founded; Walloon and Flemish respectively. In the November 1981 election, ran on joint ticket and won 4.5 percent of lower house votes (giving them two seats each) and 4.9 percent of Senate votes (giving them three and one seats respectively, plus one co-opted senator). In mid-1983, won nine regional seats and 79 municipal council seats. In October 1985 national election, increased their lower house seats to five and four respectively (6.2 percent of the vote) and returned two directly-elected senators and one co-opted senator each. In December 1987 elections, Ecolo lost two of its lower house seats, but Agalev picked up two new seats.

WEST GERMANY. *Grüne Aktion Zukunft* (GAZ) founded. In 1979, *Bremer Grüne Liste* won 5.1 percent of votes and four seats in Bremen Burgerschaft. GAZ merged with other parties in January 1980 to form *die Grünen*. Concerned at leftward drift of *die Grünen*, Herbert Gruhl and others left and in 1981 formed the *Ökologisch-Demokratische Partei (ÖDP)* (Ecological Democratic Party).

In March 1981 *die Grünen* won 5.3 percent of the vote and six seats in the Baden-Württenburg Landtag. In 1982 they won 11 seats in Lower Saxony Landtag and nine seats in Hesse Landtag. Ran unsuccessfully in Saarland, North Rhineland-Palatinate and North Rhine-Westphalia (1980), Bavaria (1982), and Rhineland-Palatinate and Schleswig-Holstein (1983). At the 1983 Bundestag elections they won 5.6 percent of the vote and 27 seats, largely at the expense of the Social Democrats. They also took 49 state and city seats, and more than 320 community seats; by 1984, *die Grünen* held 50 seats in six Land parliaments. They returned seven members in 1984 European Parliament elections.

At the 1987 Bundestag elections, *die Grünen* won 8.3 percent of the vote, and increased their number of seats to 44, only a few short of the Christian Social Union (CSU) and the Free Democratic Party (FDP).

1979

SWITZERLAND. Green parties contested the 1979 election, winning two seats and becoming the first Greens to win representation in a national assembly. In 1983, *Fédération des Partis Ecologistes de Suisse (FPE)* and *Fédération Verte* (Green Federation) founded, winning seats in cantonal assemblies in Zurich and Lucerne. At the 1983 national election, FPE won 2.9 percent of the vote and three seats in the Nationalrat.

LUXEMBOURG. *Alternative Lëscht-Wiert Iech* founded. Contested the 1979 election but won only 1.1 percent of the vote. In 1983, *Di Greng Alternativ* (The Green Alternative) founded, and at June 1984 general election won 6.8 percent of votes and two of the 64 seats in the Chamber of Deputies.

1980

FINLAND. *Vihreät* (The Greens) founded and won one seat on Helsinki City Council. Took 2.8 percent of the vote in the 1984 municipal elections, earning them 101 seats. Contested the national election in 1987, winning 4 percent of the vote and four seats in the Eduskunta (national assembly).

1981

SWEDEN. *Miljöpartiet* (Ecology Party) founded. Won 1.7 percent of vote at 1982 election and won two local council seats. Polled only 1.5 percent of the vote at 1985 general election, but won six council seats, and by 1987 enjoyed more than 8 percent support in opinion polls. At the September 1988 election, the Greens won 20 seats (largely at the expense of conservative parties), becoming the first new party to enter parliament in 70 years.

1982

AUSTRIA. *Vereinte Grüne Österreich (VGÖ)* (United Greens of Austria) and *Alternative Liste Österreich (ALÖ)* (Austrian Alternative List) founded. Won 1.9 percent and 1.3 percent of vote respectively in 1983 elections, contributing to defeat of Socialist Chancellor Bruno Kreisky. ALÖ also took four municipal council seats. At November 1986 elections, Greens increased their vote to 4.8 percent and won eight seats, bringing a fourth party into parliament for the first time since 1959.

IRELAND. *Ecology Party* founded. Fielded seven candidates in 1982 election. Since renamed *Comhaontas Glas* (Green Alliance).

1983

THE NETHERLANDS. *De Groenen* (The Greens) founded. A 1983 poll indicated that it might win 12 percent of vote in national election, but in the 1986 general election it managed barely 0.04 percent. In the 1984 European elections, *De Groenen* stood in the *Groen Progressief Akkord* (Green Progressive Alliance) with the Communists, the Pacifist Socialist Party, and the Radical Political Party, and won 5.6 percent of the vote and two seats. *De Europese Groenen* also stood but won few votes and no seats.

1984

Green parties from seven countries ran in the **EUROPEAN PARLIAMENT** elections (compared to three in the 1979 elections); Green members returned from West Germany (seven) and the Netherlands and Belgium (two each).

ITALY. Agreement reached among key Italian environmental groups to create an "antiparty" seeking qualitative rather than quantitative economic growth. In 1985 local elections, *Verdi* took 2.6 percent of the vote. In June 1987, it contested its first national election, taking 2.5 percent of the vote and returning 13 deputies and one senator. Within six months, it successfully lobbied to limit the development of nuclear power stations.

NOTE: Other Green parties have also been discussed or formed in Denmark, Canada, the United States, and Spain. The Canadian Greens fielded 60 candidates in the 1984 general election but won only 0.2 percent of the vote. In Spain, the *Partido Verde Espanol* (PVE) (Spanish Green Party) was formed in 1984 out of a coalition of pacifist, feminist, and environmentalist groups. But at its first Congress in February 1985, a number of member groups disavowed this action on the grounds that they had not been adequately consulted.

SOURCES: *Keesing's Contemporary Archives* 1973, 1974, 1976, 1978–1986; *Chronicle of Parliamentary Elections and Developments* 1978/79–1986/87; Alan J. Day and Henry W. Degenhardt, *Political Parties of the World* (Detroit: Gale Research Company, 1984); Arthur S. Banks, ed., *Political Handbook of the World: 1987* (Binghamton, NY: CSA Publications, 1987); Eva Kolinsky, "The Greens in Germany: Prospects of a Small Party," *Parliamentary Affairs* 37:4 (Autumn 1984): 434–447; Hans Lohneis, "The Swiss Election of 1983: A Glacier on the Move?" *West European Politics* 7:3 (July 1984): 117–119; Andrew Rosenbaum, "Italy's Green Party," *Environment* 29:10 (December 1987): 3, 34–35; statistical yearbooks of Luxembourg (1983/84), Austria, Switzerland, and Sweden (1986), and Finland (1987).

The Green party phenomenon has spawned numerous analytical studies, but few existing assessments are more than tentative. Cohen and Arato note how difficult it is to place the West German Greens on the traditional political map and how insufficient is the standard view of *die Grünen* as a single-issue, middle-class, left-leaning youth movement.[58] This description applies equally well to other Green parties. In the final analysis, it may prove inadequate to assess the Greens on the traditional left/right axis; they seek wide-ranging and fundamental social changes that transcend liberal/conservative or Marxist/capitalist divisions. The difficulty of making generalizations is illustrated by the varied roots of Europe's Green parties. Müller-Rommel identifies three categories of Green parties: small, preexisting socialist parties that adopted environmental policies and changed (in the public perception) into ecology parties; liberal and agrarian parties that had traditionally emphasized environmental issues (e.g. the Swedish *Centrum* party, from which the *Miljöpartiet* emerged); and the new parties specifically set up to represent an environmentally conscious electorate.[59]

The emergence of the new parties has variously been traced to the student movements of the 1960s, characterized (in the West German case at least) as the latest in a cyclical series of German youth movements,[60] and interpreted as part of the long-term value change in a postmaterial society described by Inglehart.[61] Rüdig and Lowe question the interpretation of survey data and its interplay with postmaterial explanations and suggest that an adequate analysis of the rise of the Greens would have to go beyond the traditional study of voting behavior.[62] Perhaps the most basic explanation of the rise of the Greens is the failure of older established parties simply to respond adequately to the needs and demands of the environmental movement.

ACTIVISM AND THE INTERNATIONAL ENVIRONMENT

As noted earlier, New Environmentalism had largely bypassed the established conservation movement. Although some of the older, established groups ultimately adopted activist tactics, new politicized environmental groups were needed to both feed on and service the new priorities. The change in the United States began with the creation of national organizations such as the Environmental Defense Fund and Friends of the Earth (FoE) and was then transposed to international questions through the efforts of FoE and Greenpeace, both overtly activist organizations.

The very creation of Friends of the Earth was symptomatic of the change in priorities. FoE was established in 1969 following a disagreement between the Sierra Club and its executive director, David Brower.[63] Brower had been executive director of the club since 1952, during which time the club had come to be regarded as the most influential of the traditional conservation groups,[64] and Brower among the best known conservationists. He set out to involve the club in critical public issues, such as the building of a dam that threatened the Dinosaur National Monument on the Colorado-Utah border and support for the 1964 Wilderness Act. Partly as a result, Sierra Club membership grew from 7,000 to 70,000; polls revealed that Brower's policies had the support of 85 percent of Sierra Club members.[65] His critics, however, argued that his independence of mind and his determination to follow through pet projects meant that he often let Sierra Club administrative work fall overdue. Although authorized to carry out as much political lobbying as the tax-exempt status of the club allowed, his campaigning against plans by the Bureau of Reclamation to build two dams in the Grand Canyon was instrumental in the loss of the club's tax-exempt status. In addition, his alleged dereliction of duty to the club had been associated with heavy annual deficits between 1967 and 1969. He was removed from office in 1969.

Upon his removal, Brower founded Friends of the Earth, whose philosophy was a direct reflection of New Environmentalism: that the solution to environmental problems lay not in temporary remedies but in fundamental social change. It adopted vigorous campaigning methods aimed at achieving maximum publicity and drawing attention to activities and ventures that threatened the environment. It has subsequently drawn its support from young, well-educated, middle-class discontents.[66] It was conceived from the outset as an organization that would be both overtly activist and international. The FoE "formula," according to Brower, was to find people in other countries who shared the FoE philosophy about the limits to growth, and have them set up and run independent FoE organizations.[67]

The first FoE office was opened in San Francisco in 1969, followed by offices in Paris (July 1970) and London (October 1970). Initially, Brower simply appointed friends as his overseas representatives, but the recruitment process was subsequently formalized. Two meetings in 1971 (in France and Sweden) resulted in the establishment of an international institution nominally headquartered in San Francisco. Burke notes that the primacy of self-determination and consensus decisionmaking was a defining characteristic of FoE International; "if this has, at times, resulted in a slowing down of the rate of development of FoE as an effective force internationally, it has also meant an absence of destructive divisions within the organisation."[68] Autonomous groups were subsequently set up in most western European countries and further afield (e.g. Malaysia and South Africa), with often different methods and patterns of organization, but all pursuing the aim of promoting "more rational use of our natural resources by all constructive means, and to work against those who are destroying those resources."[69] The issues FoE addressed included alternative sources of energy, wildlife issues, transport, pollution, and changes in legislation.

It was pollution—specifically that created by fallout from atmospheric nuclear tests—that led to the creation of Greenpeace, the most overt of the direct action groups. Since the Second World War, the United States, Britain, France, and China had all conducted nuclear tests in and around the Pacific. American plans to explode a nuclear device on Amchitka Island (off the coast of Alaska) in 1971 encouraged a group of American environmentalists, the Don't Make a Wave Committee, to protest by sailing a fishing boat into the area, thereby contributing to the postponement of the test and the eventual cancellation of all tests on Amchitka.[70] Similar tactics were used again in June 1972, when a crew of volunteers led by a Canadian, David McTaggart,[71] sailed a yacht toward a French test site at Moruroa Atoll, southeast of Tahiti; a bomb was detonated with the yacht only 50 miles (80 km) away.

In August 1973, the yacht again sailed into the French test site, and this time its crew was met with physical assault by French commandos. Smuggled photographs of the attack attracted considerable publicity; partly as a result of the Greenpeace activities, France announced a short moratorium on tests in November. Australia and New Zealand maintained diplomatic pressure on France throughout the 1970s, and Greenpeace continued its public protests, but France carried out regular tests throughout the 1970s. Greenpeace protest activities against the French tests took their most serious turn in July 1985, when the Greenpeace ship *Rainbow Warrior* was blown up in the harbor at Auckland, New Zealand, by members of Direction Général de la Sécurité Extérieur, the French intelligence service. One member of the Greenpeace crew (Fernando Pereira) died in the incident. The subsequent controversy seriously compromised Franco-New Zealand relations and led to the resignation of the French Defense Minister, Charles Hernu.

Greenpeace has also campaigned against whaling, sealing, nuclear power, and radioactive waste disposal. In many cases it has adopted the same tactics of direct action, such as attempting to obstruct the disposal at sea of nuclear waste, or sealing in the Arctic. The key to its activities is always the generation of often graphic and visually effective media publicity. As Greenpeace grew, so autonomous groups, rejecting the control of the original headquarters in Vancouver, were set up in Britain, France, and the Netherlands. By 1985 there were Greenpeace offices in 17 countries, with a total membership of 1.2 million,[72] and a Greenpeace International office had been set up in Lewes, on the south coast of England.

Of all the new issues addressed by the new activists, few proved so confrontational as the movement against nuclear power. The advent of nuclear power in the 1950s had been widely—but not universally—welcomed. It was portrayed as a source of energy cheaper and cleaner than traditional sources, with the potential to reduce dependence on fossil fuels. During the period of greatest optimism, it was predicted that over 100 nuclear power plants would be built each year by the 1980s. In fact, the world's nuclear power generating capacity in 1983 was less than half that projected; there were 282 commercial nuclear plants in 25 countries, with about 174,000 megawatts of generating capacity, or enough to produce 9 percent of the world's electricity.[73] Four main factors contributed to the change of heart: public opposition based on safety and environmental concerns (especially concerning the disposal of nuclear waste); operating problems (for example, with advanced gas-cooled reactors); disagreement within the industry about the relative merits of different reactor designs; and—perhaps most important—the fact that nuclear power was by the early 1980s no longer economically attractive. The building of new nuclear power stations frequently ran over budget, and it was finally admitted that nuclear power was not cheaper than coal-fired power. This had always been a contentious claim anyway.

The safety issue was almost as old as commercial nuclear power itself, although it did not attract public attention until much later. The first major reactor accident occurred in Canada in 1952, when operator confusion and technical problems combined to produce an explosion inside the core of a research reactor. There were no injuries or excessive radiation.[74] The accident at Windscale in the English Lake District in October 1957 (see chapter 3) was more public, and it was instrumental in causing a short-term cutback in British government plans for nuclear power development (other factors included the resilience of the world oil market, falling oil prices, expansion of the coal industry, and the expense of building nuclear power stations). The first accident in the United States—resulting in the deaths of three operators—occurred at a reactor in Idaho in January 1961. The exact cause of the accident has never been established, but it may have been human error.[75]

The earliest public opposition to the building of power stations came from local residents. In Britain, opposition arose initially because of fears about the safety of stations. The need to site stations well away from population centers and near a ready source of water meant that many of the stations ordered by the Central Electricity Authority were to be sited in areas of outstanding natural beauty, such as Snowdonia in Wales. This elicited protest and opposition from local residents and national pressure groups. Hall argues however that these protests were not symptomatic of a widespread desire by communities to reject nuclear power. He suggests that British opposition groups were far less successful than they were to become in the 1970s, when there was growing public perception that the nuclear power program was not a success, and plans to introduce American pressurized water reactors aroused greater and more widespread intellectual indignation than previous schemes.[76] There was considerable ignorance about nuclear power, a legacy of the secrecy that had surrounded the early research into nuclear weapons; there was also a residual naive faith in the ability of science to benefit society.

Public opposition to nuclear power was much more vocal, and often violent, in West Germany, France, and Switzerland. In 1971, for example, plans were announced to build a reactor at Whyl in southwestern Germany. Despite the opposition of local people, construction began in February 1975. Several hundred protestors immediately occupied the site, to be dispersed by police a few days later. Within days, the site was reoccupied, this time permanently. There followed several years of confrontation, and by 1982 construction had still not begun. Similar opposition met plans to build a station at Kaiseraugst in Switzerland. Mass demonstrations against plans to build a reactor at Creys-Malville in France in July 1976 were countered by forceful action by riot police, during which a demonstrator was killed.[77] Riot police were also used at Brokdorf and Grohnde in West Germany in 1976 and 1977, and at Kalkar in the Netherlands in 1977.

In the United States, safety was the fundamental issue. Public suspicion was raised by the unexplained death of Karen Silkwood, an employee at the Kerr-McGee plutonium plant near Oklahoma City, in a car crash in November 1974. She had been en route to a meeting with a union official and a reporter, at which she intended to produce evidence of malpractice at the plant. The plant was subsequently closed. Nonviolent opposition was adopted by protesters at a site in Seabrook, New Hampshire, in October 1976; more than 1,400 were arrested. The accident in March 1978 at the Three Mile Island power station in Harrisburg, Pennsylvania, gave support to the opponents of nuclear power.[78] Conflicting reports about the release of radioactivity led to the evacuation of pregnant women and young children within a five mile radius.[79] The incident raised many questions about the safety of reactors and the adequacy of safety regulations and led directly to a series of cancellations of orders for new reactors. The public effect of the accident was compounded by the release just two weeks before of the film *The China Syndrome* with Jane Fonda and Jack Lemmon, based on a fictional malfunction at a nuclear power station. In May 1979 a demonstration—the largest against nuclear power—was held in Washington DC, involving 75,000 people. Three Mile Island also had repercussions outside the United States. Two days before, the Swedish government had refused a public referendum on the Swedish nuclear program; within a week this decision had been reversed, and a referendum was held a year later.

The international scope of the antinuclear movement had been given expression in May 1977 in the convening of the nongovernmental "Conference on a Non-Nuclear Future," held alongside an International Atomic Energy Authority conference in Salzburg, Austria. An international information exchange network—the World Information Service on Energy—was founded, subsequently deriving its funding from licensing arrangements on the copyrighted symbol of the movement: a bright red smiling cartoon sun on a yellow background, surrounded by the slogan "Nuclear Power? No thanks." By 1983 the symbol was available in 40 languages;[80] its success seemed to symbolize the growing presence of a new and more activist environmental movement unconstrained by national frontiers.

The environmental movement—and specifically the antinuclear movement—had often been criticized for overstating its case, for using scare tactics to garner sympathy and support. Yet Three Mile Island had shown how close catastrophic environmental disaster might be. Confirmation of the extent to which the global environment could be contaminated by human activity was finally provided on 26 April 1986, when a reactor exploded at the Chernobyl nuclear power station, 50 miles (80 km) from Kiev in the Soviet Ukraine. The accident was caused by an experiment involving the deliberate switching off of safety systems; at least 32 deaths were ascribed to the blast, to the fire, and to radiation in the aftermath of the explosion. More than 200 people suffered severe radiation sickness, and about 135,000 had to be evacuated from the Chernobyl area. Winds carried the radiation across to Scandinavia and to parts of eastern and northwestern Europe, contaminating milk products and vegetables and compelling farmers in some areas to keep their livestock under cover. Although there is little agreement on the precise scale of the long-term threat to health, many scientists believe that the number of people likely to suffer radiation-related illnesses in the coming decades will run into the thousands.

The accident at Chernobyl was a spectacular example of how technology—if mismanaged or misdirected—could bring sudden and extreme environmental contamination. However, it is clear that most man-made environmental change is much slower, much less obvious, and more difficult to detect and measure. In most cases, it has been a function of the rate of technological development and economic growth. Where growth and development are relatively rapid and widespread, so is environmental change. Hence the marked changes evident in the environment of industrial society. In less developed countries, growth and development has often been rapid, but it has also been unequal. In their haste to provide their populations with the supposed benefits of industrialism, the governments and planners of LDCs have often put short-term benefits before long-term costs. The frequent result has been a creeping and insidious form of environmental change that has discriminated against the rural poor, bringing gradual rather than rapid degeneration: soil erosion, deforestation, siltation, the spread of desert conditions, and—ultimately—hunger, famine, and death. If industrialized nations have witnessed environmental change as a consequence of overdevelopment, LDCs are witnessing change as a consequence of unequal development. The result is that the problems and the policy responses of low-technology society are often very different from those of high-technology society.

EIGHT

The South: Environment and Development (1972–1982)

Before Stockholm, many environmentalists had questioned—and re-jected—the growth ethic. For them, economic growth was suspect and inimical to sound and rational environmental management. There was little room for compromise. A decade after Stockholm, attitudes were more conciliatory. Development and environment were no longer seen as incompatible, and it was widely agreed that an assimilation of the aims of the two was needed to create a sustainable society. Economic growth was no longer distrusted. On the contrary, it was seen as essential, pro-vided that it was sustainable. Where population growth had been re-garded in the 1960s as an obstacle to economic and social development, it was now inversely argued that a lack of development could encourage population growth. For the World Bank, the population problem was one of "a mismatch between population and income-producing ability . . . that leaves many of the world's people in a vicious circle of poverty and high fertility."[1] The Cocoyoc Declaration (see below) noted that "the huge contrasts in per capita consumption between the rich minority and the poor majority have far more effect than their relative numbers on resource use and depletion."[2] From a pre-Stockholm position of rejecting the economic and social mores of capitalist society and seeking changes outside established institutions, a new generation of environmentalists had turned a decade later toward a policy of compromise, of using polit-ical, economic, and social systems to achieve change within themselves. The new environmental slogan was "sustainable development."

Like so many "new" environmental concepts before and since, there was little new about sustainable development. It had been espoused by German and Indian foresters, and by Roosevelt and Pinchot. Delegates to Lake Success in 1949 and Bukavu in 1952 had talked of the need to man-age natural resources rationally. IUCN had suggested the need to recon-cile conservation and development policies as early as 1956. At Arusha in 1961 it was noted that "only by the planned utilisation of wildlife as a renewable natural resource . . . can its conservation and development be economically justified in competition with agriculture, stock ranching and other forms of land use."[3] IUCN had launched the African Special

Project largely because it felt that existing foreign aid programs were "prone to overlook conservation and the value of wildlife and habitat as a continuing economic, scientific, and cultural asset."[4] At the First World National Parks Conference in Seattle in 1962 it was resolved that conservation was an important element of development and that international agencies should incorporate ecological studies into their planning.[5] Also in 1962, the UN General Assembly adopted a resolution on Economic Development and the Conservation of Nature, which endorsed an earlier UNESCO resolution that, to be effective, measures to preserve nature and natural resources "should be taken at the earliest possible moment simultaneously with economic development."[6] In 1970, Paul and Anne Ehrlich argued that aid to the developing world had been "much too little and too ecologically inept";[7] the industrialized North had made the fundamental error of basing its standard of progress on expansion of the Gross National Product and had become "overdeveloped." The less developed countries would be better advised to "semi-develop," and the priority should be ecologically sound agricultural development rather than industrialization.

For all this, there is no agreed definition of sustainable development. It is usually applied to LDCs and the kind of economic and social development needed to improve the living conditions of the world's poor without destroying or undermining the natural resource base. IIED attempted a definition in 1982: "the process of improving the living conditions of the poorer majority of mankind while avoiding the destruction of natural and living resources, so that increases of production and improvements in living conditions can be sustained in the longer term."[8] It may, indeed, be an approach to the problems of LDCs, but it is equally applicable to MDCs. A more appropriate and universal definition might be development that occurs within the carrying capacity of the natural and human environment.

Prior to Stockholm, the preoccupation among European and American environmentalists with the limits to growth had led most to overlook LDC problems. The change of emphasis following Stockholm was marked and rapid. The links between environment and development were raised so often that, at the fourth session of the UNEP Governing Council in 1976, several delegations questioned the need, apparently felt by the UNEP secretariat, to continue to defend the notion. The idea was well understood and well established, they protested; it could stand restatement, but no further elaboration was needed.[9] Yet elaboration of the issue has been at the core of the environmental debate since Stockholm. Environmental problems in MDCs have been portrayed as a result of overdevelopment (i.e., the reckless and profligate exploitation of natural resources) and in LDCs as a result of underdevelopment (unequal access to national wealth, lack of economic opportunity, and the unequal exploitation of natural resources).[10] A 1976 UNEP executive-director's report argued that the worst use of the environment was occurring "at the two extremes of the scale of wealth."[11]

The roots of the changed emphasis of the post-Stockholm environmental movement must be sought in four broader developments: the changing nature of international economic and political relations, the growth of a new global view of the environment, the need felt by many northern environmentalists to accommodate the differing priorities of the LDCs, and the growing self-confidence and sophistication of environmental NGOs. Where the environmentalists of the 1960s had espoused their cause as an alternative view for those who rejected conventional economic wisdom, those of the 1970s worked to incorporate new values into the policies of existing institutions, notably industry and government.

ENVIRONMENT AND DEVELOPMENT

Following Stockholm, UNEP and the UN Conference on Trade and Development (UNCTAD) suggested the need for meetings to discuss the implementation of the ideas raised at Founex and Canberra in 1971. Gamani Corea, chairman of the UN Committee for Development Planning, suggested that the major points for discussion, given the new Third World interest in the environment, should be the urgent need to provide guidance to planners and the question of the international distribution of wealth and income.[12] The meetings would bring together social and natural scientists in an attempt to define possible lines of collaboration between them and could be followed up with a series of regional seminars and conferences on environment and development. This would all lead to a proposed (but stillborn) Stockholm II conference to be held in 1977.

Two meetings—sometimes confusingly called "Canberra II" and "Founex II"—were held. "Canberra II"[13] met in Geneva in April 1974. The meeting agreed that, given the amount and diversity of the earth's resources, their physical availability would not be a serious problem in the foreseeable future, except in short- and medium-term applications. Rather, the resource problem was "one of the technological, economic and environmental implications of making sufficient quantities of natural resources available and of using them rationally for economic development."[14] The meeting concluded that, given the complexity of international economic relations, future development was likely to be constrained by problems in the distribution of natural resources well before any problems of finite quantities arose. This was a very different conclusion from those of Paul Ehrlich and the Club of Rome. Closer and more equitable economic cooperation between countries, the group noted, could form an important prerequisite for more rational resource management on a global scale.

The meeting also noted (not surprisingly, since it was held against the background of the 1973–1974 energy crisis) that natural resources were destined to play a much more important role in international affairs. LDCs, frustrated in their efforts to negotiate substantial changes in the existing world economic order, were "seriously studying the possibilities of using their natural resource endowment as an instrument to gain a better bargaining position." MDCs, for their part, were growing increasingly aware of the importance of a continuance of supply and had made greater efforts, even in the previous year, to decrease their dependence on imported raw materials and energy. The oil crisis had given LDCs a new sense of commodity power, leading to a new phase in North-South relations.[15] In May 1974, the UN General Assembly adopted a declaration calling for the establishment of a New World Economic Order that would provide a more balanced global economic structure. That same month, a small UNEP-UNCTAD meeting on Alternative Patterns of Development was held to discuss further the agenda for Founex II. The following were among the conclusions reached:

1) The development of LDCs was governed by the availability of natural resources to a far greater extent than in MDCs, where skills, capital resources, and technological capabilities were more influential.

2) The capacity to cope with environmental disruption was more limited in less developed countries, which had fewer technological and capital resources, than in more developed countries. Hence environmental degradation could have a more immediate and more rapid impact on economic development.

3) A fundamental rethinking of planning and development strategies was needed to give higher priority to social structures, more equitable distribution of income, and environmental issues. At the local level, far greater consideration should be given to local needs and conditions before, for example, using techniques, crop varieties, agricultural methods, and so forth, that had worked elsewhere.

"Founex II"[16] was held in Cocoyoc, Mexico, between 8 and 12 October 1974. It was chaired by Barbara Ward and drew together a group of 33 delegates from 22 countries (8 MDCs, 14 LDCs), including Mostafa Tolba, Maurice Strong, and Gamani Corea. It was held to discuss the relationship between environment and development in the light of the experience of the previous few years, to analyze the impact that environmental issues—and specifically the growing awareness of the limitations to natural resources—were having (or should have) on development strategies and international economic relations, and to provide an input into the rethinking on development and international economic problems then taking place in the United Nations.[17]

A perceptive declaration (drafted largely by Barbara Ward) was issued at the end of the symposium, summing up the points raised. It noted that more people were hungry, shelterless, and illiterate than when the UN was set up to establish a new international order. The world had yet to emerge from the consequences of nearly five centuries of colonialism, which had concentrated economic power in the hands of a small group of nations. Much of the pressure on natural resources was due to the disproportionately high consumption of resources in the industrialized North: "Pre-emption by the rich of a disproportionate share of key resources conflicts directly with the longer term interests of the poor by impairing their ultimate access to resources necessary to their development and by increasing their cost. All the more reason for creating a new system of evaluating resources which takes into account the benefits and burdens for the developing countries." The lack of resources for full human development was a continuing cause of population growth, and unequal economic relationships contributed directly to environmental pressures. Any process of growth that did not lead to the fulfillment of basic human needs (food, shelter, clothing, health, and education) was a travesty of the idea of development.

The declaration recommended that:

1) policies should be instituted aimed at satisfying the basic needs of the poorest, while ensuring adequate conservation of resources and protection of the environment;

2) governments and international organizations should promote the management of resources and the environment on a global scale;

3) strong international regimes should be set up for the exploitation of the global commons, this exploitation to be taxed so as to benefit the poorest countries;

4) new priorities were needed in scientific and technological research and development;

5) new development priorities should aim at curbing overconsumption in the North and stepping up the production of essentials for the poor.

The declaration ended by challenging the assumptions of New Environmentalism. The way forward did not lie through "the despair of doom-watching nor through the easy optimism of successive technological fixes," but through careful and dispassionate assessment of the "outer limits" of the earth's physical resources and through a search for ways to achieve the "inner limits" of fundamental human rights. Though Barbara Ward felt in retrospect that the "instincts" of Cocoyoc were correct,[18] and the conference developed further the concept of the relationship between environment and development, it ultimately had little lasting influence.

DEVELOPMENT AID POLICIES AND THE ENVIRONMENT

Following Stockholm, bilateral and multilateral aid agencies began thinking more carefully about the environmental viability of their programs. The pre-Stockholm concerns with population, pollution, and flawed technology now gave way to the role and effects of poverty. The World Bank estimated in the early 1970s that about 800 million people, or one fifth of the world's population, were so deprived of income, goods, and basic needs as to be members of the "absolute poor." World Bank president Robert McNamara[19] defined absolute poverty as "a condition of life so degraded by disease, illiteracy, malnutrition, and squalor as to deny its victims basic human necessities; a condition of life so limited as to prevent realization of the potential of the genes with which one is born; a condition of life so degrading as to insult human dignity."[20]

During the 1950s and 1960s, the conventional view in the development community was that economic growth was the most effective way of eradicating poverty. The best way to help the poor was to build the capital, infrastructure, and productive capacity of an economy; the gains of economic growth would "trickle down" to the poor through market forces creating jobs, raising productivity and wages, and lowering prices. But growth did not always reduce inequality; nor did income automatically trickle down to the poor. If anything, it promoted dualism—the emergence of a modern, urban sector alongside stagnation in the rest of the economy.[21] To make matters worse, much aid was being spent on nonessential prestige projects (such as new highways, airports, and conference halls). In the 1970s, attention turned to the notion of economic growth with income redistribution,[22] and finally to the idea that the provision of basic needs (such as food, health, education, shelter, water, and sanitation) was more important to the poor than the rather more nebulous question of equality.

By the late 1960s, several development aid agencies had become aware that the efficacy of their aid was often undermined by the lack of any consideration for its environmental effects. Much aid was wasted because it either resulted in, or was undermined by, environmental degradation: soil erosion, desertification, siltation of dams, failure of irrigation systems, and so on. The Conservation Foundation in the United States had, in the 1960s, already begun thinking about the need to take ecological factors into account in development planning. In 1968 it sponsored a conference at Airlie House, Virginia, on the Ecological Aspects of International Development, which concluded that development economists, planners, engineers, and ecologists should refer more closely to one another in the design of development projects.

More meetings followed Airlie House, involving the World Bank, FAO, UNDP, IUCN, the International Biological Programme (IBP), and the Conservation Foundation. At the suggestion of Max Nicholson (on behalf of IBP) a meeting was held at FAO in Rome in 1970, involving all these groups and the aid agencies of Canada and the United States. It was decided that IUCN and the Conservation Foundation should prepare a guidebook for development planners. The book, *Ecological Principles for Economic Development*, was published in 1973, authored by Raymond Dasmann of IUCN and John Milton and Peter Freeman of the Conservation Foundation.[23] The authors examined the ecological principles that needed to be considered in instances where economic development threatened major modifications of natural systems and argued that the UNESCO/FAO definition of conservation as "the rational use of the earth's resources to achieve the highest quality of living for mankind" could equally well be used to define the goals of economic development; consequently, there should be growing convergence rather than conflict between the aims of conservation and development. Adequate consideration of ecological principles would help developers and conservationists achieve their goals with the minimum of undesirable side-effects. The ecological limitations on natural systems had to be taken into account if development was to succeed. The book set out in general terms the ecological and development needs of humid tropical areas and of pastoral lands in semi-arid and semi-humid regions, and assessed the impact of the development of tourism, agricultural development projects, and river basin projects. It explored general ideas rather than laying down comprehensive principles. IUCN subsequently pursued some of these ideas through meetings and the publication of a series of guidelines on development planning.

In the period 1977–1979, IIED undertook a series of revealing studies of the environmental policies of selected bilateral and multilateral development aid organizations.[24] Four major problems were identified in financing institutions generally: (1) the lack of any clear procedures for the environmental assessment of projects (with the exceptions of the World Bank and the Organization of American States), (2) a general lack of criteria for assessing environmental impact (stemming in large part from the lack of conceptual definitions of what constituted environmental concerns), (3) the lack of alternative forms of analysis and accountancy, which included the long-term social and environmental effects of development projects, and (4) a lack of personnel with appropriate training.

The first of the IIED studies focused on multilateral aid agencies. It concluded that, of the nine agencies studied, the World Bank had the most advanced environmental policy and practices and "undoubtedly exerts intellectual leadership on environmental matters in the whole international development community." This was thanks in large part to the personal influence and interest in environmental matters of Robert

McNamara.[25] The World Bank had established a new post of Environmental Advisor in 1970 (a move dismissed by the bank's critics as
window-dressing) and adopted the policy of considering environmental
factors in its economic assistance policy. In a 1970 address to ECOSOC,
McNamara acknowledged that finance institutions faced the problem of
making sure that development assistance avoided environmental damage
without slowing economic growth.[26] In 1972 the World Bank had published a handbook for those involved in development projects (including
engineers, planners, and finance institutions).[27] It listed, point by point,
the questions that should be raised during planning and appraisal. It was
by no means perfect. Although it covered industry, transport, utilities,
and energy, it barely touched on agriculture. It was also very general,
making little allowance for the problems of specific communities. But it
was the first major effort by a lending institution to establish criteria for
evaluating the environmental impact of its investment projects.[28]

The World Bank met early resistance to its new environmental concern
from LDCs; many feared that incorporating environmental protection
provisions in projects would add 25 to 50 percent to total project costs.
These fears were placated by the bank agreeing to cover any additional
costs involved in meeting the necessary standards.[29] In actuality, the
bank found that the additional costs were of the order of 0 to 3 percent.
World Bank policy was that the environmental and health aspects of
projects should be analyzed at the formulation and design stages. An
analysis of 1,342 projects receiving World Bank loans and credits between 1 July 1971 and 30 June 1978 found that 63 percent revealed no
apparent or potential environmental problems. In 365 cases (27 percent
of the total), those environmental problems that were identified were
dealt with by bank staff; in 110 instances (8 percent), the environmental
problems appeared sufficiently serious to require special studies by consultants, and environmental safeguards were incorporated as a condition
of lending. In the remaining 22 cases, other agencies had earlier determined the need for safeguards and appropriate action had been taken.[30]

The second IIED study examined the environmental policies of six bilateral aid organizations (those of Canada, West Germany, the Netherlands, Sweden, the United Kingdom and the United States).[31] It found
that the confusion that had existed four years earlier over the meaning of
"environment" had been resolved, and that the environment was not
being seen as an additional subject for consideration but increasingly as a
"new approach to development which gives greater weight to the sustainability of results and to the costs of destructive side effects of
projects." However wide the acceptance of this view in principle though,
it had still had "too little impact on the orientation and design of the
projects or practical development policies of the agencies studied." An
earlier study of the U.S. Agency for International Development (USAID)
had concluded that, despite the addition in 1977 of an Environment and

Natural Resources sector to the Foreign Assistance Act and the foundation of a number of USAID projects aimed at natural resource maintenance, USAID's efforts had lacked clear authority and had been "piecemeal and subject to tortuous justification."[32]

The IIED study of bilaterals concluded that environmental and resource objectives needed more thorough definition in the context of aid policies as a whole, that urgent attention was needed to help LDCs build their own capacity to study and manage their own environmental problems, that environmental enhancement projects needed support comparable to that given to traditional development sectors, and that aid agency policy documents frequently lacked adequate attention to environmental factors. Four out of the six agencies had clearly defined focal points for environmental responsibility, but only one (that of the United States) systematically screened projects for their environmental impact.[33] There was consensus in the six agencies on the need to integrate a broad concept of "environment" into development thinking and planning, but "this rhetorical commitment, with exceptions, has not been quickly matched by specific action." A separate study of the Canadian International Development Agency (CIDA) found "an informal and, at times, haphazard approach to environmental concerns."[34] The study found that CIDA lacked a strong commitment to incorporating environmental concerns in regular policy planning, that there was no systematic assessment of the environmental consequences at the project proposal stage, and that inadequate monitoring and evaluation procedures meant that there was little feedback into CIDA on the environmental consequences of projects.

British aid policy was even less enlightened. In 1982 it was Overseas Development Administration policy to "take into account" the environmental implications of aid projects and to bring the implications of these projects to the attention of recipient governments, but to give advice "strictly" on request; "it is for the governments of the developing countries themselves to decide what priority they wish to give environmental factors within their own development programmes. This is a political issue to be considered against the demands for economic and social development in any individual country."[35] The policy of Commonwealth agencies involved in development was likewise to respond to requests for advice more often than to initiate ideas and programs. Few, if any, Commonwealth activities acknowledged in any formal way the environmental dimension of development.[36]

In September 1979, nine months after the publication of the first IIED study, representatives of the nine multilateral agencies examined met in Paris under the auspices of UNEP, the World Bank, and the UN Development Programme (UNDP) and agreed upon a joint declaration (signed in New York in 1980) undertaking to pursue new policies in seven areas identified by the study, including the systematic examination of all development policies and projects to ensure that appropriate measures were proposed for compliance with the principles and recommendations of Stockholm. The declaration noted that economic development was essential to the alleviation of all major environmental problems, and acknowledged that aid agencies had a responsibility to ensure the sustainability of the economic development activities they financed.[37]

The cumulative effects of ill-advised or badly planned development, and the role in this of development aid policies, were illustrated in a report published by the World Bank in 1984 on development in sub-Saharan Africa.[38] The report concluded that the region faced serious social and economic problems, with political instability, declining gross domestic product and agricultural output, growing malnutrition, and a deteriorating natural environment. The key causative factors, it argued, were accelerating population growth, declining returns from investment, and the effect of government and aid donor policies on the efficiency of resource use. While many aid agencies, encouraged by UNEP, had agreed in principle to undertake environmental impact assessments of aid projects, "this promise has yet to be translated into widespread action—and few privately financed projects receive proper advance environmental analysis."[39] Nevertheless, UNEP believed that there had been a shift in emphasis from "an almost purely technical approach to a broader societal one, considering developmental goals from the point of view of values and ethics rather than purely from the point of view of quantitative economic growth, and the long-term rather than the short-term."[40] This had apparently reached the point at which some planners believed that real development could not be achieved by copying the West, where industrial growth had been exploitative, and so, unsustainable.[41]

ENVIRONMENTAL POLICY IN THE THIRD WORLD: KENYA AND INDIA

Just as MDCs reviewed their environmental policies in the late 1960s and early 1970s, so too did many LDCs. The number of less developed countries with environmental agencies grew from 11 in 1972 to 102 in 1980.[42] But, as with MDCs, simply creating an agency was not the same as creating an *effective* agency. The new LDC agencies not only faced many of the political and jurisdictional problems experienced by their counterparts in MDCs (notably the lack of authority given to new environmental agencies), but many had their own additional problems: all too frequent political and economic instability, the priority given to economic development at almost any cost and the lack (with some exceptions) of a substantial middle class, an environmental movement, a firm institutional or legal framework, and a solid data base. Emil Salim, the Indonesian Minister for Population Affairs and the Environment, while agreeing with the need to protect his country's genetic wealth, pointed out in 1982 that Indonesia lacked "the precise knowledge of what constitutes our own natural wealth and how to protect it."[43] Development of the legal framework (including regulatory agencies and procedures, backed up by trained personnel) for environmental action was uneven, and such legislation as existed was often difficult to enforce or was poorly implemented. Few LDCs had explicit national environmental policies. While industrialized nations had some success in carrying out environmental inventories and implementing development plans, progress in poorer countries was variable. Concepts such as sustainable development were useful guides to development projects, but did not meet with widespread application.[44]

Kenya should in theory have fared better than most. It is the site of UNEP, it has hosted key environmental conferences, it has a relatively well developed NGO network, and it has enjoyed relative economic prosperity and political stability since independence in 1963. It has a limited arable land base but enough productive land to feed (in theory at least) its rapidly growing population. It is also well endowed in other natural resources. Yet the indications are that it faces an "increasing, horrifying, long-term loss of natural resources for short-term returns."[45] The losses result from overgrazing, the expansion of cultivation into marginal rainfall areas, deforestation, the uncontrolled expansion of new settlements, the destruction of upper catchment areas, and river siltation. Kenya's population growth rate of 4.2 percent[46] is the fastest in the world, and it shows little sign of slowing. If it continues, it will double the national population every 18 years.

In their study of environmental policy in Kenya, Randall Baker and David Kinyanjui concluded that Kenya in 1980 had neither an environmental policy nor an integrated land use policy on a national scale.[47] This was despite major statements on environmental management by Presidents Kenyatta and Moi in turn, and general agreement among ministry and departmental staff that such an environment policy was a priority. The Kenyan National Environment Secretariat (NES) concluded that plans for the introduction of an environmental impact assessment requirement would have no effect as long as there was no environment policy "and so long as its implementation will be vested in the very institutions which have exacerbated, if not precipitated, existing problems."[48] In the 1979–1983 Five-Year Plan, resource use policies were listed as the responsibility of the NES and the National Council for Science and Technology, yet neither was a policymaking organ. In 1980 Kenya had 14 separate pieces of legislation relating to natural resources and resource management, but they were very rarely applied.

Baker and Kinyanjui found, among other problems, an overlap and confusion of responsibilities (e.g., 26 institutions with an interest in water alone), the nonapplication of law, a fundamental conflict between

MPs representing rural constituents facing land shortage and sectoral bodies supporting tougher and more comprehensive legislation, laws divorced from the social and economic reality of the situation they were supposed to police, an absence of organized monitoring and data gathering at the national level, and a NES lacking policies, legislative authority, local representation, and political power. The position has been further complicated by interdepartmental rivalries; seven out of a total of 20 ministries have an interest in natural resource matters: the ministries of planning and national development, environment and natural resources, lands and settlement, water development, tourism and wildlife, agriculture and livestock development, and energy and regional development.

India's problems are similar, but obviously much bigger. It has an extensive body of environmental legislation dating back to the Shore Nuisance (Bombay and Kolaba) Act of 1853.[49] A National Committee on Environmental Planning (NCEP) was set up in 1972 to act as an advisory body to the government (Indira Gandhi took an active personal interest in environmental issues). The limitations inherent in the power of an advisory body led in 1980 to the creation of a Department of the Environment (DOE) under the direct charge of the prime minister to appraise development projects, monitor pollution, and regulate and conserve marine ecosystems and biosphere reserves. The environmental appraisals have had some success, for example, the inclusion of pollution abatement measures in a fertilizer plant near Bombay and the amendment of plans to build a hydroelectric project inside a wildlife sanctuary in the state of Tamil Nadu.[50] The DOE has also identified potential biosphere reserves and made a nationwide survey of important wetlands, and the NCEP— before its closure—encouraged state governments to set up their own environmental boards. By 1985, 18 out of 22 states had their own environment departments, and there were more than 200 national and state laws relating to the environment.[51]

But the failures outweigh the successes. Ramakrishna notes the degree of uncertainty about the legislative authority of central government to implement environmental statutes, enforcement problems, and the lack of a private right of action.[52] In a survey of 30 pieces of environmental legislation, the committee responsible for the creation of the DOE noted four basic flaws: (1) many promoted development and resource use for specific economic benefits without careful analysis of the potential environmental effects; (2) several state laws had potentially adverse environmental implications for neighboring states; (3) many laws were clearly inadequate (e.g., the Insecticides Act of 1968 did not encourage a transition away from pesticides such as DDT which had been banned elsewhere and lacked adequate provision for monitoring the incidence of pesticide residues); (4) the environment was such a new policy area that it was still widely ignored or overlooked within government departments.[53] The NCEP and DOE additionally had little credibility with other government departments. For a department with such potentially enormous responsibilities, the DOE in 1983–84 had just 237 staff and an annual budget of $16 million (200 million rupees).[54] And despite the extensive body of pollution legislation, Indian industry remained either reluctant to control pollution or beyond the reach of the law; in 1985, the Minister of State for the Environment reported that there were about 4,000 polluting industries in India, of which just 200 had installed effluent treatment plants.[55]

Nowhere were the weaknesses in India's pollution control system more tragically or dramatically illustrated than in the escape of methylisocyanate gas from a Union Carbide pesticide plant in Bhopal in December 1984. Estimates of the immediate death toll varied from 1,300 to 10,000; the figure most often quoted now is about 2,500, although people continued to die from the effects several years later. UNICEF estimated that about 200,000 people in all (of whom 75 percent were local slum dwellers) were affected.[56] Three particular problems were underlined by the Bhopal accident. First, the inadequacy of regulations on pollution standards and chemical safety and of the zoning system which allows so many of India's poor to live so close to industrial plants; second, the inadequacy of the government's disaster response system ("the government's centralisation and lack of initiative," noted the Centre for Science and Environment, "so visible on ordinary days, caused it to literally collapse under stress");[57] and third, the economic and political value system that allows multinational corporations to operate plants at standards of efficiency and safety below those they would have to meet in more developed countries. The sheer number of fatalities at Bhopal was unprecedented, but similar accidents had occurred before in India and elsewhere, and the probability of future incidents remains high.[58]

Both Kenya and India have an active and vocal nongovernmental environmental movement. Of the 60 Kenyan organizations active in tree-planting alone, the most prominent is the Green Belt Movement, set up by the National Council of Women of Kenya in 1977. Headed by Wangari Maathai, a former anatomy professor, the movement helps local communities establish tree plantations on open spaces, in school grounds and along roads.[59] By 1987, there were more than 1,000 green belts, 20,000 "mini-green belts" on farmers fields, and 65 community tree nurseries. Another active group is the Kenya Energy NGOs Association (Kengo), which took part in a successful USAID-funded project to test and distribute cheaper and more efficient jikos (charcoal-burning stoves).

India boasts literally thousands of citizen groups, from local grassroots movements to broader national organizations. The power of grassroots movements is epitomized by the record of the Dasohli Gram Swarajya Mandal (DGSM).[60] Formed in 1964 to encourage forest-based cottage industries in the northern state of Uttar Pradesh, DGSM quickly found that it had no rights or control over local forests and that outside contractors were able to pay much less than the market value for local forest products. DGSM began a local public awareness campaign to draw the attention of local people to what was happening. Local resistance to the powers of outside contractors gradually became more militant, such that by 1973–74, local villagers (mainly women) were banding together to physically prevent the felling of trees. The resultant Chipko Andalan—or "movement to hug trees"—subsequently attracted worldwide attention and admiration for its nonviolent Gandhianism, although more than a decade later its goal of changing state forestry policy in Uttar Pradesh remained unfulfilled. At the national level, India also boasts one of the most energetic NGOs in the less developed world—the Centre for Science and Environment (CSE). Overseen by Anil Agarwal, CSE published reports on the state of India's environment in 1982 and 1984–85 which gave the most comprehensive and thorough assessments yet compiled of the environmental problems of an LDC (and, indeed, of almost any country).

In neither Kenya nor India does the government work as closely with NGOs as it might; NGOs thus lack the kind of access to policymaking that would give them the influence they seek. In India, the government works only with urban-based NGOs and often actively opposes the work of the rural NGOs, which are closest to the needs of India's rural majority.[61]

THE WORLD CONSERVATION STRATEGY

Stockholm placed the environment firmly on the agenda of international relations. As the identification of transboundary problems (e.g., acid pollution) and problems common to several countries (e.g., soil erosion, pollution, and deforestation) grew, so it became increasingly evident that much greater international cooperation was needed. Max Nicholson had written of the need for a world conservation program as early as 1966, although the scheme he envisaged was limited to wildlife. He observed that limited resources and an insufficient information base were discouragements to a scheme at that time, but that by 1970 a world strategy could be a practical possibility: "such a programme might be of value in focussing world opinion on the scale, nature, and distribution of the main ascertainable conservation requirements. Presumably it would be for IUCN to take the initiative here, enlisting such help as might be required and appropriate."[62]

IUCN began considering a strategic approach to conservation at its General Assembly in New Delhi in 1969.[63] Raymond Dasmann (author of the 1973 handbook on ecological guidelines) recalls that, at the time he joined IUCN in 1970 as a senior staff ecologist, there had been three changes in the Union: it had new leadership, a new organizational structure, and it had been given a major grant from the Ford Foundation. Ford had suggested the need for more centralized control by IUCN headquarters over its activities. Dasmann noted the influence of a new intercommissional marine conservation program at IUCN, which emphasized "planning, programming, strategy, and tactics."[64] This approach now pervaded the work of all IUCN commissions and was, in Dasmann's view, "one impetus that led to the strategic approach to world conservation problems." A more significant development noted by Dasmann was the shift in emphasis at IUCN toward a concern for economic development. Following the 1969 General Assembly, the 1970 Rome meeting (see above), and the publication of *Ecological Principles for Economic Development*, IUCN gave more thought to the matter. Conservation and development was the theme of the 1972 IUCN General Assembly in Banff, Canada, when Maurice Strong indicated that IUCN would receive funding from UNEP once the latter had been set up.[65]

During 1973 and 1974, a number of meetings were held within IUCN to formulate ecological guidelines for development; two sets, on tropical forests and mountains, were completed. Serious discussions on a strategic approach to conservation were begun at a meeting in 1975 between IUCN and UNEP. IUCN's Australian deputy director-general, Frank Nicholls, was keen that IUCN be clear on its future conservation policies, on the main priorities, and on the action needed to put policies into effect. At this meeting, UNEP asked IUCN to prepare a strategy for the conservation of wildlife, designed solely to determine the priority actions needed to protect and save wild species. Over the next two years, Dasmann and Duncan Poore (acting directors-general in turn) worked on drafts of the Strategy. UNEP appeared to have no clear idea of what form the Strategy should take, so the initial design of the document was left largely to Dasmann and Poore; its origins were very narrow, which Allen feels reflected to an extent IUCN's field of expertise.[66] Lee Talbot (later IUCN director-general) recalls that "the first draft was essentially a wildlife textbook," but that each subsequent draft brought the previously opposing views of developers and conservationists closer together, and that the final draft was a consensus between the two points of view.[67]

Until the late 1970s, IUCN conservation policy had been determined every three years by the General Assembly and guided in the intervening period by the Executive Board. But IUCN lacked the benefit of a coherent and integrated plan of action; its activities tended to be "a collection of projects, often individually valuable, but lacking the coherence and . . . the impact of a planned programme."[68] The first significant attempt to change this was the triennial strategy document for 1976–78, prepared by Duncan Poore and adopted at the 12th General Assembly in Kinshasa in 1975. This outlined four main objectives for the Union; the first three concerned the conservation and protection of plant and animal species, representative ecosystems and habitats, while the fourth spoke vaguely of establishing "a framework of wise use which ensures that the potential of renewable natural resources is maintained."[69] IUCN should strike a balance between "working to a long-term, phased world conservation strategy" and reacting to sudden opportunities and urgent problems. One of the guiding principles outlined in the document was that conservation programs should be treated "as an integral part of the plans for social and economic development in the regions or nations concerned."[70] Every effort should be made to involve local people in conservation projects, taking full account of their needs, attitudes, and knowledge. IUCN's priority was still clearly the conservation of nature, but there was evidence that it was becoming more interested in "ecodevelopment" (i.e., the development of a locality, taking fullest sustainable advantage of its physical, biological, and cultural resources). Writing in *IUCN Bulletin* in May 1976, Allen noted IUCN's interest in the concept, which, he observed, "appears to be the long-awaited reconciliation of conservation and development."[71]

IUCN announced that it was preparing a World Conservation Strategy (WCS) in October 1977. Dasmann left IUCN in 1977, and Poore followed in 1978; thereafter, the strategy was guided by Robert Allen (one of the authors of *A Blueprint for Survival*, now IUCN head of publications, and later senior policy adviser) and IUCN's Canadian director-general, David Munro, ostensibly in consultation with UNEP, FAO, and UNESCO, and with UNEP funding. The strategy, said IUCN, would enable international conservation action to be directed more effectively, identify the main threats to species and ecosystems, and propose action and priorities. It would be essentially a UNEP/IUCN/WWF policy document, although it would be available to other interested organizations and would also be aimed at influencing governments, UN agencies, and intergovernmental bodies. It would not be confined to threatened species or areas in need of special protection but would also cover species and areas of economic value that were being misused, such as wild and semidomesticated relatives of cultivated plant and animal species or fisheries and their supporting coastal wetlands. It would provide "for the first time a global perspective on the many problems with which conservation is concerned."[72] A first draft was to be sent to all IUCN members in December 1977, to expose it to the widest possible discussion. In an address to the 1978 General Assembly in Ashkhabad, USSR, Lee Talbot noted that this consultation on the World Conservation Strategy should be "the first of many demonstrations that the secretariat regards itself increasingly as a clearing-house of information, a presenter of opinions, and a rehearser of arguments."[73] Different economic, geographic, and conservation priorities had to be included.

A second draft had been prepared for submission to the Ashkhabad General Assembly. Its reception was generally positive, but its omissions were noted. A fuller, more focused discussion of the relationship between conservation and socio-economic factors, particularly population increase, was needed. In addition, a more thorough account was needed of the development process and of how the Strategy should influence it, and more details were needed on conservation education, planning and legislation, pollution, toxic chemicals, and soil and water conservation, Much more was needed on implementation of the Strategy—on *how* the recommended action could be achieved rather than *what* action was necessary, and more explicit and precise recommendations to governments on its implementation were needed.[74] Many LDC delegates pointed out—as they had done before and since Stockholm—that they faced more pressing environmental concerns than the protection of nature. Wildlife problems could not be treated in isolation, and there was clearly support for the idea that the Strategy should be more broadbased.

The point was also made at Ashkhabad that IUCN had the opportunity to influence multilateral and bilateral aid policies and should seize it. The Strategy did not pay enough attention to the potential for conservation-oriented development projects and to the introduction of principles of conservation into projects that might otherwise be destructive of the environment. IUCN should try to influence multilateral and bilateral aid agencies so their activities were in line with the WCS. The assembly resolved that the version of the WCS presented to the next ordinary session of the General Assembly, "while continuing to concentrate on conservation issues, shall place conservation firmly in its socio-economic context, with due reference to population and such other major influences as poverty, economic growth, the conservation of energy and raw materials, inappropriate technologies, and the satisfaction of basic human needs."[75] This, IUCN noted, was a "departure from traditional conservation concerns."[76] (Despite these hopes, the published Strategy—while including arguments about population, food, and soil erosion—remained essentially a document on nature conservation.)

A key paper before the Ashkhabad General Assembly—based on a poll of past and present IUCN executive board and council members and secretaries and directors general—summed up the successes and failures of international conservation, and particularly of IUCN. It concluded that much had been achieved in the 30 years since the foundation of IUCN, particularly in the development of national parks, legal and organizational frameworks, and data-gathering. But there had been continuing (even accelerating) destruction, degradation, and depletion of ecosystems and species, and a prevailing lack of public awareness about the importance of ecosystems and species. The achievements of the international conservation movement were small, scattered, and perhaps also temporary. In order to make real headway, much greater unity of purpose was needed, which meant agreement on a strategy of action and the implementation of that strategy.[77]

In February 1979, IUCN announced that the World Conservation Strategy (WCS) would be launched in September that year. A third draft, reflecting the views of the 14th General Assembly, had been reviewed by a panel appointed by the IUCN council in January, and the public launch of the WCS would be designed (with the help of $700,000 of UNEP funding) to attract as much media publicity as possible and achieve the greatest possible impact on decisionmakers and the public.[78] Ashkhabad had decided that the WCS should not be a definitive document, but should be revised and updated every three years and reviewed by the General Assembly. Part of the UNEP funding of IUCN was to go toward the preparation of a second edition for submission to the 15th General Assembly in 1981. In fact, the WCS was not itself updated, but, rather, was adapted through the formulation of national conservation strategies, the need for which was first realized as early as 1976.[79] By May 1979, the launch of the WCS had been postponed until March 1980; although publication had been agreed by the IUCN council panel, the penultimate draft had met with considerable criticism from UN agencies, and a number of changes had been requested. A WCS Launch Committee consisting of representatives from IUCN, UNEP, and WWF was set up in January 1979 to plan the launch, and national committees were formed in several countries to plan national launches and to discuss plans to implement the Strategy. The final draft of the Strategy went before UNEP, FAO, UNESCO, WWF, and the IUCN council in August 1979 and was finally approved in October. In December, IUCN published its policy document, which had been prepared in consultation with UNEP and WWF as a plan for IUCN policy in 1980–1982 in order to give IUCN "a more measured approach to conservation action."[80] It was based on the same principles as the WCS.[81]

The simultaneous launch of the WCS in 40 or more countries in March 1980 confirmed the trend already evident of a reappraisal of policy at an organizational level within IUCN and at a conceptual level in the conservation movement as a whole. As far as IUCN was concerned, it had been 25 years since its title had changed from "protection" to "conservation" of nature and natural resources, but until the launch of the WCS "there really was no broadly accepted platform reflecting this change, no reference base for reconciling the classical requirements of nature protection and those of sustainable economic progress."[82] The definition of IUCN's goals had, in Talbot's opinion, been long overdue. The launch of the WCS gave substance to the reformulation of IUCN's agenda. IUCN established two new ventures in the immediate wake of the Strategy. In April 1981 the Conservation for Development Centre was set up within IUCN to promote the integration of conservation in the planning and implementation of economic development. Its first tangible action on environmental impact assessment was a consultancy project to help the Natural Resources Board of Zimbabwe assess alternative energy development. In January 1982, IUCN established the Joint Environmental Service with IIED to help LDCs create or strengthen planning, education, and NGOs and legal frameworks, thereby improving their ability to promote environmentally sound land-use planning and environmental impact assessment, mainly with LDC governments and international development agencies.

By the admission of its authors, the WCS was a compromise document. It not only represented a consensus of IUCN's members and the agencies involved in its drafting, but it set out to lay down priorities for conservationists with different interests and attempted to reach an accommodation between conservation and development. It also gave a generalized and simplified view of the problems and issues involved. The Strategy's aim was to "help advance the achievement of sustainable development through the conservation of living resources."[83] It was needed, said its drafters, (a) because of the rate at which resources were being destroyed or depleted, (b) because of the rate at which demand was increasing, (c) because corrective action would take time to implement and to show results, and (d) because existing national and international conservation programs were ill-organized and fragmented, enjoying little influence over the development process. It was aimed at government policymakers, conservationists, and development practitioners (including aid agencies, industry, and commerce). Conservation was defined as "the management of human use of the biosphere so that it may yield the greatest sustainable benefit to present generations while maintaining its potential to meet the needs and aspirations of future generations." This embraced "preservation, maintenance, sustainable utilization, restoration, and enhancement of the natural environment." The specific objectives of conservation, as outlined by the WCS, were:

1) The maintenance of essential ecological processes and lifesupport systems such as soil, forests, agricultural systems, and coastal and freshwater systems. This meant reserving good cropland for crops, managing cropland to high and ecologically sound standards, protecting watersheds and coastal fisheries, and controlling the discharge of pollutants.

2) The preservation of genetic diversity for breeding projects in agriculture, forestry, and fisheries. This meant preventing the extinction of species, preserving as many varieties as possible of crop and forage plants, timber trees, animals for aquaculture, microbes and other domesticated organisms and their wild relatives, protecting the wild relatives of economically valuable and other useful species and their habitats, fitting the needs of ecosystems to the size, distribution, and management of protected areas, and coordinating national and international protected area programs.

3) Ensuring the sustainable utilization of species and ecosystems. This meant ensuring utilization did not exceed the productive capacity of

exploited species, reducing excessive yields to sustainable levels, reducing incidental take, maintaining the habitats of exploited species, regulating international trade in wild species, carefully allocating timber concessions and limiting firewood consumption, and regulating the stocking of grazing lands.

The Strategy opened by reiterating the view that conservation and development had long been seen as incompatible and that conservationists had fostered this view by appearing to resist development. Development practitioners had, as a result, come to view conservation as irrelevant, harmful, and antisocial. In fact, the Strategy argued, development that was sustainable and able to meet the needs of the world's rural poor in particular had to be based on sound conservation: "there is a close relationship between failure to achieve the objectives of conservation and failure to achieve the social and economic objectives of development—or, having achieved them, to sustain that achievement." The WCS outlined the priority areas for international action:

1) Law and international assistance. Although there were more than 40 multilateral conventions dealing with the management of living resources, few had conservation as their primary purpose.

2) More effective management of tropical forests and drylands.

3) A global program for the protection of genetic resource areas.

4) More effective management of the global commons—the open ocean, the atmosphere, and Antarctica and the Southern Ocean.

5) Regional strategies on international river basins and seas.

Everything in the WCS was in turn underwritten by the goal of sustainable development.

On a national level, the priorities included national conservation strategies, the integration of conservation and development, environmental planning, legislation, and a review of organization, training and research, public participation, education, and conservation-based rural development. National conservation strategies (NCSs) were promoted by IUCN as the best means by which individual countries could find their own way to sustainable development. Preparing an NCS would ideally be a cooperative venture in which government agencies, NGOs, private interests, and the community would take part. In this way, IUCN hoped, "sectoral interests will better perceive their interrelationship with other sectors. . . . Indeed, unless those responsible for implementing the strategy have been involved in the process and are convinced of its message, the ultimate effect of the NCS will be severely limited."[84] Furthermore, IUCN noted, an NCS could not and should not be produced according to predefined formulae—different countries had different needs. IUCN hoped that governments would take responsibility for preparing NCSs, since they would be responsible for implementation. The nation was not the only unit for a strategy—local provincial strategies or multicountry strategies were equally feasible. IUCN, UNEP, FAO, and UNESCO made themselves available to provide technical assistance and advice.

In September 1983, IUCN reported that 32 countries (including ten MDCs) had taken some form of action on national conservation strategies. Of these, 14 were "considering" the need for an NCS, 15 had either begun or completed early drafts, and three (South Africa, Spain, and the United Kingdom) had completed and launched national strategies. Britain's contribution was verbose and meandering—it did not augur well for the quality of national strategies in general. By 1987, 41 countries had acted or were thinking of action, but only five more—Australia, Madagascar, New Zealand, Vietnam, and Zambia—had published an NCS.[85] Thus, seven years after the launch of the World Conservation Strategy, only eight countries (out of more than 160) had taken tangible action. There was clearly much more to be done before the WCS could be acclaimed as a real breakthrough. IUCN's own program of technical assistance had been devoted almost entirely to LDCs, where it had only limited success, for four reasons:

1) Initial requests for assistance were normally made by natural resources or environment ministries rather than through central development planning authorities. Hence development aid agencies had found it difficult to provide financial support. The planning authorities were more inclined to deal with more conventional projects—such as energy, industry, agriculture, or rural development—than to consider the logistics of requesting financial support for the development of a conservation strategy.

2) The achievement and maintenance of a long-term view on planning was hindered by frequent changes of government in LDCs.

3) The interests supporting rapid economic growth and returns were often powerful, better organized, and more concentrated than those promoting the prevention of environmental degradation.

4) The impact of MDC demands on the global resource base was considerable, so their trade policies had a major influence on the supply and demand of resources in LDCs.

In retrospect, the Strategy will probably be seen as a useful step forward but one that was ultimately incomplete. In some ways, it was behind the times and too restricted to the more narrow traditional IUCN view of the natural world. By the late 1970s, it was already clear that environmental policy had to move well beyond the conservation of nature and natural resources and into the sphere of the human environment; Stockholm had shown that only too clearly. The WCS was a useful and manageable first move (if ultimately of variable utility and practicality); what the world would eventually need, though, was a more broad-ranging World Environment Strategy.

NINE

The Global Environment

By the mid-1970s, few countries, if any, could claim to be unaffected by environmental problems of some kind. Equally few remained untouched by the rise of the environmental movement. Whether rich or poor, industrial or agrarian, authoritarian or democratic, socialist or capitalist, almost every society felt compelled to reassess its attitudes toward resource management and the condition of the human environment. Bolstered by improved data gathering and analysis, awareness of national problems had grown to the point where it was now clear that there were many environmental problems that were either common to more than one country or were transnational, even global. Issues like marine pollution, whaling, fisheries, desertification, acid pollution, depletion of the ozone layer, and carbon dioxide build-up could not be solved by individual governments acting alone. Notice of this had been served by the nuclear fallout debate in the 1950s. The obvious response was greater international cooperation.

Stockholm had provided a compelling spur to internationalism. In a foreign policy address to Congress in 1970, Richard Nixon had said: "We know that we must act as one world in restoring the world's environment, before pollution of the skies overwhelms every nation."[1] In 1972, Falk observed that just because the most manifest impacts of environmental problems were found on the domestic level, these were not "potentially the most serious for either the United States or for the world."[2] In his Environmental Message to Congress in May 1977, President Carter noted the growing understanding that environmental problems did not stop with national boundaries and directed the CEQ and the State Department to study probable changes in global population, natural resources, and the environment to the end of the century. Their findings were to serve as the basis for longer-term U.S. planning policy. The resultant study, *The Global 2000 Report to the President*, was submitted in 1980.

GLOBAL 2000 AND THE RESOURCEFUL EARTH

Global 2000 concluded that there was "the potential for global problems of alarming proportions by the year 2000," that changes in public policy were needed, and that, "given the urgency, scope, and complexity of the challenges before us, the efforts now underway around the world fall far short of what is needed. An era of unprecedented global cooperation and commitment is essential. The necessary changes go beyond the capability of any single nation."[3] *Global 2000*, as its authors rightly noted, was not the first U.S. government investigation into natural resource futures. Theodore Roosevelt's National Conservation Commission, Franklin D. Roosevelt's National Resources Board, and Truman's Materials Policy Commission had all examined similar, though less comprehensive, questions. *Global 2000* was, however, the first attempt by any government anywhere to examine the interdependence of population, resources, and environment from a longer-term global perspective. Cleveland feels that the real importance of *Global 2000* lay not in the discovery and extrapolation of known trends in familiar categories, but in the fact that a single national government had pulled projections on a variety of issues into "a package that compels, or at least strongly encourages, a comprehensive view."[4]

Although it did not set out to make predictions, the outlining of projections in the future tense made *Global 2000* sound very much like a predictive document.[5] It warned that if "present trends continue, the world in 2000 will be more crowded, more polluted, less stable ecologically, and more vulnerable to disruption than the world we live in now. Serious stresses involving population, resources, and environment are clearly visible ahead. Despite greater material output, the world's people will be poorer in many ways than they are today."[6]

Specifically, the report concluded that by the year 2000:

1) world population would increase by a half, the greatest growth being in less developed countries;

2) the gap between the richest and the poorest—measured in terms of per capita GNP, and the consumption of food, energy, and minerals—would widen;

3) there would be fewer resources available—notably land, water, and petroleum;

4) important life-supporting ecosystems—such as forests, the atmosphere, soil, and wildlife species—would be reduced;

5) prices of many of the most vital resources would increase;

6) the world would be more vulnerable to natural disaster and to disruptions from human causes.

While *Global 2000* outlined the problems, possible solutions were listed in a subsequent document, *Global Future: Time to Act*.[7] Three reasons were given for why the United States should take an interest in global resource impoverishment and environmental degradation: the moral question of poverty and misery for the world's poorest people; the oft-quoted "future generations" argument; and self- interest, viz., the threat to U.S. political and economic security. Broadly speaking, *Global Future* recommended increased financial and scientific assistance from the United States for international programs, together, in some cases, with setting a good example at home, for example, by using its agricultural land sustainably and working toward ensuring that 20 percent of U.S. energy be derived from renewable resources by the year 2000.

If there was one clear lesson to be learned from the *Global 2000* exercise, the authors of *Global Future* noted, it was that the United States government lacked the capacity to anticipate and respond effectively to global issues. Hence—among other things—changes in governmental institutions were needed. The authors recommended the creation of a new government center to coordinate data gathering and modeling to support long-term global policy analysis, a new office in the White House devoted solely to long-term global issues, an interagency coordinating committee, and assignment of these tasks to the CEQ. But none of these recommendations was instituted, for the Reagan administration had by then come into office and chose to ignore *Global 2000*.

The report also had its detractors outside the Reagan administration. In the tradition of the earlier critics of the prophets of doom came the New Pollyannas, led by Professor Julian Simon, an economist at the University of Illinois and then of Maryland, and Herman Kahn of the Hudson Institute, New York. In 1981, Simon argued that while there had been regular warnings of deteriorating natural resources and growing human needs, the trends in both areas were in fact *positive;* the authors of *Global 2000* offered no persuasive evidence to support their case, and the facts, as he read them, pointed in quite the opposite direction.[8] Like Simon, Kahn and Schneider argued that the generally positive response to *Global 2000* served to reinforce the prevailing pessimism of society. They were concerned at the effects on social morale of reports like *Global 2000*, which, they felt, were inspired by the "prejudices, guilt feelings, and class interests . . . of the affluent, the elite, and the privileged". They regarded *Global Future* as more restrained and reasonable, "perhaps because it appears to reflect the thinking of bureaucrats more than the predispositions of professional environmentalists."[9]

In 1983, Simon and Kahn collaborated briefly in compiling *The Resourceful Earth*,[10] intended not so much to be an evaluation or criticism of *Global 2000* as an alternative view. In their commentary, they questioned all the major findings of *Global 2000* and argued, like Maddox before them (see chapter 4), that far more credit should be given to human ingenuity in solving problems. This was a valid point, but—here and elsewhere—Simon, Kahn, and Schneider revealed a perception of the world that was otherwise parochial and limited and often based on a selective use of data. For example, *Global 2000* had argued that income disparities between the wealthiest and poorest nations were projected to widen. Kahn and Schneider proclaimed that "only by consulting a statistical table in *Global 2000* can the reader learn that GNP per capita is projected to rise from $382 for the LDCs in 1975 to $587 in 2000, an increase of 50 per cent in two decades."[11] This was true enough. Yet that same table[12] shows that GNP per capita over the same period in more developed countries was projected to rise by *96 percent* and that while the 1975 per capita GNP in MDCs was over 11 times greater than that in LDCs, by the year 2000 it would be more than 14 times greater. This clearly supports the conclusion of *Global 2000*.

Simon and Kahn, for their part, suggested that "the world's people" had increasingly higher incomes, better housing, mobility, better roads, and more vehicles. If one believes that those North Americans, west Europeans, and Japanese with jobs are "the world's people," this is true. It is, however, patently not true in many LDCs. Simon and Kahn also argued that income in poorer countries was rising at a percentage rate as great or greater than in richer countries. Yet a very poor country would find it difficult *not* to increase its income proportionately faster than a very rich country, if only because it started from a much narrower base. Although the projected growth rate in LDCs in 1975–85 was 5 percent (compared to 3.9 percent in MDCs), there was a considerable difference between the projected GNP for LDCs and MDCs—respectively, $1,841 and $7,150.

AGREEMENTS ON THE GLOBAL ENVIRONMENT

One measure of the newly perceived importance of multinational responses to environmental issues was the growth in the number of international treaties and agreements in the post-Stockholm decade. Almost as many new international environmental agreements were reached in those ten years as had been reached in the previous 60 years (see Table 4). A 1984 UNEP register[13] lists 108 agreements, of which 58 date from the period 1971–83. The more comprehensive list compiled in 1985 by Burhenne[14] includes 257 multilateral treaties, 200 (77 percent) of which were signed after 1960, and 108 of those (42 percent of the total) after 1970. This proliferation was a function of four main factors: (1) the work of the new national environmental agencies and the growing body of national laws, (2) the availability of better—and more compelling—data, (3) the influence of greater public awareness, and (4) the trend toward greater international cooperation on a wide variety of issues.

But the quality of the new laws and agreements did not always match the quantity. The success of any agreement must be measured by the level of actual compliance by signatories. This in turn is a function of the

TABLE 4:

International Conventions, Protocols, Treaties and Amendments Relating to the Environment: 1911–1983.

Subject	Year signed							
	1911–20	1921–30	1931–40	1941–50	1951–60	1961–70	1971–80	1981–83
Pollution (including marine)	—	—	—	—	1	5	19	6
Marine/ fisheries	—	—	—	3	8	4	10	5
Nature/ natural resources	1	—	2	1	—	1	3	—
Toxic substances (including radiation)	—	1	—	—	3	4	2	—
Animals	—	—	—	1	1	1	6	—
Regional development	—	—	—	—	1	2	4	—
Insect pests	—	—	—	—	—	4	—	—
Plants	—	—	—	—	4	—	—	—
Ecosystems	—	—	—	—	—	—	2	—
Birds	—	—	—	—	1	1	1	—
Environment	—	—	—	—	—	—	1	—
TOTAL	1	1	2	5	19	22	47	11

SOURCE: United Nations Environment Programme, *Register of International Treaties and Other Agreements in the Field of the Environment* (UNEP/GC/INFO/11) Nairobi: UNEP, May 1984.

efficiency of enforcement, which is a function of the financial and personnel resources available, which is a function of political will. On this basis, international treaties with an environmental dimension vary in their efficacy from the Partial Test Ban Treaty (total compliance) to the Convention on International Trade in Endangered Species (CITES) (steady progress, with the benefit of a secretariat and reasonably strong funding) to the Wetlands Convention (little progress, few legally binding obligations, and no secretariat).

Most international treaties, especially multilateral agreements, are undermined by three major weaknesses. First, there is the problem of enforcement. Although international treaties are by definition firm and binding rules of law, compliance cannot be enforced in the same sense as domestic law.[15] In many cases, the appeal is made less to the letter of law than to morality and "playing the game"—signatories are influenced as much as anything by the opprobrium of attracting the criticism of other members if they do not adhere to the spirit of an agreement. Early European conventions, the Western Hemisphere Convention, and the 1968 African Convention all became "sleeping conventions" because none had established adequate systems of enforcement or administration.[16] If negotiations fail to resolve a dispute, states have recourse to international arbitration or, more rarely, to the International Court of Justice. On the whole, the best means of ensuring compliance is through nonjudicial mechanisms, for example, regular meetings of the parties to a convention (which remind them of the provisions of the treaty), the establishment of administrative bodies to oversee the treaty, and regular reporting requirements. Lyster notes also the influence of NGOs in improving compliance with treaties; by attending meetings of signatories, NGOs not only provide technical expertise, but can police the implementation of conventions and publicize contraventions or discrepancies.[17]

The second weakness of international treaties is structural: as the objects of treaties have become more complex, so their contents have become less precise, and their effectiveness less predictable.[18] Haigh cites the example of the convention on long-range transboundary air pollution (see below). A comparison of the text of the convention with that on which it was modeled—a Nordic Council convention—reveals that the greater number and variety of contracting parties produced a convention that was less precise, less constraining, and less likely to be effectively enforced than its progenitor.[19]

Finally, once an agreement has been ratified, there is the problem of transforming its principles into national law and then of actually implementing the national law. Because treaties and conventions are often no more than agreements in principle, influenced (and even weakened) by the need to accommodate the different priorities of signatory nations, there is often a great difference between what is agreed during negotiations and what is subsequently found to be acceptable to national parliaments.[20] Such treaties as CITES, for example, depend for their implementation on domestic law, which in turn depends on the effectiveness of government agencies, which is almost universally limited (see chapters 7 and 8). The bartering that precedes an international agreement often results in a text so general and nonspecific that every state can interpret it differently, producing different national legislation and different results.[21] The Stockholm Declaration provides some examples. Principle 3 observes that "the capacity of the earth to produce vital renewable resources must be maintained and, *wherever practicable*, restored or improved" (my emphasis); Principle 16 notes the need to apply demographic policies *"which are deemed appropriate* by the governments concerned"; Principle 21 notes that states have, in accordance with the principles of international law, "the sovereign right to exploit their own resources pursuant to their own environmental policies."

Some of the effects of these weaknesses are illustrated by the mixed record of international treaties on wildlife and the natural environment. Between 1900 and 1980, 18 such treaties were agreed, ten of them between 1968 and 1980 (see Table 5). The four agreements generally regarded as most important[22] were those on wetlands, the world natural and cultural heritage, international trade in endangered species, and migratory species, all signed between 1971 and 1979.

The wetlands convention was the first treaty to aim for truly worldwide participation and the first to concern itself exclusively with habitat.[23] Designed to protect a global chain of wetlands used by waterfowl in their annual migrations, it was signed on 2 February 1971 and came into force on 21 December 1975. Unlike earlier conventions touching on habitat, which emphasized the setting aside of exclusive protected areas, the convention emphasized sustainable use; the only restriction it placed on the use of wetlands was that their ecological character should not be harmed. Maltby notes that the convention was a first step toward placing international obligations on the land management decisions of sovereign states.[24] It has helped prevent development in listed wetlands of international importance, for example, plans to dam Britain's River Ouse in 1976 were changed when it was pointed out that the Ouse Washes were listed under the convention.[25] But it has also had too few legally binding obligations on its parties (Lyster notes that requiring parties to "promote the conservation of listed sites" does not legally oblige them to ensure that listed wetlands are actually protected).[26] Parties have been reluctant to list more than one or a few sites, and there have been too few non-European parties (and particularly too few from tropical regions).[27] It has also lacked adequate finance and a secretariat.

The World Heritage Convention, which is administered by UNESCO and came into force on 17 December 1975, is aimed at protecting natural and cultural sites of global significance. The convention is limited somewhat by its selectivity; listed sites must be considered to be both of

Table 5:

Multilateral International Wildlife Treaties

Name of convention	Year signed	Year came into force
Convention for the Preservation of Wild Animals, Birds, and Fish in Africa	1900	—
Convention for the Protection of Birds Useful to Agriculture	1902	1905
Treaty for the Preservation and Protection of Fur Seals	1911	—
Convention Relative to the Preservation of Fauna and Flora in their Natural State—"London Convention"	1933	—
Convention on Nature Protection and Wildlife Preservation in the Western Hemisphere	1940	1942
International Convention for the Regulation of Whaling	1946	—
International Convention for the Protection of Birds	1950	—
Interim Convention on the Conservation of North Pacific Fur Seals	1957	—
African Convention on the Conservation of Nature and Natural Resources	1968	1969
Benelux Convention on the Hunting and Protection of Birds	1970	1972
Convention on Wetlands of International Importance Especially as Waterfowl Habitat—"Ramsar Convention"	1971	1975
Convention for the Conservation of Antarctic Seals	1972	1978
Convention Concerning the Protection of the World Cultural and Natural Heritage	1972	1975
Convention on International Trade in Endangered Species of Wild Fauna and Flora—"CITES"	1973	1975
Agreement on the Conservation of Polar Bears	1973	1976
Convention on the Conservation of Migratory Species of Wild Animals - "Bonn Convention"	1979	1983
Convention on the Conservation of European Wildlife and Natural Habitats—"Berne Convention"	1979	1982
Convention on the Conservation of Antarctic Marine Living Resources	1980	

national and universal value. But listing gives sites a prestige value that provides poorer parties with the prospect of receiving financial and technical assistance for the protection of sites.[28] (In 1985 the future of the convention was cast into doubt by the withdrawal of the United States and Britain from UNESCO; the United States had been contributing 25 percent of the annual budget of the World Heritage Fund.) The Convention on International Trade in Endangered Species, which was signed on 6 March 1973 and came into force on 1 July 1975, aims to regulate or prevent trade in a specified list of endangered or threatened wild animal and plant species. By 1985, 87 states were party to CITES, which had the benefit of a full-time, paid secretariat, initially funded by UNEP but subsequently by CITES parties. Most of the major wildlife trading nations had signed CITES within a decade of its being opened for signature. The fourth major convention (the Migratory Species Convention, or Bonn Convention) was a direct product of the Stockholm conference. It was signed in Bonn on 23 June 1979, but came into force only on 1 November 1983, by which time it was clear that to be effective it needed a large number of signatories. It also faced financial and administrative constraints.

REGIONAL ORGANIZATIONS: THE ENVIRONMENT IN WESTERN EUROPE

When it comes to enforcing international agreements, regional or intergovernmental organizations have two clear advantages; they can exert moral, if not legal, pressure on national governments, and they provide administrative continuity (the OAS and the Western Hemisphere Convention being one notable exception). Western Europe has a plethora of IGOs and INGOs, many of which have addressed environmental issues. Air pollution, for example, has been addressed by the Nordic Council, the specialized UN agencies, the UN Economic Commission for Europe, the OECD, and even NATO. Declaring its intention in 1970 to change from pursuing economic growth for its own sake to pursuing qualitative growth, the OECD set up an Environment Committee to collect information to be fed into OECD policy- and decisionmaking.

The Europeans have managed to agree on shared problems—particularly ocean, river, and air pollution—more quickly than might have been the case almost anywhere else in the world. The first major body in Europe, and the first broadly-based international body anywhere,[29] to take an interest in the environment was the Council of Europe (founded in 1949). The Council set up the European Committee for Conservation of Nature and Natural Resources (CDSN) in 1963 to draw up a plan of action on the management of Europe's natural resources. In the same year, following the success of National Nature Week in Britain, the Council declared 1970 European Conservation Year (ECY) with the aim of promoting a communal European sense of the extent and value of Europe's natural resources, of the character of man's destructive abilities, and of the need for sound long-term management. ECY promoted public awareness and influenced political opinion in the period prior to Stockholm and spawned a series of European ministerial conferences on the environment (Vienna 1973, Brussels 1976, Bern 1979, Athens 1982). ECY also provided a focus for the debate on population, pollution, and growth; "thus by accident a wider and more conservative audience was provided for the radical questioning of the adequacy of man's custody of natural resources and the benefits of science and technology," notes Haigh.[30]

But ECY also had its critics. "All talk and little action—that's the state of play in European Conservation Year," noted Britain's then opposition environment spokesman Christopher Chataway.[31] "Already the cynics are calling it European Conversation Year" noted Robert Allen in the *Ecologist*. While conceding that ECY had "put new heart into the conservationists, bringing them in from the wilderness they so earnestly strive to protect," Allen argued that at the close of the year most politicians had sidestepped its deeper implications and that had the British government taken it more seriously there would already have been some constructive political action.[32]

In 1967, the Council of Europe established a European Information Centre for Nature Conservation within CDSN to promote awareness of the environment. Latterly, a project to create a network of representative European nature reserves led to the drawing up of the Convention on the Conservation of European Wildlife and Natural Habitats (the Berne Convention), which was opened for signature in 1979 and came into force in 1982. The council also promoted architectural conservation, town planning, regional planning, and pollution control (e.g., the 1968 Water Charter and the 1972 Soil Charter).

Because of its unique powers to create legislation binding upon its member states without further review or ratification, the European Economic Community (EEC) is the regional body with the greatest potential for taking effective action on the European environment. When Britain entered the Community in 1970, there were those who feared that it might have undesirable environmental implications; Brian Johnson suggested that Britain's traditionally steady but slow economic growth had left it with an essentially green and pleasant land despite the rigors of the Industrial Revolution (Britain in fact had less forest cover than any Community state but Ireland and had been losing wildlife and habitat steadily since the Second World War); the doctrine of economic growth espoused by Europe would create as many problems for Britain as it solved, he argued, and Britain's total environmental prospects might be "bargained away in political-economic package deals like the federation of Europe."[33]

For all its teething problems (notably those resulting from misplaced agricultural policies), the Community has achieved positive action on the environment. This began in October 1972, when a meeting of EEC heads of state and government concluded that economic development had resulted in inequalities in living conditions within the Community, that the ecological basis of this development was threatened, that economic expansion was not an end in itself, and that more attention should be paid to social goals such as the quality of life. So they declared themselves in support of a European environmental policy. Since then, there has been a steadily growing body of directives, regulations, and decisions on water, air, and noise pollution, waste, chemicals, wildlife, and the countryside—between 50 and 100 by 1985, depending on the criteria used.[34] These have been agreed unanimously and with only temporary blockages, notes Haigh, and without reaching the point of near immobility that tends to afflict many other areas of Community policy. Indeed, he argues, environmental policy "can now be counted as one of the quiet success stories of the Community," and is being seen to be increasingly important as acid deposition, vehicle emissions, and the movement of hazardous wastes across frontiers show that national measures are not enough.[35] The effect of EEC membership on Britain has been significant; Haigh argues that it is harder to point to changes in British domestic environmental policy resulting from Stockholm than to changes resulting from membership of the EEC.[36] Community directives on air pollution have introduced the concept of air quality standards to Britain,[37] and some of the confusion in the division of domestic responsibilities between local, regional, and national authorities in Britain has been bypassed by the transferrance of certain powers to the Community level (e.g., on setting the lead content of fuel).

Community environment policy is determined largely by the transnational nature of many European environmental problems. It is aimed, says the EEC, at bringing economic expansion "into the service of man" through environmental protection and natural resource management. The Community uses the Polluter Pays Principle, has proposed the introduction of U.S.-style environmental impact assessments, and is developing an ecological mapping project. The First Action Programme (1973–77) concentrated on control of pollution and nuisances, while the Second Action Programme (1977–81) was based on the principle of combining environmental considerations with economic policies.[38] The Third Action Programme (1982–86) included proposals for environmental coordination and recommendations on EEC foreign environmental policy: "The Community will continue to speak in various international organizations with a single voice, using to advantage the influence it has acquired in other areas of international cooperation . . . More specifically it will use this influence to ensure that plans drawn up at the international level, such as those of the UN Environment Programme and the World Conservation Strategy . . . are actually implemented."[39] The Programme went on to note the importance of environmental protection as an integral part of development policy. But Community action programs are not binding on member states, there is no guarantee that words will become actions, and no guarantee that Community members or recipients of Community aid will always agree with its priorities.[40]

EEC activities on the environment have also owed much to the role of NGOs. A key cooperative channel is the European Environmental Bureau (EEB), set up in 1974 specifically as a response to the assumption of environmental responsibilities by the European Community[41] (see chapter 5). The EEB provides environmental groups with a direct channel of access to the EEC. The European Commission regards the Bureau as a source of advice and information and provides it with funding (which to some extent determines the EEB's style of advocacy as one of reasoned and moderate argument rather than open confrontation). Its status under Belgian law means it must avoid overt political stances, has limited powers of sanction against disputed policies, and must reach a compromise between the differing tactics of its member organizations and the different national political styles of lobbying.[42]

SINGLE-ISSUE AGREEMENTS: ACID POLLUTION AND THE CONVENTION ON LONG-RANGE TRANSBOUNDARY AIR POLLUTION

No matter how much agreement there may be between two or more countries on an issue, there are some problems that cannot be solved with anything short of regional or even global agreement. Nowhere is this more clearly illustrated than in the question of air pollution, historically treated as a local issue. In an attempt to control local air pollution in Britain and other industrial countries in the 1950s, tall smokestacks were built at many power stations and factories. London happily lost its infamous yellow smog (about which George Gershwin had written so eloquently), but only at the cost of dumping the pollution further afield. Sulfur dioxide (SO_2) and nitrogen oxides given off by the burning of fossil fuels had long been implicated in the acidification of soils and surface waters. Now, as research confirmed the long-range effects of this pollution, acid pollution became one of the most serious of all international environmental issues, straining relations between governments (e.g., the United States and Canada, Britain and Norway), dividing countries into polluters and polluted, and testing political will to protect the environment.

Acid pollution is often described as a modern problem, but links between industrial emissions and the health of people and plants were noticed in England as early as the seventeenth century by John Evelyn and John Graunt.[43] They also noticed that some of the pollution was drifting across to France and suggested even then that taller chimneys be used to disperse the pollution. In the early eighteenth century, Linnaeus himself noted sulfur pollution near a smelter in Sweden. The process of acid pollution was first fully spelled out by the British chemist Robert Angus Smith,[44] who noted the correlation between coal burning and acid pollution in and around Manchester in the mid-nineteenth century. He published his findings in 1872 in *Air and Rain: the Beginnings of a Chemical Climatology*.[45] He was the first to use the term "acid rain," and to describe the connection between the burning of coal, wind direction, corrosion, and acid damage to vegetation. In 1881, a Norwegian scientist attributed "dirty snowfall" in Norway to either a large town or an industrial district in Britain.

By 1942, research on acid precipitation had spread to Austria, the United States, Canada, Sweden, Italy and Ireland.[46] In 1948, on Swedish instigation, systematic monitoring of precipitation on a Europe-wide basis was begun. In the 1960s, Svante Oden (a soil scientist at the Agricultural College, near Uppsala, Sweden) demonstrated a link between industrial emissions and environmental damage (largely to fish and lakes). He argued that precipitation over Scandinavia was becoming more acidic and that large quantities of the sulfur compounds that caused the acidification came from British and central European industrial emissions. It thus appeared conceivable that pollutants could travel 600 miles (1,000 km) or more. In April 1972 the OECD launched a four-year study into the causes, transport and effects of sulfur emissions. The results, published in 1977,[47] provided further evidence of the causes of acid pollution and confirmed that airborne pollutants could and were being transported across frontiers and were measurably affecting precipitation in other countries. In five of the 11 participating countries (Finland, Norway, Sweden, Austria, and Switzerland), more than half the total deposition of sulfur was estimated to come from foreign sources. The OECD project also revealed that the problems were not confined to Western Europe, but involved all European countries north of the Alps.

At the 1975 Helsinki Conference on Security and Cooperation in Europe, the Soviet Union suggested that attempts be made to reach agreement on three pan-European problems: energy, transport, and the environment. Western European countries concluded that only the latter was politically acceptable, and Sweden and Norway immediately took the opportunity to pursue the issue of transboundary air pollution. Their aim was to draw up a convention on long-range transboundary air pollution to be signed by all European states, the United States, and Canada.[48] The UN Economic Commission for Europe (ECE) was chosen as the best forum for discussion, mainly because it included east and west European states.

Sweden and Norway wanted a strong convention that would halt increases in SO_2 emissions (the "standstill" clause), together with a clause that specified SO_2 abatement by fixed percentage levels of up to 50 percent (the "rollback" clause). Britain and West Germany objected to legally binding controls, the former because it questioned whether Scandinavian acidification was caused by British pollution, the latter because it was reluctant to be policed by the ECE.[49] West Germany eventually accepted a compromise convention consisting of general obligations on the signatories to at least limit, and preferably reduce, air pollution, including long-range transboundary air pollution. This was to be done with the use of the "best available technology that is economically feasible" in new and retrofitted plants. These terms—"best available technology" and "economically feasible"—were subsequently given wide and loose interpretation.[50] Britain, too, finally accepted the convention, because it believed that its plans for increased reliance on nuclear power would bring a net reduction in emissions, so it could meet the terms of the convention without changing its existing energy or pollution control policies.[51] The Nordic plans for goals, timetables, abatement requirements, and enforcement provisions were excluded.

The Convention on Long-Range Transboundary Air Pollution (the LR-TAP convention) was signed in Geneva in November 1979 by 33 countries (including Britain, the United States, West and East Germany, France, and the European Community) and entered into force in March 1983. It has since been criticized for its lack of real power, yet it was the first time that the countries of East and West Europe and North America had joined in the signing of an environmental agreement. It also had the positive effect of strengthening the key European data gathering network—the Cooperative Programme for Monitoring and Evaluation of Long-Range Transmission of Air Pollutants in Europe (EMEP). EMEP, designed to provide information on the transboundary flow of air pollutants, has been operating since 1978; by 1985 it had 88 monitoring stations in 23 countries in East and West Europe.[52]

To keep up the momentum, Sweden then invited all the signatories to the convention to the Conference on the Acidification of the Environment, held in Stockholm in June 1982 (the tenth anniversary of the 1972 conference). The conference was held in two stages: a scientific and technical meeting and a ministerial meeting. The first meeting scrutinized all the evidence on the causes, transport and effects of transboundary air pollutants and concluded that man-made sulfur and nitrogen compounds were primarily responsible for acid deposition; a decrease in emissions over a large industrialized region would lead to an "approximately proportionate" decrease in acid deposition; the technology was commercially available that could radically reduce emissions of air pollutants; and the fact that improved technologies may emerge in the future did not justify waiting and delaying the use of existing technology.

The ministerial meeting adopted these conclusions, agreed that acidification problems were serious, and concluded that even if total deposition rose no further, damage to soil and water would continue to increase unless prompt action was taken within the framework of the convention. West Germany took the opportunity to announce a complete reversal of its previously lukewarm policy on acid pollution; it announced that it would try to halve its SO_2 emissions in ten years and would raise the question of the international environment at the next world economic summit. The *volte face* was ascribed to the growing momentum of *die Grünen* and the first confirmed reports of widespread West German forest damage.[53]

The 1982 Stockholm conference also speeded up the process of ratifying the LRTAP convention; within a few months, all the European Community countries had ratified. But it still had little substance, and the Nordic countries were still dissatisfied with the lack of real political action. Keeping up the pressure, they now proposed a mutual 30 percent reduction of SO_2 emissions in the ten years 1983–93, calculated from emission levels in 1980. In March 1984, representatives from ten countries met in Ottawa to sign a five-point declaration undertaking to reduce the emissions that led to acid pollution. The minimum was the 30 percent SO_2 reduction proposed by the Scandinavians—hence the agreement was dubbed the "30 Percent Club." By April 1985, 21 countries had joined the Club.[54]

A second international conference (the Multilateral Conference on the Environment) was held in Munich in June 1984, with the partial aim of encouraging more countries to join the 30 Percent Club. Pressure for a specific agreement on the reduction of annual national sulfur and nitrogen oxide emissions was growing. At the second meeting of the executive board of the LRTAP convention in September 1984, work was begun on drawing up a protocol on the reduction of sulfur emissions. This was adopted at the third board meeting in Helsinki in July 1985, committing its signatories to a 30 percent cut in annual national sulfur emissions or transboundary fluxes by 1993 at the latest, based on 1980 levels. The 21 members of the 30 Percent Club immediately signed the protocol; Britain and the United States deferred yet again. Their original accession to the LRTAP convention had now become almost meaningless.

International negotiations on the acid pollution issue were characterized by three main features. First, the level of government interest and action was often in direct proportion to the degree of domestic damage identified. The Scandinavian countries and Canada—where most of the damage had been confirmed—were the most vocal; the West Germans changed policy only when faced with proof of substantial damage to forests within their own borders; Britain, where relatively little damage was either proven or officially acknowledged, steadfastly refused to act. Second, governments were often concerned less with whether to act to curb emissions than with the costs involved and who should pay. Britain and the United States argued that too little was known about the causes and effects of acid pollution to justify the expense of controls; Britain argued that it had already reduced SO_2 emissions by 42 percent between 1970 and 1985 simply by using lower sulfur coals, using energy more efficiently, and "industrial restructuring"; Poland (another laggard) argued that for economic reasons there was very little chance of it being able to reduce its emissions.[55]

Finally, there was a marked lack of governmental interest in taking action on matters that did not have immediate national benefits. The only costs seriously considered by governments were those involved in reducing emissions. Theoretical estimates of the cost of damage to crops, forests, lakes, fisheries, health, and buildings apparently carried little weight in political decisions.

Acid pollution proved a particularly bitter issue in relations between the United States and Canada. A fundamental flaw in the Clean Air Act and U.S. pollution programs of the early 1970s was that they were designed mainly to address high pollutant concentrations near the sources and paid no heed to longer-range air pollution.[56] The use of taller smokestacks was, by implication, encouraged, with the result that 175 smokestacks over 490 feet (150 m) high were built between 1970 and 1979.[57] Research revealed that just as acid pollution was crossing national frontiers in Europe, so U.S. emissions were polluting Canada. In August 1980 the United States and Canada signed a Memorandum of Intent Concerning Transboundary Air Pollution (MOI), acknowledging the need for cooperative action to reduce pollution. Both governments agreed to take "interim actions available under current authority" to combat transboundary air pollution; the EPA however interpreted this as a commitment to control SO_2 emissions only to the extent allowed by the provisions of domestic law.[58] The MOI also established joint scientific working groups to develop a scientific data base; when their final reports were issued in February 1983, there were two sets of conclusions—one from Canada and one from the United States. Although both sets agreed on the dominant role of sulfur deposition in environmental degradation, the U.S. scientists argued that more research was needed before strict emission controls could be imposed.

Negotiations on an air quality agreement between the United States and Canada began in 1981.[59] In early 1982, the Canadian negotiators tabled a draft treaty based on a 50 percent reduction in SO_2 emissions from eastern Canada and a parallel "rollback" in the United States. This was rejected in June 1982 by the U.S. delegation; the United States questioned the sincerity of Canada's willingness to achieve such a dramatic reduction,[60] and accused Canada of being too hasty and premature in its action and accusations. The Canadians in turn accused the Americans of using delaying tactics and questioned the value of continued talks with the United States. Hopes were raised in Canada by the return to the EPA in May 1983 of William Ruckelshaus, who was directed by President Reagan to give priority to the acid pollution issue. Funding for research was even doubled.[61] Ruckelshaus worked to produce a plan that would be widely acceptable, but even his suggestion for modest cutbacks was blocked by Budget Director David Stockman and Energy Secretary Donald Hodel, who argued that it would be too costly to utility companies and their rate payers.[62] The impasse continued to place a strain on diplomatic relations between the two countries, and public statements on the issues were often characterized by rancorous language. Through the mid-1980s, acid pollution remained a major point of dispute at the regular U.S.-Canadian summits.

PROTECTING THE GLOBAL COMMONS:
THE OZONE LAYER

If agreement on shared resources or problems of transboundary air pollution seemed elusive, agreement on the much more nebulous concept of "the global commons" seemed out of the question—unless there was compelling evidence that even governments could not deny. Use of the oceans and the atmosphere was widely regarded as a free-for-all; the former as a medium of transport and a source of fish and minerals, and both as a useful dumping ground for effluents. Improved data gathering seemed to suggest new threats to the quality of the atmosphere in the post-Stockholm decade. Monitoring carried out since 1957 at the Mauna Loa observatory in Hawaii had already revealed a rise in the concentration of atmospheric carbon dioxide (CO_2), from 315 parts per million (ppm) in 1957 to 335 ppm in 1980, or 6 percent in 23 years.[63] The burning of fossil fuels was identified as the main source, but research in the late 1970s[64] suggested that deforestation and the removal of vegetation were also responsible for the release of CO_2; more CO_2 was stored in the earth's biomass than was held in the atmosphere. There were fears that the rise in CO_2 could lead to major climatic changes—including the so-called "greenhouse effect"—with profound social, economic, and political implications.

Similar fears were raised by the prospect that emissions of chlorofluorocarbons (CFCs), chlorinated compounds, carbon dioxide, and nitrogen oxides could react with stratospheric ozone, depleting the ozone layer and thereby increasing the level of harmful ultraviolet radiation reaching the surface of the earth. The effect of CFCs (compounds used in aerosol propellants, refrigeration, foam-blowing, and industrial solvents) was outlined by two University of California scientists, Mario Molina and F. S. Rowland, in 1974.[65] They warned that CFC use was on the rise and that ozone concentrations could be reduced by 20 percent. (Subsequent estimates by the National Academy of Sciences, UNEP, and the National Research Council put the figure at 16.5 percent, 10 percent and 3–5 percent respectively,[66] which says much about the difficulty of interpreting data and identifying trends.) The United States, Canada, and Sweden almost immediately banned the nonessential use of CFC propellants in sprays. The apparent result was a decrease in global CFC production between 1974 and 1979 of between 13 percent[67] and 17 percent.[68] Complete data have not been available since 1975 though, when the United States stopped reporting production levels in response to similar action by the USSR, Eastern Europe, and China. The best estimates in 1985 suggested that world production was up 6 percent on 1979 levels but was still lower than 1974 levels;[69] increased use in OECD countries and increased production and use in non-OECD countries may have accounted for this.[70]

Concerted UN action on ozone began with the launch (at a 1977 UNEP meeting of experts in Washington, DC) of the World Plan of Action on the Ozone Layer. Led by the World Meteorological Organization, the aim of the plan was to increase the number of monitoring stations. The meeting also set up a Coordinating Committee on the Ozone Layer (CCOL), which collected information about ongoing and planned research, publishing short annual summaries in the *Ozone Layer Bulletin*. By 1982, about 20 countries had taken action to control CFC emissions.[71] A study of six of those countries (including Britain and the United States) suggested that public attitudes, the presence of a strong regulatory agency, and the limited influence of CFC production on the national economy were key factors.[72] In 1981, a working group of legal and technical experts had begun work on a global ozone layer convention, following the pattern of UNEPs' Regional Seas Programme. In March 1985, the Global Convention on the Protection of the Ozone Layer was signed in Vienna by 28 countries. The adoption of protocols on control strategies was prevented by a disagreement between the EEC and Japan, and the "Toronto Group" of countries (the United States, Canada, Finland, Norway and Sweden); the former proposed a limit on production *capacity* (allowing a 30 percent growth in production), while the latter wanted more immediate and substantial reductions in aerosol use and a ceiling on per capita usage.[73]

The issue was given new urgency with the discovery in 1985 by British scientists of a thinning (or a "hole") in the Antarctic ozone layer.[74] The hole was roughly the size of the continental United States and appeared to be growing. Whether it was caused by CFCs, solar radiation, or polar meteorological conditions was unclear. Whether it was a phenomenon unique to the Antarctic or a warning of future changes in global ozone was also uncertain.[75] The scientists had noticed a dramatic drop in ozone levels ten years before, but the change had been so marked and abnormal that it had been put down to computer or human error.[76]

In February 1987, representatives of the major industrialized nations met in Vienna in an attempt to reach agreement on a freeze on CFC production levels and a gradual phasing out thereafter. By April, agreement had been reached in principle following a shift by the EEC away from a longer timetable for the freeze and reduction.[77] Final agreement was reached on 17 September 1987 at a meeting in Montreal, when 56 countries drew up an agreement to freeze consumption of the five most common types of CFC in 1990 at 1986 levels, followed by reductions of up to 50 percent by the year 2000. Two-thirds of the world's CFC consumer countries needed to sign the protocol to bring it into force. Fearing that nonsignatories would be given a competitive edge, the United States had initially argued for a minimum of 90 percent of consumer countries; to deal with this, the protocol included trade provisions allowing signatory countries to ban CFC-related imports from countries refusing to sign.[78]

THE NEED FOR SCIENTIFIC CERTAINTY

Inconsistent and incomplete scientific data has been repeatedly quoted by governments and industries opposed to action on environmental questions. The ozone issue showed how quickly governments could, in fact, agree on addressing a problem before the long-term effects were fully understood and agreed; the Ozone Convention was the first environmental agreement based on prevention rather than cure. Yet it also emphasized the problems of collecting and interpreting data on the atmosphere. Atmospheric conditions vary so much by time and place, and the combinations of factors (natural or man-made) involved in atmospheric changes can be so complex, that pin-pointing cause and effect can be very difficult. Over time, fluctuations increase, making it difficult to know whether changes are part of a new trend or a longer-term oscillation. Added problems arise from the lack of long time series, the effects of local factors on recording stations, and the relative lack of stations over the oceans.[79]

For UNEP, the application of the Stockholm Plan of Action had always demanded improved monitoring, data gathering techniques, and information exchange. Concerted attempts to improve the quality of data had begun with the International Biological Programme (see chapter 3). This closed in 1974, and the initiative passed to the UNESCO Man and the Biosphere (MAB) program. A product of the Biosphere Conference, MAB was designed as an intergovernmental and interdisciplinary research program based on 14 themes, from human interaction with ecosystems to the role of urban areas as ecological systems.[80] It had four main aims:

a) to identify and assess changes in the biosphere resulting from human activities (and the effects of those changes on man);

b) to study the interrelationships between natural ecosystems and socioeconomic processes;

c) to develop ways of measuring quantitative and qualitative changes in the environment in order to establish scientific criteria for the rational management of natural resources and the establishment of standards of environmental quality;

d) to encourage greater global coherence in environmental research.[81]

MAB had a small secretariat within UNESCO but operated in real terms through a network of 102 National Committees (made up mainly of scientists from universities or national research institutions) and representatives of relevant public and private bodies. The main policymaking body of MAB was the International Coordinating Council, elected by the General Conference of UNESCO and meeting every two years to review the program. By 1982, MAB covered 1,030 field research projects, associating over 10,000 researchers in 79 countries.[82]

The coordination and effectiveness of environmental research was helped by advances in computerized data storage and retrieval. The data collected was more precise and accurate, and many earlier assumptions based on inadequate information were undermined. For example, the rates of tropical moist forest loss assumed in the early 1970s were shown to have been exaggerated. For all its deficiencies (see chapter 6), the UNEP Earthwatch program had contributed to this progress. The MAB research and information exchange network had meanwhile helped provide a better understanding of the links between cause and effect in environmental problems at local, national, and international levels alike. It was now more clearly understood, for example (even if it was hardly a recent discovery), that the removal of forest cover on a hillside could lead to soil erosion, which could lead to siltation in rivers tens or thousands of miles downstream. The impact of environmental changes on food chains was better understood and appreciated, as were the mechanics of phenomena like acid pollution.

In 1979, the World Meteorological Organization, in conjunction with a number of UN specialized agencies, including UNEP and FAO, launched the World Climate Programme with the object of determining the extent of human influence on the climate. Different components of the program would work to improve the availability and reliability of climatic data and promote consideration of climatic factors in development planning. By 1981, a network of 109 regional monitoring stations in 71 countries had been set up in cooperation with UNEP to monitor, for example, CO_2 and contaminants in precipitation. There were growing suspicions that the world's climate was changing. Climatic variability is a natural phenomenon, and while climatic extremes are no evidence of climatic change, it seemed to many in the 1970s and 1980s that such extremes were becoming more common: severe droughts, low rainfall, high rainfall, heatwaves, "the hottest summer for 50 years," "the driest/mildest winter this century", and so on.

By 1986, greater consensus was emerging on the question of global climatic change. New and more sophisticated computer models suggested that the climate was not only growing warmer, but was doing so faster than scientists had predicted.[83] There were suggestions that the greenhouse effect could lead to increased temperatures of 3.5–4.2° C by the mid-twenty-first century[84] and that global sea levels could rise accordingly by 8–16 inches (20–40 cm).[85] Scientists recommended that regional studies be carried out on the impact and possible policy responses of such changes and warned that ozone depletion and climatic changes could no longer be considered unrelated issues.[86]

Meanwhile, the data in other areas remained incomplete or unreliable. Wildlife conservation provides an example. Without a complete inventory of the world's species, it is difficult to know which are endangered, to what extent they are endangered, and why they are endangered. Only about 1.6 million species have been classified and named; estimates of the actual total range from 5 to 30 million.[87] It is increasingly accepted that except in the cases of the rarest species, where captive breeding may be essential, wildlife can only be effectively protected in its natural habitat. Yet that habitat is being constantly changed and exploited. Given the rate of habitat destruction and the limited range of many species, it is conceivable that species extinction is a daily event. As recently as the 1960s, national parks were regarded as an effective method of protecting wildlife; by the late 1970s it was clear that few national parks in LDCs could continue to exist without more obvious economic benefits to local communities. Natural areas could not last "as fortress islands in seas of hungry people," noted Eckholm.[88] "Where large numbers lack a means to make a decent living, some are sure to invade national parks to grow food and cut wood. . . . Nature reserves cannot be successfully managed in isolation from local society. They must be planned within the context of broader regional development."

One area of particular concern was the narrowing of the genetic base of many of the world's crops and livestock, making them more vulnerable to pests, diseases, and changes in soils and climate. The destruction of wetlands and tropical moist forests, and the pollution of coastal waters, posed critical threats to wild genetic resources. In 1974 the International Board for Plant Genetic Resources (IBPGR) was set up in Rome to coordinate and encourage the collection, preservation, and exchange of plant genetic material. It made field collections of genetic material and rethought the best means for conserving genetic resources. The register of sites for *in situ* conservation was incomplete, and protection was not always adequate; hence *ex situ* germplasm collections were considered necessary. Much more progress was made in *ex situ* conservation; the IBPGR promoted base collections covering more than 20 of the world's most important crops, including wheat, rice, maize and barley.[89] In 1975, only eight institutions had the facilities for long-term seed storage; by 1983, the number had risen to 33.[90]

In 1982, UNEP warned that "the number of environmental parameters for which global trends can be stated quantitatively can be counted on one hand."[91] Holdgate and colleagues concluded that while there was relatively complete data on food production, fisheries, population growth, and industrial development, there was little reliable information on marine pollution and the status of inland waters and conflicting evidence on rates of tropical deforestation. Writing in 1982, they concluded that the world community had not yet achieved one of the major goals of the Stockholm conference: "the compilation, through a global programme of monitoring, research and evaluation, of an authoritative picture of the state of the world environment."[92]

Furthermore, while the new data which had been collected were now more accurate, they had the unfortunate effect of casting doubt on many earlier environmental assessments; Holdgate and colleagues note that "these advances hampered comparisons that might have revealed changes in the world environment between 1970 and 1980 because they cast doubt on so much of the earlier information."[93] Nonetheless, there were few who could now deny the global scope of many environmental problems. In a 1982 report, the OECD concluded that "a major implication of economic and ecological interdependence is that, as it inevitably increases, the ability of governments to deal unilaterally with problems on a national scale will diminish."[94] There would always be local or national problems demanding appropriate responses, but bilateral and regional responses had been proved to be workable if well planned. At the end of the day, the problems of the global environment demanded workable global responses.

THE WORLD COMMISSION ON ENVIRONMENT AND DEVELOPMENT

In September 1983, 38 years after UNSCCUR and 11 years after Stockholm, the UN General Assembly passed a resolution calling for the creation of a new independent commission charged with addressing the question of the relationship between environment and development, and with listing "innovative, concrete and realistic" proposals to deal with the question. The resulting World Commission on Environment and Development held its first meeting in Geneva in October 1984, chaired by Gro Harlem Brundtland, the Labor prime minister of Norway for nine months in 1981 (and again from May 1986). The Commission had 23 members—12 from the Third World, seven from the industrialized world (among them Maurice Strong), and four from the Communist bloc.

An unprecedented growth in pressures on the global environment had made grave predictions about the future commonplace, the Commission noted; a more prosperous, just, and secure future demanded policies aimed at sustaining the ecological basis of development, and at changing the nature of cooperation between governments, business, science, and people. Avoiding a reiteration of problems and trends, which had already been well covered by *Global 2000* and other reports, the Commission selected eight key issues (including energy, industry, food security, human settlements, and international economic relations) and examined them from the perspective of the year 2000. Between March 1985 and February

1987, it sponsored more than 75 studies and reports and held meetings or public hearings in ten countries, garnering the views of an impressive selection of individuals and organizations. In 1987, the report of the Commission was published as *Our Common Future*.[95]

The report concluded that environment and development were inextricable, and that existing policy responses were handicapped by the fact that existing institutions tended to be independent, fragmented, too narrowly focused, and too concerned with addressing effects rather than causes. (Hence problems like acid pollution were too often addressed as discrete policy problems.) The goals of these agencies were too often focused on increasing investment, employment, food, energy, and other economic and social goods rather than on sustaining the environmental resource capital on which these goals depended.[96] National frontiers had become so porous that the distinctions between local, national, and international issues had become blurred; domestic policies increasingly had effects well beyond national frontiers (e.g., acid pollution again). Greater international cooperation was needed, but international agencies—notably the UN system—were under siege at the time they were most needed.

Furthermore, the Commission concluded, environmental policy was too often accorded a secondary status; environmental agencies often learned of new initiatives in economic, trade, or energy policy (with possible consequences for resources) long after the effective decisions had been taken. It was time that "the ecological dimensions of policy [were] considered at the same time as the economic, trade, energy, agricultural, industrial, and other dimensions—on the same agendas and in the same national and international institutions."[97] National environmental protection agencies needed urgent strengthening, particularly in LDCs; UNEP's work needed to be reinforced and extended (notably through increased funding); monitoring and assessment needed better focus and coordination; policymakers needed to work more closely with NGOs and industry; law and international conventions needed strengthening and better implementation; and the UN should work toward a universal declaration and later a convention on environmental protection and sustainable development.

In the Brundtland Commission's critique of conventional environmental management and in its global view, Redclift sees the most radical departure yet from previous approaches to sustainable development. Yet, even before the final publication of the report, he felt it unlikely that MDCs or LDCs would act on the measures recommended by Brundtland; they could not do so "without involving themselves in very radical structural reform, not only of methodologies for costing forest losses or soil erosion, but of the international economic system itself."[98] Whether this process of reform had begun, or whether it could make headway against conventional political and economic attitudes to natural resources, struck at the very heart of the goals and philosophies of the environmental movement.

It had been nearly 125 years since the creation of the first government pollution agency, and 101 years since the first international environmental agreement. In the 20 years before Brundtland reported, more than 130 countries had created new environmental agencies, more than 180 international agreements had been signed, several thousand environmental NGOs had been formed, 113 countries had attended a landmark conference on the environment, and the United Nations had created a new global environmental program. Much of the structure was in place. The process of reform had surely begun.

CONCLUSION

Into the Twenty-First Century

The environmental movement has come a long way in a century. Its beginnings were truly humble: a group of Englishwomen concerned about the toll their fashions imposed upon wild birds, men of letters railing in coffee houses at the smogs that gagged their cities, isolated foresters and botanists working in Africa and Asia to curb the uncontrolled cutting of forests, a bearded backwoodsman and a Yale Brahmin bickering over the natural splendors of North America, and a bevy of naturalists, illustrators, and photographers striving to educate society about the beauties of untamed nature.

Out of these and other events grew a global mass movement which has left few societies untouched. The environment has become a policy issue that cuts across traditional policy fields, the *raison d'etre* of whole new bureaucracices and whole new political parties, the object of complex new bodies of legislation, the subject of national and multinational research programs, and the cause of a mass movement numbering in the tens of millions. Through all this, the environmental movement has wrought three significant changes in human values.

First, it has prompted the rediscovery of one of the most fundamental realities of human existence: that humanity is utterly dependent on a healthy natural environment. Appreciation of this basic truth had been lost over the millennia as a function of progress in agricultural and industrial development. Primitive man saw untamed nature as threatening and dangerous. As he strove first to control nature, and then to exploit natural resources more efficiently and profitably, so nature became less threatening. But the threat of an untamed environment was removed only to be replaced by the threat of an over-controlled environment.

Technological man has begun to understand the irony, and herein lies the second significant facet of environmentalism: it represents a readjustment to the legacy of technology. The earliest environmentalists felt that the changes spawned by the agricultural and industrial revolutions ultimately exerted too great a cost on nature. Educated Victorians, with their new appreciation of nature, were the first to rebel in any significant numbers to air and water pollution, and to the loss of wildlife and wilderness. But there was no universal sense of alarm, and two world wars, several regional wars, and a severe economic depression combined to divert attention back to more immediate problems. It was not until the second half of this century, with the rise of a new middle class, the expansion of education, and the emergence of two-thirds of the world's population from the shadows of colonialism, that questions of social, economic, and political justice began to be addressed by more than a privileged few. The environment was one of several such questions.

Inglehart characterizes the change in attitude as "a silent revolution," a shift from an overwhelming emphasis on material values and physical security towards greater concern for the quality of life.[1] There were suggestions that the traditional yardstick by which the progress of industrial societies was measured—economic growth—was no longer appropriate. Ophuls and others argued that many dominant social beliefs, formed in times of abundance, needed to be reassessed in the light of growing ecological scarcity.[2] For Pirages, environmental problems in industrial societies had their roots in the Dominant Social Paradigm, a set of beliefs and values that included private property rights, faith in science and technology, individualism, economic growth, and the subjection of nature and exploitation of natural resources.[3] Pollution, energy shortages, and even inflation, economic recession, and unemployment posed challenges to the Dominant Social Paradigm.[4] Fears about the limits to growth and the implications of environmental mismanagement gave rise to a new world view more compatible with environmental limits. This view, which may even be an ideology, has been called the New Environmental Paradigm.[5] At its heart is a call for an entirely new kind of society based on carefully considered production and consumption, resource conservation, environmental protection, and the basic values of compassion, justice, and quality of life.

Milbrath suggests that environmentalists constitute a vanguard, using education, persuasion, and politics to try to lead people to their vision of a new, more sustainable society.[6] In this they are opposed by a rearguard (exemplified by Julian Simon and Herman Kahn) which believes that modern industrial societies are working quite well, that there is no limit to human ingenuity, and that industrial society produces the most wealth and the most equitable economic, social, and political arrangements.

The third significant facet of environmentalism lies in the challenge it poses to orthodox models of economic growth, whether capitalist or socialist. In MDCs, it is a direct challenge to unthinking and unregulated production and consumption; in LDCs, it is a challenge to the assumption that the industrial model is the most effective route to rapid and equal development. In a much-discussed 1966 paper, the medieval historian Lynn White linked the historical destruction of nature to Judeo-Christian anthropomorphism.[7] Christianity, he argued, was the most anthropocentric of religions, teaching that it was God's will that man exploit nature for his proper ends; man had a God-given dominion "over all the earth and over every creeping thing that creepeth upon the earth" (Genesis 1:26). Man was to be "fruitful and multiply and replenish the earth and subdue it" (Genesis 1:28). Western science and technology, argued White, were "so tinctured with orthodox Christian arrogance towards nature that no solution can be expected from them alone."

Moncrief disputes White's thesis, arguing that cultures outside the Judeo-Christian sphere experienced similar instances of dramatic environmental change: "no culture has been able to completely screen out the egocentric tendencies of human beings."[8] This may be true enough, but in terms of breadth and volume, the most severe environmental problems have come only in the last 150 years, in proportion to the spread of the industrial revolution and of European settlement and colonization to other continents. In sub-Saharan Africa, the most serious problems have come at the interface of traditional and industrial societies, where the demands of the latter have been imposed with little thought about the implications for the former.

Certainly, environmentalism has forced a reconsideration of the priorities and principles of growth. From the late 1960s, the nature of the debate was fundamentally altered by the competing perspectives of "more" and "less" developed nations and communities within nations. Western environmentalists may still be more immediately concerned with domestic issues, but—at the global level—some of the most fundamental philosophical changes in environmentalism have derived from the influence of LDCs. In 1972, note Holdgate, Kassas, and White, environmental problems tended to be seen "individually, simplistically, and overwhelmingly from a developed western country's standpoint,"[9] where environmentalists warned of the evils of economic growth. For the less developed countries, meanwhile, the potential benefits of economic growth were unquestioned. Faced as they were by the immediate and visible problems of poverty, LDCs viewed environmental management as a distant concern, if not actually a brake on development.

A decade later, by contrast, there was much wider acceptance (in word if not in deed) of the concept of sustainable development. At the UNEP Session of a Special Character (held in Nairobi in 1982 to mark the tenth anniversary of Stockholm), Sandbrook recalls that governments "expressed concern" at the damage being done to their natural environments "which adversely affect their development and the conditions of many of their peoples' lives."[10] India's Centre for Science and Environment argued that there could be no "rational and equitable economic development without environmental conservation. Environmental degradation invariably results in increased economic inequalities in which the poor suffer the most. Environmental degradation and social injustice are two sides of the same coin."[11]

Not only did many LDCs now appear convinced of the economic benefits of environmental management, but the contribution they made to the international debate on the environment had the additional effect of injecting a note of realism into environmentalism in western Europe and North America. The simplistic initial view of some New Environmentalists that all growth was wrong and that the aims of economic development and sound environmental management were incompatible was replaced by the more realistic view that the aims of the two had to be reconciled. Rather than being mutually exclusive, the aims of development and environmental management were mutually dependent. The often reactionary categorization of environmental issues that took place before Stockholm was gradually (if not wholly) replaced by more conciliatory attitudes and attempts to achieve realistic compromises.

THE FUTURE OF ENVIRONMENTALISM

"The report of my death," once observed a robust Mark Twain, "was an exagerration." He might have been speaking for the environmental movement. With a persistent and misguided regularity, environmentalism has been declared dead, dying, or defunct since almost before it was born. As early as 1954, Grant McConnell lamented that America would never again see the like of the Progressive Conservation movement.[12] In 1972, Anthony Downs warned that most social issues eventually enter a stage of prolonged limbo (although he conceded that environmental issues might retain their interest longer).[13] In 1975, James Bowman perceived a gradual decline of intense interest in the environment.[14] In 1976, Riley Dunlap and Donald Dillman wrote of a "dramatic decline in support of environmental protection programs."[15] In 1980, Francis Sandbach, quoting opinion polls and diminishing newspaper inches, saw no reason to disagree with Bowman.[16]

Against this background, the views of Clay Schoenfeld were in a notable minority. Far from being a passing fad, he argued in 1972, the environmental movement (in America at least) seemed destined to be a permanent fixture,[17] for several reasons. First, environmental degradation was a high-visibility problem that millions could see, smell, taste, and hear. Second, environmentalism was not a wholly new movement; it had a long-established and solid infrastructure from which to operate and expand. Third, the diversity inherent in the movement boded well for its survival. Fourth, affluence gave more people the opportunity to make hard choices. Finally, the movement had a good deal of internal integrity in that it was part of a coherent, fundamental shift in values.

Certainly there were opinion polls in the 1970s that seemed to indicate declining support for the environmental movement. There have been as many since that indicate exactly the opposite.[18] They are all missing the point. The robustness and significance of a social movement cannot always be measured in opinion polls, because too many look at the environmental movement from a perspective limited both in historical and geographical terms.

For those Europeans or Americans who lived through the emotional heyday of mass environmentalism in the 1960s and 1970s, the relative sobriety of the late 1970s and early 1980s—distracted as they were by economic recession and the energy crisis, and then by returning affluence and political conservatism—must have seemed anticlimactic. The environmentalism of the streets declined, it is true; but the broader movement did not. Rather, it was transformed. During the 1960s, it was fixed in the arena of mass protest and citizen action; by the early 1980s, it had scaled (and in some places breached) the citadel of public policy. During the 1960s, activists demanded changes in policymaking, planning goals, and economic and social values; by the late 1970s, their demands were slowly being met. Qualitatively, the actions of governments and the efficacy of legislation often have left much to be desired, but there is no denying the advent of "the environment" as a public policy issue. In manifestos, platforms, and campaign speeches, energy and the environment regularly take their place alongside statements on economic and foreign policy, welfare, education, crime, health, agriculture, and other more "traditional" policy areas. By 1987, it was even being suggested that the West German Greens were on the wane because their environmental policies were being adopted by the older, larger parties.[19] The environment was becoming increasingly nonpartisan.

However, as the twenty-first century approaches, and as the nature of environmentalism continues to change, it is difficult to know whether to be optimistic or pessimistic about the future. The signals are mixed. In the credit column, there has been a notable change of attitude.

- At the most fundamental level, the lifestyle of the Western middle classes is changing: people are driving more fuel-efficient cars, conserving energy at home, reducing the size of their families, and supporting environmental groups and their aims. Environmental awareness is taken increasingly for granted.

- There are more examples of corporate responsibility, notably through the growing incidence of environmental impact assessments. The record is still far from perfect, and the roots of such change may not always be as honorable as they appear (social responsibility does not yet always exceed the profit motive), but the trend is hopeful.

- Citizen and grassroots movements in MDCs and LDCs alike are building impressive records of achievement. In Britain, the National Trust alone has ensured the protection in perpetuity of thousands of acres of countryside. In Kenya, the Green Belt Movement has helped turn tree-planting into a national crusade. In Mexico, Malaysia, and India, citizens movements play a growing role in planning decisions. In the United States, environmental groups have proved effective lobbyists, and have repeatedly made the environment an issue in national, state, and local politics.

- Although still far from perfect, the number of government agencies and institutions dealing with the environment has grown. These agencies have been supported by a growing body of local, national and international legislation. Environmental policy-making—while still bound too often by the confines of ideology and incomplete data—is improving. Alongside the successes of Green parties in Western Europe, older established parties have given more thought to the environment as a policy area. The environment has traditionally fallen more easily into the constituency of moderate/liberal political ideology, but 1988 saw signs of a new interest among anti-regulation conservatives. During the 1988 US presidential campaign, George Bush made considerably stronger statements on the environment than Ronald Reagan ever felt inclined to do (although the issue remained the intellectual preserve of his Democratic opponent Michael Dukakis).

  Even more surprisingly, Margaret Thatcher—after years of ardent opposition to government regulation (especially on environmental questions) and growing pressure from environmentalists and members of her own party—apparently underwent an abrupt conversion to environmentalism. In October 1988, she suddenly declared that protecting the balance of nature was one of "the great challenges" of the late 20th century, and called for emergency action to safeguard the ozone layer, curb acid pollution, and avoid global climatic warming. The announcement took many environmentalists by surprise; it seemed to some that the Conservatives were launching an attempt to claim the environment as the natural preserve of the right.

- The data are still far from complete, but much more is known than even a decade ago about the state of the environment and about the kind of protection it needs. Environmental research is more coordinated and effective; IBP, MAB, Earthwatch, and GEMS have brought a better understanding of the interconnectedness of cause and effect in environmental problems. The new data have revealed more clearly the geographical scope of environmental problems.

- Whether Green parties continue to exist in their present form, or wither away as their policies are adopted by the older parties, the advent of Green politics has already shaken our assumptions about the old left/right axis in politics. Many Greens argue that an entirely new political philosophy is needed to respond adequately to the needs of environmentalism, and that conservatism, liberalism and socialism in all their existing hues are too "un-ecological." Jonathon Porritt, a prominent figure in the British Green Party, argues that Green politics "challenges the integrity of [existing] ideologies, questions the philosophy that underlies them, and fundamentally disputes today's accepted notions of rationality."[20]

- Environmentalism has moved beyond the despair of the prophets of doom and has entered a more mature and measured phase in which the accumulated knowledge of the past two centuries, and particularly of the past two decades, is increasingly being put to considered and effective use. Planners in MDCs and LDCs have begun to agree in seeing many environmental problems as being as much global as local concerns. The nature and scope of the work of international agencies is evidence in itself of a broader and more rational view of environmental issues and problems.

Yet despite such progress, there are problems on the debit side of the balance sheet which cannot be ignored. Although there is more certainty about the threats to the environment, there is perhaps less certainty about the prospects for addressing those threats.

- Despite the creation of new environmental agencies and the passage of new legislation in MDCs, the political will to implement the spirit—let alone the letter—of environmental protection, is patchy. The ascendancy of materialist, antiregulation forces under Reaganism and Thatcherism, giving priority to short-term over long-term interests, combined in the mid-1980s with an economic recession to reduce the resources allocated to addressing environmental problems. Holdgate, Kassas, and White argue that the ratio of words to action is weighted too heavily toward the former.[21] Eckholm notes that while public understanding of environmental imperatives increased in the post-Stockholm decade and needed new institutions had evolved, "many of the social, economic, and technological forces that underly environmental difficulties [had] scarcely been checked."[22]

- It is often difficult to know what is happening in the centrally planned economies. Air pollution in Poland and Czechoslovakia is almost unprecedented in its severity;[23] the Chernobyl accident raised questions about the priorities of Soviet planners and administrators; combined with reports of the severe pollution of Lake Baikal, it also raised questions about the quality of the environment elsewhere in the Soviet Union.

  There may be hope for the future, however; during 1988 and 1989, environmental management and protection featured increasingly prominently in the policy statements of President Gorbachev. There was an emerging forthrightness, honesty and assurance about Soviet environmental policy that had been missing under Leonid Brezhnev; rational environmental management seemed to capture the very essence of *glasnost* and *perestroika*.

- The litany of problems afflicting LDCs meanwhile grows with worrying persistence. Incidents such as Bhopal and Ixhuatepec not only cast a shadow over planning and development priorities, but—as most of their victims were shanty-dwellers—also underline the dire social and economic problems of Third World cities, where economic inequality is creating a growing underclass, and where population growth frequently outpaces the provision of housing, clean water, and sanitation.

Sub-Saharan Africa gives the greatest cause for concern. Such problems as spiraling population growth, widespread soil erosion, falling food production, political instability, bureaucratic incompetence, unequal terms of trade, misguided development priorities, civil war, and economic corruption and mismanagement have all too often combined to produce a sub-continent in crisis. If current trends continue, the region is promised nothing less than a human and environmental catastrophe.

• Overarching almost everything has been the emergence first of problems affecting many different parts of the planet (acid pollution, toxic wastes, nuclear contamination, deforestation, and the killing of wildlife), and then of problems affecting the planet as a whole. Agreement on dealing with the threats to the ozone layer was reached remarkably quickly; more serious now, though, is the greenhouse effect. With the increased use of coal, oil and natural gas, the concentration of carbon dioxide (CO_2) in the earth's atmosphere has risen steadily since the Industrial Revolution. Acting like a greenhouse, this CO_2 has been trapping solar radiation in the earth's atmosphere.

Warnings of a global warming were made as early as 1970. Then, they sounded very much like science fiction, with seemingly fantastic suggestions that a warmer climate would lead to changes in crop production patterns, the melting of the polar ice caps, and a rise in global sea levels, inundating many coastal areas. By the last 1980s, those warnings had begun to seem much more real. For many who lived through the American drought of 1988, it must have been difficult not to believe that climatic change had finally begun in earnest. Temperatures soared, hovering in the 95–105°F (35–40°C) range for weeks on end. The lack of rain caused vegetation to burn up, and led to a shortfall in maize and soybean production across much of the midwest. Water levels in the Mississippi fell, leaving barges stranded along the upper reaches. For much of August and September, swathes of forest in the mountain West burned; among the worst damaged regions was Yellowstone National Park. Smoke from the fires reached as far east as St Louis and Chicago. Whether this really was part of the greenhouse effect, or simply the latest cyclical extreme in continental weather patterns, it provided many with a taste of the possible consequences of a man-made global warming. A truly planetary problem like this demands policy responses very different from anything that has come before.

In 1982, UNEP published *The World Environment 1972–1982* as an audit of "the first ten years in which mankind [had] consciously and co-operatively attempted the rational management" of the earth. In his fore-word, UNEP Executive Director Mostafa Tolba noted that "preventive rather than curative actions have been gaining momentum and wide acceptance" and that the importance of international cooperation had been brought into focus. But, he warned, "ten years after Stockholm it is clear that we still have a very imperfect knowledge of the state of the major components of our environment and of the interacting mechanisms," and he emphasized the need for long-term planning: "the problems which overwhelm us today are precisely those which, through a similar [lack of foresight], we failed to solve decades ago."[24]

At the global level, finding out and understanding what is needed in the management of resources is much easier than actually implementing multinational management programs. Science provides an understanding of the mechanics of environmental problems, but the causes and solutions are ultimately a question of human values and human behavior. In the final analysis, the environment is a political issue. Whether or not solutions are effectively applied will continue to rely upon politics and policy, upon the attitudes of leaders, parties, and their constituents and upon a complex cross-referencing and cooperative system involving international agencies, national environmental agencies, non-governmental organizations, and a series of often non-binding international conventions and agreements.

Whatever the short-term prognosis however, the longer-term changes in attitude have been heartening for the environmental movement. Bowman sees environmentalism as the last stage in a process that has taken man "from fearing, to understanding, to using, to abusing, and now, to worrying about the physical and biological world around him."[25] There has been a marked trend away from the notion of environment as divorced from humanity and toward a new focus on the *human* costs of environmental deterioration and mismanagement. It is no longer simply a question of what man is doing to the environment, but of what the despoliation of the environment is doing to man. Environmentalists argue that we can no longer take the environment for granted. It is already too late to save many species and habitats, and more will undoubtedly suffer through ill-advised development. Pollution has been curbed or reduced in some parts of the world, but it is worsening in others. Forests and fertile land are being lost in some parts, and restored in others. Sooner or later, a workable balance must be achieved between the needs of humanity and the needs of nature. However long this takes, the rise of the environmental movement has made sure that the relationship between humans and their environment will never be quite the same again.

Notes

INTRODUCTION

1. Earthscan, *Cropland or Wasteland: The Problems and Promises of Irrigation* (London: Earthscan, 1984) 22–23.

2. H. C. Darby, "The Clearing of the Woodland in Europe," in William L. Thomas, *Man's Role in Changing the Face of the Earth* (Chicago: University of Chicago Press, 1956), 185.

3. J. Donald Hughes, *Ecology in Ancient Civilizations* (Albuquerque: University of New Mexico, 1975), 97.

4. Earthscan, note 1 above, 23.

5. E. S. Deevey, Don S. Rice, Prudence M. Rice, H. H. Vaughan, Mark Brenner, and M. S. Flannery, "Mayan Urbanism: Impact on a Tropical Karst Environment," *Science* 206:4416 (19 October 1979): 298–306.

6. Darby, note 2 above, 187.

7. John Evelyn, *Fumifugium: or the Inconvenience of the Aer and Smoake of London Dissipated*, reproduced in James P. Lodge, *The Smoake of London: Two Prophecies* (New York: Maxwell Reprint Company, 1969), 14–16.

8. Council on Environmental Quality, *Environmental Quality 1980* (Washington, DC: U.S. Government Printing Office, 1980), 418–419.

9. Philip Lowe and Jane Goyder, *Environmental Groups in Politics* (London: George Allen & Unwin, 1983), 37.

10. For the American movement, see particularly the work of Huth, Hays, Fox, Nash, and Petulla; for British ideas and developments, see Lowe, O'Riordan, Sheail, Allen, Thomas, and others.

11. See especially Max Nicholson, *The Environmental Revolution* (London: Hodder and Stoughton, 1970); Max Nicholson, *The New Environmental Age* (Cambridge: Cambridge University Press, 1987); Lynton K. Caldwell, *In Defense of Earth: International Protection of the Biosphere* (Bloomington: Indiana University Press, 1972); and Lynton K. Caldwell, *International Environmental Policy: Emergence and Dimensions* (Durham, NC: Duke University Press, 1984).

12. Donald Worster, *Nature's Economy* (San Francisco: Sierra Club Books, 1977), 261.

13. Roderick Nash, "The American Invention of National Parks," *American Quarterly* 22:3 (Fall 1970): 726–735.

14. William Wordsworth, *A Guide through the District of the Lakes* (Bloomington: Indiana University Press, 1952), 127.

15. Sir William Petty, *Mankind and Political Arithmetic* (New York: The Mershon Co., n.d).

16. Peter Kropotkin, *Fields, Factories, and Workshops (Tomorrow)* edited by Colin Ward (London: Unwin, 1974).

17. Roger Scruton, *A Dictionary of Political Thought* (New York: Harper & Row, 1982), 150.

18. *New Republic*, 1 March 1970, 8–9.

19. Joseph M. Petulla, *American Environmentalism: Values, Tactics, Priorities* (College Station: Texas A & M University Press, 1980).

20. Timothy O'Riordan, *Environmentalism* (London: Pion Limited, 1981), 1–19, 375–377.

ONE. THE ROOTS OF ENVIRONMENTALISM

1. Keith Thomas, *Man and the Natural World: Changing Attitudes in England 1500–1800* (Harmondsworth: Penguin, 1983).

2. David Elliston Allen, *The Naturalist in Britain* (Harmondsworth: Penguin, 1978), 52.

3. William Gilpin, *Observations on the Highlands of Scotland* (Richmond, Surrey: Richmond, 1973), 112.

4. Thomas, note 1 above, 284.

5. Philip Lowe, "Values and Institutions in the History of British Nature Conservation," in Andrew Warren, and F. B. Goldsmith, *Conservation in Perspective* (London: Wiley, 1983), 333.

6. Donald Worster, *Nature's Economy* (San Francisco: Sierra Club Books, 1977), 170–171.

7. Ibid, 179.

8. Lowe, note 5 above, 337.

9. Philip Lowe and Jane Goyder, *Environmental Groups in Politics* (London: George Allen & Unwin, 1983), 19.

10. Ibid, 19.

11. Lowe, note 5 above, 333.

12. John Sheail, *Nature in Trust* (London: Blackie, 1976), 4.

13. Ibid, 9.

14. Allen, note 2 above, 197–198.

15. Lowe, note 5 above, 331.

16. Sheail, note 12 above, 12.

17. Ibid, 13.

18. Friedrich Engels, *The Condition of the Working Class in England* (Stanford: Stanford University Press, 1958).

19. Lowe, note 5 above, 338.

20. Eric Ashby and Mary Anderson, *The Politics of Clean Air* (Oxford: Clarendon Press, 1981), 23.

21. Allen, note 2 above, 199–200.

22. Sheail, note 12 above, 60.

23. Ibid, 63.

24. Ibid, 70.

25. Ann MacEwen and Malcolm MacEwen, *National Parks: Conservation or Cosmetics?* (London: George Allen & Unwin, 1982), 5.

26. H. Verney Lovett, "The Development of the Services 1858–1918," in *The Cambridge History of India* vol. 6 (Cambridge: Cambridge University Press, 1932), 364.

27. Dietrich Brandis (1824–1907) was born in Bonn, Prussia, and trained as a botanist. He was forest superintendent in Lower Burma from 1856 to 1862, and inspector-general of forests for India from 1864 to 1883, when he returned to Germany. It was with the help of Brandis that Gifford Pinchot studied forestry in France and Switzerland in 1889–1890. Both Brandis and William Schlich were knighted for their services to Indian forestry.

28. Quoted in Guy Bolton, *Spoils and Spoilers* (Sydney: George Allen & Unwin, 1981), 37.

29. Ibid, 46.

30. Ibid, 15.

31. Captain John Lort Stokes, to Sir Francis Beaufort, 31 January 1849 (Hydrography Office, Taunton), quoted by Bolton, note 28 above, 55.

32. J. G. Mosley, "Towards a History of Conservation in Australia," in Amos Rapoport, ed., *Australia as Human Setting* (Sydney: Angus and Robertson, 1972), 147.

33. Richard Grove, "Incipient Conservationism in the Cape Colony and the Emergence of Colonial Environmental Policies in Southern Africa." Unpublished paper presented to conference: The Scramble for Resources: Conservation Policies in Africa, 1884–1984, Cambridge, April 1985.

34. Ibid.

35. John Pringle, *The Conservationists and the Killers* (Cape Town: Books of Africa, 1982), 44, 11.

36. Eric C. Tabler, *The Far Interior* (Cape Town: A. A. Balkema, 1955).

37. Ibid., 51–52.

38. Hans Huth, *Nature and the American: Three Centuries of Changing Attitudes* (Berkeley: University of California Press, 1957), 9.

39. Roderick Nash, *Wilderness and the American Mind* (New Haven: Yale University Press), 1973.

40. Worster, note 6 above, 67.

41. Huth, note 38 above.

42. Worster, note 6 above, 71.

43. Ibid., 82.

44. George Perkins Marsh (1801–1882) was born in Vermont and taught briefly before entering law, then politics. As a Whig member of Congress (1843–1859), he helped found and shape the Smithsonian Institution. He was United States Minister to Turkey (1848–1854) and to Italy (1861–1882), the latter posting giving him time to write copiously. *Man and Nature* was an immediate bestseller.

45. George Perkins Marsh, *Man and Nature* (Reprint; Cambridge: Harvard University Press, 1965), 36.

46. David Lowenthal, in introduction, ibid., xxii.

47. Stewart L. Udall, *The Quiet Crisis* (New York: Holt, Rinehart & Winston, 1963), 94.

48. Huth, note 38 above, 148.

49. Laura Wood Roper, *FLO: A Biography of Frederick Law Olmsted* (Baltimore: Johns Hopkins University Press, 1973), 285.

50. George Catlin, *North American Indians* (Philadelphia: Leary, Stuart & Co., 1913), 294–295.

51. Henry David Thoreau, *The Maine Woods*, (Reprint; New York: W. W. Norton, 1950), 321.

52. Nash, note 39 above, 102.

53. Marsh, note 45 above, 203.

54. Roderick Nash, "The American Invention of National Parks," *American Quarterly* 22:3 (Fall 1970): 726–735.

55. Alfred Runte, *National Parks: The American Experience* (Lincoln: University of Nebraska Press, 1979), 7–9, 11–18.

56. John Muir (1838–1914) was born in Dunbar, Scotland, and emigrated with his family to Wisconsin in 1849. Following university (he did not graduate), he wandered through Canada and the southern United States before arriving in San Francisco in 1868 and moving to Yosemite. In mid-life he took to writing and was instrumental in the protection not only of Yosemite but of Petrified Forest and Grand Canyon national parks in Arizona.

57. Nash, note 39 above, 132.

58. Ralph L. Rusk, ed., *The Letters of Ralph Waldo Emerson* vol. 6 (New York: Columbia University Press, 1939), 155.

59. Harold T. Pinkett, *Gifford Pinchot: Private and Public Forester* (Urbana: University of Illinois Press, 1970), 9.

60. Gifford Pinchot (1865–1946) was born in Connecticut and brought up in Paris and Pennsylvania. After education at Yale, he studied forestry in Germany and France before setting up as a forestry consultant in New York. He

was appointed to the board of the new National Forestry Commission in 1896. His family helped him establish a forestry school at Yale. Pinchot first met John Muir (twenty-three years his elder) in 1893; the two were to become bitter opponents.

61. Pinkett, note 59 above, 10–11.

62. Worster, note 6 above, 266.

63. Nash, note 39 above, 135.

64. Gifford Pinchot, *The Fight for Conservation* (New York: Doubleday Page & Co., 1910), 40–52.

65. Worster, note 6 above, 267–268.

66. Grant McConnell, "The Conservation Movement: Past and Present," *Western Political Quarterly* 7:3 (Sept. 1954): 463–478.

67. Maldwyn A. Jones, *The Limits of Liberty* (New York: Oxford University Press, 1983), 369.

68. James L. Bates, "Fulfilling American Democracy: The Conservation Movement, 1907–1921," *Mississippi Valley Historical Review* 44 (June 1957): 29–57.

69. Samuel P. Hays, *Conservation and the Gospel of Efficiency* (Cambridge: Harvard University Press, 1959), 271–276.

70. Ibid.

71. Jones, note 67 above, 369.

72. Carroll Pursell, ed., *From Conservation to Ecology: The Development of Environmental Concern* (New York: Thomas Y. Crowell Co., 1973), 2.

73. Stephen Fox, *John Muir and His Legacy: The American Conservation Movement* (Boston: Little, Brown & Co., 1981), 128.

74. Theodore Roosevelt, *An Autobiography* (New York: Macmillan, 1913), 402.

75. Hays, note 69 above, 8, 108–109.

76. James Penick, *Progressive Politics and Conservation* (Chicago: University of Chicago Press, 1968), 9.

77. Report of the National Conservation Commission, Senate Doc. 676, 60th Cong., 2d sess., 1, quoted in Martin N. McGeary, *Gifford Pinchot: Forester-Politician* (Princeton, NJ: Princeton University Press, 1960), 100.

78. McGeary, ibid., 100.

79. Robert Boardman, *International Organization and the Conservation of Nature* (Bloomington: Indiana University Press, 1981), 27.

80. Richard S. R. Fitter, *The Penitent Butchers* (London: Collins, 1978), 24.

81. Boardman, note 79 above, 28.

82. Fitter, note 80 above, 7–8.

83. Ibid., 8.

84. In Carl G. Schillings, *With Flashlight and Rifle* (London: Hutchinson, 1905), xv.

85. Fitter, note 80 above, 13.

86. Carl G. Schillings, *In Wildest Africa* (London: Harper & Brothers, 1907), 111.

87. Richard Tjader, *The Big Game of Africa* (New York: D. Appleton & Co., 1910), 299–303.

88. Lord Cranworth, *Profit and Sport in British East Africa* (London: Macmillan, 1919), 391.

89. Ibid., 208.

90. James Sleeman, *From Rifle to Camera: The Reformation of a Big Game Hunter* (London: Jarrolds, 1947), 192–193.

91. Boardman, note 79 above, 146.

92. Fox, note 73 above, 187.

93. Worster, note 6 above, 269.

94. Aldo Leopold (1887–1948) was born in Iowa and graduated from Yale For-

estry School before joining the U.S. Forest Service in Arizona. He was influential in having the Forest Service adopt more carefully considered techniques of game management. After four years in Wisconsin, he left the Forest Service in 1928 to conduct a series of game surveys. In 1933, the chair of game management was created for him at the University of Wisconsin, a post he retained until his death.

95. Aldo Leopold, *Game Management* (New York: Scribner's, 1933), 21.

96. Aldo Leopold, *Sand County Almanac* (New York: Oxford University Press, 1949), 204, 214.

97. Ibid., viii.

98. Fox, note 73 above, 199.

99. Worster, note 6 above, 222.

100. Ibid., 226.

101. Great Plains Committee, *The Future of the Great Plains* (Washington, DC: U.S. Government Printing Office, 1936).

102. David Anderson, "Depression, Dust Bowl, Demography, and Drought: The Colonial State and Soil Conservation in East Africa During the 1930s," *African Affairs* 83:332 (July 1984): 321–343.

103. Boardman, note 79 above, 29.

104. The Central Correlating Committee for the Protection of Nature was set up in Britain in January 1924 specifically to act as a clearing-house for information, as a coordinating body, and to facilitate international liaison. Representatives from its ten constituent bodies were to meet annually to discuss national and international problems and policies, and this they did for three years, discussing, among other things, the problems faced by whales and migratory species. In order to avoid giving the impression that it was an international body, it changed its name to the British Correlating Committee. By 1926 there was no longer any point in holding annual meetings because there was felt to be nothing to discuss; its members made less and less use of the committee as a forum, and it was disbanded in 1936. (Sheail, note 12) above, 20.

105. Lowe and Goyder, note 9 above, 165.

106. Ibid.

107. Boardman, note 79 above, 31.

108. Simon Lyster, *International Wildlife Law* (Cambridge: Grotius Publications, 1985), 110–111.

TWO. PROTECTION, CONSERVATION, AND THE UNITED NATIONS (1945–1961)

1. Martin N. McGeary, *Gifford Pinchot: Forester-Politician* (Princeton: Princeton University Press, 1960), 426.

2. Edgar B. Nixon, ed., *Franklin D. Roosevelt and Conservation 1911–1945*, vol. 2 (New York: Franklin D. Roosevelt Library, 1957), 599.

3. Ibid., 607.

4. Ibid., 627.

5. Ibid., 635.

6. Ibid., 641.

7. Ibid., 644–647.

8. McGeary, note 1 above, 426.

9. UNSCCUR, UNSCCUR Memorandum from Chairman to members of NRC Co on UNESCO, 8–9, quoted in Robert Boardman, *International Organization and the Conservation of Nature* (Bloomington: Indiana University Press, 1981), 39.

10. United Nations, *United Nations Yearbook 1946–47* (New York: Department of Public Information, United Nations, 1947), 491.

11. Ibid., 492.

12. Gove Hambidge, *The Story of FAO* (New York: Van Nostrand, 1955).

13. Sir John Boyd Orr (1880–1971) was a Scottish-born physician who specialized in nutrition after seeing the suffering of Glasgow slum-dwellers. He was active in League of Nations activities on nutrition. He resigned from FAO in 1948, and in 1949, in recognition of his work at FAO, was awarded the Nobel Peace Prize and elevated to the peerage, becoming Lord Boyd Orr.

14. Hambidge, note 12 above, 14.

15. United Nations, note 10 above, 694.

16. Kenneth Ingham, *A History of East Africa* (London: Longman, 1963), 379–380.

17. Sir John Russell, "World Population and World Food Supplies." Presidential Address to the British Association for the Advancement of Science, in *Advancement of Science* 6:23 (October 1949): 173–183.

18. John Boyd Orr, *The White Man's Dilemma: Food and the Future* (London: George Allen & Unwin, 1953), 71.

19. Stuart Chase, *Rich Land, Poor Land* (New York: McGraw-Hill, 1936).

20. Paul B. Sears, *Deserts on the March* (Norman: University of Oklahoma Press, 1935).

21. Hugh H. Bennett, *Soil Conservation* (New York: McGraw-Hill, 1939).

22. R. O. Whyte and G. V. Jacks, *Vanishing Lands* (New York: Doubleday, 1939).

23. Frank Pearson and Floyd Harper, *The World's Hunger* (Ithaca: Cornell University Press, 1945).

24. Fairfield Osborn, *Our Plundered Planet* (Boston: Little, Brown & Co., 1948), 201.

25. Fairfield Osborn, *The Limits of the Earth* (Boston: Little, Brown & Co., 1953), 6.

26. Stephen Fox, *John Muir and His Legacy: The American Conservation Movement* (Boston: Little, Brown & Co., 1981), 307.

27. William Vogt, *Road to Survival* (New York: William Sloane & Associates, 1948), 34–37.

28. Ibid., 284–288.

29. Fox, note 26 above, 310.

30. Sir Julian Sorell Huxley (1887–1975) was a biologist and writer. He lectured at Oxford (1910–1925) and King's College, London (1925–1935) before becoming Secretary of the Zoological Society of London (1935–1942). In 1946 he served briefly on the National Parks Committee and was first director-general of UNESCO (1946–1948). He was knighted in 1958.

31. Edward Max Nicholson (b. 1904) is an ornithologist and former civil servant. His enormously influential role in the evolution of British and international environmentalism has been consistently underestimated in the literature. Cofounder of the British Trust for Ornithology and the Council for Nature, he was also instrumental in the creation of IUCN and the World Wildlife Fund, was second director-general of the Nature Conservancy (1952–1966), and was closely involved in the environment/development debate of the 1970s (see chapter 8).

32. Johann Büttikofer, *Report on the Conference for the International Protection of Nature* (Basle: Swiss League for the Protection of Nature, 1946), 34.

33. Max Nicholson, personal communication, Sept./Nov. 1981.

34. Büttikofer, note 32 above, 35.

35. Ibid., 39.

36. Nicholson, note 33 above.

37. Sir Julian Huxley, *Memories II* (New York: Harper & Row, 1973), 127.

38. E. D. Adrian, "Activities of UNESCO in the Natural Sciences During 1948," *Advancement of Science* 6:22 (July 1949): 90–104.

39. United Nations, note 10 above, 707.
40. Huxley, note 37 above, 50–51.
41. Nicholson, note 33 above.
42. Johann Büttikofer, *Proceedings of the International Conference for the Protection of Nature* (Basle: Swiss League for the Protection of Nature, 1947), 12.
43. Ibid. 152.
44. Ibid. 160.
45. Ibid. 211.
46. UNESCO, Minutes of the Natural Resources Panel of the U.S. National Commission for UNESCO, 27 September 1948.
47. Nicholson, note 33 above.
48. IUCN, *IUCN Yearbook 1973* (Morges: IUCN, 1974), 20.
49. UNESCO, *Preparatory Documents to the International Technical Conference on the Protection of Nature, August 1949* (Paris: UNESCO, 1949).
50. Ibid.
51. F. Dixey, "Conservation and Utilization of World Resources: United Nations Conference," *Nature* 164:4176 (12 November 1949): 813–815.
52. Max Nicholson, *The Environmental Revolution* (London: Hodder & Stoughton, 1972), 196.
53. UNESCO, note 49 above.
54. UNESCO, *Proceedings and Papers of the International Technical Conference on the Protection of Nature, August 1949* (Paris/ Brussels: UNESCO, 1950), 181.
55. Max Nicholson, *The First World Conservation Lecture* (London: World Wildlife Fund, 1981).
56. IUPN, *Proceedings and Reports of the 2nd Session of the IUPN General Assembly, 1950* (Morges: IUPN, 1951), 71.
57. Nicholson, note 33 above.
58. IUCN, note 48 above, 19.
59. Jean-Paul Harroy, "A Pioneer's Reward," *IUCN Bulletin* 14:4–6 (1983): 35–43.
60. Nicholson, note 33 above.
61. Enrique Beltran, "A Forgotten Chapter in IUCN's History," *IUCN Bulletin* 14:10–12 (1983): 108–109.
62. Lee Merriam Talbot (b. 1930), a zoologist and ecologist, was IUCN's first staff ecologist. He joined CEQ in 1970 as senior scientist. In 1978 he became director of conservation of the World Wildlife Fund, and from 1980 to 1983 was director-general of IUCN.
63. UNESCO, note 54 above, 183.
64. Boardman, note 9 above, 60.
65. Nicholson, note 33 above.
66. Robert Allen, *How to Save the World* (London: Kogan Page, 1980), 96.
67. Harold J. Coolidge, "The Growth and Development of International Interest in Safeguard Endangered Species," *Proceedings XV International Congress of Zoology*, London, 16–23 July 1958, 58.
68. Nicholson, note 52 above, 201.
69. Nicholson, note 55 above.
70. IUCN, note 48 above, 44.
71. Nicholson, note 55 above.
72. Harold Coolidge, "Profile," *The Environmentalist* 1:1 (1981): 65–74.
73. Ibid.
74. Ibid.
75. World Wildlife Fund, *The Ark Under Way: 2nd Report of the World Wildlife Fund 1965–1967* (Morges: WWF, 1967), 49.
76. World Wildlife Fund, *World Wildlife Fund Yearbook 1969* (Morges: WWF,

1969), 16.

77. Ibid., 167.

78. World Wildlife Fund, note 75 above, 212.

79. *IUPN Bulletin*, II:6 (1953): 2.

80. *Proceedings of the 5th IUCN General Assembly, Edinburgh 1956* (Morges: IUCN, 1956), 22.

81. Gerald Watterson, ed., *Report of the Pan-African Symposium on the Conservation of Nature and Natural Resources in Modern African States, September 1961* (Morges: IUCN, 1963), 61.

82. *IUCN Bulletin*, No. 1 (August 1961): 1.

83. IUCN had nonetheless been concerned about the weighting in favor of European discussion leaders; the difficulty was said to have been one of finding outstanding African speakers, which in turn was seen as a reflection on colonial education policies. "Correcting Misconceptions about Conservation," *New Scientist* 11:250 (31 August 1961): 504.

84. *IUCN Bulletin*, No. 2 (December 1961): 7.

85. John Hillaby, "Conservation in Africa: A Crucial Conference," *New Scientist* 11:250 (31 August 1961): 536–538.

86. Watterson, note 81 above, 19.

87. Ibid., 49.

88. *IUCN Bulletin*, No. 4 (July/September 1962): 2.

89. The Asian equivalent of the ASP, the South-East Asia Project (SEAP), was launched in 1964. Lee Talbot undertook fieldwork during 1964–65, and the Conference on Conservation of Nature and Natural Resources in Tropical South-East Asia was held in Bangkok 29 November to 4 December 1965. A Latin American equivalent, the Latin American Conference on Conservation of Renewable Natural Resources, was held in San Carlos de Bariloche, Argentina, from 27 March to 2 April 1968.

90. *IUCN Bulletin*, No. 6 (January/March 1963): 7.

91. *IUCN Bulletin*, No. 8 (July/September 1963): 1.

92. *IUCN Bulletin*, No. 9 (October/December 1963): 3.

93. Russell E. Train, "A World Heritage Trust," in World Wildlife Fund, note 75 above, 36.

94. Boardman, note 9 above, 151.

95. World Wildlife Fund, *World Wildlife Fund Yearbook 1968* (Morges: WWF, 1968), 46–47.

96. IUCN, note 48 above, 47.

97. Ibid., 47. This definition appeared almost unchanged in the preamble to the World Conservation Strategy in 1980.

THREE. THE ENVIRONMENTAL REVOLUTION (1962–1970)

1. Stephen Fox, *John Muir and His Legacy: The American Conservation Movement* (Boston: Little, Brown & Co., 1981), 292.

2. *Time*, 4 January 1971, 21–22.

3. *Life*, 30 January 1970, 23.

4. Few of the new groups had large memberships; a 1973 EPA survey found that 72 percent of the groups had memberships of less than 500, and 45 percent fewer than 100. Clem L. Zinger, Richard Dalsemer, and Helen Magargle, *Environmental Volunteers in America* (Washington, DC: EPA, 1973), 5.

5. Denton E. Morrison, Kenneth E. Hornback, and W. Keith Warner, "The Environmental Movement: Some Preliminary Observations and Predictions," in William R. Burch, Neil H. Cheek, and Lee Taylor, *Social Behavior, Natural Resources and the Environment* (New York: Harper & Row, 1972), 261–262.

6. Richard L. Means, "The New Conservation," *Natural History*, 78:7 (August-September 1969): 16–25.

7. Roderick Nash, *Wilderness and the American Mind* (New Haven: Yale University Press, 1973), 251–252.

8. Stephen Cotgrove, *Catastrophe or Cornucopia* (London: Wiley, 1982), 5.

9. Francis Sandbach, *Environment: Ideology and Policy* (Oxford: Basil Blackwell, 1980), 21–22.

10. John Maddox, *The Doomsday Syndrome* (London: Macmillan, 1972), 135.

11. Quoted in Carroll Pursell, ed., *From Conservation to Ecology: The Development of Environmental Concern* (New York: Thomas Y. Crowell Co., 1973), 4.

12. Philip Lowe, Jane Clifford and Sarah Buchanan, "The Mass Movement of the Decade," *Vole*, January 1980, 26–28.

13. Philip Lowe and Jane Goyder, *Environmental Groups in Politics* (London: George Allen & Unwin, 1983), 25.

14. Timothy O'Riordan, *Environmentalism* (London: Pion Ltd., 1981), 37.

15. Cotgrove, note 8 above, 74–100.

16. Stephen Raushenbush, "Conservation in 1952," *The Annals of the American Academy of Political and Social Science* 281 (May 1952); 1–9.

17. William E. Leuchtenburg, *A Troubled Feast: American Society Since 1945* (Boston: Little, Brown & Co., 1979), 37–38.

18. William H. Chafe and Harvard Sitkoff, eds., *A History of Our Time: Readings on Postwar America* (New York: Oxford University Press, 1983), 10.

19. Lawrence S. Wittner, *Cold War America: From Hiroshima to Watergate* (New York: Praeger, 1974), 112.

20. John Kenneth Galbraith, *The Affluent Society* (Boston: Houghton Mifflin, 1958).

21. Anthony Downs, "Up and Down with Ecology—The 'Issue-Attention' Cycle," *The Public Interest* 28 (1972): 38–50.

22. Earl H. Voss, *Nuclear Ambush: The Test-Ban Trap* (Chicago: Henry Regnery Company, 1963), 33.

23. The revival of interest in the issue in the late 1970s resulted in the setting up of a Royal Commission, which reported in December 1985, revealing that the tests had been carried out without adequate attention to meteorological conditions or to the dangers posed to aborigines, and that British attempts to clean up remaining toxic wastes in 1967 had been wholly inadequate; large areas of land surrounding the sites of the tests remained contaminated and inaccessible.

24. Graham Baines, "Nuclear Games in the South Pacific," *The Ecologist* 1:18 (December 1971): 9–11.

25. American Society for the Advancement of Science, *Report of the Air Conservation Commission* (Washington, DC: ASAS, 1965).

26. Barbara Ward and René Dubos, *Only One Earth* (Harmondsworth: Penguin, 1972), 297; Barry Commoner, *The Closing Circle: Nature, Man and Technology* (New York: Knopf, 1971), 56.

27. Maddox, note 10 above, 13.

28. Voss, note 22 above, 33.

29. Commoner, note 26 above, 50.

30. Ibid., 49.

31. Voss, note 22 above, 37.

32. Gwyn Prins, ed., *Defended to Death: A Study of the Nuclear Arms Race* (Harmondsworth: Penguin, 1983), 75.

33. Mary Milling Lepper, *Foreign Policy Formulation: A Case Study of the Nuclear Test Ban Treaty of 1963* (Columbus, Ohio: Charles E. Merrill, 1971), 51.

34. Ibid., 33–34.

35. Commoner, note 26 above, 53.

36. American Institute of Public Opinion, December 1961, quoted in Ronald J. Terchek, *The Making of the Test Ban Treaty* (The Hague: Martinus Nijhoff, 1970), 116.

37. American Institute of Public Opinion, April 1955 and December 1961, quoted in Terchek, note 36 above, 116.

38. Harris Survey, 16 December 1963, quoted in Terchek, note 36 above, 121.

39. Terchek, note 36 above, 119–120; Arthur M. Schlesinger, *A Thousand Days: John F. Kennedy in the White House* (Boston: Houghton Mifflin, 1965), 460, 895; Glenn T. Seaborg, *Kennedy, Krushchev and the Test Ban* (Berkeley: University of California Press, 1981), 31–32.

40. Terchek, note 36 above, 149–150.

41. Ibid., 149, 169.

42. Lepper, note 33 above, 40.

43. Harold Karan Jacobson and Eric Stein, *Diplomats, Scientists and Politicians: The United States and the Nuclear Test Ban Negotiations* (Ann Arbor: University of Michigan Press, 1966), 382.

44. Commoner, note 26 above, 57–58. This concept was elaborated in the nuclear winter debate of the early 1980s.

45. Trevor N. Dupuy and Gay M. Hammerman, *A Documentary History of Arms Control and Disarmament* (New York: R.R. Bowker Co, 1973), 525.

46. See Terchek, note 36 above, 200.

47. Rachel Carson (1907–1964) was a marine biologist by training. She studied genetics at Johns Hopkins University before teaching at Johns Hopkins and the University of Maryland. In 1936 she joined the U.S. Bureau of Fisheries. She began writing for journals in 1937. Her first book, *Under the Sea Wind*, was published in 1941. She became editor-in-chief of U.S. Fish and Wildlife Service publications and became a full-time writer and literary celebrity in 1951 with the publication of *The Sea Around Us*.

48. Kevin P. Shea, "A Celebration of Silent Spring," *Environment* 15:1 (January-February 1973): 4–5.

49. Allen Schnaiberg, "Politics, Participation and Pollution: The 'Environmental Movement,' " in John Walton and Donald E. Carns, eds., *Cities in Change: Studies in the Urban Condition* (Boston: Allen and Bacon Inc., 1977), 466.

50. Frank Graham, *Since Silent Spring* (Boston: Houghton Mifflin, 1970), 17.

51. Rachel Carson, *Silent Spring* (Boston: Houghton Mifflin, 1962), 8.

52. Ibid., 13.

53. Paul Brooks, *The House of Life: Rachel Carson at Work* (Boston: Houghton Mifflin, 1972), 228–229.

54. During 1945, *Harper's*, the *Atlantic Monthly*, and the *New Yorker* had all run articles on the dangers posed by DDT to nature. Colleagues of Carson at the Fish and Wildlife Service wrote in scientific papers of the possible long-term consequences of DDT. Rachel Carson had herself submitted an article on DDT to *Reader's Digest*, but it had been rejected. Ibid, 230–231.

55. Ibid., 294.

56. George Claus and Karen Bolander, *Ecological Sanity* (New York: David McKay Co, 1977), 10.

57. Brooks, note 53 above, 308.

58. Graham, note 50 above, 53–54.

59. Fox, note 1 above, 292.

60. Ibid., 298.

61. Nash, note 7 above, 252.

62. Eric Ashby and Mary Anderson, *The Politics of Clean Air* (Oxford: Clarendon Press, 1981), 104.

63. Roy Herbert, "The Day the Reactor Caught Fire," *New Scientist*, (October 14, 1982): 84–87; Tony Hall, *Nuclear Politics* (Harmondsworth: Penguin, 1986), 57–

63.

64. Stanley Johnson, *The Politics of Environment: The British Experience* (London: Tom Stacey, 1973), 82.

65. Erich R. Gundlach, "Oil Tanker Disasters," *Environment* 19:9 (December 1977): 16–27.

66. Johnson, note 64 above, 84.

67. Philip Lowe, "Science and Government: The Case of Pollution," *Public Administration* (Autumn 1975): 287–298.

68. M. Foster, M. Neushul, and R. Zingmark, "The Santa Barbara Oil Spill, Part 2: Initial Effects on Intertidal and Kelp Bed Organisms," *Environmental Pollution* 2:2 (October 1971): 115–134.

69. Council on Environmental Quality, *Environmental Quality 1979* (Washington, DC: U.S. Government Printing Office, 1979), 10–11.

70. Harvey Molotch and Marilyn Lester, "Accidental News: The Great American Oil Spill as Local Occurrence and National Event," *American Journal of Sociology* 81:2 (September 1975): 235–260.

71. Johnson, note 64 above, 84.

72. Molotch, note 70 above.

73. Ibid.

74. Council on Environmental Quality, *Environmental Quality 1970* (Washington, DC: U.S. Government Printing Office, 1970), 38.

75. Ibid., 38.

76. Commoner, note 26 above, 94–111.

77. Eutrophication occurs when organic wastes enter a lake, consuming the oxygen and leaving too little for the fish to survive. Eutrophication is a natural process that normally takes thousands of years to evolve; pollution in Lake Erie had compacted the process into a matter of decades. (Over time, eutrophic lakes become swamp and then solid land.)

78. Council on Environmental Quality, *The Global 2000 Report to the President* (Harmondsworth: Penguin, 1982), 318.

79. Norie Huddle and Michael Reich, "The Octopus That Eats Its Own Legs," *The Ecologist* 3:8 (August 1973): 292–295.

80. Ibid.

81. Fox, note 1 above, 302.

82. C. H. Waddington, in E. Barton Worthington, ed., *The Evolution of IBP* (Cambridge: Cambridge University Press, 1975), 11.

83. Ibid., 8–10.

84. Ibid., 126.

85. Ibid., 60, 137.

86. Martin Holdgate, Mohammed Kassas, and Gilbert White, *The World Environment 1972—82* (Dublin: Tycooly, 1982), 230.

87. Francois Bourliére, in Worthington, note 82 above, 138–139.

88. Schnaiberg, note 49 above, 465.

89. A 1973 survey by the National Center for Voluntary Action found that 98 percent of the members of American environmental organizations were white, 61 percent were college graduates, 35 percent were professionals, and 53 percent had family incomes greater than $15,000. Zinger, et al., note 4 above, 20–21. For other studies, see also Fox, note 1 above, 345–346, 355–357; Joseph Harry, Richard Gale, and John Hendee, "Conservation: An Upper-Middle Class Social Movement," *Journal of Leisure Research* 1 (Summer 1969): 246–254; William B. Devall, "Conservation: An Upper-Middle Class Social Movement: A Replication," *Journal of Leisure Research* 2 (Spring 1970): 123–126; Stephen Cotgrove and Andrew Duff, "Environmentalism, Middle-Class Radicalism and Politics," *Sociological Review* 28 (1980): 333–351; Lowe and Goyder, note 13 above, 27–31.

90. James Ridgeway, *The Politics of Ecology*, (New York: E. P. Dutton and Co.,

1970), 204.

91. Richard Taylor, and Colin Pritchard, *The Protest Makers: The British Nuclear Disarmament Movement of 1958–1965 Twenty Years On* (Oxford: Pergamon, 1980), 3.

92. Ibid., 45–46.

93. Jerome H. Skolnick, *The Politics of Protest: A Task Force Report Submitted to the National Commission on the Causes and Prevention of Violence* (New York: Simon and Shuster, 1969), xx.

94. Ibid., 79.

95. Cox Commission, *Crisis at Columbia: Report of the Fact-Finding Commission Appointed to Investigate the Disturbances at Columbia University in April and May 1968* (New York: Vintage Books, 1968), 4.

96. Skolnick, note 93 above, 79–81.

97. Seymour Martin Lipset, "Student Activism," *Current Affairs Bulletin* 42:4 (15 July 1968): 52–58.

98. John Searle, *The Campus War* (Harmondsworth: Pelican, 1972), 14–17.

99. Nash, note 7 above, 252–253.

100. Cotgrove, note 8 above, 12.

101. Charles Reich, *The Greening of America* (New York: Random House, 1970).

102. Nash, note 7 above, 257–258.

103. Fox, note 1 above, 325.

104. Downs, note 21 above.

105. See Sandbach, note 9, and Downs, note 21 above.

106. James S. Bowman, "The Environmental Movement: An Assessment of Ecological Politics," *Environmental Affairs* 5:4 (1976): 649–667.

107. Ibid.

108. Means, note 6 above.

109. Schnaiberg, note 49 above, 466.

110. Downs, note 21 above.

111. Hans Magnus Enzensberger, "A Critique of Political Ecology," *New Left Review* 84 (March-April 1974): 3–31.

112. William Solesbury, "The Environmental Agenda," *Public Administration* 54 (Winter 1976): 379–397.

113. Charles M. Hardin, "Observations on Environmental Politics," in Stuart S. Nagel, ed., *Environmental Politics* (London: Prager, 1974), 182.

114. Robert Golub and Jo Townsend, "Malthus, Multinationals and the Club of Rome," *Social Studies of Science* 7 (1977): 201–222.

115. Fox, note 1 above, 315.

116. *Time*, 2 February 1970, 56.

117. *New Republic*, 7 March 1970, 9; and 31 October 1970, 5.

118. Stewart L. Udall, *The Quiet Crisis* (New York: Holt, Rinehart and Winston, 1963), viii.

119. Kenneth S. Davis, *The Politics of Honor: A Biography of Adlai E. Stevenson* (New York: G. P. Putnam's Sons, 1967), 500.

120. Kenneth E. Boulding, "The Economics of Coming Spaceship Earth," in Henry Jarrett, ed., *Environmental Quality in a Growing Economy* (Baltimore: Johns Hopkins University Press, 1966), 9.

121. Arthur C. Clarke, *The Promise of Space* (New York, Harper and Row, 1968), 149.

FOUR. THE PROPHETS OF DOOM (1968–1972)

1. Michael Barkun, *Disaster and the Millenium* (New Haven: Yale University Press, 1974), 74–89.

2. Sir William Petty, *Mankind and Political Arithmetic* (New York: The Mershon

Co., n.d.).

3. Although best remembered as a demographer, the Rev. Thomas Robert Malthus (1766–1834) wrote and studied in many different fields and was a professor of history and political economy at the East India College, Hertfordshire. The fact that he was a clergyman earned him the epithet "that dismal parson."

4. Thomas Malthus, *An Essay on the Principle of Population*, edited by Philip Appleman (New York: W. W. Norton, 1976).

5. David Brower, quoted in *Newsweek*, 3 October 1966, 108.

6. Paul Ehrlich (b. 1932), a biologist, has been on the faculty of the Department of Biological Sciences at Stanford University since 1959. He became professor in 1966 and Bing Professor of Population Studies in 1976.

7. Curiously, a remarkably similar book published three years before—*The Silent Explosion* by Philip Appleman (Boston: Beacon Press, 1965), an English professor at Indiana University—sold well, but achieved nothing like the impact of *The Population Bomb*. Ehrlich made no reference to Appleman's work.

8. Paul R. Ehrlich, in *Playboy* 17:8, August 1970, 56.

9. Paul R. Ehrlich, *The Population Bomb* (New York: Ballantine Books, 1968), xii.

10. Barry Commoner (b. 1917), a biologist, has been on the faculty of Washington University, St. Louis, since 1947. Initially professor of plant pathology, he campaigned in the 1950s for freer information on the effects of nuclear tests and founded the St. Louis Committee for Nuclear Information in 1958. He wrote *Science and Survival* in 1966 and *The Closing Circle* in 1971.

11. Barry Commoner, *The Closing Circle: Nature, Man and Technology* (New York: Knopf, 1971), 140–177.

12. Constance Holden, "Ehrlich versus Commoner: An Environmental Fallout," *Science* 177:4045 (21 July 1972): 245–247.

13. Ibid.

14. Commoner, note 11 above, 128–133.

15. Paul R. Ehrlich and John P. Holdren, "The Closing Circle," *Environment* 14:3 (April 1972): 24–39.

16. Barry Commoner, "The Closing Circle," *Environment* 14:3 (April 1972): 23–52.

17. Nicholas Pole, "An Interview with Paul Ehrlich," *The Ecologist* 3:1 (January 1973): 18–24.

18. Paul R. Ehrlich and Anne H. Ehrlich, *The End of Affluence* (New York: Ballantine Books, 1974).

19. Pole, note 17 above.

20. Ehrlich, note 8 above.

21. Pole, note 17 above.

22. Ehrlich, note 9 above, 26.

23. Paul R. Ehrlich and Richard L. Harriman, *How to be a Survivor: A Plan to Save Spaceship Earth* (New York: Ballantine Books, 1971), authors' note.

24. Pole, note 17 above.

25. Garret Hardin (b. 1915), a biologist, joined the faculty of the University of California at Santa Barbara in 1946, becoming professor of biology in 1956 and professor of human ecology in 1964.

26. Garrett Hardin, "The Tragedy of the Commons," *Science* 162:3859 (13 December 1968): 1243–1248.

27. See, for example, Mancur Olson, *The Logic of Collective Action* (Cambridge: Harvard University Press, 1965).

28. Hardin, note 26 above.

29. For further discussion, see Francis Sandbach, "The Rise and Fall of the *Limits to Growth* Debate," *Social Studies of Science*, 8:4 (November 1978): 495–520.

30. Samuel H. Ordway, *Resources and the American Dream* (New York: Ronald Press Co., 1953).

31. Jay Wright Forrester (b. 1918) has spent almost his entire professional career at MIT. He was on the research staff from 1939 to 1956 (directing the MIT Digital Computer Laboratory between 1946 and 1951) and became professor of management at the Sloan School of Management in 1956. He developed the system dynamics model of social and economic change in the United States.

32. Walter E. Hecox, "Limits to Growth Revisited: Has the World Modelling Debate Made Any Progress?" *Environmental Affairs* 5:1 (Winter 1976): 65–96.

33. Ibid.

34. Aurelio Peccei (1908–1985) was born in Turin and graduated in economics from the University of Turin. He worked for Fiat from 1930 to 1973, was President of Olivetti from 1963 to 1967, and Chairman of the Board of Italconsult from 1971. After cofounding the Club of Rome, he devoted his time to the study of macroproblems of the technological age and of the changes needed in human society in order to find answers to those problems.

35. Aurelio Peccei, *The Chasm Ahead* (London: Macmillan, 1969).

36. S. I. Schwartz and T. C. Foin, "A Critical Review of the Social System Models of Jay Forrester," *Human Ecology* 1:2 (September 1972): 161–173.

37. Donella H. Meadows, Dennis L. Meadows, Jorgen Randers, and William W. Behrens III, *The Limits to Growth* (New York: New American Library, 1972), xi.

38. Study of Critical Environmental Problems, *Man's Impact on the Global Environment: Assessment and Recommendations for Action* (Cambridge, MA: MIT Press, 1970), 5.

39. Ibid., 253.

40. Jay W. Forrester, "Counterintuitive Behavior of Social Systems," *Technology Review* 73:3 (January 1971): 53–68.

41. Jay W. Forrester, *World Dynamics* (Cambridge, MA: Wright-Allen Press, 1971).

42. Dennis Lynn Meadows (b. 1942) was assistant professor of management at MIT between 1969 and 1972. He then moved to the Department of Engineering at Dartmouth College, New Hampshire. His wife Donella (b. 1941) was a researcher in nutrition and food science at MIT (1970–72) and then moved to the Department of Environmental Studies at Dartmouth.

43. Meadows, et al., note 37 above, 29.

44. Ibid., 159.

45. Ibid., 194–198.

46. The World Conservation Strategy, the *Global 2000* report, and the reports of the Brandt and Brundtland Commissions—published respectively in 1980, 1982, 1980, and 1987—can be seen as steps in this direction.

47. Meadows, et. al., note 37 above, 189.

48. Hardin, note 26 above.

49. Meadows, et al., note 37 above, 195.

50. *The Ecologist, Blueprint for Survival* (Harmondsworth: Penguin, 1972).

51. Ibid., 9.

52. E. F. Schumacher, *Small is Beautiful: Economics as If People Mattered* (London: Abacus, 1974).

53. Paul R. Ehrlich and Anne H. Ehrlich, *Population, Resources, Environment* (San Francisco: W.H. Freeman and Co., 1970), 1.

54. Barbara Ward and René Dubos, *Only One Earth* (Harmondsworth: Penguin, 1972), 25.

55. Barclay Inglis, "Concorde: The Case Against Supersonic Transport," in John Barr, ed., *The Environmental Handbook* (London: Ballantine/Pan, 1971), 180.

56. *Life*, 30 January 1970, 22.

57. Lester Brown, ed., *State of the World 1984* (New York: W.W. Norton, 1984), 188.

58. Paul R. Ehrlich, *The Population Bomb*, rev. ed. (New York: Ballantine Books, 1978), 203.

59. David L. Sills, "The Environmental Movement and Its Critics," *Human Ecology* 3:1 (1975): 1–41.

60. C. Kaysen, "The Computer That Printed Out W*O*L*F*," *Foreign Affairs* 50:4 (1972): 660–668.

61. Timothy O'Riordan, *Environmentalism* (London: Pion Ltd., 1981), 59.

62. Robert Allen, "European Con Year," *The Ecologist* 1:6 (December 1970): 4–7.

63. See National Caucus of Labor Committees, *Blueprint for Extinction* (New York: NCLC, 1972).

64. A. Martin, *The Last Generation: The End of Survival?* (London: Fontana, 1975); John Maddox, *The Doomsday Syndrome* (London: Macmillan, 1972).

65. Council on Environmental Quality, *The Global 2000 Report to the President* (Harmondsworth, Penguin, 1982), 607.

66. H. S. D. Cole, Christopher Freeman, Marie Jahoda, and K. L. R. Pavitt, *Thinking About the Future: A Critique of* The Limits to Growth (London: Chatto & Windus, for Sussex University Press, 1973).

67. Ibid., 12.

68. Aurelio Peccei, *The Human Quality* (Oxford: Pergamon, 1977), 85.

69. Meadows, et al., note 37 above, 28.

70. Cole, et al., note 66 above, 5–13.

71. Ibid., 12.

72. Francis Sandbach, *Environment: Ideology and Policy* (Oxford: Basil Blackwell, 1980), 205.

73. O'Riordan, note 61 above, 60–72.

74. Meadows, et al., note 37 above, 191.

75. E. W. Pehrson, "The Mineral Position in the United States and the Outlook for the Future," *Mining and Metallurgy Journal* 26 (1945): 204–214.

76. See Sandbach, note 29 above, 205 for many examples.

77. For discussion of the strengths and weaknesses of the model, see Hecox, note 32 above.

78. John McCormick, *Acid Earth: The Global Threat of Acid Pollution* (London: Earthscan, 1985).

79. Council on Environmental Quality, note 65 above, 608.

80. Ibid., 609.

81. Hecox, note 32 above. The Club of Rome sponsored a more optimistic follow-up to *The Limits to Growth*, entitled *Mankind at the Turning Point* by Mihaljo Mesarovic and Eduard Pestel (New York: Dutton, 1974). Dividing the world into sub-regions, it offered a gaming technique by which policymakers could actually test their strategies. Deliberately low-key, the report was all but ignored.

82. Maddox, note 64 above, vii.

83. Melvin J. Grayson and Thomas R. Shepard, Jr., *The Disaster Lobby: Prophets of Ecological Doom and Other Absurdities* (Chicago: Follett Publishing Co., 1973), 21–43.

84. Petr Beckmann, *Eco-hysterics and the Technophobes* (Boulder, CO: Golem Press, 1973), 8–9, 206–212.

85. "Aurum," "British Architects and the Environment," *Bulletin of the Atomic Scientists* 28:3 (March 1972): 42.

86. Lewis M. Killian, "Social Movements," in Robert E. L. Faris, ed., *Handbook of Modern Sociology* (Chicago: Rand McNally, 1964), 450.

87. *Newsweek*, 4 May 1970, 27.

88. Carl E. Bagge, "Radicalism Perils Supply of Minerals." Speech quoted in

ɔuɪt *Lake City Tribune*, 29 June 1971, 6.

89. Stan L. Albrecht, "Environmental Social Movements and Counter-Movements: An Overview and an Illustration," *Journal of Voluntary Action Research* 1 (October 1972): 2–11.

90. Allen, note 62 above.

91. Maddox, note 64 above, 236–237.

92. Daniel B. Luten, quoted in *The Boston Globe*, 12 May 1985, A21.

93. Meadows et al., note 37 above, 198.

94. Karl Marx, *The Poverty of Philosophy* (New York: International Publishers, 1963), 195.

FIVE. THE STOCKHOLM CONFERENCE (1970–1972)

1. UN Economic and Social Council, Annexes, Agenda Item 12 (Doc E/4466/Add.1) at 2 (New York: ECOSOC, 1968).

2. Robert Boardman, *International Organization and the Conservation of Nature* (Bloomington: Indiana University Press, 1981), 82.

3. UNESCO, *Use and Conservation of the Biosphere* (Proceedings of the Biosphere Conference) (Paris: UNESCO, 1970), foreword.

4. Ibid., 201.

5. Ibid., 210.

6. UNESCO, *Backgrounder: The MAB Programme* (Paris: UNESCO, 1982), 2.

7. Alden L. Doud, "International Environmental Developments: Perceptions of Developing and Developed Countries," *Natural Resources Journal* 12 (October 1972): 520–529.

8. As with UNSCCUR in 1949, the Stockholm conference was called initially to focus attention on an issue but not necessarily to recommend action. It was not until 1970 that any talk of action entered into the deliberations of the organizing committee. Peter Stone, *Did We Save the Earth at Stockholm?* (London: Earth Island, 1973), 18.

9. United Nations, Resolution 2398 (XXIII) of the General Assembly, 3 December 1968.

10. Ibid.

11. United Nations, *Yearbook of the United Nations 1970* (New York: Office of Public Information, United Nations, 1970), 449.

12. United Nations Environment Programme, *Review of the Areas of Environment and Development and Environmental Management*, UNEP Report No. 3 (Nairobi: UNEP, 1978), 6.

13. United Nations, Report of the Secretary-General to the Third Session of the Preparatory Committee (UN Doc A/CONF.48/PC.11) (New York: United Nations, 1971).

14. MDCs apparently had their own concerns about what the conference might achieve. Just before the conference, the *Ecologist* suggested that MDCs were "anxious to limit international action on the environment as far as possible to anti-pollution measures, (fearing) that the conference would turn into yet another platform for poor country demands for further economic aid." *The Ecologist* (June 1972): 4.

15. K. Rodgers, "With the Developing Countries at Founex," *Uniterra* 1 (1982), 6.

16. Martin Holdgate, Mohammed Kassas, and Gilbert White, *The World Environment 1972–1982* (Dublin: Tycooly, 1982), 7.

17. Maurice F. Strong (b. 1929) is a Canadian businessman and self-made millionaire with interests in a number of business ventures, including Petro-Canada. From 1966 to 1971 he was director-general of the Canadian External Aid Office

(later Canadian International Development Agency). He was first executive-director of UNEP, from 1973 to 1975.

18. Maurice F. Strong, "The International Community and the Environment," *Environmental Conservation* 4:3 (Autumn 1977): 165–172.

19. United Nations, note 11 above.

20. Brian Johnson, "The Bureaucrat and the Biosphere," *The Ecologist* 2:6 (June 1972): 30–36.

21. United Nations, note 13 above.

22. United Nations, *The UN System and the Human Environment* (Gen. Ass. Doc A/CONF.48/12, 17 December 1971), 71.

23. Ibid., 5.

24. Ibid., 72.

25. Hans H. Landsberg, "Reflections on the Stockholm Conference," (unpubl. paper; Washington, DC: August 1972).

26. Ibid.

27. United States Department of State, *Stockholm and Beyond* (Department of State Publication 8657, Washington, DC: 1972), 129.

28. Johnson, note 20 above.

29. National Academy of Sciences, *International Arrangements of International Environmental Co-operation* (Washington, DC: NAS, 1972), 4.

30. Louis B. Sohn, "The Stockholm Declaration on the Human Environment," *The Harvard International Law Journal* 14:3 (Summer 1974): 423–515.

31. Landsberg, note 25 above.

32. Ibid.

33. Ibid.

34. Barbara Ward (1914–1982), also known as Baroness Jackson of Lodsworth, was a journalist and author. She was assistant editor of the *Economist* from 1940 to 1950 and in 1968 was appointed Schweitzer Professor of International Economic Development at Columbia University. In 1973 she became president of IIED. Her last two books were *The Home of Man* (1976) and *Progress for a Small Planet* (1979). René Dubos (1901–1983) was a French-born American biologist and philosopher and a winner of the Pulitzer Prize.

35. Barbara Ward, Interview with Jon Tinker, 1981 (unpubl.).

36. Barbara Ward and René Dubos, *Only One Earth* (Harmondsworth: Penguin, 1972).

37. International Institute for Environmental Affairs, Minutes of the fifth meeting of the International Institute for Environmental Affairs Board of Directors, Paris, February 1972 (unpubl.).

38. Thomas W. Wilson, Draft Plan for the International Institute for Environmental Affairs, 21 September 1970 (unpubl.).

39. Ibid.

40. Thomas W. Wilson, Proposal to Establish an International Center for Environmental Affairs, 26 June 1970 (unpubl.).

41. IIEA, note 37 above.

42. United Nations, *Yearbook of the United Nations 1972* (New York: Office of Public Information, United Nations, 1972), 319.

43. Ward and Dubos, note 36 above, 24.

44. In Erik Eckholm, *Down to Earth* (New York: W.W. Norton, 1982), xii.

45. Lee M. Talbot, "A Remarkable Melding of Contrasts and Conflicts," *Uniterra* 1 (1982), 2.

46. Martin Holdgate, "Beyond the Ideals and the Vision," *Uniterra* 1 (1982), 3.

47. Barbara Ward, Speech to the UN Conference on the Human Environment, June 1972 (unpubl.).

48. In Eckholm, note 44 above, xi.

49. International Union for Conservation of Nature and Natural Resources, *IUCN Yearbook 1971* (Morges: IUCN, 1972), 14.

50. Gerardo Budowski, "A Certain Pre-Event Anxiety," *Uniterra* 1 (1982), 5–6.

51. International Union for Conservation of Nature and Natural Resources, *IUCN Yearbook 1972* (Morges: IUCN, 1973), 20.

52. Keith Johnson, "A Second Copernican Revolution," *Uniterra* 1 (1982), 4–5.

53. Terri Aaronson, "World Priorities," *Environment* 14:6 (July/August 1972): 4–13.

54. Landsberg, note 25 above.

55. Aaronson, note 53 above.

56. Ibid.

57. Reported in *Stockholm Conference Eco*, 14 June 1972, 1.

58. Aaronson, note 53 above.

59. Mary Jean Haley, ed., *Open Options: A Guide to Stockholm's Alternative Environmental Conferences* (Stockholm: 29 May 1972), 3.

60. Landsberg, note 25 above.

61. Talbot, note 45 above.

62. Richard Sandbrook, "NGOs and the UNEP Council - Governments No Longer Listen," *IUCN Bulletin* 11:6 (June 1980): 65.

63. United Nations Environment Programme, *Review of Major Achievements in the Implementation of the Action Plan for the Human Environment*, UNEP Doc. Na.82-0006-1142C (Nairobi, UNEP, 26 January 1982), 46.

64. Philip Lowe and Jane Goyder, *Environmental Groups in Politics* (London: George Allen & Unwin, 1983), 163.

65. European Environmental Bureau, *Reports 1975/1976* (Brussels: EEB, 1976), 163.

66. Lowe and Goyder, note 64 above, 165.

67. Holdgate, note 46 above.

68. Ward, note 35 above.

69. Ibid.

70. In Eckholm, note 44 above, xi–xii.

71. Talbot, note 45 above.

72. Holdgate, et al., note 16 above, 7.

73. Ward, note 35 above.

74. Sohn, note 30 above.

75. United Nations, note 42 above, 320–321.

76. Landsberg, note 25 above.

77. Richard Sandbrook, "The UK's Overseas Environmental Policy," in *The Conservation and Development Programme for the UK: A Response to the World Conservation Strategy* (London: Kogan Page, 1983), 390.

SIX. THE UNITED NATIONS
ENVIRONMENT PROGRAMME (1972–1982)

1. United Nations, Resolution 2997 (XXVII) of the General Assembly, 15 December 1972.

2. United Nations, Resolution 3004 (XXVII) of the General Assembly, December 1972.

3. Michael Hardy, "The United Nations Environment Program," *Natural Resources Journal* 13 (April 1973): 235–255.

4. United Nations, note 1 above.

5. Richard Sandbrook, "The UK's Overseas Environmental Policy," in *The Conservation and Development Programme for the UK: A Response to the World Conser-*

vation Strategy (London: Kogan Page, 1983), 391.

6. Robin Clarke and Lloyd Timberlake, *Stockholm Plus Ten* (London: Earthscan, 1982), 50.

7. Sandbrook, note 5 above, 390.

8. Ibid., 391.

9. United Nations Environment Programme, *The Environment in 1982: Retrospect and Prospect,* Paper prepared for the Session of a Special Character, Nairobi (UNEP, Doc UNEP/GC [SSC]/2, 29 January 1982, Nairobi), 22; Sandbrook, note 5 above, 391.

10. United Nations Environment Programme, *Review of the Areas of Environment and Development and Environmental Management,* UNEP Report No. 3 (Nairobi: UNEP, 1978), 3.

11. Sandbrook, note 5 above, 392.

12. United Nations Environment Programme, *Earthwatch: An In-depth Review,* UNEP Report No. 1 (Nairobi: UNEP, 1981).

13. Ibid., 76.

14. United Nations Environment Programme, *Review of Major Achievements in the Implementation of the Action Plan for the Human Environment,* UNEP Doc. Na.82-0006-1142C (Nairobi: 26 January 1982), 58.

15. Sandbrook, note 5 above, 388.

16. United Nations Environment Programme, Report on the Present State of UNEP, prepared by the Permanent Representatives of the European Community Countries, 1980 (unpubl.).

17. Mostafa Kamal Tolba (b. 1928) was born in Egypt. He held the chair of microbiology at the University of Cairo and served as a government minister and aide to Anwar Sadat before heading the Egyptian delegation to Stockholm. He served as deputy to Maurice Strong at UNEP for three years before being appointed UNEP executive director in 1976.

18. United Nations Environment Programme, note 16 above.

19. David L. Sills, "The Environmental Movement and Its Critics," *Human Ecology* 3:1 (1975): 1–41.

20. United Nations Environment Programme, note 14 above, 61.

21. Clarke and Timberlake, note 6 above, 48.

22. Martin Holdgate, "UNEP: Some Personal Thoughts," *Mazingira,* March 1984, 17–20.

23. Clarke and Timberlake, note 6 above, 48.

24. Ibid., 52.

25. Ibid., 56.

26. United Nations Environment Programme, note 9 above, 20.

27. United Nations Environment Programme, note 9 above, 21; Clarke and Timberlake, note 6 above, 47.

28. Holdgate, note 22 above.

29. Ibid.

30. Ibid.

31. Clarke and Timberlake, note 6 above, 49.

32. United Nations Environment Programme, note 14 above, 61.

33. United Nations Environment Programme, *Report of the Environmental Coordination Board on its Sixth Session, New York, 20–21 October 1976* (UNEP/GC/89) (Nairobi: UNEP, 1976), 1–2.

34. United Nations Environment Programme, *Memoranda of Understanding between the UN Environment Programme and Other Organisations of the United Nations System, 19 December 1977* (UNEP/GC/INFO/6) (Nairobi: UNEP, 1977).

35. Nicholas A. Robinson, Prepared statement before the Subcommittee on

Human Rights and International Organizations, Committee on Foreign Affairs, U.S. House of Representatives, 20 April 1982.

36. Clarke and Timberlake, note 6 above, 70.

37. United Nations Environment Programme, note 9 above, 74.

38. The principle of a regional approach to marine management was not new; the International Council for the Exploration of the Seas, for example, had been active in the North Atlantic and Baltic as early as 1902.

39. Earthscan, *The Polluted Seas* (London: Earthscan, 1978), 12.

40. Clarke and Timberlake, note 6 above, 43.

41. Earthscan, note 39 above, 14.

42. Peter Hulm, "The Regional Seas Program: What Fate for UNEP's Crown Jewels?" *Ambio* 12:1 (1983): 2–13.

43. United Nations Environment Programme, *Achievements and Planned Development of UNEP's Regional Seas Programme and Comparable Programmes Sponsored by Other Bodies,* UNEP Regional Seas Reports and Studies No. 1 (Nairobi: UNEP, 1982).

44. Hulm, note 42 above.

45. Ibid.

46. Clarke and Timberlake, note 6 above, 43.

47. Alan Grainger, *Desertification* (London: Earthscan, 1982), 5.

48. Ibid., 8.

49. Lloyd Timberlake, *Africa in Crisis* (London: Earthscan, 1985), 61.

50. Amartya Sen, *Poverty and Famines* (Oxford: Clarendon Press, 1981).

51. Timberlake, note 49 above.

52. Nigel Twose, *Why the Poor Suffer Most: Drought and the Sahel* (Oxford: Oxfam, 1984), 4.

53. William W. Murdoch, *The Poverty of Nations: The Political Economy of Hunger and Population* (Baltimore: Johns Hopkins University Press, 1980), 293.

54. Ibid., 298.

55. Grainger, note 47 above, 19.

56. Mostafa K. Tolba, "Desertification is Stoppable." Speech delivered to UNEP Governing Council, Nairobi, May 1984.

57. Ibid.

58. Grainger, note 47 above, 88.

59. United Nations Environment Programme, *General Assessment of Progress in the Implementation of the Plan of Action to Combat Desertification 1978-1984* (UNEP/GC.12/9) (Nairobi: UNEP, 1984), 32.

60. Grainger, note 47 above, 88.

61. United Nations Environment Programme, note 59 above, 32.

62. Grainger, note 47 above, 51.

63. United Nations Environment Programme, note 59 above, 33.

64. Ibid., 33.

65. Lloyd Timberlake, "Alone in the Wastelands" (Earthscan News Feature) London: Earthscan, May 1984.

66. Grainger, note 47 above, 53.

67. International Institute for Environment and Development, *Report on the African Emergency Relief Operation 1984–1986* (Draft) (London: IIED, 1986), 213, 221.

68. World Bank, *Toward Sustained Development in Sub-Saharan Africa* (Washington, DC: World Bank, 1984), 4.

69. Timberlake, note 49 above, 7.

70. Erik Eckholm, *Down to Earth* (New York: W. W. Norton, 1982), 5.

71. United Nations Environment Programme, note 9 above, 22.

72. United Nations Environment Programme, note 14 above, 68–69.

73. Clarke and Timberlake, note 6 above, 50.

SEVEN. THE NORTH: POLITICS AND ACTIVISM (1969–1980)

1. Organization for Economic Cooperation and Development, *The State of the Environment in OECD Member Countries* (Paris: OECD, 1979).

2. Australia, Britain, Canada, France, West Germany, India, Japan, Kenya, New Zealand, Singapore, Switzerland, and the United States. Council on Environmental Quality, *Environmental Quality 1971* (Washington, DC: U.S. Government Printing Office, 1971), 28.

3. World Environment Center, *The World Environment Handbook* (New York: WEC, 1983).

4. Francis Sandbach, "The Rise and Fall of the *Limits to Growth* Debate," *Social Studies of Science* 8:4 (November 1978): 495–520.

5. World Resources Institute/International Institute for Environment and Development, *World Resources 1986* (New York: Basic Books, 1986), 191.

6. Organization for Economic Cooperation and Development, *The State of the Environment 1985* (Paris: OECD, 1985), 241.

7. WRI/IIED, note 5 above, 192.

8. This to some extent influenced the perception of national movements toward the issues. A 1974 survey of 635 local amenity societies in Britain, for example, revealed that 83 percent saw their work as connected with universal problems of pollution, over-population, and shortages of natural resources (e.g., local traffic schemes linked to global oil consumption). Of these, 44 percent said they could make their main contribution through public education and publicity, and 20 percent said local issues could be used as examples of global problems. A. Barker, "Local Amenity Societies, A Survey and Outline Report," in Civic Trust, *The Local Amenity Movement* (London: Civic Trust, 1976).

9. Roy Gregory, *The Price of Amenity* (London: Macmillan, 1971), 38.

10. Jon Tinker, "Britain's Environment: Nanny Knows Best," *New Scientist* 53:786 (9 March 1972): 530.

11. Howard A. Scarrow, "The Impact of British Domestic Air Pollution Legislation," *British Journal of Political Science* 2:3 (July 1972): 261–282.

12. Stanley Johnson, *The Politics of Environment: The British Experience* (London: Tom Stacey, 1973), 172–173.

13. Royal Commission on Environmental Pollution, *Second Annual Report* (London: Her Majesty's Printing Office, Cmnd 4894, 1972).

14. Cynthia Enloe, *The Politics of Pollution in Comparative Perspective* (New York: David McKay, 1975), 273.

15. Johnson, note 12 above, 98–99.

16. Sir Frank Fraser Darling, *Wilderness and Plenty* (Boston: Houghton Mifflin Co., 1970).

17. *White Paper on the Reorganisation of Central Government* (London: Her Majesty's Printing Office, Cmnd 4506, October 1970).

18. Graham Bennett, "Pollution Control in England and Wales: A Review," *Environmental Policy and Law* 5:2 (12 April 1979): 93–99.

19. Tony Aldous, *Battle for the Environment* (London: Fontana Books, 1972), 16.

20. E. Pollard, M. D. Hooper, and N. W. Moore, *Hedges* (London: Collins, 1974), 42.

21. Charlie Pye-Smith and Chris Rose, *Crisis and Conservation: Conflict in the British Countryside* (Harmondsworth: Penguin, 1984), 83.

22. Marion Shoard, *The Theft of the Countryside* (London: Temple Smith, 1980), 99.

23. Philip Lowe and Jane Goyder, *Environmental Groups in Politics* (London: George Allen and Unwin, 1983), 75.

24. Barker, note 8 above, 3.

25. Lowe and Goyder, note 23 above, 1.

26. Council on Environmental Quality, *Environmental Quality 1970* (Washington, DC: U.S. Government Printing Office, 1970), vii.

27. R. V. Dunenberg, *Understanding American Politics* (London: Fontana, 1984), 99–100.

28. Walter A. Rosenbaum, *Environmental Politics and Policy* (Washington, DC: CQ Press, 1985), 52–54.

29. Geoffrey Wandesforde-Smith, "National Policy for the Environment: Politics and the Concept of Stewardship," in *Congress and the Environment* ed. Richard Cooley and Geoffrey Wandesforde-Smith, (Seattle: University of Washington Press, 1970), 210.

30. J. Clarence Davies and Barbara S. Davies, *The Politics of Pollution* (Indianapolis: Pegasus, 1975), 108.

31. Ibid.

32. See annual Council on Environmental Quality reports.

33. Nixon had preempted Congress by creating, in May 1969, his own Cabinet-level advisory Environmental Quality Council. This consisted of the president as chairman, the vice-president, and the secretaries of six departments (including agriculture and the interior). The council met only a few times and accomplished little. Council on Environmental Quality, *The Global 2000 Report to the President: Entering the Twenty-First Century* (Harmondsworth: Penguin, 1982), 695.

34. Davies and Davies, note 30 above, 117.

35. John Quarles, *Cleaning Up America* (Boston: Houghton Mifflin, 1976), 19–20.

36. Rosenbaum, note 28 above, 51.

37. Council on Environmental Quality, *Environmental Quality 1979* (Washington, DC: U.S. Government Printing Office, 1979), 177.

38. Ibid., 181.

39. Norman J. Vig and Michael E. Kraft, "Environmental Policy from the Seventies to the Eighties," in *Environmental Policy in the 1980s: Reagan's New Agenda*, ed. Norman J. Vig and Michael E. Kraft (Washington, DC: CQ Press, 1984), 4.

40. Paul J. Culhane, "Sagebrush Rebels in Office: Jim Watt's Land and Water Politics," in Vig and Kraft, ibid., 294.

41. Rosenbaum, note 28 above, 54.

42. Conservation Foundation, *State of the Environment 1982* (Washington, DC: Conservation Foundation, 1982), 387–392.

43. Vig and Kraft, note 39 above, 3.

44. Rosenbaum, note 28 above, 73-74.

45. Council on Environmental Quality, *Environmental Quality 1980* (Washington, DC: U.S. Government Printing Office, 1980), 418–419.

46. Ibid., 421–422.

47. Eva Kolinsky, "The Greens in Germany: Prospects of a Small Party," *Parliamentary Affairs* 37:4 (Autumn 1984): 434–447.

48. Fritjhof Capra and Charlene Spretnak, *Green Politics* (London: Hutchinson, 1984), 3.

49. Ibid., 28.

50. Elim Papadakis, "The Green Party in Contemporary West German Politics," *Political Quarterly* 54:3 (July–September 1983): 302–307.

51. Petra Kelly (b. 1947) was born in West Germany and educated there, in the United States, and the Netherlands. From 1972 she worked as an administrator with the EEC in Brussels. Resigning her membership of the German Social Democratic Party in 1979, she joined the newly formed Greens, becoming one of its early and best known leaders. She won a Bundestag seat in 1983 and was replaced as leader in 1984 in the rotational system used by *die Grünen*.

52. Hans Lohneis, "The Swiss Election of 1983: A Glacier on the Move?," *West*

European Politics 7:3 (July 1984): 117–119.

53. Tony Brunt, "In Search of Values," in *Right Out—Labour Victory '72: The Inside Story*, ed. Brian Edwards (Wellington: A.H. & A.W. Reed Ltd., 1973), 79.

54. Colin C. James, "Social Credit and the Values Party," in Howard R. Penniman, *New Zealand at the Polls: The General Election of 1978* (Washington, DC: American Enterprise Institute for Public Policy Research, 1980), 164.

55. Stephen Levine, *The New Zealand Political System: Politics in a Small Society* (Sydney: George Allen & Unwin, 1979), 82.

56. James, note 54 above, 166; Levine, ibid., 81.

57. Wolfgang Rudig and Philip Lowe, "The Withered 'Greening' of British Politics: A Study of the Ecology Party," *Political Studies* 34:2 (June 1986): 262–284.

58. Jean L. Cohen and Andrew Arato, "The German Green Party: A Movement Between Fundamentalism and Modernism," *Dissent* 31:3 (Summer 1984): 327–332.

59. Ferdinand Muller-Rommel, "Ecology Parties in Western Europe," *West European Politics* 5:1 (January 1982): 68–74.

60. See Capra and Spretnak, note 48 above, 10.

61. Ronald Inglehart, *The Silent Revolution: Changing Values and Political Styles among Western Publics* (Princeton: Princeton University Press, 1977).

62. Rudig and Lowe, note 57 above.

63. David Brower (b. 1912) became one of the most respected conservation activists in the United States. After dropping out of university, Brower spent six years working in Yosemite before joining the University of California Press as an editor. In 1952 he was appointed first full-time executive-director of the Sierra Club, a post he retained until compelled to resign in 1969. He then founded Friends of the Earth.

64. Stephen Fox, *John Muir and His Legacy: The American Conservation Movement* (Boston: Little, Brown & Co., 1981), 316.

65. Peter Wild, *Pioneer Conservationists of Western America* (Missoula, MT: Mountain Press, 1979), 157.

66. Stephen Cotgrove and Andrew Duff, "Environmentalism, Middle-Class Radicalism and Politics," *Sociological Review* 32 (1980): 92–110.

67. David Brower, Personal communication, December 1984; Tom Burke, "Friends of the Earth and the Conservation of Resources," in Peter Willetts, *Pressure Groups in the Global System* (London: Francis Pinter, 1982), 106.

68. Burke, note 67 above, 107.

69. Friends of the Earth, "Newsletter," *The Ecologist* 1:18 (December 1971): 33.

70. Robin Morgan and Brian Whitaker, *Rainbow Warrior* (London: Arrow Books, 1986), 115–116.

71. David McTaggart (b. 1933) was born in Canada and ran a number of business ventures in the United States before abandoning his career and moving to Tahiti. Following the 1972–73 Moruroa Atoll protests, McTaggart moved to Vancouver and created Greenpeace, latterly becoming director of Greenpeace International.

72. Morgan and Whitaker, note 70 above, 120–121.

73. Christopher Flavin, *Nuclear Power: The Market Test* (Washington, DC: Worldwatch Instituute, December 1983), 6–7.

74. Walter Patterson, *Nuclear Power* (Harmondsworth: Penguin, 1983), 120–122.

75. Ibid., 132–133.

76. Tony Hall, *Nuclear Politics* (Harmondsworth: Penguin, 1986), 135.

77. Patterson, note 74 above, 154.

78. The accident, involving both mechanical failure and human error, was triggered by the failure of a valve and the closure of a pump supplying water to a generator, leading to shutdown of the reactor. This was exacerbated by the failure

of a pressure relief valve to close (leading to reactor coolant being released), by the fact that auxiliary feedwater pumps were not operating (in violation of regulations), by the failure of operators to respond promptly, and by faulty instrument readings.

79. Council on Environmental Quality, *Environmental Quality 1979* (Washington, DC: U.S. Government Printing Office, 1979), 361.

80. Patterson, note 74 above, 162–163.

EIGHT. THE SOUTH: ENVIRONMENT AND DEVELOPMENT (1972–1982)

1. World Bank, *Toward Sustained Development in Sub-Saharan Africa* (Washington, DC: World Bank, 1984), 17.

2. United Nations Environment Programme, *In Defence of the Earth: The Basic Texts on Environment: Founex, Stockholm, Cocoyoc* (Nairobi: UNEP, 1981), 110.

3. Gerald Watterson, ed., *Report of the Pan-African Symposium on the Conservation of Nature and Natural Resources in Modern African States, September 1961* (Morges: IUCN, 1963), 19.

4. Ibid., 61.

5. National Parks Service, *First World Conference on National Parks* (Washington, DC: Department of the Interior, 1962), 381.

6. *IUCN Bulletin*, No. 6 (January/March 1963).

7. Paul Ehrlich and Anne Ehrlich, *Population, Resources, Environment* (San Francisco: W.H. Freeman and Co., 1970), 298.

8. International Institute for Environment and Development, *IIED Annual Report 1981–1982* (London: IIED, 1982), 7.

9. United Nations Environment Programme, *Report of the Governing Council of the United Nations Environment Programme, Fourth Session, 30 March-14 April 1976* (Nairobi: UNEP, 1976).

10. United Nations Environment Programme *Report of the Governing Council of the United Nations Environment Programme, Fifth Session, 9-25 May 1977* (Nairobi: UNEP, 1977).

11. UNEP, note 9 above.

12. Founex II, *Report of the Advisory Group Meeting*, 7 March 1973 (unpubl.).

13. The UNEP-UNCTAD Expert Group on the Impact of Resource Management Problems and Policies in Developed Countries on International Trade and Development Strategies.

14. UNEP-UNCTAD, *Report of the Expert Group on the Impact of Resource Management Problems and Policies in Developed Countries on International Trade and Development Strategies*, April 1974.

15. Joan Edelman Spero, *The Politics of International Economic Relations* (New York: St Martin's Press, 1985), 293–342.

16. The Symposium on Patterns of Resource Use, Environment, and Development Strategies.

17. Gamani Corea and Maurice Strong, Letter to Barbara Ward, 18 July 1974.

18. Barbara Ward, Interview with Jon Tinker (unpublished, 1981).

19. Robert McNamara (b. 1916) was educated at the University of California and at Harvard Business School. He was an executive with the Ford Motor Company from 1946 to 1961, rising to the position of president before being appointed Secretary of Defense in the first Kennedy cabinet. He stayed on under Johnson and in 1968 became chairman of the World Bank, a position he held until 1981.

20. Erik Eckholm, *Down to Earth* (New York: W.W. Norton, 1982), 15.

21. Paul Streeten, "From Growth to Basic Needs," *Finance and Development* (September 1979): 28–31.

22. Hollis Chenery, Montek S. Ahluwalia, C. L. G. Bell, John H. Duloy, and Richard Jolly, *Redistribution with Growth* (Oxford: Oxford University Press, 1974).

23. Raymond F. Dasmann, J. P. Milton, and P. H. Freeman, *Ecological Principles for Economic Development* (London: John Wiley, 1973).

24. Robert E. Stein and Brian Johnson, *Banking on the Biosphere?* (Lexington, MA: Lexington Books, 1979); Brian Johnson and Robert O. Blake, *The Environment and Bilateral Development Aid* (London: IIED, 1980).

25. Stein and Johnson, ibid., 11, 22.

26. World Bank, *Environment and Development* (Washington, DC: World Bank, 1979), 3.

27. World Bank, *Environmental, Health and Human Ecologic Consideration in Economic Development Projects* (Washington, DC: World Bank, 1972).

28. "World Bank Group Committed to Protecting Environment of Underdeveloped Countries," *Environment Reporter* 8:16 (19 August 1977).

29. Stein and Johnson, note 24 above, 12.

30. World Bank, note 26 above, 9.

31. Johnson and Blake, note 24 above, iii.

32. Thomas B. Stoels, Jacob Scherr, and Diana C. Crowley, *Environment, Natural Resources and Development: The Role of the US Agency for International Development* (Washington, DC: Natural Resources Defense Council, 1978), 30.

33. Johnson and Blake, note 24 above, v.

34. R. Ehrhart, A. Hanson, C. Sanger, and B. Wood, *Canadian Aid and the Environment* (Halifax, Nova Scotia: Dalhousie University, 1981), 59.

35. Richard Sandbrook, "The UK's Overseas Environmental Policy," in *The Conservation and Development Programme for the UK: A Response to the World Conservation Strategy* (London: Kogan Page, 1983), 381.

36. Ibid., 396.

37. *Declaration of Environment Policies and Procedures Relating to Economic Development*, reproduced ibid., 383.

38. World Bank, note 1 above.

39. Eckholm, note 20 above, 9.

40. UNEP, *A Review of the Major Achievements in the Implementation of the Stockholm Action Plan on the Human Environment*, UNEP Doc. Na. 81-4960 (Nairobi: UNEP, 1981), 67.

41. Robin Clarke and Lloyd Timberlake, *Stockholm Plus Ten* (London: Earthscan, 1982), 61.

42. Center for International Environment Information, "Government Agencies with Environmental Responsibilities in Developing Countries," *World Environment Report* 6 (April 1980): 9.

43. Emil Salim, *Conservation and Development*. The Second World Conservation Lecture (London: World Wildlife Fund, 1982).

44. UNEP, note 40 above, 69.

45. Randall Baker and David Kinyanjui, "Recommendations on the Institutional Framework for Environmental Management in Kenya," School of Development Studies, University of East Anglia, Occasional Paper No. 9 (November 1980), 3.

46. World Resources Institute/International Institute for Environment and Development, *World Resources 1987* (New York: Basic Books, 1987), 248.

47. Baker and Kinyanjui, note 45 above, 7.

48. National Environment Secretariat, quoted in Baker and Kinyanjui, id., 7.

49. Kilaparti Ramakrishna, "The Emergence of Environmental Law in the Developing Countries: A Case Study of India," *Ecology Law Quarterly* 12:4 (1985): 907–935.

50. Centre for Science and Environment, *The State of India's Environment 1982*

(New Delhi: CSE, 1982), 84, 178.

51. Centre for Science and Environment, *The State of India's Environment 1984–85* (New Delhi: CSE, 1985), 327, 343.

52. Ramakrishna, note 49 above.

53. CSE, note 50 above, 180–181.

54. CSE, note 51 above, 327.

55. Ibid., 348.

56. Ibid., 206–226.

57. Ibid.

58. The attention drawn by Bhopal overshadowed another serious incident only the month before: the death of more than five hundred people in the explosion of a liquefied petroleum gas store in Ixhuatepec, a shanty suburb of Mexico City. As many as one hundred thousand people—most of them migrants from rural areas—were settled in makeshift homes as close as 130 metres from the storage facility. (Pearce, Fred, "After Bhopal, Who Remembered Ixhuatepec?" *New Scientist*, 18 July 1985, 22–23.) At fault in the accident were many of the same problems that underlay Bhopal.

59. Paul Harrison, *The Greening of Africa* (Harmondsworth: Penguin, 1987), 187–188.

60. CSE, note 51 above, 338–339.

61. Ibid., 330.

62. Max Nicholson, "Requirements for a World Conservation Programme" (unpublished paper, IBP, 1966).

63. Duncan Poore, Personal communication, April 1986; Lee M. Talbot, "The World Conservation Strategy," in *Sustaining Tomorrow*, ed. F. R. Thibodeau and H. H. Field (Hanover: University Press of New England, 1985), 14.

64. Raymond Dasmann, "An Introduction to World Conservation," in Thibodeau and Field, Ibid., 17, 19.

65. Poore, note 63 above.

66. Ibid; Robert Allen, Personal communication, April 1984.

67. Talbot, note 63 above, 14.

68. International Union for Conservation of Nature, *IUCN Yearbook 75–76* (Morges: IUCN, 1976), 2.

69. Ibid., 3.

70. Ibid.

71. Robert Allen, "Ecodevelopment: A Long-Awaited Concept," *IUCN Bulletin* 7:5 (May 1976): 30.

72. "IUCN Prepares World Strategy," *IUCN Bulletin* 8:10 (October 1977): 59.

73. Lee M. Talbot, Introductory remarks to the 14th IUCN General Assembly, Ashkhabad, USSR, 25 September 1978.

74. "The Strategy Gets a Warm Welcome," *IUCN Bulletin* 9:10/11 (October/November 1978): 64.

75. IUCN, "Resolutions of the 14th Session of the General Assembly of IUCN," *IUCN Bulletin* 9:10/11 (October/November 1978).

76. *IUCN Bulletin*, note 74 above.

77. IUCN, Report on International Conservation, submitted to the 14th Session of the General Assembly of IUCN, Gen. Ass. paper GA.78/11, 18 August 1978.

78. "Strategy Launched in September," *IUCN Bulletin* 10:2 (February 1979): 15.

79. Poore, note 63 above.

80. IUCN, *A Conservation Programme for Sustainable Development: 1981–83* (Gland: IUCN, 1980).

81. IUCN, Director-General's Report, June-December 1979.

82. IUCN, *Achievements 1978–81* (Report of the director-general) (Gland: IUCN, 1981).

83. *World Conservation Strategy* (Gland: IUCN/UNEP/WWF, 1980), iv.

84. IUCN, *National Conservation Strategies: A Framework for Sustainable Development* (Gland: CDC/IUCN, 1984), 3.

85. WRI/IIED, note 46 above, 344–345.

NINE. THE GLOBAL ENVIRONMENT

1. Council for Environmental Quality, *Environmental Quality 1971* (Washington, DC: U.S. Government Printing Office, 1971), viii.

2. Richard A. Falk, "Environmental Policy as a World Order Problem," *Natural Resources Journal* 12:2 (April 1972): 161–171.

3. Council on Environmental Quality, *The Global 2000 Report to the President: Entering the Twenty-First Century* (Harmondsworth: Penguin, 1982), Letter of Transmittal.

4. Harlan Cleveland, "The Extrapolation of Metaphors: A 'Book Review' of the US Government's Global 2000 Study." Unpublished address to OECD, 1 April 1981.

5. Ibid.

6. Council on Environmental Quality, note 3 above, 1.

7. Council on Environmental Quality, *Global Future: Time to Act* (Washington, DC: CEQ, 1981).

8. Julian L. Simon, "Global Confusion, 1980: A Hard Look at the Global 2000 Report," *The Public Interest* 62 (Winter 1981): 3–20.

9. Herman Kahn and Ernest Schneider, "Globaloney 2000," *Policy Review* 16 (Spring 1981): 129–147.

10. Julian L. Simon and Herman Kahn, eds., *The Resourceful Earth: A Response to Global 2000* (Oxford: Basil Blackwell, 1984).

11. Kahn and Schneider, note 9 above.

12. Council on Environmental Quality, note 3 above, 16.

13. United Nations Environment Programme, *Register of International Treaties and Other Agreements in the Field of the Environment* (UNEP/GC/INFO/11) Nairobi: UNEP, May 1984.

14. Wolfgang Burhenne, ed., *International Environmental Law: Multilateral Treaties* (Berlin: Erich Schmidt Verlag, 1985).

15. Simon Lyster, *International Wildlife Law* (Cambridge: Grotius Publications, 1985), 10–11.

16. Ibid.

17. Ibid., 151.

18. Nigel Haigh, *Vienna Centre Project ECO I. Collaborative Arrangements for Environmental Protection in Western Europe* (London: IEEP/European Cultural Foundation, 1985), 4.

19. Ibid., 4.

20. Ibid.

21. Ibid., 5.

22. *World Conservation Strategy* (Gland: IUCN, UNEP, WWF, 1980), 15; Lyster, note 15 above, xxiii.

23. Lyster, note 15 above, 206.

24. Edward Maltby, *Waterlogged Wealth* (London: Earthscan, 1986), 94.

25. *Proceedings of the Conference on the Conservation of Wetlands of International Importance Especially as Waterfowl Habitat* (Doc. CONF/4) Cagliari, Italy, November 1980.

26. Lyster, note 15 above, 191.

27. Maltby, note 24 above, 94–95.

28. Lyster, note 15 above, 209, 237.

29. Haigh, note 18 above, 8.

30. Nigel Haigh, *EEC Environmental Policy and Britain* (London: Environmental Data Services, 1983), 4.

31. Robert Allen, "European Con Year," *The Ecologist* 1:6 (December 1970): 4–7.

32. Ibid.

33. Brian Johnson, "Common Market v Environment," *The Ecologist* 1:11 (May 1971): 10–14.

34. Haigh, note 18 above, 14.

35. Nigel Haigh, "Devolved Responsibility and Centralization: Effects of EEC Environmental Policy," *Public Administration* 64:2 (Summer 1986): 197–207.

36. Haigh, note 30 above, 1.

37. Haigh, note 35 above.

38. Athleen Ellington and Tom Burke, *Europe: Environment* (London: Ecobooks, 1981), 10.

39. Richard Sandbrook, "The UK's Overseas Environmental Policy," in *The Conservation and Development Programme for the UK: A Response to the World Conservation Strategy* (London: Kogan Page, 1983), 330–331.

40. Ibid., 331.

41. Philip Lowe and Jane Goyder, *Environmental Groups in Politics* (London: George Allen & Unwin, 1983), 164–165.

42. Ibid., 171.

43. Ellis B. Cowling, "Acid Precipitation in Historical Perspective," *Environmental Science and Technology* 16:2 (1982): 110A–123A.

44. Robert Angus Smith (1817–1884) was a Scottish-born chemist. Educated in Germany, he lived most of his life in Manchester, earning a living as a consultant chemist and researching public health issues such as the contamination of water supplies and air pollution. During the 1850s and 1860s he outlined the process of acid pollution, and during his twenty years with the Alkali Inspectorate (of which he was the first inspector), he campaigned assiduously for controls on industrial air pollution.

45. Robert Angus Smith, *Air and Rain: The Beginnings of a Chemical Climatology* (London: Longmans, Green & Co., 1872).

46. Cowling, note 43 above.

47. Organization for Economic Cooperation and Development, *The OECD Programme on Long Range Transport of Air Pollutants* (Summary Report) (Paris: OECD, 1977).

48. John McCormick, *Acid Earth: The Global Threat of Acid Pollution* (London: Earthscan, 1985), 61.

49. Gregory S. Wetstone and Armin Rosencranz, *Acid Rain in Europe and North America* (Washington, DC: Environmental Law Institute, 1984), 142.

50. McCormick, note 48 above, 61.

51. Wetstone and Rosencranz, note 49 above, 142–143.

52. UN Economic Commission for Europe, *Progress in Selected Areas of Cooperation* (Executive Body for the Convention on Long-Range Transboundary Air Pollution, Doc. EB AIR/R.12) UNECE, 1985.

53. McCormick, note 48 above, 63.

54. The original members were Austria, Canada, Denmark, Finland, France, West Germany, the Netherlands, Norway, Sweden, and Switzerland. Denmark and the Netherlands went further by committing themselves to 40 percent reductions, and Austria, Canada, France, West Germany, and Norway to 50 percent reductions. In June 1984, the ten were joined by Belgium, Bulgaria, Byelorussia, East Germany, Liechtenstein, Luxembourg, Ukraina, and the USSR. In September, Czechoslovakia and Italy joined, and in April 1985 Hungary joined.

55. McCormick, note 48 above, 68.

56. Wetstone and Rosencranz, note 49 above, 97.

57. Ibid., 101.

58. Ibid., 125.

59. Jurgen Schmandt and Hilliard Roderick, *Acid Rain and Friendly Neighbors: The Policy Dispute between Canada and the United States* (Durham: Duke University Press, 1985), 63–65.

60. Wetstone and Rosencranz, note 49 above, 128.

61. "President Reagan Assigns EPA Four Priority Tasks," *EPA Journal* 10 (July 1983).

62. Schmandt and Roderick, note 59 above, 66.

63. John Gribbin, *Carbon Dioxide, Climate and Man* (London: Earthscan, 1981), 12.

64. Bert Bolin, "Changes of Land Biota and Their Importance for the Carbon Cycle," *Science* 196:4290 (6 May 1977): 613–615; George M. Woodwell, "The Carbon Dioxide Question," *Scientific American* 238:1 (January 1978): 34–43.

65. Mario J. Molina and F. S. Rowland, "Stratospheric Sink for Chlorofluoromethanes: Chlorine Atom-Catalysed Destruction of Ozone," *Nature* 249:5460 (28 June 1974): 810–812.

66. *Stratospheric Ozone Depletion by Halocarbons: Chemistry and Transport Panel on Stratospheric Chemistry and Transport,* (Washington, DC: National Academy of Sciences, 1979); "Environmental Assessment of Ozone Layer Depletion and Its Impact," *Ozone Bulletin* 6 (1981); National Research Council, *Causes and Effects of Changes in Stratospheric Ozone: Update* (Washington, DC: National Research Council, 1984).

67. Organization for Economic Cooperation and Development, *The State of the Environment 1985* (Paris: OECD, 1985), 36.

68. Chemical Manufacturers Association, quoted in Martin Holdgate, Mohammed Kassas, and Gilbert White, *The World Environment 1972-82* (Dublin: Tycooly, 1982), 44.

69. James K. Hammitt, et al., *Product Uses and Market Trends for Potential Ozone-Depleting Substances 1985–2000* R-3386-EPA (Washington, DC: Rand Corporation, 1986), 2–3.

70. OECD, note 67 above, 36.

71. Stephen H. Schneider and Starley L. Thompson, "Future Changes in the Atmosphere," in Robert Repetto, ed., *The Global Possible: Resources, Development and the New Century* (New Haven: Yale University Press, 1985), 405.

72. Thomas E. Downing and Robert W. Kates, "The International Response to the Threat of Chlorofluorocarbons to Atmospheric Ozone," *American Economic Review* 72:2 (May 1982): 267–272.

73. World Resources Institute/International Institute for Environment and Development, *World Resources 1987* (New York: Basic Books, 1987), 195.

74. Robert T. Watson, et al., *Present State of Knowledge of the Upper Atmosphere: An Assessment Report,* Publ. 1162 (Washington, DC: NASA, 1986), 14–15.

75. Ibid., 15.

76. Jim Ylisela, "Scientists Probe the Ozone Hole for Clues to Its Cause," *Christian Science Monitor,* 6 October 1987, 18.

77. In the United States, meanwhile, ozone—and the dangers of ultra violet radiation and skin cancer—became a major talking point, prompted at least in part by the discovery of skin cancer on President Reagan's nose.

78. Timothy Aeppel, "Ozone Accord Shows Concern Over Global Climate," *Christian Science Monitor,* 17 September 1987, 8.

79. Holdgate, et al., note 68 above, 30–31.

80. Francesco di Castri, Malcolm Hadley, and Jeanne Damlamian, "MAB: The Man and the Biosphere Program as an Evolving System," *Ambio* 10:2-3 (1981): 52–57.

81. UNESCO, *Backgrounder: The MAB Programme* (Paris: UNESCO, 1982), 3.

82. Ibid., 5.

83. World Resources Institute/International Institute for Environment and Development, note 73 above, 158–159.

84. Richard A. Kerr, "Greenhouse Warming Still Coming," *Science* 232:4750 (2 May 1986): 573–574.

85. UNEP/WMO/ICSU, An Assessment of the Role of Carbon Dioxide and of Other Greenhouse Gases in Climate Variations and Associated Impacts (Geneva: World Meteorological Organization, 1985), 12.

86. WRI/IIED, note 73 above, 159.

87. Ibid., 78.

88. Erik Eckholm, *Down to Earth* (New York: W. W. Norton, 1982), 8.

89. International Board for Plant Genetic Resources: Consultative Group on International Agricultural Research, *Annual Report 1981* (Rome: IBPGR, 1981).

90. D. L. Plucknett, N. J. H. Smith, J. T. Williams and N. Murthi Anishetty, "Crop Germplasm Conservation and Developing Countries," *Science* 220:4593 (8 April 1983): 163–169.

91. United Nations Environment Programme, *The Environment in 1982: Retrospect and Prospect*, Paper prepared for the Session of a Special Character, Nairobi. Doc. UNEP/GC (SSC)/2, 29 January 1982, 34.

92. Holdgate, et al., note 68 above, 622–623.

93. Ibid., 15.

94. Organization for Economic Cooperation and Development, *Economic and Ecological Interdependence* (Paris: OECD, 1982), 3.

95. World Commission on Environment and Development, *Our Common Future* (Oxford: Oxford University Press, 1987).

96. Ibid., 310–312.

97. Ibid., 313.

98. Michael Redclift, *Sustainable Development: Exploring the Contradictions* (London: Methuen, 1987), 14.

CONCLUSION: INTO THE TWENTY-FIRST CENTURY

1. Ronald Inglehart, *The Silent Revolution: Changing Values and Political Styles Among Western Publics* (Princeton: Princeton University Press, 1977).

2. William Ophuls, *Ecology and the Politics of Scarcity* (San Francisco: W. H. Freeman, 1977); Dennis C. Pirages, *The Sustainable Society* (New York: Praeger, 1977); Jeremy Rifkin, *Entropy: A New Worldview* (New York: Viking Press, 1980); J. Robertson, *The Sane Alternative: A Choice of Futures* (St. Paul, MN: River Basin, 1979).

3. Dennis C. Pirages, ibid., 26. See also Thomas Kuhn, *The Structure of Scientific Revolutions* (Chicago: University of Chicago Press, 1970).

4. Daniel Yankelovich and Bernard Lefkowitz, "The Public Debate on Growth: Preparing for Resolution," *Technological Forecasting and Social Change* 17:2 (June 1980): 95–140.

5. Riley E. Dunlap and Kent D. Van Liere, "The 'New Environmental Paradigm': A Proposed Measuring Instrument and Preliminary Results," *Journal of Environmental Education* 9 (1978): 10–19; Stephen Cotgrove, *Catastrophe or Cornucopia: The Environment, Politics and the Future* (Chichester: John Wiley & Sons, 1982); Lester W. Milbrath, *General Report: US Components of a Comparative Study of Environmental Beliefs and Values* (Buffalo: State University of New York Environmental

Studies Center, 1981).

6. Lester W. Milbrath, "Environmental Beliefs and Values, in *Political Psychology* ed. Margaret G. Hermann, (San Francisco: Jossey-Bass, 1986).

7. Lynn White, "The Historical Roots of Our Ecologic Crisis," *Science* 155:3767 (10 March 1967): 48–56.

8. Lewis W. Moncrief, "The Cultural Basis for Our Environmental Crisis," *Science* 170:3957 (30 October 1978): 57–64.

9. Martin Holdgate, Gilbert White, and Mohammed Kassas, *The World Environment, 1972–1982* (Dublin: Tycooly, 1982), 626.

10. Richard Sandbrook, "The UK's Overseas Environmental Policy," in *The Conservation and Development Programme for the UK: A Response to the World Conservation Strategy* (London: Kogan Page, 1983), 322.

11. Centre for Science and Environment, *The State of India's Environment 1982* (New Delhi: CSE, 1982), 190.

12. Grant McConnell, "The Conservation Movement—Past and Present," *Western Political Quarterly* 7:3 (Sept. 1954): 463–478.

13. Anthony Downs, "Up and Down With Ecology—The 'Issue-Attention' Cycle," *The Public Interest* 28 (Summer 1972): 38–50.

14. James S. Bowman, "The Ecology Movement: A Viewpoint," *International Journal of Environmental Studies* 8:2 (1975): 91–97.

15. Riley E. Dunlap and Don A. Dillman, "Decline in Public Support for Environmental Protection: Evidence from a 1970–1974 Panel Study," *Rural Sociology* 41:3 (Fall 1976): 382–390.

16. Francis Sandbach, *Environment, Ideology and Policy* (Oxford: Basil Blackwell, 1980), 1–10. See also Riley E. Dunlap and Kent D. Van Liere, "Further Evidence of Declining Public Concern with Environmental Problems: A Research Note," *Western Sociological Review* 8 (1977): 108–112; J. Honnold and L. D. Nelson, "Age and Environmental Concern: Some Specification of Effects," Paper presented at annual meeting of the American Sociological Association, Toronto, 1981.

17. Clay Schoenfeld, "Environmentalism: Fad or Fixture," *American Forests* 78:3 (March 1972): 17–19.

18. See, for example, Lester W. Milbrath, *Environmentalists: Vanguard for a New Society* (Albany: State University of New York Press, 1984), and Council on Environmental Quality, *Environmental Quality 1980* (Washington, DC: U.S. Government Printing Office, 1980), 401–423.

19. *The Economist*, 19 December 1987, 45.

20. Jonathon Porritt, *Seeing Green* (Oxford: Basil Blackwell, 1984), xix–xv.

21. Martin Holdgate, et al., note 9 above, 629.

22. Erik Eckholm, *Down to Earth* (New York: W. W. Norton and Co., 1982), 199.

23. John McCormick, *Acid Earth: The Global Threat of Acid Pollution* (London: Earthscan, 1985), 120–131.

24. Martin Holdgate, et al., note 9 above, xvi.

25. James S. Bowman, note 14 above.

Bibliography

Aaronson, Terri. "World Priorities." *Environment* 14:6 (July/August 1972): 4–13.
Adrian, E. D. "Activities of UNESCO in the Natural Sciences during 1948." *Advancement of Science* 6:22 (July 1949): 90–104.
Aeppel, Timothy. "Ozone Accord Shows Concern over Global Climate." *Christian Science Monitor* (17 September 198): 8.
Ågesta Group, The. *Twenty Years After Stockholm: Summary of Comments Received.* Farsta, Sweden: Ågesta Gammelgard, April 1982.
Albrecht, Stan L. "Environmental Social Movements and Counter-Movements: An Overview and an Illustration." *Journal of Voluntary Action Research* 1 (October 1972): 2–11.
Aldous, Tony. *Battle for the Environment.* London: Fontana Books, 1972.
Allen, David Elliston. *The Naturalist in Britain.* Harmondsworth: Penguin, 1978.
Allen, Robert. "European Con Year." *The Ecologist* 1:6 (December 1970): 4–7.
———. "Ecodevelopment: A Long-Awaited Concept." *IUCN Bulletin* 7:5 (May 1976): 30.
———. *How to Save the World.* London: Kogan Page, 1980.
American Society for the Advancement of Science. *Report of the Air Conservation Commission.* Washington, DC: ASAS, 1965.
Anderson, David. "Depression, Dust Bowl, Demography, and Drought: The Colonial State and Soil Conservation in East Africa during the 1930s." *African Affairs* 83:332 (July 1984): 321–343.
Appleman, Philip. *The Silent Explosion.* Boston: Beacon Press, 1965.
Ashby, Eric, and Mary Anderson. *The Politics of Clean Air.* Oxford: Clarendon Press, 1981.
"Aurum." "British Architects and the Environment." *Bulletin of the Atomic Scientists* 28:3 (March 1972): 42.
Bagge, Carl E. "Radicalism Perils Supply of Minerals." Speech quoted in *Salt Lake City Tribune,* 29 June 1971.
Baines, Graham. "Nuclear Games in the South Pacific." *The Ecologist* 1:18 (December 1971): 9–11.
Baker, Randall, and David Kinyanjui. "Recommendations on the Institutional Framework for Environmental Management in Kenya." School of Development Studies, University of East Anglia, Occasional Paper No. 9, November 1980.
Banks, Arthur S., ed. *Political Handbook of the World: 1987.* Binghamton, NY: CSA Publications, 1987.
Barker, A. "Local Amenity Societies—A Survey and Outline Report." In *The Local Amenity Movement.* London: Civic Trust, 1976.
Barkun, Michael. *Disaster and the Millenium.* New Haven: Yale University Press, 1974.
Bates, James L. "Fulfilling American Democracy: The Conservation Movement, 1907–1921." *Mississippi Valley Historical Review* 44 (June 1957): 29–57.
Beckmann, Petr. *Eco-hysterics and the Technophobes.* Boulder, CO: Golem Press, 1973.
Beltran, Enrique. "A Forgotten Chapter in IUCN's History." *IUCN Bulletin* 14:10-12 (1983): 108–109.
Bennett, Graham. "Pollution Control in England and Wales: A Review." *Environmental Policy and Law* 5:2 (12 April 1979): 93–99.
Bennett, Hugh H. *Soil Conservation.* New York: McGraw-Hill, 1939.

Boardman, Robert. *International Organization and the Conservation of Nature*. Bloomington: Indiana University Press, 1981.

Bolin, Bert. "Changes of Land Biota and Their Importance for the Carbon Cycle." *Science* 196:4290 (6 May 1977): 613–615.

Bolton, Guy. *Spoils and Spoilers*. Sydney: George Allen & Unwin, 1981.

Boulding, Kenneth E. "The Economics of Coming Spaceship Earth." In *Environmental Quality in a Growing Economy*, ed. Henry Jarrett. Baltimore: Johns Hopkins University Press, 1966.

Bowman, James S. "The Ecology Movement: A Viewpoint." *International Journal of Environmental Studies* 8:2 (1975): 91–97.

———. "The Environmental Movement: An Assessment of Ecological Politics." *Environmental Affairs* 5:4 (1976): 649–667.

Boyd Orr, Sir John. *The White Man's Dilemma: Food and the Future*. London: George Allen & Unwin, 1953.

Brooks, Paul. *The House of Life: Rachel Carson at Work*. Boston: Houghton Mifflin, 1972.

Brown, Lester, ed. *State of the World 1984*. New York: W. W. Norton, 1984.

Brunt, Tony. "In Search of Values." In *Right Out—Labour Victory '72: The Inside Story*, ed. Brian Edwards. Wellington : A. H. & A. W. Reed Ltd., 1973.

Budowski, Gerardo. "A Certain Pre-Event Anxiety." *Uniterra* 1 (1982).

Burhenne, Wolfgang, ed. *International Environmental Law: Multilateral Treaties*. Berlin: Erich Schmidt Verlag, 1985.

Burke, Tom. "Friends of the Earth and the Conservation of Resources." In *Pressure Groups in the Global System*, ed. Peter Willetts. London: Francis Pinter, 1982.

Büttikofer, Johann. *Report on the Conference for the International Protection of Nature*. Basle: Swiss League for the Protection of Nature, 1946.

———. *Proceedings of the International Conference for the Protection of Nature*. Basle: Swiss League for the Protection of Nature, 1947.

Caldwell, Lynton K. *In Defense of Earth: International Protection of the Biosphere*. Bloomington: Indiana University Press, 1972.

———. *International Environmental Policy: Emergence and Dimensions*. Durham, NC: Duke University Press, 1984.

Capra, Fritjhof, and Charlene Spretnak. *Green Politics*. London: Hutchinson, 1984.

Carson, Rachel. *Silent Spring*. Boston: Houghton Mifflin, 1962.

di Castri, Francesco, Malcolm Hadley, and Jeanne Damlamian. "MAB: The Man and the Biosphere Program as an Evolving System." *Ambio* 10:2-3 (1981): 52–57.

Catlin, George. *North American Indians*. Philadelphia: Leary, Stuart & Co, 1913.

Center for International Environment Information. "Government Agencies with Environmental Responsibilities in Developing Countries." *World Environment Report* 6:9 (April 1980).

Centre for Science and Environment. *The State of India's Environment 1982*. New Delhi: CSE, 1982.

———. *The State of India's Environment 1984–85*. New Delhi: CSE, 1985.

Chafe, William H., and Harvey Sitkoff, eds. *A History of Our Time: Readings on Postwar America*. New York: Oxford University Press, 1983.

Chase, Stuart. *Rich Land, Poor Land*. New York: McGraw-Hill, 1936.

Chenery, Hollis, Montek S. Ahluwalia, C. L. G. Bell, John H. Duloy, and Richard Jolly. *Redistribution with Growth*. Oxford: Oxford University Press, 1974.

Clarke, Arthur C. *The Promise of Space*. New York: Harper and Row, 1968.

Clarke, Robin, and Lloyd Timberlake. *Stockholm Plus Ten*. London: Earthscan, 1982.

Claus, George, and Karen Bolander. *Ecological Sanity*. New York: David McKay Co., 1977.

Cleveland, Harlan. "The Extrapolation of Metaphors: A 'Book Review' of the US Government's Global 2000 Study." Unpublished address to OECD, 1 April 1981.

Cohen, Jean L., and Andrew Arato. "The German Green Party: A Movement between Fundamentalism and Modernism." *Dissent* 31:3 (Summer 1984): 327–332.

Cole, H. S. D. Christopher Freeman, Marie Jahoda, and K. L. R. Pavitt. *Thinking about the Future: A Critique of* The Limits to Growth. London: Chatto & Windus, for Sussex University Press, 1973.

Commoner, Barry. "The Closing Circle." *Environment* 14:3, (April 1972): 23–52.

———. *The Closing Circle: Nature, Man and Technology*. New York: Knopf, 1971.

Conservation Foundation. *State of the Environment 1982*. Washington, DC: Conservation Foundation, 1982.

Coolidge, Harold J. "The Growth and Development of International Interest in Safeguarding Endangered Species." In *Proceedings XV International Congress of Zoology*, London, 16–23 July 1958.

———. Profile. *The Environmentalist* 1:1 (1981): 65–74.

Corea, Gamani, and Maurice Strong. Letter to Barbara Ward, 18 July 1974.

Cotgrove, Stephen. *Catastrophe or Cornucopia: The Environment, Politics and the Future*. Chichester: John Wiley & Sons, 1982.

Cotgrove, Stephen, and Andrew Duff. "Environmentalism, Middle-Class Radicalism and Politics." *Sociological Review* 32 (1980): 92-110.

Council on Environmental Quality. *Environmental Quality 1970*. Washington, DC: U.S. Government Printing Office, 1970.

———. *Environmental Quality 1971*. Washington, DC: U.S. Government Printing Office, 1971.

———. *Environmental Quality 1979*. Washington, DC: U.S. Government Printing Office, 1979.

———. *Environmental Quality 1980*. Washington, DC: U.S. Government Printing Office, 1980.

———. *Public Opinion on Environmental Issues: Results of a National Public Opinion Survey*. Washington, DC: U.S. Government Printing Office, 1980.

———. *Global Future: Time to Act*. Washington, DC: CEQ, 1981.

———. *The Global 2000 Report to the President: Entering the Twenty-First Century*. Harmondsworth: Penguin, 1982.

Cowling, Ellis B. "Acid Precipitation in Historical Perspective." *Environmental Science and Technology* 16:2 (February 1982): 110A–123A.

Cox Commission. *Crisis at Columbia: Report of the Fact-Finding Commission Appointed to Investigate the Disturbances at Columbia University in April and May 1968*. New York: Vintage Books, 1968.

Cranworth, Lord. *Profit and Sport in British East Africa*. London: Macmillan, 1919.

Culhane, Paul J. "Sagebrush Rebels in Office: Jim Watt's Land and Water Politics." In *Environmental Policy in the 1980s: Reagan's New Agenda*, ed. Norman J. Vig and Michael E. Kraft. Washington, DC: CQ Press, 1984.

Darby, H. C. "The Clearing of the Woodland in Europe." In *Man's Role in Changing the Face of the Earth*, ed. William L. Thomas. Chicago: University of Chicago Press, 1956.

Dasmann, Raymond. "An Introduction to World Conservation." In *Sustaining Tomorrow*, ed. F. R. Thibodeau and H. H. Field. Hanover: University Press of New England, 1985.

Dasmann, Raymond F., J. P. Milton, and P. H. Freeman. *Ecological Principles for Economic Development*. London: John Wiley, 1973.

Davies, J. Clarence, and Barbara S. Davies. *The Politics of Pollution*. Indianapolis: Pegasus, 1975.

Davis, Kenneth S. *The Politics of Honor: A Biography of Adlai E. Stevenson*. New York: G.P. Putnam's Sons, 1967.

Day, Alan J., and Henry W. Degenhardt. *Political Parties of the World*. Detroit: Gale Research Company, 1984.

Deevey, E. S., Don S. Rice, Prudence M. Rice, H. H. Vaughan, Mark Brenner, and M. S. Flannery. "Mayan Urbanism: Impact on a Tropical Karst Environment." *Science* 206:4416 (19 October 1979): 298–306.

Devall, William B. "Conservation: An Upper-Middle Class Social Movement: A Replication." *Journal of Lesire Research* 2 (Spring 1970): 123–126.

Dixey, F. "Conservation and Utilization of World Resources: United Nations Conference." *Nature* 164:4176 (12 November 1949): 813–815.

Doud, Alden L. "International Environmental Developments: Perceptions of Developing and Developed Countries." *Natural Resources Journal* 12 (October 1972): 520–529.

Downing, Thomas E., and Robert W. Kates. "The International Response to the Threat of Chlorofluorocarbons to Atmospheric Ozone." *American Economic Review* 72:2 (May 1982): 267–272.

Downs, Anthony. "Up and Down with Ecology—The 'Issue-Attention' Cycle." *The Public Interest* 28 (Summer 1972): 38–50.

Dunenberg, R. V. *Understanding American Politics*. London: Fontana, 1984.

Dunlap, Riley E., and Don A. Dillman. "Decline in Public Support for Environmental Protection: Evidence from a 1970–1974 Panel Study." *Rural Sociology* 41:3 (Fall 1976): 382–390.

Dunlap, Riley E., and Kent D. Van Liere. "Further Evidence of Declining Public Concern with Environmental Problems: A Research Note." *Western Sociological Review* 8 (1977): 108–112.

———. "The 'New Environmental Paradigm': A Proposed Measuring Instrument and Preliminary Results." *Journal of Environmental Education* 9 (1978): 10–19.

Dupuy, Trevor N., and Gay M. Hammerman. *A Documentary History of Arms Control and Disarmament*. New York: R.R. Bowker Co., 1973.

Earthscan. *The Polluted Seas*. London: Earthscan, 1978.

———. *Cropland or Wasteland: The Problems and Promises of Irrigation*. London: Earthscan, 1984.

Eckholm, Erik. *Down to Earth*. New York: W. W. Norton and Co., 1982.

Ecologist, The. A Blueprint for Survival. Harmondsworth: Penguin, 1972.

Ehrhart, R., A. Hanson, C. Sanger and B. Wood. *Canadian Aid and the Environment*. Halifax, Nova Scotia: Dalhousie University, 1981.

Ehrlich, Paul R. *The Population Bomb*. New York: Ballantine Books, 1968.

———. Interview in *Playboy* 17:8 (August 1970).

Ehrlich, Paul R., and Anne H. Ehrlich. *Population, Resources, Environment*. San Francisco: W. H. Freeman and Co., 1970.

———. *The End of Affluence*. New York: Ballantine Books, 1974.

Ehrlich, Paul R., and Richard L. Harriman. *How to Be a Survivor: A Plan to Save Spaceship Earth*. New York: Ballantine Books, 1971.

Ehrlich, Paul R., and John P. Holdren. "The Closing Circle." *Environment* 14:3 (April 1972): 24–39.

Ellington, Athleen and Tom Burke. *Europe: Environment*. London: Ecobooks, 1981.

Engels, Friedrich. *The Condition of the Working Class in England*. Reprint. Stanford: Stanford University Press, 1958.

Enloe, Cynthia. *The Politics of Pollution in Comparative Perspective*. New York: David McKay, 1975.

Environmental Protection Agency. *Analysis of Issues Concerning a CFC Protocol*. Washington, DC: EPA, 1985.

Enzensberger, Hans Magnus. "A Critique of Political Ecology." *New Left Review* 84 (March–April 1974): 3–31.

European Environmental Bureau. *Reports 1975/1976*. Brussels: EEB, 1976.

Evelyn, John. *Fumifugium: Or the Inconvenience of the Aer and Smoake of London Dissipated*. Reproduced in James P. Lodge, *The Smoake of London: Two Prophecies*. New York: Maxwell Reprint Company, 1969.

Falk, Richard A. "Environmental Policy as a World Order Problem." *Natural Resources Journal* 12:2 (April 1972): 161–171.

Fitter, Richard S. R. *The Penitent Butchers*. London: Collins, 1978.

Flavin, Christopher. *Nuclear Power: The Market Test*. Washington, DC: Worldwatch Institute, December 1983.

Forrester, Jay W. "Counterintuitive Behavior of Social Systems." *Technology Review* 73:3 (January 1971): 53–68.

———. *World Dynamics*. Cambridge, MA: Wright-Allen Press, 1971.

Foster, M., M. Neushul, and R. Zingmark. "The Santa Barbara Oil Spill, Part 2: Initial Effects on Intertidal and Kelp Bed Organisms." *Environmental Pollution* 2:2 (October 1971): 115–134.

Founex II. *Report of the Advisory Group Meeting*, 7 March 1973 (unpublished).

Fox, Stephen. *John Muir and His Legacy: The American Conservation Movement*. Boston: Little, Brown & Co., 1981.

Fraser Darling, Sir Frank. *Wilderness and Plenty*. Boston: Houghton Mifflin Co., 1970.

Friends of the Earth. Newsletter. *The Ecologist* 1:18 (December 1971).

Galbraith, John Kenneth. *The Affluent Society*. Boston: Houghton Mifflin, 1958.

Gilpin, William. *Observations on the Highlands of Scotland*. Reprint. Richmond, Surrey: Richmond Publishing, 1973.

Golub, Robert, and Jo Townsend. "Malthus, Multinationals and the Club of Rome." *Social Studies of Science* 7 (1977): 201–222.

Graham, Frank. *Since Silent Spring*. Boston: Houghton Mifflin, 1970.

Grainger, Alan. *Desertification*. London: Earthscan, 1982.

Grayson, Melvin J., and Thomas R. Shepard, Jr. *The Disaster Lobby: Prophets of Ecological Doom and Other Absurdities*. Chicago: Follett, 1973.

Great Plains Committee. *The Future of the Great Plains*. Washington, DC: U.S. Government Printing Office, 1936.

Gregory, Roy. *The Price of Amenity*. London: Macmillan, 1971.

Gribbin, John. *Carbon Dioxide, Climate and Man*. London: Earthscan, 1981.

Grove, Richard. "Incipient Conservationism in the Cape Colony and the Emergence of Colonial Environmental Policies in Southern Africa." Unpublished paper presented to conference: The Scramble for Resources: Conservation Policies in Africa, 1884–1984, Cambridge, April 1985.

Gundlach, Erich R. "Oil Tanker Disasters." *Environment* 19:9 (December 1977): 16–27.

Haigh, Nigel. *EEC Environmental Policy and Britain*. London: Environmental Data Services, 1983.

———. *Vienna Centre Project ECO I. Collaborative Arrangements for Environmental Protection in Western Europe*. London: IEEP/European Cultural Foundation, 1985.

———. "Devolved Responsibility and Centralization: Effects of EEC Environmental Policy." *Public Administration* 64:2 (Summer 1986): 197–207.

Haley, Mary Jean, ed. *Open Options: A Guide to Stockholm's Alternative Environmental Conferences*. Stockholm: 29 May 1972.

Hall, Tony. *Nuclear Politics*. Harmondsworth: Penguin, 1986.

Hambidge, Gove. *The Story of FAO*. New York: Van Nostrand, 1955.

Hammitt, James K., et al. *Product Uses and Market Trends for Potential Ozone-Depleting Substances 1985–2000*. R-3386-EPA. Washington, DC: Rand Corporation, 1986.

Hardin, Charles M. "Observations on Environmental Politics." In *Environmental Politics* ed. Stuart S. Nagel. London: Prager, 1974.

Hardin, Garrett. "The Tragedy of the Commons." *Science* 162:3859 (13 December 1968): 1243–1248.

———. "Living on a Lifeboat." *Bioscience* 24:10 (October 1974): 561–568.

Hardy, Michael. "The United Nations Environment Program." *Natural Resources Journal* 13 (April 1973): 235–255.

Harrison, Paul. *The Greening of Africa*. Harmondsworth: Penguin, 1987.

Harroy, Jean-Paul. "A Pioneer's Reward." *IUCN Bulletin* 14:4–6 (1983): 35–43.

Harry, Joseph, Richard Gale, and John Hendee. "Conservation: An Upper-Middle Class Social Movement." *Journal of Leisure Research* 1 (Summer 1969): 246–254.

Hays, Samuel P. *Conservation and the Gospel of Efficiency*. Cambridge: Harvard University Press, 1959.

———. *Beauty, Health and Permanence: Environmental Politics in the United States, 1955–1985*. Cambridge: Cambridge University Press, 1987.

Hecox, Walter E. "Limits to Growth Revisited: Has the World Modelling Debate Made Any Progress?" *Environmental Affairs* 5:1 (Winter 1976): 65–96.

Herbert, Roy. "The Day the Reactor Caught Fire." *New Scientist*, (14 October 1982): 84–87.

Hillaby, John. "Conservation in Africa: A Crucial Conference." *New Scientist* (31 August 1961): 536–538.

Holden, Constance. "Ehrlich versus Commoner: An Environmental Fallout." *Science* 177:4045 (21 July 1972): 245–247.

Holdgate, Martin. "Beyond the Ideals and the Vision." *Uniterra* 1 (1982).

———. "UNEP: Some Personal Thoughts." *Mazingira* (March 1984): 17–20.

Holdgate, Martin, Mohammed Kassas, and Gilbert White. *The World Environment 1972–1982*. Dublin: Tycooly, 1982.

Honnold, J., and L. D. Nelson. "Age and Environmental Concern: Some Specification of Effects." Paper presented at annual meeting of the American Sociological Association, Toronto, 1981.

Huddle, Norie, and Michael Reich. "The Octopus That Eats Its Own Legs." *The Ecologist* 3:8 (August 1973): 292–295.

Hughes, J. Donald. *Ecology in Ancient Civilizations*. Alberquerque: University of New Mexico, 1975.

Hulm, Peter. "The Regional Seas Program: What Fate for UNEP's Crown Jewels?" *Ambio* 12:1 (1983): 2–13.

Huth, Hans. *Nature and the American: Three Centuries of Changing Attitudes*. Berkeley: University of California Press, 1957.

Huxley, Sir Julian. *Memories II*. New York: Harper & Row, 1973.

Ingham, Kenneth. *A History of East Africa*. London: Longman, 1963.

Inglehart, Ronald. *The Silent Revolution: Changing Values and Political Styles among Western Publics*. Princeton: Princeton University Press, 1977.

Inglis, Barclay. "Concorde: The Case Against Supersonic Transport." In *The Environmental Handbook*, ed. John Barr. London: Ballantine/Pan, 1971.

International Board for Plant Genetic Resources: Consultative Group on International Agricultural Research. *Annual Report 1981*. Rome: IBPGR, 1981.

International Institute for Environmental Affairs. Minutes of the fifth meeting of the International Institute for Environmental Affairs Board of Directors, Paris, February 1972 (unpublished).

International Institute for Environment and Development. *IIED Annual Report 1981–1982*. London: IIED, 1982.

———. *Report on the African Emergency Relief Operation 1984–1986*. (Draft). London: IIED, 1986.

International Union for Conservation of Nature and Natural Resources. *Proceedings of the 5th General Assembly, Edinburgh 1956*. Morges: IUCN, 1956.

———. *IUCN Yearbook 1971*. Morges: IUCN, 1972.

———. *IUCN Yearbook 1972*. Morges: IUCN, 1973.

———. *IUCN Yearbook 1973*. Morges: IUCN, 1974.

———. *IUCN Yearbook 1975–76*. Morges: IUCN, 1976.

———. Report on International Conservation, submitted to the 14th Session of the General Assembly of IUCN, Gen. Ass. paper GA.78/11, 18 August 1978.

———. Resolutions of the 14th Session of the General Assembly of IUCN. In *IUCN Bulletin* 9:10/11 (October/November 1978).

———. Director-General's Report, June-December 1979.

———. *A Conservation Programme for Sustainable Development: 1981–83*. Gland: IUCN, 1980.

———. *Achievements 1978–81*. (Report of the Director-General). Gland: IUCN, 1981.

———. *National Conservation Strategies: A Framework for Sustainable Development*. Gland: CDC/IUCN, 1984.

International Union for the Protection of Nature. *Proceedings and Reports of the 2nd Session of the IUPN General Assembly, 1950*. Morges: IUPN, 1951.

Jacobson, Harold Karan, and Eric Stein. *Diplomats, Scientists and Politicians: The United States and the Nuclear Test Ban Negotiations*. Ann Arbor: University of Michigan Press, 1966.

James, Colin C. "Social Credit and the Values Party." In *New Zealand at the Polls: The General Election of 1978*, ed. Howard R. Penniman. Washington, DC: American Enterprise Institute for Public Policy Research, 1980.

Johnson, Brian. "Common Market v Environment." *The Ecologist* 1:11 (May 1971): 10–14.

———. "The Bureaucrat and the Biosphere." *The Ecologist* 2:6 (June 1972): 30–36.

Johnson, Brian, and Robert O. Blake. *The Environment and Bilateral Development Aid*. London: IIED, 1980.

Johnson, Keith. "A Second Copernican Revolution." *Uniterra* 1 (1982).

Johnson, Stanley. *The Politics of Environment: The British Experience*. London: Tom Stacey, 1973.

Jones, Maldwyn A. *The Limits of Liberty*. New York: Oxford University Press, 1983.

Kahn, Herman, and Ernest Schneider. "Globaloney 2000." *Policy Review* 16 (Spring 1981): 129–147.

Kaysen, C. "The Computer That Printed Out W*O*L*F*." *Foreign Affairs* 50:4 (1972): 660–668.

Kerr, Richard A. "Greenhouse Warming Still Coming." *Science* 232:4750 (2 May 1986): 573–574.

Killian, Lewis M. "Social Movements." In *Handbook of Modern Sociology*, ed. Robert E. L. Faris. Chicago: Rand McNally, 1964.

Kolinsky, Eva. "The Greens in Germany: Prospects of a Small Party." *Parliamentary Affairs* 37:4 (Autumn 1984): 434–447.

Kropotkin, Peter. *Fields, Factories and Workshops (Tomorrow)*. Edited by Colin Ward. London: Unwin, 1974.

Kuhn, Thomas. *The Structure of Scientific Revolutions*. Chicago: University of Chicago Press, 1970.

Landsberg, Hans H. "Reflections on the Stockholm Conference." Unpublished paper. Washington, DC: August 1972.

Leopold, Aldo. *Game Management*. New York: Scribner's, 1933.

―――. *Sand County Almanac*. New York: Oxford University Press, 1949.

Lepper, Mary Milling. *Foreign Policy Formulation: A Case Study of the Nuclear Test Ban Treaty of 1963*. Columbus, OH: Charles E. Merrill, 1971.

Leuchtenburg, William E. *A Troubled Feast: American Society since 1945*. Boston: Little, Brown & Co., 1979.

Levine, Stephen. *The New Zealand Political System: Politics in a Small Society*. Sydney: George Allen & Unwin, 1979.

Lipset, Seymour Martin. "Student Activism." *Current Affairs Bulletin* 42:4 (15 July 1968): 48–52.

Lohneis, Hans. "The Swiss Election of 1983: A Glacier on the Move?" *West European Politics*, 7:3 (July 1984): 117–119.

Lovett, H. Verney. "The Development of the Services 1858-1918." In *The Cambridge History of India*. Vol. 6. Cambridge: Cambridge University Press, 1932.

Lowe, Philip. "Science and Government: The Case of Pollution." *Public Administration* (Autumn 1975): 287–298.

―――. "Values and Institutions in the History of British Nature Conservation." In *Conservation in Perspective*, ed. Andrew Warren and F. B. Goldsmith. London: Wiley, 1983.

Lowe, Philip, Jane Clifford, and Sarah Buchanan. "The Mass Movement of the Decade." *Vole* (January 1980): 26–28.

Lowe, Philip, and Jane Goyder. *Environmental Groups in Politics*. London: George Allen & Unwin, 1983.

Lyster, Simon. *International Wildlife Law*. Cambridge: Grotius Publications, 1985.

MacEwen, Ann, and Malcolm MacEwen. *National Parks: Conservation or Cosmetics?* London: George Allen & Unwin, 1982.

Maddox, John. *The Doomsday Syndrome*. London: Macmillan, 1972.

Maltby, Edward. *Waterlogged Wealth*. London: Earthscan, 1986.

Malthus, Thomas. *An Essay on the Principle of Population*. Edited by Philip Appleman. New York: W. W. Norton, 1976.

Marsh, George Perkins. *Man and Nature*. Reprint. Cambridge: Harvard University Press, 1965.

Martin, A. *The Last Generation: The End of Survival?* London: Fontana, 1975.

Marx, Karl. *The Poverty of Philosophy*. New York: International Publishers, 1963.

McConnell, Grant. "The Conservation Movement: Past and Present." *Western Political Quarterly* 7:3 (Sept 1954): 463–478.

McCormick, John. *Acid Earth: The Global Threat of Acid Pollution*. London: Earthscan, 1985.

McGeary, Martin N. *Gifford Pinchot: Forester-Politician*. Princeton, NJ: Princeton University Press, 1960.

Meadows, Donella H., Dennis L. Meadows, Jorgen Randers, and William W. Behrens III. *The Limits to Growth*. New York: New American Library, 1972.

Means, Richard L. "The New Conservation." *Natural History* 78:7 (August–September 1969): 16–25.

Mesarovic, Mihaljo, and Eduard Pestel. *Mankind at the Turning Point*. New York: Dutton, 1974.

Milbrath, Lester W. *General Report: US Components of a Comparative Study of Environmental Beliefs and Values*. Buffalo, NY: State University of New York Environmental Studies Center, 1981.

―――. *Environmentalists: Vanguard for a New Society*. Albany State University of New York Press, 1984.

——. "Environmental Beliefs and Values." In *Political Psychology*, ed. Margaret G. Hermann. San Francisco: Jossey-Boss, 1986.

Molina, Mario J., and F. S. Rowland. "Stratospheric Sink for Chlorofluoromethanes: Chlorine Atom-Catalysed Destruction of Ozone." *Nature* 249:5460 (28 June 1974): 810–812.

Molotch, Harvey, and Marilyn Lester. "Accidental News: The Great American Oil Spill as Local Occurrence and National Event." *American Journal of Sociology* 81:2 (September 1975): 235–260.

Moncrief, Lewis W. "The Cultural Basis for Our Environmental Crisis." *Science* 170:3957 (30 October 1978): 57–64.

Morgan, Robin, and Brian Whitaker. *Rainbow Warrior.* London: Arrow Books, 1986.

Morrison, Denton E., Kenneth E. Hornback, and W. Keith Warner. "The Environmental Movement: Some Preliminary Observations and Predictions." In *Social Behavior, Natural Resources and the Environment*, ed. William R. Burch, Neil H. Cheek, and Lee Taylor. New York: Harper & Row, 1972.

Mosley, J. G. "Towards a History of Conservation in Australia." In *Australia as Human Setting*, ed. Amos Rapoport. Sydney: Angus and Robertson, 1972.

Muller-Rommel, Ferdinand. "Ecology Parties in Western Europe." *West European Politics* 5:1 (January 1982): 68–74.

Murdoch, William W. *The Poverty of Nations: The Political Economy of Hunger and Population.* Baltimore: Johns Hopkins University Press, 1980.

Nash, Roderick. "The American Invention of National Parks." *American Quarterly* 22:3 (Fall 1970): 726–735.

——. *Wilderness and the American Mind.* New Haven: Yale University Press, 1973.

National Academy of Sciences. *International Arrangements of International Environmental Co-operation.* Washington, DC: NAS, 1972.

National Parks Service. *First World Conference on National Parks.* Washington, DC: Department of the Interior, 1962.

National Research Council. *Causes and Effects of Changes in Stratospheric Ozone: Update.* Washington, DC: National Research Council, 1984.

Nicholson, Max. "Requirements for a World Conservation Programme." Unpublished paper, IBP, 1966.

——. *The Environmental Revolution.* London: Hodder & Stoughton, 1972.

——. *The First World Conservation Lecture.* London: World Wildlife Fund, 1981.

——. *The New Environmental Age.* Cambridge: Cambridge University Press, 1987.

Nixon, Edgar B., ed. *Franklin D. Roosevelt and Conservation 1911–1945.* New York: Franklin D. Roosevelt Library, 1957.

Olson, Mancur. *The Logic of Collective Action.* Cambridge: Harvard University Press, 1965.

Ophuls, William. *Ecology and the Politics of Scarcity.* San Francisco: W. H. Freeman, 1977.

Ordway, Samuel H. *Resources and the American Dream.* New York: Ronald Press Co., 1953.

Organization for Economic Cooperation and Development. *The OECD Programme on Long Range Transport of Air Pollutants* (Summary Report). Paris: OECD, 1977.

——. *The State of the Environment 1979.* Paris: OECD, 1979.

——. *Economic and Ecological Interdependence.* Paris: OECD, 1982.

——. *The State of the Environment 1985.* Paris: OECD, 1985.

O'Riordan, Timothy. *Environmentalism.* London: Pion Ltd., 1981.

Osborn, Fairfield. *Our Plundered Planet.* Boston: Little, Brown & Co., 1948.

———. *The Limits of the Earth.* Boston: Little, Brown & Co., 1953.

Papadakis, Elim. "The Green Party in Contemporary West German Politics." *Political Quarterly* 54:3 (July–September 1983): 302–307.

Patterson, Walter. *Nuclear Power.* Harmondsworth: Penguin, 1983.

Pearce, Fred. "After Bhopal, Who Remembered Ixhuatepec?" *New Scientist,* (18 July 1985): 22–23.

Pearson, Frank, and Floyd Harper. *The World's Hunger.* Ithaca: Cornell University Press, 1945.

Peccei, Aurelio. *The Chasm Ahead.* London: Macmillan, 1969.

———. *The Human Quality.* Oxford: Pergamon, 1977.

Pehrson, E. W. "The Mineral Position in the United States and the Outlook for the Future." *Mining and Metallurgy Journal* 26 (1945): 204–214.

Penick, James. *Progressive Politics and Conservation.* Chicago: University of Chicago Press, 1968.

Petty, Sir William. *Mankind and Political Arithmetic.* New York: The Mershon Co, n.d.

Petulla, Joseph M. *American Environmentalism: Values, Tactics, Priorities.* College Station: Texas A&M University Press, 1980.

Pinchot, Gifford. *The Fight for Conservation.* New York: Doubleday Page & Co., 1910.

Pinkett, Harold T. *Gifford Pinchot: Private and Public Forester.* Urbana: University of Illinois Press, 1970.

Pirages, Dennis C. *The Sustainable Society.* New York: Praeger, 1977.

Plucknett, D. L., N. J. H. Smith, J. T. Williams, and N. Murthi Anishetty. "Crop Germplasm Conservation and Developing Countries." *Science* 220:4593 (8 April 1983): 163–169.

Pole, Nicholas. An Interview with Paul Ehrlich. *The Ecologist* 3:1 (January 1973): 18–24.

Pollard, E., M. D. Hooper, and N. W. Moore. *Hedges.* London: Collins, 1974.

Porritt, Jonathon. *Seeing Green: The Politics of Ecology Explained.* Oxford: Basil Blackwell, 1984.

Pringle, John. *The Conservationists and the Killers.* Cape Town: Books of Africa, 1982.

Prins, Gwyn, ed. *Defended to Death: A Study of the Nuclear Arms Race.* Harmondsworth: Penguin, 1983.

Proceedings of the Conference on the Conservation of Wetlands of International Importance Especially as Waterfowl Habitat (Doc. CONF/4), Cagliari, Italy, November 1980.

Pursell, Carroll, ed. *From Conservation to Ecology: The Development of Environmental Concern.* New York: Thomas Y. Crowell Co., 1973.

Pye-Smith, Charlie, and Chris Rose. *Crisis and Conservation: Conflict in the British Countryside.* Harmondsworth: Penguin, 1984.

Quarles, John. *Cleaning Up America.* Boston: Houghton Mifflin, 1976.

Ramakrishna, Kilaparti. "The Emergence of Environmental Law in the Developing Countries: A Case Study of India." *Ecology Law Quarterly* 12:4 (1985): 907–935.

Raushenbush, Stephen. "Conservation in 1952." *The Annals of the American Academy of Political and Social Science* 281 (May 1952): 1–9.

Reich, Charles. *The Greening of America.* New York: Random House, 1970.

Ridgeway, James. *The Politics of Ecology.* New York: E. P. Dutton & Co., 1970.

Rifkin, Jeremy. *Entropy: A New Worldview.* New York: Viking Press, 1980.

Robertson, J. *The Sane Alternative: A Choice of Futures.* St. Paul, MN: River Basin, 1979.

Robinson, Nicholas A. Prepared statement before the Subcommittee on Human

Rights and International Organizations, Committee on Foreign Affairs, U.S. House of Representatives, 20 April 1982.

Rodgers, K. "With the Developing Countries at Founex." *Uniterra* 1 (1982).

Roosevelt, Theodore. *An Autobiography.* New York: Macmillan, 1913.

Roper, Laura Wood. *FLO: A Biography of Frederick Law Olmsted.* Baltimore: Johns Hopkins University Press, 1973.

Rosenbaum, Andrew. "Italy's Green Party." *Environment* 29:10 (December 1987): 3, 34–35.

Rosenbaum, Walter A. *Environmental Politics and Policy.* Washington, DC: CQ Press, 1985.

Royal Commission on Environmental Pollution. *Second Annual Report.* London: Her Majesty's Printing Office, Cmnd. 4894, 1972.

Rudig, Wolfgang, and Philip Lowe. "The Withered 'Greening' of British Politics: A Study of the Ecology Party." *Political Studies* 34:2 (June 1986): 262–284.

Runte, Alfred. *National Parks: The American Experience.* Lincoln: University of Nebraska Press, 1979.

Rusk, Ralph L., ed. *The Letters of Ralph Waldo Emerson.* New York: Columbia University Press, 1939.

Russell, Sir John. "World Population and World Food Supplies" (Presidential Address to the British Association for the Advancement of Science). *Advancement of Science* 6:23 (October 1949): 173–183.

Salim, Emil. *Conservation and Development* (The Second World Conservation Lecture). London: World Wildlife Fund, 1982.

Sandbach, Francis. "The Rise and Fall of the *Limits to Growth* Debate." *Social Studies of Science* 8:4 (November 1978): 495–520.

———. *Environment: Ideology and Policy.* Oxford: Basil Blackwell, 1980.

Sandbrook, Richard. "NGOs and the UNEP Council—Governments No Longer Listen." *IUCN Bulletin* 11:6 (June 1980): 65.

———. "The UK's Overseas Environmental Policy." *The Conservation and Development Programme for the UK: A Response to the World Conservation Strategy.* London: Kogan Page, 1983.

Scarrow, Howard A. "The Impact of British Domestic Air Pollution Legislation." *British Journal of Political Science* 2:3 (July 1972): 261–282.

Schillings, Carl G. *With Flashlight and Rifle.* London: Hutchinson, 1905.

———. *In Wildest Africa.* London: Harper & Brothers, 1907.

Schmandt, Jurgen, and Hilliard Roderick. *Acid Rain and Friendly Neighbors: The Policy Dispute between Canada and the United States.* Durham, NC: Duke University Press, 1985.

Schnaiberg, Allen. "Politics, Participation and Pollution: The 'Environmental Movement'." In *Cities in Change: Studies in the Urban Condition,* ed. John Walton and Donald E. Carns. Boston: Allen and Bacon Inc., 1977.

Schneider, Stephen H., and Starley L. Thompson. "Future Changes in the Atmosphere." In *The Global Possible: Resources, Development and the New Century,* ed. Robert Repetto. New Haven: Yale University Press, 1985.

Schoenfeld, Clay. "Environmentalism: Fad or Fixture." *American Forests* 78:3 (March 1972): 17–19.

Schumacher, E. F. *Small is Beautiful: Economics as If People Mattered.* London: Abacus, 1974.

Schwartz, S. I., and T. C. Foin. "A Critical Review of the Social System Models of Jay Forrester." *Human Ecology* 1:2 (September 1972): 161–173.

Searle, John. *The Campus War.* Harmondsworth: Pelican, 1972.

Sears, Paul B. *Deserts on the March.* Norman: University of Oklahoma Press, 1935.

Sen, Amartya. *Poverty and Famines.* Oxford: Clarendon Press, 1981.

Shea, Kevin P. "A Celebration of Silent Spring." *Environment* 15:1 (January–February 1973): 4–5.

Sheail, John. *Nature in Trust*. London: Blackie, 1976.

Shoard, Marion. *The Theft of the Countryside*. London: Temple Smith, 1980.

Sills, David L. "The Environmental Movement and Its Critics." *Human Ecology* 3:1 (1975): 1–41.

Simon, Julian L. "Global Confusion, 1980: A Hard Look at the Global 2000 Report." *The Public Interest* 62 (Winter 1981): 3–20.

Simon, Julian L., and Herman Kahn, eds. *The Resourceful Earth: A Response to Global 2000*. Oxford: Basil Blackwell, 1984.

Skolnick, Jerome H. *The Politics of Protest: A Task Force Report Submitted to the National Commission on the Causes and Prevention of Violence*. New York: Simon and Shuster, 1969.

Sleeman, James. *From Rifle to Camera: The Reformation of a Big Game Hunter*. London: Jarrolds, 1947.

Smith, Robert Angus. *Air and Rain: The Beginnings of a Chemical Climatology*. London: Longmans, Green & Co., 1872.

Sohn, Louis B. "The Stockholm Declaration on the Human Environment." *The Harvard International Law Journal* 14:3 (Summer 1974): 423–515.

Solesbury, William. "The Environmental Agenda." *Public Administration* 54 (Winter 1976): 379–397.

Spero, Joan Edelman. *The Politics of International Economic Relations*. New York: St. Martin's Press, 1985.

Stein, Robert E., and Brian Johnson. *Banking on the Biosphere?* Lexington, MA: Lexington Books, 1979.

Stoel, Thomas B., S. Jacob Scherr, and Diana C. Crowley. *Environment, Natural Resources and Development: The Role of the U.S. Agency for International Development*. Washington, DC: Natural Resources Defense Council, 1978.

Stone, Peter. *Did We Save the Earth at Stockholm?* London: Earth Island, 1973.

Stratospheric Ozone Depletion by Halocarbons: Chemistry and Transport Panel on Stratospheric Chemistry and Transport. Washington, DC: National Academy of Sciences, 1979.

Streeten, Paul. "From Growth to Basic Needs." *Finance and Development* (September 1979): 28–31.

Strong, Maurice F. "The International Community and the Environment." *Environmental Conservation* 4:3 (Autumn 1977): 165–172.

Study of Critical Environmental Problems. *Man's Impact on the Global Environment: Assessment and Recommendations for Action*. Cambridge, MA: MIT Press, 1970.

Tabler, Eric C. *The Far Interior*. Cape Town: A. A. Balkema, 1955.

Talbot, Lee M. Introductory remarks to the 14th IUCN General Assembly, Ashkhabad, USSR, 25 September 1978.

———. "A Remarkable Melding of Contrasts and Conflicts." *Uniterra* 1 (1982).

———. "The World Conservation Strategy." In *Sustaining Tomorrow: A Strategy for World Conservation and Development*, ed. F. R. Thibodeau and H. H. Field. Hanover: The University Press of New England, 1984.

Taylor, Richard, and Colin Pritchard. *The Protest Makers: The British Nuclear Disarmament Movement of 1958–1965 Twenty Years On*. Oxford: Pergamon, 1980.

Terchek, Ronald J. *The Making of the Test Ban Treaty*. The Hague: Martinus Nijhoff, 1970.

Thomas, Keith. *Man and the Natural World: Changing Attitudes in England 1500–1800*. Harmondsworth: Penguin, 1983.

Thoreau, Henry David. *The Maine Woods*. New York: W. W. Norton, 1950.

Timberlake, Lloyd. "Alone in the Wastelands" (Earthscan Feature). London: Earthscan, May 1984.

———. *Africa in Crisis*. London: Earthscan, 1985.

Tinker, Jon. "Britain's Environment: Nanny Knows Best." *New Scientist* 53:786 (9 March 1972): 530.

Tjader, Richard. *The Big Game of Africa*. New York: D. Appleton & Co., 1910.

Tolba, Mostafa K. "Desertification is Stoppable." Speech delivered to UNEP Governing Council, Nairobi, May 1984.

Train, Russell E. "A World Heritage Trust." In World Wildlife Fund, *The Ark Under Way: 2nd Report of the World Wildlife Fund 1965–1967*. Morges: WWF, 1967.

Twose, Nigel. *Why the Poor Suffer Most: Drought and the Sahel*. Oxford: Oxfam, 1984.

Udall, Stewart L. *The Quiet Crisis*. New York: Holt, Rinehart and Winston, 1963.

United Nations. *United Nations Yearbook 1946–47*. New York: Office of Public Information, United Nations, 1947.

———. *Yearbook of the United Nations 1970*. New York: Office of Public Information, United Nations, 1970.

———. *The UN System and the Human Environment*. General Assembly Doc A/CONF.48/12, 17 December 1971.

———. *Yearbook of the United Nations 1972*. New York: Office of Public Information, United Nations, 1972.

———. *Report of the United Nations Conference on the Human Environment*. A/CONF.48/14/Rev.1, 1972.

United Nations Economic and Social Council. UN (ECOSOC), Annexes, Agenda Item 12 (Doc E/4466/Add.1) at 2. New York: ECOSOC, 1968.

United Nations Economic Commission on Europe. *Progress in Selected Areas of Cooperation* (Executive Body for the Convention on Long-Range Transboundary Air Pollution, Doc. EB AIR/R.12). Geneva: UNECE, 1985.

United Nations Environment Programme. *Report of the Governing Council of the United Nations Environment Programme, Fourth Session, March 30–April 14 1976*. Nairobi: UNEP, 1976.

———. *Report of the Environmental Coordination Board on its Sixth Session, New York, 20–21 October 1976* (UNEP/GC/89). Nairobi: UNEP, 1976.

———. *Report of the Governing Council of the United Nations Environment Programme, Fifth Session, May 9–25, 1977*. Nairobi: UNEP, 1977.

———. *Memoranda of Understanding between the UN Environment Programme and Other Organisations of the United Nations System, 19 December 1977* (UNEP/GC/INFO/6). Nairobi: UNEP, 1977.

———. *Report of the Governing Council of the United Nations Environment Programme, Fifth Session, 9–25 May 1977*. Nairobi: UNEP, 1977.

———. *Review of the Areas of Environment and Development and Environmental Management* (UNEP Report No. 3). Nairobi: UNEP, 1978.

———. Report on the Present State of UNEP, prepared by the permanent representatives of the European Community Countries, 1980. Unpublished.

———. *Earthwatch: An In-depth Review* (UNEP Report No. 1). Nairobi: UNEP, 1981.

———. *In Defence of Earth: The Basic Texts on Environment: Founex, Stockholm, Cocoyoc*. Nairobi: UNEP, 1981.

———. *Review of Major Achievements in the Implementation of the Action Plan for the Human Environment* (UNEP Doc. Na.82-0006-1142C). Nairobi: UNEP, 1982.

———. *The Environment in 1981: Retrospect and Prospect*. Paper prepared for the Session of a Special Character, Nairobi. Doc. UNEP/GC (SSC)/2, 29 January 1982.

———. *Achievements and Planned Development of UNEP's Regional Seas Programme and Comparable Programmes Sponsored by Other Bodies* (UNEP Regional Seas Reports and Studies No. 1). Nairobi: UNEP, 1982.

———. *Register of International Treaties and Other Agreements in the Field of the Environment* (UNEP/GC/INFO/11). Nairobi: UNEP, 1984.

———. *General Assessment of Progress in the Implementation of the Plan of Action to Combat Desertification 1978–1984* (UNEP/GC.12/9). Nairobi: UNEP, 1984.

UNEP-UNCTAD. *Report of the Expert Group on the Impact of Resource Management Problems and Policies in Developed Countries on International Trade and Development Strategies.* Nairobi: UNEP, 1984.

UNEP/WMO/ICSU. *An Assessment of the Role of Carbon Dioxide and of Other Greenhouse Gases in Climate Variations and Associated Impacts.* Geneva: World Meteorological Organization, 1985.

UNESCO. *Proceedings and Papers of the International Technical Conference on the Protection of Nature, August 1949.* Paris and Brussels: UNESCO, 1950.

———. *Use and Conservation of the Biosphere* (Proceedings of the Biosphere Conference). Paris: UNESCO, 1970.

———. *Backgrounder: The MAB Programme.* Paris: UNESCO, 1982.

United States Department of State, *Stockholm and Beyond.* Department of State Publication 8657, Washington, DC, 1972.

Vig, Norman J., and Michael E. Kraft. "Environmental Policy from the Seventies to the Eighties." In *Environmental Policy in the 1980s: Reagan's New Agenda*, ed. Norman J. Vig and Michael E. Kraft. Washington, DC: CQ Press, 1984.

Vogt, William. *Road to Survival.* New York: William Sloane, 1948.

Voss, Earl H. *Nuclear Ambush: The Test-Ban Trap.* Chicago: Henry Regnery, 1963.

Wandesforde-Smith, Geoffrey. "National Policy for the Environment: Politics and the Concept of Stewardship." In *Congress and the Environment*, ed. Richard Cooley and Geoffrey Wandesforde-Smith. Seattle: University of Washington Press, 1970.

Ward, Barbara. Speech to the UN Conference on the Human Environment, June 1972. Unpublished.

Ward, Barbara. Interview with Jon Tinker, 1981. Unpublished.

Ward, Barbara, and René Dubos. *Only One Earth.* Harmondsworth: Penguin, 1972.

Watson, Robert T. et al. *Present State of Knowledge of the Upper Atmosphere: An Assessment Report* (Publ. 1162). Washington, DC: NASA, 1986.

Watterson, Gerald, ed. *Report of the Pan-African Symposium on the Conservation of Nature and Natural Resources in Modern African States, September 1961.* Morges: IUCN, 1963.

Wetstone, Gregory S., and Armin Rosencranz. *Acid Rain in Europe and North America.* Washington, DC: Environmental Law Institute, 1984.

White, Lynn. "The Historical Roots of Our Ecologic Crisis." *Science* 155:3767 (10 March 1967): 48–56.

White Paper on the Reorganisation of Central Government. London: Her Majesty's Printing Office, Cmnd 4506, October 1970.

Whyte, R. O., and Jacks, G. V. *Vanishing Lands.* New York: Doubleday, 1939.

Wild, Peter. *Pioneer Conservationists of Western America.* Missoula, MT: Mountain Press, 1979.

Wilson, Thomas W. Proposal to Establish an International Center for Environmental Affairs, 26 June 1970. Unpublished.

———. Draft Plan for the International Institute for Environmental Affairs, 21 September 1970. Unpublished.

Wittner, Lawrence S. *Cold War America: From Hiroshima to Watergate.* New York: Praeger, 1974.

Woodwell, George M. "The Carbon Dioxide Question." *Scientific American* 238:1 (January 1978): 34–43.

Wordsworth, William. *A Guide through the District of the Lakes*. Bloomington: Indiana University Press, 1952.

World Bank. *Environmental, Health and Human Ecologic Consideration in Economic Development Projects*. Washington, DC: World Bank, 1972.

———. *Environment and Development*. Washington, DC: World Bank, 1979.

———. *Toward Sustained Development in Sub-Saharan Africa*. Washington, DC: World Bank, 1984.

World Conservation Strategy. Gland: IUCN/UNEP/WWF, 1980.

World Environment Center. *The World Environment Handbook*. New York: WEC, 1983.

World Resources Institute/International Institute for Environment and Development. *World Resources 1986*. New York: Basic Books, 1986.

———. *World Resources 1987*. New York: Basic Books, 1987.

World Wildlife Fund. *The Ark Under Way: 2nd Report of the World Wildlife Fund 1965–1967*. Morges: WWF, 1967.

———. *World Wildlife Fund Yearbook 1968*. Morges: WWF, 1968.

———. *World Wildlife Fund Yearbook 1969*. Morges: WWF, 1969.

Worster, Donald. *Nature's Economy*. San Francisco: Sierra Club Books, 1977.

Worthington, E. Barton, ed. *The Evolution of IBP*. Cambridge: Cambridge University Press, 1975.

Yankelovich, Daniel, and Bernard Lefkowitz. "The Public Debate on Growth: Preparing for Resolution." *Technological Forecasting and Social Change* 17:2 (June 1980): 95–140.

Ylisela, Jim. "Scientists Probe the Ozone Hole for Clues to Its Cause." *Christian Science Monitor* (6 October 1987): 18.

Zinger, Clem, Richard Dalsemer, and Helen Magargle. *Environmental Volunteers in America*. Washington, DC: EPA, 1973.

Index

development, 149–150, 159, 167–168, 193, 197. *See also* desertification, World Conservation Strategy
Dickens, Charles, 5
Dominant Social Paradigm, 196
Donora, Pennsylvania, 57
Don't Make a Wave Committee, 144
Doomsday Syndrome, The, 84–85
Downs, Anthony, 64–66, 198
Dubos, René, 79, 95–96; biographical note, 221
Dukakis, Michael, 200
Dumont, René, 139, 140
Dust Bowl, 22, 29

Earth Day 1970, 47, 67, 86
Earthscan, 109, 122
Earthwatch. *See* UNEP
East Riding Association for the Protection of Sea Birds (UK), 4, 15
Ecological Principles for Economic Development, 155, 163
Ecologist, The, 78, 100, 180
Ecology Party (UK). *See* Green parties, in Britain
economic development and the environment. *See* development and the environment
ECOSOC. *See* United Nations Economic and Social Council
Ehrlich, Paul, 30–31, 67, 79–80, 151; and Barry Commoner, 69–73; biographical note, 217
Einstein, Albert, 52
Emergency Committee for Direct Action Against Nuclear War (UK), 63
Emerson, Ralph Waldo, 10, 13
Engels, Friedrich, 5, 74
environment and development. *See* development and environment
Environment Coordination Board. *See* UNEP
Environment, Department of the (India), 160–161
Environment, Department of the (UK), 126, 127, 129–130
Environment Forum. *See* Stockholm conference
Environment Liaison Centre, 101
Environmental Defense Fund (US), 137, 143
environmental movement: and other social movements, 61–64; achievements, 195–198, 203; future prospects, 198–199. *See also* Britain, United States, non-governmental organizations, New Environmentalism
environmental policy, 199–200; in MDCs, 125–127, 201; in Britain, 57–58, 126,

127–132, 200; in United States, 29–30, 126, 132–135; in European Community, 180–182; in Soviet bloc, 201; in LDCs, 126, 148, 154, 158–162, 193, 201–202; in Kenya, 159–160; in India, 160–161; and environmental movement, 199
environmental impact statement, 134, 181
environmental treaties. *See* treaties, environmental
Environmental Protection Agency. See US Environmental Protection Agency
Erie, Lake, pollution of, 59
European Commission, 182
European Committee for Conservation of Nature and Natural Resources (CDSN), 179
European Community: environmental policy, 180–182; and UNEP, 111; Common Agricultural Policy, 130; and NGOs, 101, 181–182; and threats to ozone layer, 188
European Conservation Year, 129, 179–180
European Economic Community. *See* European Community
European Environmental Bureau (EEB), 101–102, 181–182
Evelyn, John, vii, 182
Everglades National Park, 60

fallout, nuclear. *See* nuclear tests
Fauna and Flora Preservation Society, 15, 18, 24, 39
Fauna Preservation Society. *See* Fauna and Flora Preservation Society.
Fernow, Bernhard, 13
First World Conference on National Parks 1962, 40–41, 45, 88, 150
fisheries, 80
Flamborough Head, 4
Fontainebleu Conference 1948, 35
Food and Agriculture Organization (FAO), 25–26, 37, 44, 91, 113, 155, 190, 210; founded, 27–28, 36; and natural resources, 28–29; and African convention 1968, 46; and World Conservation Strategy, 164, 166, 169
Ford Foundation, 162–163
forest clearance, 28; East Africa, 19–20; United States, 10; Australia, 7–8
forest protection: United States, 13; South Africa, 8–9; India, 6–7, 161–162; Germany, 6–7
Forrester, Jay, 74, 75, 81; biographical note, 218
Founex meeting 1971, 92, 95, 151
"Founex II", 151, 152
France: and nuclear tests, 51, 144–145; and Greenpeace, 144–145; Green